GHOST RIDER

Published by ECW PRESS
2120 Queen Street East, Suite 200, Toronto, Ontario, Canada M4E 1E2

NATIONAL LIBRARY OF CANADA CATALOGUING IN PUBLICATION DATA

Peart, Neil
Ghost rider: travels on the healing road / Neil Peart
ISBN 1-55022-546-4 (cloth)   1-55022-548-0 (paper)
1. Peart, Neil — Journeys — North America. 2. North America — Description and travel.
3. Motorcycling — North America. I. Title.
E27.5.P42 2002   917.04´539   C2002-902178-2

Editors: Paul McCarthy and Kevin Connolly
Cover design: Hugh Syme
Text design: Tania Craan
Production and typesetting: Mary Bowness
Printing: Webcom
Author photo: Steven Taylor
Cover and interior photos by author,
except pages 233 and 267 which are by Brad French.

Second Printing

This book is set in John Handy, Mason and Minion

The publication of *Ghost Rider* has been generously supported by the Canada Council, the Ontario Arts Council, and the Government of Canada through the Book Publishing Industry Development Program.

DISTRIBUTION

CANADA: Stewart House, 195 Allstate Parkway, Markham, ON L3R 4T8

UNITED STATES: Independent Publishers Group, 814 North Franklin Street, Chicago, Illinois 60610

PRINTED AND BOUND IN CANADA

ECW PRESS
ecwpress.com

GHOST RIDER

Travels On The Healing Road

neil peart

ECW PRESS

Dedicated to the future
with honor to the past

We're only immortal for a limited time

DREAMLINE, 1991

Book 1
RIDING THE HEALING ROAD

Book 2

HOMEWARD ANGEL, ON THE FLY

Book 1

RIDING
THE HEALING ROAD

Suddenly
You were gone
From all the lives
You left your mark upon

AFTERIMAGE, 1984

İΠΤ⊙ EΧİLE

You can go out, you can take a ride
And when you get out on your own
You get all smoothed out inside
And it's good to be alone

FACE UP, 1991

Outside the house by the lake the heavy rain seemed to hold down the darkness, grudging the slow fade from black, to blue, to gray. As I prepared that last breakfast at home, squeezing the oranges, boiling the eggs, smelling the toast and coffee, I looked out the kitchen window at the dim Quebec woods gradually coming into focus. Near the end of a wet summer, the spruce, birch, poplars, and cedars were densely green, glossy and dripping.

3

For this momentous departure I had hoped for a better omen than this cold, dark, rainy morning, but it did have a certain pathetic fallacy, a sympathy with my interior weather. In any case, the weather didn't matter; I was going. I still didn't know where (Alaska? Mexico? Patagonia?), or for how long (two months? four months? a year?), but I knew I had to go. My life depended on it.

Sipping the last cup of coffee, I wrestled into my leathers, pulled on my boots, then rinsed the cup in the sink and picked up the red helmet. I pushed it down over the thin balaclava, tightened the plastic rainsuit around my neck, and pulled on my thick waterproof gloves. I knew this was going to be a cold, wet ride, and if my brain wasn't ready for it, at least my body would be prepared. That much I could manage.

The house on the lake had been my sanctuary, the only place I still loved, the only thing I had left, and I was tearing myself away from it unwillingly, but desperately. I didn't expect to be back for a while, and one dark corner of my mind feared that I might *never* get back home again. This would be a perilous journey, and it might end badly. By this point in my life I knew that bad things could happen, even to me.

I had no definite plans, just a vague notion to head north along the Ottawa River, then turn west, maybe across Canada to Vancouver to visit my brother Danny and his family. Or, I might head northwest through the Yukon and Northwest Territories to Alaska, where I had never travelled, then catch the ferry down the coast of British Columbia toward Vancouver. Knowing that ferry would be booked up long in advance, it was the one reservation I had dared to make, and as I prepared to set out on that dark, rainy morning of August 20th, 1998, I had two and a half weeks to get to Haines, Alaska — all the while knowing that it didn't really matter, to me or anyone else, if I kept that reservation.

Out in the driveway, the red motorcycle sat on its centerstand, beaded with raindrops and gleaming from my careful preparation. The motor was warming on fast idle, a plume of white vapor jetting out behind, its steady hum muffled by my earplugs and helmet.

I locked the door without looking back. Standing by the bike, I checked the load one more time, adjusting the rain covers and shock cords. The proverbial deep breath gave me the illusion of commitment, to the day and to the journey, and I put my left boot onto the footpeg, swung my right leg high over the heavily laden bike, and settled into the familiar saddle.

My well-travelled BMW R1100GS (the "adventure-touring" model) was packed with everything I might need for a trip of unknown duration, to unknown destinations. Two hard-shell luggage cases flanked the rear wheel, while behind the saddle I had stacked a duffel bag, tent, sleeping bag, inflatable foam pad, groundsheet, tool kit, and a small red plastic gas can. I wanted to be prepared for anything, anywhere.

Because I sometimes liked to travel faster than the posted speed limits, especially on the wide open roads of the west — where it was safe in terms of visible risks, but dangerous in terms of hidden enforcement — I had decided to try using a small radar detector, which I tucked into my jacket pocket, with its earpiece inside the helmet.

A few other necessities, additional tools, and my little beltpack filled the tankbag in front of me, and a roadmap faced up from a clear plastic cover on top. The rest of the baggage I would carry away with me that morning had less bulk, but more weight — the invisible burdens that had driven me to depart into what already seemed like a kind of exile.

But at that moment, before I'd turned a wheel or even pushed off the centerstand, I reaped the first reward of this journey, when my thoughts and energies contracted and narrowed their focus to riding the machine. My right hand gently rolled on the throttle a little more, left hand wiped away the raindrops already collecting on my clear faceshield, then pulled in the clutch lever. My left foot toed the shifter down into first gear, and I moved slowly up the lane between the wet trees. At the top I paused to lock the gate behind me, wiped off my faceshield again, and rode out onto the muddy gravel road, away from all that.

Just over a year before that morning, on the night of August 10, 1997, a police car had driven down that same driveway to bring us news of the first tragedy. That morning my wife Jackie and I had kissed and hugged our nineteen-year-old daughter, Selena, as she set out to drive back to

Toronto, ready to start university that September. As night came on, the hour passed when we should have heard from her, and Jackie became increasingly worried. An incorrigible optimist (back then, at least), I still didn't believe in the possibility of anything bad happening to Selena, or to any of us, and I was sure it was just teenage thoughtlessness. She would call; there'd be some excuse.

When I saw headlights coming down the driveway to where the house lights showed the markings of a police car, I remembered the previous summer when the provincial police came to ask about a robbery down the road, and I thought it must be something like that. A mother has a certain built-in radar detector, however, and the moment I announced that it was the police, I saw Jackie's eyes go wide and her face turn white; she knew.

Instinctively, I took her hand as we went out to the driveway to face the local police chief, Ernie Woods. He led us inside and showed us the fax he had received from the Ontario Provincial Police, and we tried to take in his words: "bad news," "maybe you'd better sit down." Then we tried to read the black lines on the paper, tried to make sense of the incomprehensible, to believe the unacceptable. My mind was reeling in a hopeless struggle to absorb those words. "Single car accident," "apparently lost control," "dead at the scene."

"No," Jackie breathed, then louder, "NO," again and again, as she collapsed to the floor in the front hall. At first I just stood there, paralyzed with horror and shock, and it was only when I saw Jackie start to get up that I felt afraid of what she might do, and I fell down beside her and held her. She struggled against me and told me to let her go, but I wouldn't. Our big white Samoyed, Nicky, was frightened and confused by all this, and he barked frantically and tried to push between us. Chief Ernie was afraid to touch the dog, I wouldn't let go of Jackie, and Nicky was trying to protect *somebody*, to make us *stop* this, so it was pandemonium as the two of us kicked and yelled at him while his shrill barks echoed through the house.

I held onto Jackie until she was overcome by the numbing protection of shock, and asked Chief Ernie to call our local doctor. Time was all meaningless now, but at some point Nicky crept away to hide somewhere and Dr. Spunt came and tried to say comforting things, but we were unreceptive. Sometime later, Chief Ernie left, then Dr. Spunt too, and for the rest of the night I walked endlessly around the living-room carpet (what I learned later is called the "search mode," in which I was unconsciously "trying to find the lost one," just as some animals and birds do), while Jackie sat and stared into space, neither of us saying anything. In the gray twilight of morning we put the downcast Nicky in the car and headed for Toronto, driving through the rain to face the end of the world.

Just before those headlights came down the driveway to turn our relatively pleasant and tranquil lives into a waking nightmare, Jackie had been fretting on the porch while I blithely watched a ᴛv documentary about the Mormon trek west in 1847. It quoted a woman who had survived the ordeal about the terrible hardships they had endured, and the last words I remember were, "The only reason I am alive is because I could not die." That terrible phrase would come back to haunt me in the months that followed. It soon became apparent that Jackie's world was completely shattered forever; she had fallen to pieces, and she never came back together again.

And neither did the two of us, really, though I tried to do everything I could for her. As my life suddenly forced me to learn more than anyone ever wanted to know about grief and bereavement, I learned the sad fact that most couples do not stay together after losing a child. Outrageous! So wrong, so unfair, so cruel, to heap more pain and injustice on those who had suffered so much already. In my blissful ignorance, I would have imagined the opposite — that those who most shared the loss would cling to each other. But no.

Maybe it's because the mutually bereaved represent a constant reminder to each other, almost a reproach, or it might run as deep as the "selfish genes" rejecting an unsuccessful effort at reproduction. Whatever it was, it was harsh to think that Jackie and I had survived 22 years of common-law marriage; had managed to stay together through bad times and good (with only a couple of "temporary estrangements"); through poverty and wealth, failure and success, crises of youth and midlife and middle age (she was 42; I was 45); through all the stages of Selena's childhood and adolescence; and even my frequent absences, both as a touring musician and an inveterate traveller. We had made it through all that, and now the loss of what we each treasured most would drive us apart.

During those first awful weeks in Toronto our friends and family filled the House of Mourning day and night, trying to distract us and help us deal with this unbearable reality as best they could, but Jackie remained inconsolable, pining and withering visibly into a fragile, suffering wraith. One time she shook her head and looked up at me, "Don't be hurt, but I always knew this was the one thing I just couldn't handle."

She wouldn't let me comfort her, and didn't want anything to do with me really. It was as though she knew she needed me, but her tortured heart had no place in it for me, or anybody. If she couldn't have Selena, she no longer wanted anything — she just wanted to die. She had to be coaxed into eating anything at all, and talked of suicide constantly. I had to keep a close watch on her sedatives and sleeping pills, and make sure she was never left alone. When she did surrender to a drugged sleep, she held a framed picture of Selena in her arms.

After a couple of weeks I took Jackie away to London, England, accompanied by our friends Brad and Rita. I had known Brad since childhood, and in the early '70s he and I had shared a flat in London, where he had met Rita, a refugee from the Shah's Iran, and brought her back to Canada. Brad and Rita had known great tragedy in their own lives, so they were a good choice to help Jackie and me begin our exile. After they went home, other friends came to stay with us for a week or two at a time, and eventually we moved into a small flat near Hyde Park, where we stayed for six months. We started seeing a grief counsellor, "Dr. Deborah," several times a week at the Traumatic Stress Clinic, which seemed to help a little, and at least got us *outside* occasionally. It was hard for me to try to force Jackie even to take a walk, for she was tortured by everything she saw — by advertisements for back-to-school clothes (Selena!), children playing in the park (Selena!), young girls on horseback taking riding lessons (Selena!), pretty young women in the full pride of youth (Selena!). These same triggers stabbed me too, of course, and I also felt bleak and morose and often tearful, but it seemed I was already building a wall against things which were too painful for me to deal with, wearing mental blinkers when I was outside in the busy streets of London. I would just flinch and turn away from such associations, but Jackie remained raw and vulnerable, unable to protect herself from the horror of memory.

In an effort to keep her eating nutritiously, I even learned to cook simple meals in our little kitchenette (thanks to the food hall in the Marks and Spencer store on Oxford Street, which offered cooking instructions with every item, even fresh fish and vegetables), calling myself "Chef Ellwood," after my unfortunate middle name. But none of it was enough. As I tried to look after Jackie in every way I could, only ever leaving her alone for a fast afternoon walk around the park or through the London streets (with the pills locked in the safe), or to buy the day's groceries, it was like witnessing a suicide brought on by total apathy. She just didn't care.

The following January, when we were finally thinking about returning from London to try to find some kind of life back in Canada, Jackie began to suffer from severe back pain and nocturnal coughing. She refused to let me get a doctor, saying, "They'll just say it's stress," but Dr. Deborah finally prevailed on me to make an executive decision and get a doctor anyway. On the eve of our departure, Jackie was diagnosed with terminal cancer (the doctors called it cancer, but of course it was a broken heart), and a second nightmare began.

Jackie's brother Steven met us in Toronto and soon took over the household, controlling the number of visitors (who called him "The Gatekeeper"), and supervising Jackie's care as I felt myself slipping into a kind of "protective insanity," a numb refuge of alcohol and drugs.

Jackie, however, received the news almost gratefully — as though this was the only acceptable fate for her, the only price she could pay. After months of misery, despair, and anger (often directed at *me,* as the handiest "object"), she never uttered a harsh word after that diagnosis, and rarely even cried. To her, the illness was a terrible kind of justice. To me, however, it was simply terrible. And unbearable.

After two months of dissipation in Toronto, I pulled myself together, and we fulfilled Jackie's wish to go to Barbados. Two years previously we had enjoyed a memorable family vacation in that pleasant island-nation, and it offered sufficient medical services to allow us to continue providing home care for Jackie, even when she began to decline sharply, needing oxygen most of the time, slipping away both mentally and physically, until a series of strokes brought a relatively merciful end.

Exhausted and desolated, I flew back to Toronto, staying there just long enough to organize the house and put it on the market, with more help from family and friends, then got away to the house on the lake, still not knowing what I was going to do. Before she died, Jackie had given me a clue, saying, "Oh, you'll just go travelling on your motorcycle," but at that time I couldn't even *imagine* doing that. But as the long, empty days and nights of that dark summer slowly passed, it began to seem like the only thing to do.

I didn't really have a *reason* to carry on; I had no interest in life, work, or the world beyond, but unlike Jackie, who had surely willed her death, I seemed to be armored with some kind of survival instinct, some inner reflex that held to the conviction that "something will come up." Because of some strength (or flaw) of character, I never seemed to question "why" I should survive, but only "how" — though that was certainly a big enough question to deal with at the time.

I remember thinking, "How does anyone *survive* something like this? And if they do, what kind of person comes out the other end?" I didn't know, but throughout that dark time of grief, sorrow, desolation, and complete despair, something in me seemed determined to carry on. Something would come up.

Or maybe it was more like the Mormon woman's statement, "The only reason I am alive is because I could not die."

In any case, I was now setting out on my motorcycle to try to figure out what kind of person I was going to be, and what kind of world I was going to live in. Throughout that first day on the road, as I traced the rain-slick highway north across the rocky face of Quebec, my shaky resolve would be tested a few times. Tense and shivering, peering through the turbulent wash of spray behind a lumber truck for a chance to pass, more than once I thought about packing it in. "Who needs this? I'm really not having fun, and I don't think I'm strong enough to deal with this right now. Why not turn around and go back to the house by the lake, hide there a little longer?"

But no. That too would be a perilous road.

When I allowed myself to consider turning back, the thought that kept me riding on was, "Then what?" For over a month I had tried living there alone, with occasional visits from friends to help take me out of myself, and I had still felt myself beginning to slip into a deep, dark hole. Various stimulants and depressants could help me get through the days and nights, but as I had recently written to a friend, "That's okay for a temporary escape hatch, but it's no kind of a *life*."

I had tried the Hermit mode, now it was time to try the Gypsy mode. I tried not to think of what I would do if that didn't work.

Travelling had always been a more or less normal condition for me, not only as the necessary environment of a touring musician for the past 23 years with Rush, but also as a kind of escape from all that. Between concert tours I had travelled the roads of China, Africa, Europe, and North America, at first by bicycle, and later by motorcycle, and that kind of self-contained journeying had fired my imagination with curiosity and challenge.

From the beginning, I kept daily journals during my travels, and when I returned home I used them to exercise my interest in prose writing, experimenting with different approaches to telling the story of a journey. My interest in writing had begun with composing lyrics for the band, and had grown from a taste for writing letters into a serious love of stringing words together on the page. As I continued to develop the craft through my travel stories, I would print up a few copies of them for friends and fellow travellers, until after learning my way through about five privately printed books, I finally felt ready to publish one in 1996: *The Masked Rider*, about cycling in West Africa.

Lately, though, I hadn't been doing much writing of any kind, except for a few letters to distant friends, but during our stay in London the grief counsellor, Dr. Deborah, had encouraged me to start a daily journal of "letters to Selena," and that had proved to be good therapy. On this tentative beginning to a new kind of travel (purposeful, yet aimless) I doubted I would feel the old urge to document what I saw and felt, or any ambition to make this sad journey into a book, but just in case I had brought one of my little black notebooks with me, and that first day I made an experimental entry:

[August 20, '98]

Ach. Cold and wet. Lunch in Cadillac, Que. Heavy rain last few hours, surprisingly heavy traffic. Trucks roaring in spray plume. Scenery? Dark, wet, gloomy — like me. Much-logged face of Canadian Shield, occasional lake flooded or drained, mines and factories up around here, Val d'Or and Noranda. Barely 10° [50 F] this a.m., not much more now.

As I crossed into Ontario the rain let up at last, but the day remained chilly, and I finally sought refuge at the Northern Lites Motel, in Cochrane. 850 kilometres (531 miles) was plenty for that kind of day. Pouring a measure of The Macallan from my little flask into a plastic cup, I felt its warmth inside as I hung my wet riding gear around the room.

In the shower I thought about Cochrane, isolated at the northern edge of Ontario's grid, and ghosts came out of the memory of a concert the band had played there back in the mid-'70s. After driving all night from Winnipeg, we'd played our set to a spattering of applause, and at the end we left the stage, figuring that was that. However, when we got to the dressing room, the promoter, a squat and hairy French Canadian, descriptively named "Hunk," came running in, distressed we hadn't played an encore. He said the agent had promised him we would.

We protested that an encore was usually a request for another song from the audience, and there had been no response that night to indicate any such desire. Hunk became more distraught, saying, in his thick accent, "I never t'ought Rush would do dis to me!" The three of us looked at each other, shrugged, and went back onstage. The audience was waiting quietly, we played another song, and everyone went home. No one seemed excited, but everyone seemed satisfied. We knew that everyone in town knew how much we were getting paid (probably a thousand dollars), and that the agent had promised Hunk an encore. After the gear was packed up and loaded into the truck, seven of us from the band and crew piled into a rented station wagon and drove all night back to Toronto.

Cochrane. Hunk. Ghosts.

All that seemed so far away and long ago, part of another life. Even after my first terrible loss I had felt no urge to work with the band anymore, and the day of Selena's funeral I had told my partners in Rush, Geddy and Alex (all of us in tears), that they should "consider me retired." I hadn't worried about whether or not I could *afford* not to work again; it was simply unthinkable. After 23 years together, Geddy and Alex were loyal and caring friends through my sequence of nightmares, and they were, of course, nothing but supportive and understanding of whatever I wanted to do. Now that I was trying to carry the weight of yet another unbearable tragedy, I had even less reason to care about the future — or even if I *had* a future.

Certainly I had no interest in playing the drums, or writing lyrics for rock songs. Before that night when my world crashed down around me I had been working on a book about my motorcycle adventures with my friend Brutus on the just-finished Rush tour, *Test For Echo*, and now I couldn't imagine taking up that project again.

That night in Cochrane, I took refuge in my journal notes once more, as I sat in the Northern Lites dining room after my fried pickerel (usually the tastiest of freshwater fish, but not this specimen). The only other diners were a pair of retired couples, and I heard them marvelling to discover that they hailed from two Ontario towns, Brantford and Peterborough, that were all of a two-hour drive apart. One of the ladies was even moved to remark, "It's a small world."

One of the men also tried to be sociable to the solitary diner, and leaned toward me to say, "You're bein' awful quiet over there."

Startled, a dozen possible replies zipped through my answer index, all of them true, but some of them real conversation-enders. In the end I gave a shy chuckle, nodded toward my dinner, and said, "Oh . . . I'm okay."

Then I wrote in my journal: "Perils of solitude #1: People *talk* to you. I'd rather *listen*."

The next morning, I continued west across Ontario, on the road from dawn until late afternoon, pausing only for fuel, and an occasional pause at the roadside for a stretch and a cigarette. Just kept moving, afraid to stop for too long, afraid to give myself time to think. Riding a motorcycle with total concentration, devoting infinite attention to the ever-changing road and other traffic; that was sufficient to keep most of my little brain busy.

My mind was also lulled into tranquility by the motion, the trance-like effect of steady vibration, occasional bumps and curves, and the world coming at me mile after mile, hour after hour.

Earlier that summer, contemplating the wreckage of my life, I had determined that my mission now was to protect a certain essence inside me, a sputtering life force, a meager spirit, as though I held my cupped hands around a guttering candle. In letters I had begun calling that remnant spark "my little baby soul," and the task before me now, I decided, was to nurture that spirit as well as I could.

My little baby soul was not a happy infant, of course, with much to complain about, but as every parent learns, a restless baby often calms down if you take it for a ride. I had learned my squalling spirit could be soothed the same way, by motion, and so I had decided to set off on this journey into the unknown. Take my little baby soul for a ride.

When I had arrived in Quebec from Toronto, after everything else was gone, I didn't have much interest in the world around me. I didn't like anything, didn't care about anything, and didn't want to do anything. The first hint of a possible upturn came one afternoon when I was sitting on the dock with a glass of The Macallan in one hand and a cigarette in the other.

Way down at the far end of the shining lake, near one of the islands, my eyes fastened on two wedge-shaped rocks sticking out of the water. Those two rocks had always reminded me of a pair of ducks facing each other, and somehow that day my little baby soul decided to imbue them with *meaning*. A voice spoke inside my head, "You know, I still like those two rocks."

My eyebrows lifted at the realization: I actually *liked* something; and thus from that pair of rocks I began to build a new world. It would have to be a world my little baby soul could stand to live in, and a world that included the possibility of all that had happened, so it was going to be very different from the world I had lived in before. However, I was starting with first principles, the Earth, and now that I was travelling westward I began to respond to the landscapes around me too, the rugged cliffs and forests around Lake Nipigon and the north shore of Lake Superior.

If I wasn't exactly finding *joy* in that scenic splendor the way I used to, I was at least "resonating" again, feeling the beauty around me, and curious about what that next line on the map might look like.

But as I rode toward that line on the map, my serenity, my thoughts, and my internal music were suddenly interrupted by the ugliest of sounds. Even through earplugs, helmet, and wind noise, there was no mistaking that loud electronic whooping and bleating, and my eyes darted to the rear-view mirror, which was filled with the insistent flash of red-and-blue lights behind the grille of a provincial police cruiser. Cursing, I pulled to the side of the road and straddled the bike. The officer walked up beside me, held out his hand and said, "May I have your radar detector please?"

Flustered, I protested, "But it's supposed to be undetectable!"

He shook his head, "They shouldn't be allowed to get away with saying that. Someone should go after them. I knew it was an 'undetectable' one because it gave off a weird signal."

Damn. Then worse. As he looked over my Ontario driver's licence, I saw his head give a little jerk upward, then move in closer. He peered into my helmet, smiling now.

"You a *musician?*"

I mentally rifled through the answer index again, looking for a truthful evasion (not an easy task when you're answering a man with a uniform and a gun).

Eventually I mumbled, "Um . . . not any more."

He paused a moment, looking over my insurance and registration.

"You *used* to be a musician, though?"

"Um . . . years ago."

He went on talking about some place in Toronto where he used to live that was apparently close by something that was supposed to be meaningful to the person he thought I was, but I was still thinking of alternatives from the answer index.

"I used to be a lot of things."

Lately I had written to one of my friends, "I don't know who I am, what I'm doing, or what I'm *supposed* to do." Time would tell, I could only hope, and if time was supposed to be the great healer, then the best thing I could do was try to "let it pass" as painlessly as possible, try to minimize the self-destructive urges, and stay away from the house on the lake for awhile.

Let time pass. Take my little baby soul for a ride.

The policeman finished writing out my ticket, and I went riding on.

The road unwinds toward me
What was there is gone
The road unwinds before me
And I go riding on
It's my turn to drive

DRIVEN, 1996

Chapter 2

WESTERİNG

What a fool I used to be

PRESTO, 1990

Before dawn had reached Thunder Bay and the northern shore of Lake Superior, I was carrying my bags and helmet out to the hotel parking lot. I paused beside the bike to watch a spectacular display of aurora borealis — shimmering veils of greenish light draped across the northern sky. Setting off through the forests of northwestern Ontario, the lonely road cast its hypnotic, soothing effect over my mood. The steady droning of the engine, the constant wind noise, the cool, forest-scented air, and my visual fixation on the road ahead occupied most of my senses, while my mind wandered above its monitoring function into the fields of memory.

The Ghost of Christmas Past carried me back to a snowy December afternoon in 1993, a few days before Christmas. Selena and Jackie and I lived most of the year in Toronto, but we usually spent our summers and holidays at the house by the lake in Quebec, and for our tight little family, Christmas was a special time there.

The snow had been heavy that winter, already laying two feet deep in the woods and over the frozen lake. The house was carefully decorated indoors and out, with lights strung in the snow-covered trees, and the living room dominated by a tall, glittering Christmas tree. Selena was 15 then, and covered a large table with her annual tableau of "Christmas Town," an array of porcelain houses on snowy cotton hills, miniature trees with tiny colored lights, a toy train puffing real smoke as it circled through the houses, and even little figures skating magnetically on a mirrored pond. Christmas Town was different every year, but even into Selena's late teens it was an expression of her love for the rituals of Christmas.

She was always so excited to arrive from Toronto and start decorating, the fireplace blazing as we played the Christmas CDs by Frank Sinatra, Nat King Cole, the Harlem Boys Choir, and a special favorite, *A Charlie Brown Christmas.* That year the house was filled with live music too. Our guests were Jackie's mother, her sister Deb, and her partner Mark, a musician and recording engineer, and we had made up a little orchestra of Selena on flute and acoustic guitar, Mark on acoustic guitar, and me attempting to play the marimba — a wooden-keyed percussion instrument on which I was only a "dabbler" — and the easier, more familiar time-keeping, with wire brushes on snare drum and high-hat.

That afternoon we were rehearsing our repertoire of five or six Christmas songs, preparing to give a private concert for Jackie, Deb, and Grandma on Christmas Eve. I was struggling over a difficult marimba part while Selena complained that I was "a loser" (her usual style of endearment for those she loved), when I heard the rumble of an engine in the driveway and a door slamming. Jackie called to me from the kitchen, "Neil, it's for you," but I was preoccupied with trying to get my mallets to hit the right keys on the marimba, and just grumbled, "How do you know?"

What a fool I used to be. (The truest words I ever wrote, and they get truer every day.)

With an impatient sigh, I walked over to the front door and looked out to see the pickup truck driven by Jackie's brother, Keith, who worked for us looking after the Quebec house, and perched in the back of it was a red BMW motorcycle. I immediately realized that it was a present to me from Jackie, for I had long claimed that I was going to try motorcycling when I "grew up," and that my choice of machine would be a BMW. Mouth agape, and still wearing my slippers, I ran into the snowy driveway and climbed into the truck bed, then up to the saddle of the beautiful red R1100-RS. I didn't know *anything* about motorcycles then, had never even ridden one, but I just sat on it and looked at the controls and instruments and closed my hands around the grips. A phrase came into my head, full blown, right out of a novel: "And nothing was ever the same again . . ."

During the rest of that winter of 1994 I was away working with Rush on our *Counterparts* tour, so all I could do was read the motorcycle magazines while I dreamed about riding that beautiful red beast. In April, I attended a riding class at a Toronto college with Rush guitarist Alex, who had been bitten by "the bug" himself that same winter, and had bought a Harley-Davidson.

A strange and ironic part of my physical-mental interface was that although I had made my living playing drums for 20 years, with hands and feet doing this and that and the other thing, more-or-less independently of one another, all my life I had trouble with physical coordination — sports, for example, at which I had always been very poor. I attempted to comfort this wounded self-image by theorizing that while playing the drums I had to divide my limbs in a kind of four-way independence, and thus it was more like "dis-coordination," but of course that didn't really wash, for they all had to work together eventually. In any case, even on the small motorcycles provided by the riding school I had difficulty coordinating the balance of clutch and throttle controls, and I struggled rather pathetically for the three days of the program.

Alex was already a licensed pilot by then, and something of a natural athlete, so he aced the final test easily, but I failed on that first attempt. I felt humiliated and dismayed, and even more so when I failed on my second try, during the next break in the tour. Before my third attempt I finally engaged an instructor for a private lesson, and he quickly helped me understand my difficulties and correct them. How proud and happy (and relieved) I was when I finally passed that riding test.

It was another quality of my physical-mental interface that any activity in which I developed an interest became a positive *obsession*. This had been true of playing the drums, reading every great book ever written, writing lyrics, writing prose, cross-country skiing, bicycling, and now, motorcycling. Selena, Jackie, and I spent that whole summer of 1994 at the house on the lake, and several mornings a week I got up before dawn and went riding for a couple of hours on the empty, winding roads of the Laurentians, slowly gaining skill and confidence.

That summer, we had friends renting a cottage on a nearby lake: Jackie's best friend Georgia, her husband, Brutus, and their son, Sam. At that time Brutus and I were friends in the "my-wife's-friend's-husband" sense, but when he saw me having so much fun with my new motorcycle he went out and bought one of his own, a BMW K-1100RS. That September, he joined me on my first motorcycle journey, through Quebec, Newfoundland, and the Maritime provinces, and we met up with Jackie and Georgia in Nova Scotia. They flew into Halifax and rented a car (neither of them seemed to enjoy riding behind us on the motorcycles — at least farther than to the store for a newspaper — they said they didn't *like* being cramped, overdressed, uncomfortable, and cold) to follow us for a few days around the Cabot Trail on Cape Breton Island and back to Halifax, whence they flew home while Brutus and I rode back to Quebec.

Brutus and I discovered two important things on that first trip together: we liked travelling by motorcycle, and we liked travelling together. He gave our two-man gang the name "Scooter Trash," and we began to spin more dreams and plans for adventures together. In the Spring of '95 we shipped our bikes to Mexico for a three-week tour (where

Brutus crashed and broke a couple of ribs, then later set his luggage cases on fire), and in the early summer of that year we squeezed in another adventure. (We both had the time professionally, for I was between tours and Brutus was a self-employed entrepreneur, but there was some serious bargaining and bribery going on between us and our families.)

That June, we set off across Canada on a two-week blast up to Yellow-knife, in Canada's Northwest Territories (where both of us fell over in the mud repeatedly, a story published as "Catching Some Midnight Rays" in *Cycle Canada* magazine), before rejoining our families for the summer in Quebec. My birthday present from Jackie that September was a card reading "Seven days of freedom," and we took advantage of that, and Georgia's tacit resignation, to ride east again, to New Brunswick and Nova Scotia. After another winter of work and family time, in the spring of 1996 we shipped the bikes across the Atlantic to Munich, where we began another three-week tour through Bavaria and the Austrian Alps (where Brutus crashed), Italy, Sicily, and Tunisia (where Brutus broke down in the middle of the Sahara), then back through Sardinia, France, and Switzerland.

But all of that was just preparation for the Really Big Tour. During the summer of 1996 plans were coming together for Rush's *Test For Echo* concert tour, which would eventually span 67 shows in the United States and Canada. I began to think about how I was going to endure yet another rock tour, which I had always perceived as a combination of crushing tedium, constant exhaustion, and circus-like insanity, none of which suited my restless, independent, and private temperament.

Paradoxically, I enjoyed the preparation for a tour, for I liked rehearsing with the band with the shared intensity of working toward "the perfect show," and the first few shows certainly got the adrenaline pumping when we hit the stage in front of 10 or 12 thousand people in a big arena. However, by about the third show we would get it *right,* the band and crew and audience locked together in a transcendent perform-ance, and as far as I was concerned, that was *it.* If my job was to play a good show, then I had done it. Goal achieved, challenge met, case dismissed. Can I go home now?

Nothing is ever that simple, of course, but it felt to me that for the rest of the tour I would only be going up there night after night and trying to repeat that experience, at best. Not to say that was simple, either. When a particular show fell short of that standard I felt deflated and disgusted with myself, while if I played well enough to meet that benchmark, it was only what I expected of myself — nothing to get excited about. So for me, touring could be a long, relentless grind, exhausting and soul-destroying. And that only refers to the onstage time, a small fraction of the chaos of travelling, waiting, and shifting from hotel to bus to arena to hotel for months on end.

For several tours through the '80s and early '90s I had carried a bicycle with me on the tour bus, which had provided a great escape and diversion. During the days off between shows I might spend the whole day riding from city to city, if they were within 100 miles or so, and on the afternoons before a show I often pedaled through the various cities to the local art museum, to feed my growing interest in paintings, art history, and African carvings.

This time I was thinking about how the motorcycle would make it possible for me to cover some *real* distances, and I conceived a plan of using a tour bus with a trailer for the motorcycles, and convinced Brutus to join me on the tour as navigator, machine supervisor, and (most important) riding companion. From the tour's opening show in Albany, New York, we made our own journey around the band's itinerary, eventually riding about 40,000 miles, in nearly every state in the lower 48 (excepting only North Dakota, for some reason, which never seemed to cross our path) and several Canadian provinces.

The main logo of that *Test For Echo* tour was taken from the cover art of the album, which portrayed a humanoid icon of piled stones, a gigantic version of an Inuit *inukshuk,* which means "in the likeness of a man." My suggestion that we use this image had been inspired by that long ride up to Yellowknife the previous year, when I had seen one of those mystical-looking cairns of rock overlooking the remote northern town, at the very edge of true wilderness. Knowing that these stone figures traditionally marked travel and hunting routes across the barren Arctic, I had been struck by the power of this human symbol in a hostile land.

Now, just over a year after the final show of the *Test For Echo* tour, which we played in Ottawa on July 4, 1997, it was the dark summer of 1998, and everything was changed so very much, at least through my eyes. I was riding again, but I was riding alone, motivated partly by my desire to see if solitary travelling might help to soothe the torment of my little baby soul, and partly because Brutus couldn't get away, and was hoping to meet up with me somewhere later on.

On the first day of my journey westward from Quebec, I saw a small *inukshuk* placed at the roadside, high on a rocky cut, and then another the second day, and again on the third. Perhaps they had been assembled by another solitary traveller, a hitchhiker passing time until the next ride came along. A good omen, I liked to think, although it gave me a wry smile to think about that definition, "in the likeness of a man."

For that was surely how I felt, so hollow and dispirited that I could hardly imagine what it had been like to be "the fool I used to be." Sometimes I tried to steer my mind away from memories of the past, but in other moods they now seemed so remote, so unreal, that I could dare to think about the past without breaking down.

The Ghost of Summer Past took me back to the summer of 1996, probably the most productive time of my life. *Test For Echo* had just been released, and I considered it to be my masterpiece as a drummer, for I had worked hard on my playing during the two years prior to those sessions. That summer, I was settling the post-production details of an instructional video on drumming, *A Work in Progress,* and at the same time correcting the proofs for my first published book, *The Masked Rider.* (I had made an agreement with Jackie and Selena that I could work in my office until noon, then stop and spend the afternoons and evenings with them — fair enough.) Just two summers later, all that was ashes, and I felt little connection with any of those accomplishments.

My current struggles weren't about creating or producing, or planning adventures, only about surviving. When I reflected on that old life I tended to think of the protagonist as "that guy," for I shared only his memories. And some of those memories I was now trying to hide from, escape from, ride away from.

I could ride — but I couldn't hide.

On the third morning, I crossed into Manitoba and pulled off the Trans-Canada Highway into a rest area in a grove of evergreens (fir trees, I decided when I rolled the needles in my hand — woodsman's lore: "fir's flat, spruce spins"). There, a diner had been converted from an old school bus, and I bought a hot dog, milkshake, and fries (feeding my inner child), and carried them to a picnic table in the shade. A hairy woodpecker probed for his own protein (no empty carbohydrates for him) in a nearby tree, while a flock of cedar waxwings, pearl-gray and crested with natty markings, darted among the branches of the grove.

Birds had attracted me since boyhood, when I used to trace the little illustrations from my grandmother's bird books, and try to name the species I saw flitting around the suburbs and woodlands of southern Ontario, and it was a youthful enthusiasm that had actually grown in my adulthood. Even on this wretched journey I travelled with a small pair of binoculars and a field guide, as I always had for whatever part of Africa, Europe, North America, or Mexico I was visiting. During our time in Barbados, while I was mostly confined to our rented villa and the lush gardens around it, I could sit with Jackie while she read, scanning the trees with my binoculars, and eventually identifying 22 of Barbados's 24 native species.

Back on the highway, the forests fell behind like a wall and the roadside fanned open into wide green prairie. The sun warmed the air, carrying the delicious scent of wet hay, and I watched the farmers at work with balers, combines, windrowers, and disc harrows. Part of me envied the straightforward nature of their task, guiding their machines along geometric lines between earth and sky, but part of me envied *everybody*.

Soon the empty skyline would be regularly punctuated by "prairie skyscrapers," the tall grain elevators that sprouted like exclamation marks beside the train tracks in every prairie town. Once, I saw an example of the massive scale of modern farming, automobile-sized bales of hay in stacks the size of apartment buildings, with wide lanes between them for flatbed semis. I had so many childhood memories of the farms of relatives and my parents' friends, for they had only left the farm when I was a year or two old, when my father started his career in the farm equipment business. That too had filled part of my life, working summers and holidays at my father's International Harvester dealership, and then as his parts manager in my early 20s, right up until the time I joined Rush.

That evening I called my Mom and Dad, and talked to my Dad about what I had been seeing and remembering. He told me that when his Dad and Uncle John were young they used to come west to Manitoba from southern Ontario on the "harvest trains," which gathered young men from as far east as the Maritimes to help bring in the wheat — especially during wartime, when farm labor was scarce. He also told me how after the war, when the first self-propelled combine harvesters appeared in the United States, the operators would work their way north from Texas to Manitoba, like crop-sprayer pilots or cattle drovers, following the harvest and hiring themselves out all the way.

After Winnipeg, I turned northwest on the Yellowhead Highway, just because I'd never gone west that way, and started to think about where to stop for the night. I'd left Thunder Bay that morning at 6:00, under the shimmering arc of the northern lights (as opposed to the "Northern Lites" in Cochrane), then gained an hour as I crossed my first time zone. So when the bike's digital clock showed 4:30, I'd been on the road almost twelve hours, and had covered 945 kilometres (590 miles), so it was time to start looking for a place to roost.

On the prairies, as in the desert, a clump of trees in the distance usually means a town, and I decided to stop at the next grove of trees on the horizon. Closer up, Neepawa looked welcoming, and my motel room was a memorable time warp. The screen door squeaked open to reveal three double beds with buttoned naugahyde headboards, "mahogany" paneled walls, with a feed-mill calendar and a religious sampler ("For God so loved the world"), sparkly-tile ceiling, and shag carpeting of an orangy-brown hue that used to be called "whisky" (though it didn't match my plastic cup of The Macallan).

I took my drink outside to the covered walkway and watched the dark clouds looming in from the northwest, trailing ghostly tendrils of rain. Dust swirled beside the highway, whipped along by the wind that heralded the coming storm, and soon the rain swept in, pounding on the roof and bouncing on the shiny pavement. Distant thunder rumbled, and lightning flashed off to the south. I stood and watched for awhile, delighted, then put on my rain jacket and walked up the road to "Mr. Ribs" restaurant.

That morning I had written a hopeful title in the front of my journal, "The Healing Road," and after a salad and "triple combo" of ribs, souvlaki, and shrimp, I offered these reflections on that theme:

> *Thinking while I stuffed my face that I feel better tonight than I've felt in — more than a year. I've achieved "immersion" in The Journey, which used to be a necessarily limited state of mind: especially when interrupted by work. Or the end of the journey. Neither applies at this point.*
>
> *590 miles of healing today, maybe. "Isn't it pretty to think so."*

That closing line from Hemingway's *The Sun Also Rises* had acquired a fresh resonance for me lately, in the conscious irony of entertaining a wish without believing in its *possibility*. I did not really believe in a destination called "healing," but at least I had begun to believe in the *road*, and that was enough to keep me riding westward. Through those days and nights I wasn't always feeling "better," as the process of grieving oscillated, even through each day, from a little better to a little worse, from total existential despair to those occasional rays of hope and *interest*, which was definitely a spark of healing.

The next morning carried me into another positive response to worldly beauty, as I left Neepawa at sunrise on a fine prairie morning, cool and cloudy, the road still wet from the night's showers. The Yellowhead Highway meandered gently with the contours of the land, then ran straight and endless to the horizon, as I kept pace with a long train to the south. The sun peeked through the clouds behind me and flared in my mirrors, turning the shiny pavement to a gold ribbon between the rich green fields. My helmet filled with the fresh, nostalgic scent of damp hay.

And sometimes there was music playing in my helmet, too, as my "mental jukebox" transformed the white noise of the wind passing into a soundtrack in richly detailed high fidelity. Sometimes the same song seemed to repeat all day long; other times the playlist moved through different ones; the only distinction seemed to be that none of them were from the "family soundtrack," for of course I tried to steer the day's selections toward the pop hits from my youth or Sinatra standards. Otherwise the choice seemed random, though sometimes triggered by the scenery (*"The wheatfields and the clotheslines and the junkyards and the highways come between us"),* the weather ("Here's That Rainy Day"), a road sign ("By the Time I Get to Phoenix"), or my mood ("Everything Happens to Me"). When the riding became demanding, the music receded into the background, but when it was just me and the motorcycle on a pretty stretch of road, my brain would turn up the radio.

So early on a Sunday morning there was almost no traffic, and I cruised with my legs stretched in front of me, resting on the cylinder heads. Occasional ponds and marshes were dotted with waterbirds, and near Yorkton I saw my first magpie, a sure sign of the West.

> *Breakfast at Russell Inn: nice-looking motel and "family restaurant." Wasn't thinking of stopping yet, but couldn't resist. Just after 8:00, done over 100 miles very pleasantly. Rheostatics' "prairie music" in head, occasional sad thoughts, a few tears, but otherwise, couldn't be better (?).*

Obviously I hadn't lost my sense of irony or humor, and that was a good thing, for after covering a personal record 1,176 kilometres (735 miles) to make it into Edmonton that day, I would be sorely tested the following day. After having a leaky boot repaired, getting an oil change at the BMW dealer, and replenishing my stock of The Macallan, I made a late start out of Edmonton. Riding north now, making my way toward the Alaska Highway, I stopped at a rural gas station and pulled the bike back onto its centerstand in front of the pump. While I fiddled with getting my tankbag out of the way, the young attendant handed me the nozzle, and I started filling the tank. I noticed that the fuel seemed kind of foamy, but didn't think too much about it until the boy came out again and said, "Your bike runs on *diesel?*"

I looked down at the nozzle's handle and noticed it was green, which often (though not always) means diesel, and at the oily fuel foaming up from the filler neck. I shook my head in disbelief and said, *"No."*

Then through gritted teeth, "Do you have a siphon?"

We drained the poisonous diesel from the tank and refilled it with gasoline, but when I started the bike and tried to ride away, it died at the edge of the parking lot. On the good side of the balance sheet for this particular obstacle, the owner of the station, a stocky man whose features suggested a Native heritage, was quietly efficient, and his country garage was well equipped with the tools we would employ to try to get the dead machine running again. I started by unloading all the luggage from the bike and pulling out my toolkit, then we went to work.

Other customers stopped by in their high-wheeled, mud-spattered pickups, many of them with the same backwoods dress and Native features, and offered useful theories and suggestions. Siphon the tank out again. Remove the spark plugs and clean them, twice. Remove the injectors and spray them clean, twice. Tie a rope around the forks and tow the bike behind a car, like a water-skier, while the terrified rider tries to jumpstart it. (Sounded like a good idea . . .) Still the starter cranked impotently.

As for the teenage boy who had caused all this, he stayed out of sight for awhile, and I hoped his boss hadn't been too harsh with him. After all, it was his first day on the job, and something inside me could relate to his gangly, scrawny, pimply self-consciousness.

Call it memory.

I knew how I would have felt at that age: embarrassed, afraid, and ignorant. I felt the ghost of the fool I used to be.

But if I didn't get mad at the *boy,* I sure got angry at the *situation,* especially as the hours passed. By 4:30 I decided to call the BMW dealer back in Edmonton, while they were still open, to see about getting a truck sent out to pick up the dead bike. I described the problem to the mechanic, and he agreed that we had tried all the right things, then suggested one last desperate remedy, though he warned me to "be careful."

At my request, the taciturn owner produced a can of ether starting fluid, and he sprayed it into the air intake while I cranked the tired starter one more time. A couple of loud explosions had us ready to dive for cover, but suddenly the motor caught in clouds of thick white smoke, and I turned the throttle wide to keep it going.

While I was frantically reloading the bike and putting on my riding gear, eager to get back on the road and get *moving* again, one of the more talkative Natives remarked on the height of the bike, and said with a quiet laugh, "Too tall for orientals."

With a start I realized that those bush-wise young men who had helped me so willingly and knowledgeably were not "natives" in either sense, but were actually *Chinese,* probably only a generation or two away from an ancestor who raised millet and spoke Mandarin, or grew rice and spoke Cantonese. Their grandfathers might have worn the long braid of the Mongol emperor; their grandmothers might have woven conical hats to keep off the sun in the paddies. Now these young men had become so "native" that I had actually mistaken them for the "first immigrants," those who had been there the longest (in this area, probably Cree).

These rough-and-ready individuals looked and acted so wonderfully unstereotypical in their work boots and bush clothes, their muddy pickups with ATVs in the back, their talk of hunting season and snow machines, and I realized that these Canadians absolutely *were* "natives" now, in every sense, fully adapted to their environment. For the first time it was clear to me that when we try to classify others by stereotypes of race, what we really mean is *culture.* The modes of behavior, dress, and habits of "The Other" that we find strange and exotic, or sometimes contemptible, are cultural patterns developed over hundreds of generations in a specific locale, under local influences of weather, livelihood, diet, and daily customs.

Something I had long felt instinctively, without being able to articulate it, could finally be put into words. I saw that it was plain *wrong* to evaluate people according to race, for it was clear that *culture* was the real divider among peoples. Given enough time, a generation or two, we could all become "The Other," no more different in behavior from our neighbors and peers than they were from each other. Even the cosmetic differences would disappear in the course of a few more generations of "assimilation," adopting the local diet, mores, and chromosomes, and eventually dissolving into the gene pool.

The word *race* comes from the same Latin root as the French word *rascin* — root. Hence the English word *deracinated,* "to be uprooted." Exiled, perhaps. Well, exile is better than imprisonment, after all, and it seems to me that roots are highly overrated anyway. But *racemus* is Latin for "bunch of grapes," and perhaps those are sour ones. I no longer had any roots; I only had the road.

And on the current stretch of that road, I had hoped to make it to Dawson Creek, British Columbia, but that was out of the question now. Still, after such a frustrating setback I was determined to make some distance before dark, and I rode like a demon, passing trucks, RVs, pickups, and cars.

Behind one long line of traffic I waited tensely for an opportunity to zip into the oncoming lane, when I noticed the driver in front of me stick his hand up through his open sunroof and rotate his index finger. Recognizing the warning of a police car ahead, I backed off, but it was too late. Once again my mirrors were filled with flashing red-and-blue lights, a Royal Canadian Mounted Police car this time, and my adrenaline deflated with a sad little curse as I signalled my turn onto the shoulder of the road.

I hit the kill switch and stood slumped over the bike, helmeted head hanging down. The Mountie obviously read my body language as he walked up beside me, and with a good-humored note of mock hesitation, he said, "Well, I *was* going to ask for your licence and registration . . ."

I slowly lifted my helmet off, removed my sunglasses, and turned to look him in the eyes. "Just this once, you have *got* to hear my story." I recounted my three-hour ordeal back at the Cottonwood gas station, and explained that I was trying to make up some time and get to Grande Prairie before dark.

The mustachioed Mountie was friendly and sympathetic, and this time my Ontario driver's licence only elicited a story about how he had once lived in Toronto, and had owned a motorcycle, but had given it up as "too dangerous." His radar unit had clocked me at 140 kilometres-per-hour in a 100-kph zone, which would have been a $174 fine and some serious demerit points, but he gave me a break.

"I've got to give you a ticket, but I'll cut it down considerably."

He wrote it up as a generic "disobeying a sign" infraction, for an even $100. Fair enough, and he was nice about it too, advising me that if I took it slow, steady, and safe, I would get to Grande Prairie just as quickly. I followed his advice, though more out of dispirited resignation — and a heightened fear of further encounters with authority — than any wish to be slow, steady, and safe.

By 6:30 I'd had enough, and felt a strong desire for a large whisky and a hot shower, so I pulled into the Horizon Motel, in Valleyview. Like many of the motels I'd passed on this journey, the parking lot was full of construction pickups, carrying laborers for road-repair projects. (Given the attrition of brutal weather, Canada is said to have two seasons: Winter and Construction.) Dirty work clothes were sprawled over the railings on the upper walkway, boots and beer cases stood outside the doors, and above my ground-floor room there was much stomping around near the designated "party room."

If such rowdy groups of "men on the loose" were common in these backroad motels, solitary women of any age were certainly rare, and as I took a table in the neighboring Chinese restaurant I noticed a middle-aged woman sitting alone, hunched over a wine glass. Her face was puffy and crusted with lurid make-up, hair a too-young shade of red unknown to nature, and I wondered idly if she might be an aging hooker, winding down her career as a camp follower for the construction crews.

No doubt there was a story there, but I soon realized it wouldn't be a happy one, for she was grumbling at length to a red-faced young waiter who had apparently forgotten her order. She seemed to take it as a personal insult, and summoned the manager and complained to him indignantly, with boozy repetition. He brought her another glass of wine to mollify her, and explained that it was the boy's first day on the job. Another rookie having a bad day.

The boy's cheeks were burning when he came to my table, and his voice shook when he asked if I'd like something to drink. The woman's thoughtless cruelty angered me (how had *her* first day on the job gone?), and I tried to be extra nice to the poor boy. I told him what had happened to me that day, and said "Don't be upset about *her*." He breathed a sincere "thanks," and I felt better, and hoped he did too.

Back in my room, I flicked through the TV channels looking for the weather and stopped at an old Sinatra special from the late '60s. Frank was in splendid voice, and his tour-de-force on "Old Man River" played on my overwrought emotions and left me feeling weepy. Because he was so great, and, I suppose, because he was *dead*. Another ghost.

I was away before 6:00 on a cold morning, riding past hay farms, scrub forest, and some bald-looking areas of clearcut. (A roadside sign informed me that some of these had been cut to fight against a parasite on the spruce trees, and to eliminate the stands of deadwood left behind.)

Magpies, crows, a coyote, and a fox kept me company as I covered 250 kilometres (156 miles) before stopping for gas and breakfast in Dawson Creek, British Columbia. The poor violated GS backfired a few times when I downshifted, but seemed to be running smoothly again. I noticed my thumb was sore from working the starter button so much trying to get it started the previous day, and that made me worry about the starter itself; I hoped its brushes and windings hadn't been worn too badly by all that abuse. We were now officially getting "out there," for a sign in Dawson Creek announced "Mile 0 of the Alaska Highway," and there was no BMW dealer until the other end of it, in Fairbanks, over 1,000 miles away.

The morning remained cold, and a light overcast let through just enough glare to require sunglasses. A steady 120 kph (75 mph) was fast enough to cover the miles, though still moderately legal, but I was soon feeling bone-chilled, even with my heated vest (wired like an electric blanket and plugged into the bike's electrics), the heated grips under my heavy gloves, and my plastic rainsuit over the leathers.

In Fort Nelson, I stopped at The Pantry for a bowl of soup and a chance to warm myself, and wrote in my journal,

> *The best two-lane highway you can imagine so far — wide,*
> *well-paved, lightly travelled. Some nice bits of scenery, but I*
> *know the spectacular stuff will just be starting, as I head west*
> *into the mountains.*
>
> RV *bumper sticker:* WHERE ARE WE GOING?
> AND WHY ARE WE IN THIS HANDBASKET?

Back beside my motorcycle in the parking lot, I dug out my emergency cell phone and called Sheila, the band's bookkeeper, back at our office in Toronto. Sheila had been part of our family life in past times, for she used to come to our house to update our books every two weeks, on Tuesday evenings, the same night as Selena's flute lesson, when the house would be filled with the rich chords of the teacher's piano accompaniment and Selena's sometimes-halting performances (like her father, she loved to play, but with an impatience more like her mother's, she hated to *practise*).

Sheila had been a dear and supportive friend through all my troubles, and I had taken advantage of her kindness by gradually shifting all my business to her desk, and making her my "central liaison" for messages from friends and family. I might have been a solitary traveller, feeling completely detached from everything around me, but I was never really *alone* — always there were people thinking of me, worrying about me, and looking after the necessary business of my abandoned life.

When my whole world was pulled out from under me so completely I was left feeling so flat and weak and helpless that I was unable to cope with the details of everyday life at all, and had to accept the help that was offered so willingly by family and friends. Once I was able to accept the idea, I was amazed how much they would and could do to help me survive those dark days. John Steinbeck once wrote that sometimes the nicest thing you can do for someone is to allow them to do something for *you*, and I learned the truth of that insight too. For perhaps the first time in my life I surrendered my independence and my proud self-sufficiency, and once I had opened that window to the warm breeze of compassion, my world-view was utterly transformed. I fell into their open arms.

My brother Danny was one of those caregivers, and he sent me a quote from Thoreau, "At death, our friends and relatives either draw nearer to us, and are found out, or depart farther from us, and are forgotten." Nearly everyone close to me had drawn nearer through that time, and one day in the House of Mourning I remember saying to my friend Brad, "You know, I used to think, 'Life is great, but people suck,' but now I've had to learn the opposite, 'Life sucks, but *people* are great.'"

In my former shallow, perhaps callous, world-view, I had enjoyed my life and appreciated my family and my friends, but I had often been annoyed by the feeling that everyone else just *wanted* something from me. But now life, which I had once idealized as a generous deity offering adventure and delight, had betrayed my faith viciously, and in the aftermath it was *people* who had held me up and held me together with unstinting care and unimagined affection.

With regard to "unimagined affection," I confess that I am one of those people who, in a deep and secret place, can never imagine why anyone would actually *like* them. Respect maybe, or even appreciate, but not really *care* for. This psychology (or psychosis, or neurosis) is not about self-esteem or pride, for most people seem to possess sufficient reserves of those qualities, or some facsimile thereof, but it is more a sense of one's ineptitude in the social graces, a perceived "disability" in what seemed to be the normal social routines of being charming, funny, entertaining, and *forthcoming* with another person.

This existential discomfort causes more social awkwardness than the contrary self-image (as evinced by one friend of mine who, in that same deep and secret place, can't imagine why anyone *wouldn't* like him). And for those of us who feel deficient in such socially valued qualities, it can also be that the effort of opening ourselves up to another is so difficult we're willing to at least attempt the operation in close relationships, but not for casual encounters.

That part of me remained the same, it seemed, but I had learned that it could be *worthwhile* to try to give yourself to others. They had certainly given themselves to me. Even some who had never been that close to me before were moved, and I remembered one former employee of the band's who I hadn't seen for years showing up at the House of Mourning and tearfully rambling through a speech that basically expressed what many others must have felt, "I don't know what to say, but here's my heart."

Also in the spirit of doing others the "favor" of letting them help me, I had taken advantage of Sheila's boss, and Rush's manager, Ray, by asking him to look after the selling of the family house in Toronto. During my first meeting with a realtor, barely two weeks after Jackie's death, I had faced the raw wound of having to tell her why I was selling the house — one of the first times I was forced to tell my sad story in brief, painful words — and after offering a formulaic expression of sympathy, she told me how that might affect a buyer's response to the house, then went on to argue repeatedly against my objection to holding "open house" showings, when anyone could walk in and take a tour through that haunted house, from serious buyers to the merely curious and the outright *ghouls.*

So I was glad to avoid any more realtor-dealings, and the constant reawakening of happy family memories from that house. During our cell phone conversation that day Sheila said, "Ray wants to talk to you; I think he has pretty much got the house sold." That set my mind reeling. It was what I wanted, of course, but now it seemed so . . . final.

I tried to call Ray, but couldn't reach him, so I suited up and got back on the Alaska Highway, thinking about all those things as I rode west, the road narrowing as it twisted through the conifer forests and into the northern reaches of the Rockies. The day remained cold under looming clouds, and sometimes the road was shiny with rain, so the mountains were sensed more often than seen. When they did appear, they were bare of trees, for at this latitude the treeline was very near; at the 4,000-foot elevation of Summit Lake, the trees seemed to end right at the roadside.

After days of riding across the horizontal plane of the prairies, my journal described this three-dimensional scenery as "monumental" and "glorious," and after all those straight roads, I described the riding as "way more entertaining." This late in the season (August 25th) the traffic was light, and most of it gigantic RVs travelling in the other direction, away from Alaska. Rounding one thickly forested bend in the road, I was startled to see a small herd of caribou browsing at the roadside, and I slowed enough to look at them, but not scare them off.

I was still responding to the landscapes, highways, and wildlife, "creating" the world as I rode. I was even starting to respond to *people,* it seemed, even strangers. Apparently I could even *care* about them, like the kid at the gas station, the Oriental "natives," the hapless waiter, "the fool I used to be." This empathy had been a rare feeling for me lately, as all of my emotions were bound up in one paradigm (Loss!), and my attitude toward strangers tended more toward bitterness and envy, and could be summed up by the angry accusation, *"Why are you alive?"* (And not "them," of course.)

Now, it seemed, I was beginning to include strangers in my brave new world, and maybe as I travelled down the Healing Road I would start to *like* them again too. Anything was possible. However, despite these occasional precious moments of Truth and Beauty I was finding on the road, I often felt lost and alone, and each day I was attacked by spells of dark, weepy desolation.

So it was that cold, wet day on the Alaska Highway, and after 622 miles I was glad to arrive at the Northern Rockies Lodge, on the shore of Muncho Lake. Billed as "the largest log structure in British Columbia," with a 45-foot-high central dining room, it had been built only two years previously, in 1996, just before my friend Brutus and I happened to make a brief stop there on our motorcycling trip to Yellowknife. Back then I had thought it would be a great place to stay, an outpost of civilization on a pretty little lake cradled among tall trees and rugged gray peaks, and when I set out that morning I remembered it, and hoped to make it that far.

The gravel parking lot in front was lined with cars and sport-utility vehicles bearing licence plates from South Dakota, New York, Washington, Colorado, Texas, Utah, Florida, and Alaska. Between the lodge and the lake a few tiny, weathered log cabins, maybe 12 feet square and 10 feet high, remained from a previous enterprise, and these were offered to pariah smokers like me. "Fabulous," I wrote in my journal, and began to think seriously of staying another day. I had been afraid to consider staying in one place longer than a night, not wanting to give myself time to *think* too much, but in the six days since leaving the house on the lake I had covered 5,000 kilometres (3,000 miles), and apart from giving myself a rest at another house on a lake, there were practicalities to consider — I carried only six changes of socks, underwear, and T-shirts. The Northern Rockies Lodge offered guest laundry facilities; there were small motorboats for rent, hiking possibilities, and my little log cabin made an inviting sanctuary to hide away with a measure of The Macallan and a book.

Still uncertain about the wisdom of this notion, I left the decision to the morning, which was cold (8°C [48°F]) and threatened rain. Not the kind of day that invited travel, so I made up my mind to try staying. Walking up to the lodge for breakfast, I stopped at the desk to book another night.

The Northern Rockies Lodge was owned by a Swiss pilot named Urs and his wife Marianne, both apparently in their late 40s, and photographs on display indicated that Urs had flown for the oil company AGIP in Libya. Perhaps he had earned enough money there to buy this remote property, build the new lodge, and purchase the two float planes of Liard Air that were tied up at the dock, available for charter to sightseers and sportsmen.

With my laundry washed and dried and rolled away again, I asked Marianne about a place to hike, and she directed me across the highway to what she called "the wash." The morning was still cold and overcast, but I was soon warmed by the effort of climbing over the tumbled rocks, stones, and gravel at the bottom of a narrow canyon, like a glacial moraine or scree, where the snowmelt obviously came pouring down in spring. The lower part had been bulldozed into levees to channel the flow, and I scrambled over them and up into the larger boulders, following the banks of a small stream up into the ragged forest.

A little bird called a dipper, or water ouzel, retreated ahead of me upstream, easily identifiable by its habit of ducking under the water, or "dipping," to hunt its food of insects and small crustaceans. Seeing a new species like that was always a mild thrill for a longtime bird lover, and later that afternoon when I rented a small motorboat to tour the lake I saw a bald eagle soaring against the dark forest, and another first sighting, an Arctic loon, sleeker and lighter-colored than the common loons that lived on my lake at home. There were also slender mergansers fishing on the lake, and a large flock of small, puffin-like ducks which flew off before I was close enough to identify them.

A brief rainshower during my boat ride made me grateful for my waterproof jacket and hat, but the clouds finally passed off to the east, leaving a rainbow and bright washes of sunlight on the barren gray peaks above the forest. When I got back to the lodge I said to Marianne at the front desk, "A place like this is supposed to be relaxing, but I'm *exhausted*; so much to do!"

Exhausted I may have been, but I was also relaxed; my first day staying in one place had turned out pretty well. As always, the main thing was to keep *moving*; keep active, take that little baby soul for a ride. It just took *will*, and I knew I was always just barely hanging on to that necessary resolve. I was still overcome by tears and abject sorrow several times a day, but I tried to let those spells pass, and to avoid the hopeless tailspin of spiralling down into the abyss of memories.

Those memories were always with me, of course, and it seemed that part of what Freud called "grief work" involved calling up and processing every memory I had of the lost ones. Every shared laugh and every harsh word had to be recalled and assigned a new, final judgement, something I could eventually feel good about, maybe, or something I would have to keep replaying in my mind, like my mental video-loop of Selena's accident or the memory of Jackie's last breath, until I could lay it to rest in a peaceful garden of memory.

For some reason, as part of that grief work it also seemed necessary for me to replay every single incident of my own life, and once when I was awake in the middle of the night in a motel, stewing over these things, I tried to write it down.

> *Notice in these "watches of the night," or while riding (or anytime), pattern of torment (*tormente, *Spanish for storm). Not only have to relive and examine every episode of life with Jackie and Selena, but every single episode of my own life. Every embarrassment, act of foolishness, wrong-headedness, error, idiocy etc. going back to childhood and all the way forward to now.*
>
> *I physically flinch, say "ow" out loud, or "fuck," as the case may be, and can hardly bear it. Such stupid things sometimes, but it seems my confidence, or belief in myself, or something, is so shaken, so undermined, so tenuous, that I have no tolerance, no understanding, no* forgiveness: *for myself or anyone else.*
>
> *No forgiveness . . .*

Without knowing it, I had identified a subtle but important part of the healing process. There would be no peace for me, no *life* for me, until I learned to forgive life for what it had done to me, forgive others for still being alive, and eventually, forgive *myself* for being alive.

With such currents in the existential sea to swim through, a day spent in motion helped keep me afloat, forcing me to be moderately curious about my surroundings, and to concentrate on what I was doing, especially when I was riding the motorcycle and dealing with the balancing act, literally and figuratively, of its operation, the road, the weather, other traffic, the background of inspiring scenery, and the occasional glimpses of birds and animals.

Landscapes, highways, and wildlife — my new holy trinity. From those simple elements it did seem I was finding enough to get moderately excited about, and each of those moments of Truth and Beauty was an important baby step along the Healing Road, and other strands to weave into the day's fabric of grief and despair.

Just as when I was alone at the house on the lake, I never felt consciously *lonely*, for I had always enjoyed my own company, and reading had always served as a diversion, escape, and solace for me. I did notice that I was doing a lot of journal writing, which made for a kind of companion during solitary meals, and I had also been uncharacteristically active on the telephone, calling two or three friends or family members every day, and that was very unlike me.

Or at least, it was very unlike the fool I *used* to be.

"Mr. Gregarious," I laughed at myself in my journal.

> *Probably good for me, though. I do find I'm talking to myself fairly often, which makes me laugh (crazy old coot). But that's okay. Just watch it!*

> *Fortune is random — fate shoots from the hip*
> *I know you get crazy, but try not to lose your grip*
> NEUROTICA, 1991

Chapter 3

∩·O·RTH T·O İ∩UVİK

The point of the journey
Is not to arrive —
Anything can happen

PRIME MOVER, 1987

Parking my motorcycle in front of a motel at the end of a long day on the road could certainly be sweet, like finally exhaling after holding my breath all day, but best of all was setting out in the morning. Whatever torments the night had brought; whatever weather the new day threw at me, when I loaded up the bike and swung my leg over the saddle, my whole perspective changed. Focus tightened into the mechanics and mentality of operating the machine, and awareness contracted to that demanding paradigm. As I let in the clutch and turned the throttle, my world-view expanded as I moved into a whole new paradigm of landscapes, highways, and wildlife. Infinite possibilities.

Travel writers often feel compelled to try to explain and justify the difference between being a tourist and being a traveller. They cite the etymology of "travel" in the French word *travail*, labor, and point out that any independent journey outside the well-worn tourist routes requires extreme will and endurance simply *to keep moving forward.* One of the most indefatigable of serious travellers, Paul Theroux, explains that after one of his journeys, he hasn't *had* a vacation; he *needs* a vacation. But for most of his readers, the "armchair travellers," it's only the vicarious, pristine experience they want to share, not the unhygienic, exhausting reality.

The solitary traveller is frequently invested by others with an aura of romance, myth, and *desire.* So many people feel trapped in the workaday predictability of their lives, and their frustrations and dissatisfactions can be simultaneously stimulated and soothed by a non-specific fantasy of "getting away." But like all fantasies, this dream vision remained free of consequences, and that alone was the deep, cold distinction between fantasy and reality: No consequences.

Watching a movie or reading a novel might make you feel sad, or frightened, or inspired, but at the end of that experience, nothing has actually *happened* in your life. The experiences of real life were not like that, as I had certainly come to know. The fantasy image of a free spirit drifting without care or effort through some IMAX movie of breathtaking scenery not only ignored the darker possibilities (breakdown, accident, injury, death), it also omitted the simple joy-killers of bad weather, indigestion, toothache, or diesel in your fuel tank. Anything can happen, and scenery is never "neutral."

So if I always felt a quiet thrill as I set off into the mysteries of a new day, it was often tempered by such realities, both potential and immediate. Leaving Muncho Lake before 6:00 on a chilly, overcast morning, for example, the danger was potential, but the cold was immediate. I wore my full foul-weather outfit of long underwear under the armored leather suit, heated vest and handgrips on full, thin balaclava under my full-face helmet, and the plastic rainsuit over it all to help shield me from the cruel wind.

A different journey was beginning as I left behind the relatively secure environment of highways and cities and struck off into remote areas of rough roads and widely scattered little settlements. From that day on, I felt less like a traveller and more like an adventurer (or misadventurer), for I was very much aware that out here the consequences of "pilot error" or accident were increasingly severe. Fear was my co-pilot, and there was much to worry about now, in both imagination and reality.

Highway construction, or rather *de*construction, was the day's first obstacle. When I saw the pavement ending at a long stretch of soft-looking dirt, I held myself tense and breathless as my wheels plowed into the deep, heavy morass of ruts that could so easily knock me down. For several miles my eyes were fixed on nothing but the brown dirt approaching my wheels, steering toward the more packed-down areas as smoothly as I could, easy on the brakes, easy on the gas, balance, balance, balance.

Then came the day's first reward. As I crossed a bridge high above the wide Liard River, I glanced down and saw something large and dark in the middle of the water. It seemed to be swimming across, trailing a vee-shaped wake of silver, so I slowed down for a better look. At first it resembled a cow, but that seemed unlikely, so I decided it was probably a moose, and I slowed even more, then put my feet down and stopped to watch. As the dark mass reached the far shore and climbed up on the bank, my eyes widened as I saw that it was a huge black bear, shaking itself and lumbering off into the forest.

The characteristic birds of the far north were the ravens flapping heavily across the gray sky, and occasionally a spruce grouse standing dumbly at the roadside. The morning seemed gradually to brighten a little, and I began to hope that some solar warmth might ease my shivering, but the day remained bitter.

I stopped at a roadside clearing for a break, and as I stood looking over the expansive view of the river and its banks of green and yellow forest, a big RV pulled in behind me. Its driver, a friendly older man, came over to look at my bike, and told me he had owned a BMW in 1960, and now rode a Honda Gold Wing back home in southern Illinois. As we discussed our travels, I learned that he and his wife were on their way home from Alaska, and when I told him I was thinking of heading off the highway that day to some gravel roads, he hooked a thumb back toward the RV and said with a rueful smile, *"She* won't let me leave the highway!"

The destination I had in mind was Telegraph Creek, because . . . well, because I liked the name. I first heard of it in an article in *Equinox* ("The Magazine of Canadian Discovery," now defunct, unfortunately) in which the writer had pointed out that map-makers seemed to like Telegraph Creek because it gave them a name to put on an otherwise empty region, where northern British Columbia met the Alaska Panhandle.

The settlement had flourished briefly twice, first during the Klondike gold rush when it was the head of navigation for steamboats carrying hopeful prospectors up the Stikine River. From there, they could travel overland to the Yukon goldfields on what came to be known as "The Bughouse Trail," its history replete with Jack London-style tales of starvation, scurvy, frostbite, and madness. The town's second life, and the source of its name, came from an American scheme to run a telegraph cable overland through Alaska, under the Bering Strait, and across Russia to connect with Europe, but shortly after the surveying was completed the project was rendered pointless by the laying of the transatlantic cable. Telegraph Creek once again lapsed into a virtual ghost town, and the only present-day visitors seemed to be attracted by boat, raft, and kayaking expeditions on the Stikine River. Or by the name.

Another siren-call for me was the romantic lure of an isolated, storied destination which lay "at the end of the road." Telegraph Creek was a dot on the map at the end of a long unpaved road, far from anywhere, the kind of place Brutus and I used to dream about exploring (in fact, it was Brutus, in a recent telephone conversation, who had urged me to go there). The guidebooks disagreed on whether I would have to navigate 74 miles or 74 kilometres of that road, but they agreed that it was "rough" and "often treacherous." In fact it turned out to be 112 kilometres (near enough 74 miles) of dirt and gravel winding through deep forest and steep switchbacks up and down the walls of "The Grand Canyon of the Stikine." In some places, the sheer cliffs of eroded, multi-layered rock did resemble a modest version of that famed stretch of the Colorado River, and sometimes the road was a mere ledge perched on those vertical walls, dropping off into a frightening abyss.

My journal described it as a "scary, scary road," and I was fairly rattled when I pulled up in front of the Stikine Riversong café, general store, lodge, and boat-tour headquarters. All this was housed in one large white frame building facing the swift-moving river, and I learned later that it had been the original Hudson's Bay Company trading post, situated just downriver, and had been moved piece by piece to Telegraph Creek. A few other abandoned-looking houses and a small church clustered on the river bank, but only the Riversong showed any signs of life.

The guidebooks said that a few rooms were available there, but if they happened to be filled it would be a long way back to any other lodgings. The cold, gloomy weather made the idea of camping uninviting, but once again I was glad to be carrying my little tent and sleeping bag, especially when the owner told me he was closing for the weekend and taking the staff upriver in his tour boat to celebrate the end of their season. Then, after a moment's thought, he said that I was welcome to rent one of the rooms and stay there on my own. That was thoughtful, hospitable, and trusting of him, and I only asked what I might do for food. He told me there was a kitchen upstairs where I could prepare my own meals, so I bought a few provisions in the general store in the back of the building, including some fresh salmon from the river, and carried my bags to a small bedroom upstairs.

I watched through the café window as the owner and his three employees loaded their camping gear into the motor boat, and my only regret was missing the opportunity for a tour of the river myself. I stood on the riverbank and watched the boat speed away upriver against the strong current, and felt a little excited, and a little fearful.

Apparently the only other enterprise, Trina Anne Excursions, was also abandoned for the weekend, so the only living souls in town were the

Mountie and his wife at the RCMP post at the other end of town. (Because the Stikine River flowed down to the Alaskan town of Wrangell, Telegraph Creek was a kind of frontier outpost between the two countries.) I was virtually alone in my own private ghost town, watching the river flow.

Upstairs in the empty old building the silence seemed almost oppressive, and only accentuated by the amazingly creaky floors as I walked around between my small bedroom at the front, the shared bathroom, and the common area of kitchen and sitting room. On the payphone I called my friend and colleague, Alex, on his birthday, and he was pleased to hear from me, though a little bemused by my tale of where I was calling from. The delay on the line made me feel even more like a voice from the wilderness. *Vox clamatis in deserto.*

As I wrote in my journal, "Well, I've fetched up in some strange places in my travels, and some places that were a serious adventure to *get* to, but this . . . this is one of them."

I slept soundly with my window open to the cool, fresh air and the murmuring of the river, and took a walk before breakfast on another chilly, overcast morning. Past ruined cabins and abandoned, moss-covered cars and pickups from the 1950s, a narrow path led up a high, lava-rock cliff above a steep scree to an old graveyard overlooking the town. As I walked among the stones reading the inscriptions, the bare facts of names and dates had a whole new resonance for me, for I felt them as part of a story like mine, a story of love and loss. I thought about "Honey Joe," who had died at the age of 105 and was buried beside "Mrs. Joe," who he had outlived by 40 years. Then there were all the babies, children, teenagers, and young men and women, and I found myself weeping for all the lost ones, theirs and mine. Ghost town indeed.

High on the other side of the main road was a Native settlement of prefab houses, and the map showed a road leading from there another 15 miles downriver to the ruins of a town called Glenora, where the Hudson's Bay Company post, now the Riversong, had originally been located. In the afternoon I suited up and took a ride out that way, to see if there was anything to see, but as I picked my way along the narrow dirt road, rain began to fall, turning the surface under my wheels to mud. Where the road ended I found only a couple of pickup trucks and boat trailers, and I straddled the bike and tried to turn it around. The tires slid in the mud and I lost my footing, then leapt aside as the motorcycle fell over, leaving us both laying in the mud. Even with all the bags removed the bike still weighed about 600 pounds, and it took all my strength, slipping around in my muddy boots, to haul it upright. One mirror was broken and hanging loose, but there didn't seem to be any other damage, and I slithered my way back to the Riversong through the steady rain.

I hunted up a piece of scrap wood to put under the centerstand, to prevent the bike from sinking into the liquefying surface and falling over again, tried unsuccessfully to fix the mirror, then had a closer look for other damage. Nothing was apparent, but I did notice the brake pads were looking a little thin, and it was possible that all the wet, gritty riding I'd been doing had worn them more quickly than usual. It was hard to tell with everything gummed up with mud, and there was nothing I could do about it anyway, but it was something else to worry about.

And still the rain kept falling, hour after hour, and I began to fear the ride out of there the following day. If that 70-mile dirt road had been treacherous and scary when it was *dry,* what would it be like as a slippery mire clinging to a precipice? I didn't like to think about it; but I did.

From the payphone at the Riversong I finally got a call through to Ray to find out what was going on with the sale of the Toronto house. Apparently the day before, while I had been hiding out there in the wilderness, unconcerned with any news from the outside world, the stock market had taken its own tumble into the mud, the Canadian dollar had plummeted again, and the formerly committed buyer had found an excuse to back out of the deal at the last minute. Just when I had grown used to the idea of saying goodbye to that "haunted house," with all its years of family memories, it was back on the market, and back on my mind.

Just what I needed. It's hard not to feel like Mr. All-Time Loser sometimes.

Rain and despair, bad combination.
Have the feeling of being "driven to the edge of a deep, dark
hole," so to speak. Very aware of backing away: "Don't go there."

After a troubled night, I was up at 5:00, nervous and edgy, fixing a quick breakfast of orange juice, cereal, and strong coffee. It was still dark as I carried my bags out to the bike, and though the ground was sodden, I was glad to see the rain had stopped, and looked up to a clear patch of sky with stars and a planet.

As I walked back to the door after the first load, I was stopped in my tracks at the sight of a fox, small and brown with a white-tipped tail, standing by the door and watching me calmly. At first I was thrilled to see this elusive wild animal up close, but I realized this was unnatural behavior, and it made me uneasy. The fox might have been rabid, or it might have been tamed by someone from the staff feeding it; I couldn't know. When I came out with the second load it was still sitting there, just looking at me. I worried about it sneaking inside in search of food, so I kicked the door closed behind me. Just as the latch clicked shut I felt a start of fear and cringed, remembering the door was self-locking, and that I had left the key on the kitchen table.

Oh man. It was 5:30 in the morning; no one from the Riversong was expected back until later that day, and short of breaking something, my only hope of getting the door unlocked was the Mountie, and I couldn't very well go knocking on *his* door at this hour.

I remembered seeing a ladder nailed to the front of the building, plank rungs leading up to the second floor — a primitive fire escape. My bedroom window was still cracked open, maybe I could raise it all the way from outside. Wearing all my riding gear except the helmet (at least I'd be armored if I fell!), I climbed up the side of the building, squeezed through the window, and rescued myself.

In the gloomy twilight the bike's headlight glittered on the puddles and dripping vegetation as I threaded slowly and nervously through the soggy gravel and mud of the Stikine Valley. Higher up, the road seemed as dry as it had been on the way in, and I made my careful way out to the main road at Dease Lake. The morning was windy and cold, but I was glad to be back on pavement as I sped north once more, toward breakfast in Watson Lake, just over the border in the Yukon.

Back on the Alaska Highway, I stopped to marvel at the famed "Sign Forest," where more than 30,000 town signs from all over the world were displayed in a vast open area, a custom apparently inspired by a single sign posted by a homesick G.I. during the construction of what had originally been called the Alcan Highway, during World War II.

Continuing westward, bursts of yellow aspen dotted the dark green forest, and above the low treeline, the higher elevations of the rounded mountains were dusted with snow. Occasional lakes gleamed in the dull light, and once I saw a bald eagle swooping over the turquoise shallows. A few motorcycles passed me in the other direction, including three BMW GSes like mine, and we exchanged big waves of recognition.

My own GS, apart from being muddy and missing a mirror, needed a new indicator bulb and another oil change, which I tried to do every 3,000 kilometres, so I decided to go without lunch and get to Whitehorse early enough in the day for that operation. By early afternoon I had covered the 858 kilometres (536 miles) and circled the wide, neat streets of downtown Whitehorse in search of the necessary facilities. I carried tools and a spare filter to do the oil change myself, but I needed a place to buy some oil and drain the old stuff. At the Canadian Tire store I found the bulb I needed, but the mechanics were off on Saturday and no one else seemed to know where I could empty my old oil. They sent me to the "Enviro-Lube" shop, who said they didn't "do" motorcycles (even if I "did" it myself), and they sent me to the Honda dealer, which was closed. I surrendered to fate, and went in search of lodging.

The Westmark Hotel made for a sharp contrast with my previous two nights in Telegraph Creek, for the busy high-rise was filled with people on bus tours, and my room had a view across an airshaft to the blank windows of other rooms. The restaurant was also put to shame by the previous night's meal (the fresh local salmon prepared by *moi*, Chef

Ellwood), and my own service had been a lot better too, for this waitress was inattentive, forgetful, and unaware of her own ineptitude. In my journal-writing during dinner I toyed with the crazy idea of actually telling her the truth, "You know, you're a lousy waitress."

But, I noted, "Like so many other truths, pointless."

However, the music that was playing in the restaurant caught my ear. In previous years I had always kept abreast of new music, not so much professionally but as a music lover, but in the wake of my tragedies I had left all that behind too. After being outside the pop-culture loop for over a year, I was just starting to hear some of what I had missed.

> *Surprisingly decent music — unfamiliar, countryish, but kind of, um, "smart." Heartfelt too. Different artists and singers, male and female, intriguing lyrics, interesting arrangements. Most unusual and unexpected, here in Whitehorse. With everything else going on within and without, it has a surreal effect somehow.*
>
> *Is all this the pop music I've missed in the past year? If so, I'm pleasantly surprised.*

Next morning the Weather Network showed -3° [28°F] and there was frost on my saddle, so I decided to stay around for awhile, have breakfast, and call my Mom on her birthday. No one answered the phone at my parents' house that morning, and after a couple of hours of sitting around, I was restless and anxious to get moving. As I set off on the Klondike Highway toward Dawson, passing many ravens and a couple of coyotes, the weather had not warmed up much, but at least it was bright and sunny.

At the Braeburn Lodge, one of those "everything" places that dot the far north (café, gas station, general store, humble-looking motel rooms, road-maintenance depot, and shortwave radio station), the owner sold me some oil and gave me a bucket to drain mine into. I spread my blue plastic ground sheet on the gravel lot to lay upon, peeled off some of my overclothes, and completed a successful oil and filter change in about 20 minutes.

Reloaded and resuited, I rode off feeling the small satisfaction of having looked after the motorcycle's needs. I crossed the Yukon River at Carmack, and now I was out of the mountains again, for the low forest stretched to the horizon in every direction, the deciduous trees in full autumn color already, at the end of August. Stopping at a roadside stand called "Penny's Place," I sat on a picnic bench and enjoyed an excellent burger, the best lunch of the journey so far. While discussing the weather with Penny, she told me that up there, spring and fall each lasted about a week.

Three other motorcyclists pulled in behind me on heavily-loaded Kawasaki dual-sport bikes (like my GS, designed with high clearance, long-travel suspension, and stout wheels to handle heavy baggage and bad roads). We shared some of our travel stories, and I learned that they were a father and his two sons from southern British Columbia on their way to Alaska, where they were planning to ride to the Arctic Circle on the Dalton Highway, the service road which followed the Alaska Pipeline up to Prudhoe Bay (not a "highway" at all, of course, but a gravel haul road for the oil company's vehicles). I told them I had my eye on the Dempster Highway, the equally misnamed dirt road on the Canadian side, which also crossed the Arctic Circle on its way to Inuvik, in the Northwest Territories. As I prepared to ride away, we wished each other good riding. "Keep the shiny side up and the rubber side down."

More snow-dusted mountains came into view as I approached Dawson, at the end of a relatively easy day's ride on a dry, paved highway under sunny skies. It was still early in the afternoon, and I'd only covered 565 kilometres (350 miles) that day, but Dawson was the starting point for the Dempster Highway, and I needed to make some decisions, and maybe some preparations. In any case, it was pleasant having an early end to a day that wasn't quite so "epic," and I was glad to check into another Westmark Hotel (also filled with bus tours, probably the same group), do some laundry, and walk around the town.

Except for Front Street, the main road in, all the streets were unpaved and lined with boardwalks, otherwise the permafrost would heave the paving up every year like a wrinkled carpet. The boardwalk helped to give the place a real frontier town feel, along with a couple of genuine older buildings like the court house and the bank. Although the main part of town was a little tarted up for tourists, with "Klondike Days" saloons and such, behind the facades Dawson had the rugged, weather-beaten look of any small town in the far north. Several camper trucks were parked along the levees beside the Yukon River, among them a few vw microbuses with British Columbia and California plates, one with a "smiley-face" tire cover. Neo-hippies.

Another attraction in Dawson was the Jack London Centre, which commemorated the writer's time in the area as a young prospector during the Klondike gold rush, in 1897. The stories and novels inspired by that part of his life, including *The Call of the Wild* and *White Fang*, had brought him his first success and fame. By chance I had recently come across a Jack London story in an anthology called *The Very Richness of That Past*, a collection of writing about Canada by "visitors." (The title came from a story by another American writer, Wallace Stegner, whose writing I would also come to love after that first taste of his work.) The opening of London's story, "In a Far Country," had relevance to my present journey both literally and metaphorically:

When a man journeys into a far country, he must be prepared to forget many of the things he has learned, and to acquire such customs as are inherent with existence in the new land; he must abandon the old ideals and the old gods, and oftentimes he must reverse the very codes by which his conduct has hitherto been shaped. To those who have the protean faculty of adaptability, the novelty of such change may even be a source of pleasure; but to those who happen to be hardened to the ruts in which they were created, the pressure of the altered environment is unbearable, and they chafe in body and in spirit under the new restrictions which they do not understand. This chafing is bound to act and react, producing diverse evils and leading to various misfortunes. It were better for the man who cannot fit himself to the new groove to return to his own country; if he delay too long, he will surely die.

The lady curator was just getting ready to close the museum for the day, but she talked with me for a few minutes about London's life and writing, and dismissed the biography I'd read as "sensationalized." She recommended a couple of others, and when I named the few books of his that I had read so far, she said I was in for a treat when I got to his masterworks, like *The Sea Wolf* and *Martin Eden*.

Outside the museum was a replica of the small log cabin in which London was said to have waited out his long, dark winter in the bush farther up the Yukon River. The ruins had been identified by a carved inscription, "Jack London, Writer and Miner," he had allegedly left on a board inside it, and two copies of the cabin had been assembled from the original pieces, one in Dawson, and one in London's home town of Oakland, California.

Back in the hotel parking lot I talked to a man who had just come back from the Dempster Highway in his Jeep, and he shook his head as he told me it had been a rough journey, and he had barely made it even in his four-wheeler. Five hundred miles of dirt road each way, he said, with only one gas station in the middle, and there had been some muddy construction zones where he had seen a few other motorcyclists having a hard time, falling down and pushing each other through the muck.

That night, I finally reached my mother on the phone and wished her a happy birthday, and she sounded worried when I told her my plans. After Selena's death I had leaned on my Mom the most, not surprisingly, and my Dad had been there for me too, giving strength and help and comfort when he could. (I would never forget that first night back in Toronto, standing in the front hall in my father's arms and sobbing, "It's so *bad!*")

Even after Jackie and I went to London I had called my mother every day, just needing the refuge of her voice, and recently, when I had apologized for not calling so often, she had said, "That's okay — when I don't hear from you I know you're all right!" She and Dad had come to London to help us through that first awful Christmas, and later visited us in Barbados, not long before Jackie's passing. Earlier that August, when I hadn't felt up to facing the anniversary of Selena's death by myself, I had ridden my motorcycle across Ontario to Mom and Dad's house to spend the night with them.

On the telephone in Dawson, partly to calm her, and partly to calm myself, I made the decision out loud that I would go for the Arctic Circle at least (just over halfway), and turn around the first time I fell down. Neither of us was much comforted by that idea, but at least I had committed myself to a plan.

At 9:30 at night the sun was still hitting the hilltop behind the town, even that late in the summer (August 30th), and at 10:15, when I was still trying to catch up with my journal-writing, I noted that it was still fairly light outside.

> *Still hard to keep up with this trip, journalizing-wise, even when I think I'm taking it easy. Too much happens in a day, that's all, as Selena once observed.*

In late June of 1997, toward the end of the *Test For Echo* tour, Selena joined Brutus and me in our "Scooter Trash" gang for a few days, sleeping on the bus, travelling by motorcycle to the shows, then getting herself all dolled up for "show time."

At the end of a show at Greatwoods Amphitheater, near Boston, I ran straight off the stage and into the "Scooter Trash" bus. Brutus and Selena were already aboard, and our driver, Dave, set off across New England while I dried off and changed, then sat in the front lounge talking and listening to music. Brutus and I raised a glass of The Macallan and Selena sipped a beer.

Soon we melted off to our bunks (Selena claimed her favorite place to sleep was in the bunk of a moving bus) and jostled through the night in the classic rest of the touring musician. Brutus had chosen a "staging area" for the next morning's ride in a corner of Maine, and Dave drove to a rest area nearby, where we could enjoy some motionless sleep for another few hours.

At daylight, I roused the sleepy Selena, and we all crowded into the narrow lounge and struggled into our riding gear. Brutus and I backed the bikes off the trailer, Selena climbed on behind me, and we rode into the

White Mountains of New Hampshire, where Brutus had arranged a rendezvous with a helicopter pilot and a videographer.

For the next six hours Selena traded her uncomfortable seat behind me on the motorcycle for an uncomfortable seat beside the helicopter pilot, while he performed all kinds of aerobatics for the videographer and Andrew, the still photographer (who didn't much enjoy hanging out the side of the helicopter to shoot pictures of Brutus and me riding together).

After that ordeal, poor Selena climbed on the back of the motorcycle again, and we rode another six hours to the Wheatcroft Inn, in Lenox, Massachusetts. It was way, way too long of a day for her, and she was sore and tired and miserable; we all were. However, in one of her greatest moments, within three minutes my little girl had changed from her leather riding suit into a pretty green dress, given her hair a quick "up-do," and was transformed into her elegant-lady persona. "Selena the Warrior Princess," we called her.

At dinner that night the three of us were limply good-humored, and Selena kept teasing Brutus about his bad planning, and how tired and sore she was. Then, as we discussed the events of that day, Selena shook her head and said, "I can't believe how much can happen in *one day!*" She made me proud.

A few days later, before the second half of the show at an amphitheatre near Buffalo, New York, Selena was leaving to go back to Toronto, and I said goodbye to her outside the trailer dressing room. As I hugged and kissed her, I told her, "I love you, and I'm proud of you — in so many ways." And the last time I saw her, on the morning of August 10th, 1997, I had ridden ahead of her on my motorcycle to guide her through the back roads of Quebec to a gas station in Hawkesbury, Ontario, and once again I hugged and kissed her, and told her I loved and was proud of her. Now I was so glad those words had been spoken, and I was grateful for other good memories too.

Most of our family travels had tended to be at *my* convenience, at the end of one of my solo adventures, for example, when Jackie and Selena would meet me in Hong Kong, Nairobi, the Ivory Coast, or Paris, or join me for a break in a Rush tour in Boston, St. Louis, or San Francisco. But just the year before, in the spring of 1997, I had taken Jackie alone to Tahiti, Bora Bora, and Moorea for a couple of weeks, and at the end of it she told me that the nicest thing about it was that for the whole time she had felt like she'd had all my attention. Typically, I hadn't thought of that as being an important factor, but in retrospect, I was sure glad I had done that. Sometimes — however unknowingly — I *hadn't* been such a fool.

Aug. 31 Dawson

Up at 5:30, chipping the ice off saddle. Now at Klondike River Lodge for breakfast, at turnoff for Dempster. Should I try it or not? 380 kms (238 miles) to first gas stop. Current fuel range makes that . . . marginal. Then there's the mud story — deep, slippery clay up here on the permafrost, the worst possible hazard when wet.

Well, I'm here at "Mile 0" anyway, so something (stubbornness? optimism? stupidity?) is pushing me that way. There've been at least two dry days since the Jeep guy was up there, so . . . maybe.

One guy at the Klondike River Lodge just asked a truck driver, "How was the trip?"

He just shrugged, "Muddy."

Oh boy.

At the start of the Dempster Highway a large sign announced that there were no emergency facilities available on this road, and that, basically, "You're on your own." Fuel was my main concern, and I kept the engine speed below 3,000 RPMS, went as light as I could on the throttle, and even pulled in the clutch on downhills. The surface varied from loose gravel, where I tried to follow the firmer ruts left by the trucks, to long stretches of hard-packed clay, which were almost like pavement. About once an hour I encountered another vehicle — big semis trailing long dust clouds, camper trucks, and the odd car or pickup — but, I noted, it was "a lonely old road."

Low spruce forest rolled for miles in every direction, gradually giving way to stretches of barren tundra, and I described the landscape as "spectacularly bleak and barren." Small ponds at the roadside had a skin of ice at the edges, and the air was so cold that the bike's oil temperature hardly registered on the gauge. I covered half the oil cooler with a piece of cardboard torn from a cigarette package, and that worked fine.

Apart from the usual ravens, I saw a few gray jays and many willow ptarmigans, a grouse-like bird, which at this season were halfway between their plumage of summer brown and winter white. I was riding slowly enough to identify the many birds of prey: peregrine falcons, gyrfalcons, rough-legged hawks, and harriers hovering over the open areas. A fox crossed the road in front of me, brown with a white-tipped tail, like the friendly one back at Telegraph Creek, and I spotted a few hares and ground squirrels, and a couple of caribou melting into the bush in the distance. I was a few weeks early for the big caribou migration, and I saw none of the bison and bears Brutus and I had encountered on our way to Yellowknife.

Eagle Plains marked the halfway point on the Dempster, and I was relieved to see the long, low complex of buildings come into view. Another "everything" sort of oasis in the wilderness, it included a gas station, restaurant, motel, several big outbuildings for road-maintenance equipment, a tall radio tower, and a windsock for helicopter landings. I pulled up to the gas pumps at about 1:30, glad to see that my fuel-sparing measures had worked; I had covered the first 380 kilometres without even hitting my reserve tank, never mind having to use my spare gallon can. It looked as though I could make it to Inuvik in another six hours or so, if everything went well, but I was aware that the rough stretches of mud and construction would still be ahead of me, so I was taking nothing for granted.

A sign at the restaurant door said "Please remove wet, muddy, or bloody footwear," the last of which gave me pause, but I presumed they meant hunters. Large areas of land at the roadside had been sign-posted as native reserves, with hunting "by written permit only."

The walls were covered with framed photos and documents telling the story of "The Lost Patrol," a group of Royal Canadian Mounted Police who had become disoriented and died of starvation just north of there, in the winter of 1910. The Dempster Highway was named after the Mountie who had found their remains the following spring.

In open areas I had noticed a long straight line of discolored vegetation cutting across the landscape, and from other old photographs on display at Eagle Plains I learned that this track had been left by a "cat train," a bulldozer-drawn caravan that had followed the seismic lines in search of oil. However, this cat-train had passed only once, *44 years ago*, which demonstrated the fragility of the Arctic landscape.

> *Amazing sweeping views from here: hills, rolling tundra, distant low mountains. The open area after Eagle Plains in crimson and rust colors, among rounded, elephantine hills. Brutal wind, sweeping through the grasses and shrubs, and shoving me all over the road. When it was strong and steady, I was practically riding side-saddle, on the corner of the seat.*
>
> *Up and down and around, the road like a gravel dike laid over the tundra.*

Just north of Eagle Plains, a sign announced the crossing of the Arctic Circle, and I stopped to mark my claim to this new territory in the primitive animal fashion. A van pulled into the bitterly cold, windswept parking area, and its solitary driver offered to take one of the few photographs from my travels which had *me* in it, standing in front of the sign and spreading my rainsuit-covered arms.

The next sign I passed announced the border with the Northwest Territories, and the wind seemed to suddenly switch to the opposite direction, then it died altogether as I descended to the wide delta of the Mackenzie River. I followed the track of dirt and gravel through walls of shoulder-high spruce, with a few stunted tamaracks and shrubs in yellow and orange. The evenly spaced dwarf birch and scrub willow reminded me of the creosote bushes in the Mojave Desert in California, one of many reminders of a desert landscape in the lower Arctic.

The road worsened considerably as I rode on, particularly in the areas of road construction. Just after a small ferry carried me over the Mackenzie River to Fort McPherson, a long stretch of the road had been graded bare of gravel and soaked by water trucks, presumably to hold down the dust. An older "flag lady" with a walkie-talkie was controlling the traffic on the one open lane, and when she waved me forward, my wheels sank into the greasy clay ruts. I rode as slowly as I could, gently fighting for control, but with zero traction available, my rear wheel slipped sideways, and in an instant I was down and sliding in the mud, the bike bearing down on me from behind in a slow circle.

In those few seconds of slow-motion perception, I was sure that the bike was going to end up on *top* of me, but it slid to a stop just behind, both of us painted with reddish-brown slime. I was muddy but unbowed, seemingly unhurt, and grateful once again for my strong boots and the armored padding inside the leathers, which protected my elbows, shoulders, knees, and hips.

The only apparent damage to the bike was a snapped-off turn signal, which a little duct tape would remedy, but the tipover in Telegraph Creek had shown that I could barely raise the bike even without its load. I removed the tankbag, the tent and sleeping bag, the gas can and the right-side luggage case, but the one on the left side was trapped under the fallen machine.

It occurred to me then that one of my *legs* might easily have been caught like that, wedged under the hot exhaust pipe even, and I felt lucky for a moment. But I still faced the problem of getting *moving* again. My boots flailed in the viscous goop as I took hold of the bars and leaned down to wedge my knee under the bike. I put my body into it and strained mightily, risking heart attack and hernia, but despite my grunting efforts the glutinous muck refused to let it go. Now I considered the reality that I should never have tried that journey alone, if I couldn't even lift the bike if it fell. Judging from my experiences with Brutus on our first journey into the land of permafrost mud and rainy construction zones, it was likely to happen again.

A tractor-trailer came looming down on me from the other direction, so I skated my way through the mud and off the road, out of its way. I took a moment to collect myself and consider my plight, hoping the big truck could squeeze past the fallen bike. The flag lady came running from her post a quarter-mile back to see that I was all right, and I was touched by this neighborly concern. I didn't like to ask her to help me lift the bike, and was trying to decide if I would swallow my pride and flag down the oncoming truck and ask for help.

I didn't have to. The semi came slithering to a stop beside me, and a short, dark man in coveralls hopped down from the cab, asked if I was okay, then bent to help me lift the bike. He had obviously recognized my situation, and on remote roads in the Arctic, travellers helped one another, knowing that one day they might be stranded themselves and need assistance from a stranger. The job was easy enough with two backs and four feet on the ground, and my Good Samaritan of the North helped me get the mud-covered mess back on its wheels and pushed to the roadside.

I put the bike back together and soldiered on, making it to the next little ferry at Arctic Red River. During the short ferry crossing I had a chance to look more carefully at the poor muddy motorcycle, and I saw there was more damage than just the broken signal light. The handlebars and shifter pedal were slightly bent, the plastic engine guard was broken, and the clear plastic headlight protector had been cracked by a flying stone, probably from a passing semi. The repair list for Fairbanks was growing.

The ferry attendant, a friendly man who was probably from the Dene (den-ay) people of the Gwi'chin Nation (unless he was Chinese), told me the other motorcyclists I had heard about from the Jeep driver were Belgians, and one of them had "hitched a ride out on an eighteen-wheeler." Injured, apparently. The ferryman seemed surprised that they could make it all this way and then crash on the *Dempster*, but I wasn't. I was worried.

The ferryman produced a rag and cleaned my lights and licence plate, then fetched some clear tape to fix the headlight protector. Tactfully, I asked if I could "buy him a coffee," but he gracefully declined, speaking in the direct, almost monotonal cadences of the far north. When he asked how I was enjoying my journey, I told him it was tough going, but very beautiful. "Especially at this time of year," he agreed, then gestured up toward the rolling tundra above the delta, and said, "From up there, it's like a *painting*."

From then on the road was better (which is to say, not under construction), and I had a smooth, fast cruise (with only a few of what my journal called "yikes moments") on the narrow, hard-packed tracks between the gravel berms left by the big rigs.

Having lost a time zone at the territorial border, it was nearly 9:00 by the time I approached Inuvik, but when I hit the short stretch of paved road which connected Inuvik's airport with the town, I felt relieved and exhilarated. Fourteen hours it had taken, but I had made it, all 820 kilometres (512 miles), and but for those last ten kilometres of sweet black asphalt, it had all been gravel and dirt (and mud).

The first building I encountered was the Finto Motor Inn, and with no wish to explore any further that day, I stopped right there.

> *The Dempster is mine (one way, anyway) and the Arctic Circle is mine, forever.*
>
> *Late dinner in Cabin Lounge, large whisky, decent Caesar salad, chicken on kaiser, red wine.*
>
> *Good music playing once again, Nirvana* Unplugged. *Makes me think of Kurt Cobain: he shot himself, left wife and daughter behind. Hard for me to imagine, but I still feel for the guy.*
>
> *Thoughts so often wandering to Jackie and Selena, especially their ends, and have to consciously try to steer away from that direction.*

The next morning, September 1st, was dark and gloomy, and I felt tired and worried. The weather forecast had changed from "rainy" to "cloudy," but the waitress told me she thought it was going to rain. I was truly fatigued and in need of a rest, sore all over from tension and exertion, and I had hoped to spend a day in Inuvik, way up there at the end of the northernmost road in Canada. Maybe I would find a way to visit Tuktoyaktuk, a nearby Inuit community on the Arctic Ocean.

But if it rained heavily, I would be in trouble. There was only one way out again, the Dempster Highway, and if that road was no longer a mystery, it was still an obstacle. On a rainy day I would not be able to make it, and I could be stuck somewhere for days, unless I hitched a ride out on a truck, like the Belgian had. So I was afraid, but my fear was not about falling, or getting hurt, or breaking down, or having a flat tire (though those hazards were certainly on my mind). Much more dangerous to me was the idea of being *stuck* somewhere, with too much time to think and the feeling of being trapped. I decided I would take a chance on one more dry day, and make my escape.

Just as I started loading the bike, the raindrops began, and I leaned on the motel doorway, bags in hand, dressed to go. What to do? Stay and wait it out, or go and hope I wouldn't get stuck somewhere? No answer, really. You can't guess the weather. I made a brief circuit of the little town, through the main crossroads with a few stores, another big hotel, and the famed igloo-shaped church, then filled up with gas and headed south.

On the short paved stretch of road leading out of town, I remembered riding the other way the previous night, feeling proud and exhilarated. Now I was frightened, weak, and weepy, truly dispirited, and as the paving ended, I found myself swearing out loud at the road, the rain, my life, and whatever Power might be responsible for all my bad fortune.

But lacking the solace of faith, I also lacked anyone to blame.

You can drive those wheels to the end of the road
You will still find the past
Right behind you

CARVE AWAY THE STONE, 1996

Chapter 4

WEST TO ⊙ ALASKA

Shadows on the road behind
Shadows on the road ahead
Nothing can stop you now

GHOST RIDER, 2001

The sun came out by the time I made the Arctic Red River ferry, and the day remained bright (and *dry*), though I had to curse the water truck I had to follow through the same construction area where I had fallen the previous day. In the early afternoon I reached the halfway point, Eagle Plains, and knew the worst was behind me. I decided to stop there for the night and get some rest, and as I checked in, I said to the man at the front desk, "Yesterday this seemed like wilderness; today it seems like civilization."

At sunset, I poured a glass of whisky and walked outside to enjoy the spectacular view, looking far over rolling billows of green, gray, and dark red. Peace settled over the land as the wind fell off at last, for that ceaseless, roaring wind had felt harsh and chaotic, at least to my little baby soul. In Bruce Chatwin's *Songlines* he writes about an Australian who goes crazy and starts *shooting* the wind, and I could always relate to that — especially when I was battling a headwind on a bicycle, but even when I was just trying to be still.

Leaving Eagle Plains early on a sunny morning, the rest of the way back to Dawson passed fairly quickly through the low forest dotted with crimson and yellow and the sharp-etched gray mountains. Still pools near the road reflected the clear sky, and I noticed ice around their edges, though I felt cool rather than cold. Getting used to it, I decided, or getting used to wearing *all* my clothes. With more confidence and less concern about fuel conservation, I made it back to Dawson in an hour less than the six it had taken going out, though I did have to use my spare can of gas. However, I noted, that's what it's there for.

In Dawson I stopped for a quick sandwich at Nancy's, then found a payphone to call the BMW dealer in Fairbanks, hoping to make an appointment for a couple of days later for new tires, an oil change, a look at the front brake pads, and some damage repair. The voice on the phone was gruff and laconic, and when I told him I was travelling his way and wanted to get some service work done, he growled, "Left it a bit *late,* didn't you?"

Thinking he meant that I should have called him sooner for an appointment, I told him that I'd just arrived back in Dawson, and was only now able to predict when I might get to Fairbanks.

"No," he said, "I mean late in the *season.*"

"Well," I said, "this is when I *got* here."

"It's September now, you know. It could snow any day. What you gonna do then?"

"Well, load the bike on a truck and haul it out, I guess. I don't know."

I began to think of him as Mister Dismal, though time would prove me wrong. His manner was only the voice of the "old Alaska hand," impatient with naive travellers from Down South. When I mentioned my concern about the front brake pads, he asked the year of the bike. I told him it was three years old, and he said he didn't think they could be worn yet. Then he asked "How many miles on it?", and when I told him "just over 40,000," his tone softened. "Oh, you're a *rider*. You're a *real* rider." Evidently I was now worthy of respect, and he agreed to do what he could for me when I arrived in Fairbanks.

I rode down to the Yukon River and caught the ferry across, then headed up to the "Top of the World Highway." I had been skeptical about that name, thinking maybe it was another northern exaggeration, like "highway" often was, and by "top of the world" they only meant so far *north*, but the hyperbole was justified.

The narrow paved road twisted along the top of a high ridge with sweeping views on either side, looking down steep green mountain slopes and far off to distant ranges of purple and gray. It truly *felt* like the top of the world, and I decided it was one of the most spectacular roads I had ever travelled. Banking smoothly into the corners with the revs up high and the bike down low, looking ahead through the turn for the proper apex (and the occasional scattering of gravel), I reflected that this was more like the *sport* of motorcycling, as opposed to the "survival course" of something like the Dempster. (Though I must confess that having made it all the way to Inuvik and back, I felt a little proud. In a foolish sort of way.)

The paving gave way to graded gravel near the Alaska border, where I stopped at a temporary-looking, prefab building (a seasonal, summer-only frontier) and switched off the engine to talk to the friendly officer. Riding away with a stamp in my passport reading "Poker Creek, Alaska," I had finally managed to visit all 50 of the United States. During 23 years of touring, Rush had performed in the other 49; I'd even bicycled in about 40; and during the *Test For Echo* tour, Brutus and I had managed to ride our motorcycles through 47 of the lower 48. But up until then, I had never made it to Alaska, so this too made me a little proud. In a foolish sort of way.

Now I was on the Taylor Highway (Jackie and Selena's last name, alas), another overstated title for a winding gravel road leading down through forested mining country (including the tiny settlement of Chicken) and back to the Alaska Highway (which, after three days of dirt roads, I described as "plush"). On the last stretch I began to see big RVs parked at the roadside, often with a trailer of ATVs with rifle cases. The caribou migration was just beginning in this area, and the hunters could park their luxurious rigs nearby, climb on their ATVs, drive right to the migration route, and ready, aim, fire, all without even having to *stand up*, never mind the discomforts of stalking elusive prey through the bush. Personally, I've never been against the idea of hunting game that is plentiful and good to eat, especially when it is actually *eaten*, but I was a little disenchanted with these "sportsmen."

"That's not hunting," I wrote, "that's just *shooting*."

In the hotel bar that night I heard a man say to his neighbor that hunting was "our national heritage," and that hunters replaced the natural predators, like bears and wolves, that had been wiped out. Although it might be argued that those predators had been wiped out by hunters, there was some truth to that claim, but it still sounded like the sort of self-serving rationalization the lumber companies used in claiming that clear-cutting (sorry, "harvesting") the forests offered the benefits of naturally occurring forest fires.

In the little crossroads town of Tok (pronounced "toke," with the "e" sometimes graffitied onto signs, presumably by superannuated pot-heads), the Westmark Motel ought to have been a quiet Wednesday-night destination, but once again I was in "bus-tour land," and the bar and restaurant were packed with a nametag-wearing crowd of middle-aged, overweight, loud-voiced tourists. I squeezed into a stool at the bar for a quick dinner of margarita and enchiladas, then slipped off to my room for an early sleep, waking several times during the night with an upset stomach and troubled dreams.

Sept 3 Tok — Fairbanks
66,627 (357 kms) [223 miles]

Got to sleep for another hour, but I'm crabby. Restaurant crowded with bus tour people, Holland America sheep (hardly older than me, for Cri-yi), so service is glacial, buffet line backed up with browsing hippos. They wear fucking nametags, and clump together, as if for security. Kill them all. (I'm allowed to have feelings like that!)

If I can get to Fairbanks and convince Mr. Dismal (no, not me!) to do the work on my bike today, then get my laundry done, that'll do. I'll have time to visit "Los Anchorage." [As the locals call it.]

Before leaving home I had committed myself to that one reservation, for a cabin on the ferry from Haines, Alaska, to Prince Rupert, British Columbia, on September 7th. Now that date was only four days away, so I wanted to see as much of Alaska as I could, then get to the port of Haines.

I rode out of Tok very early on another cold morning, this one punctuated by intervals of sun, clouds, and spatters of rain. The highway to Fairbanks led me through green and yellow forest with snow-covered peaks, and once a cow moose trotted across the road ahead.

Making Fairbanks by noon, I took a quick ride around the downtown area and pulled up at the Visitors' Center beside the Chena River. After a scan of the brochures for local lodgings, I settled on another of the Westmark chain, this one a large, modern-looking place. Checked-in, bags dropped, I set off to get the bike looked after.

Trail's End BMW was on the farthest edge of town behind a grove of tall conifers, and at first it seemed the image of a trapper's cabin, with an old house-trailer built onto it. Under the trees to one side, a rustic shelter covered a few new bikes and older sidecar bits and pieces. George, the owner, salesman, mechanic, parts manager, and gruff voice on the telephone, was a grizzled old prospector type, though with neatly trimmed beard and mustache, and he was friendly in his laconic, somewhat distracted manner. Though obviously very knowledgeable about all things BMW, he seemed scattered, so that I often had the disconcerting feeling he was chasing his own thoughts and hardly hearing what I said.

When I pulled the luggage cases off the bike to make it easier to work on, and asked where I could put them, George pulled open the creaky door of a dilapidated pickup, shoved some stuff aside, and said, "They'll be okay in here." He offered me a ride back to the hotel in his vintage BMW sidecar outfit, which would have been a new experience for me, but the bike wouldn't run. "Water in the carbs," he said, and drove me in his old diesel Mercedes instead.

Fairbanks seemed a pleasant little city, with about 30,000 friendly people, judging by the ones I met while walking the downtown streets and poking around the shops for stickers and postcards. When Brutus and I travelled together, we often sought out those colorful, and sometimes nostalgic, souvenir stickers as small and easily carried mementoes, and on this trip I was starting to use that quest as an excuse to go out and look around.

Another mission on my past travels had been sending a postcard to my grandfather, who was in his 90s and confined to a "home." After Selena's funeral, Gramps had whispered in my mother's ear, "Tell Neil to run for the woods," and though I wasn't able to follow that advice at the time, I was certainly running for the woods now.

Back at the hotel, I did some laundry, sent off a few cards, and had an excellent meal downstairs at the Bear 'n' Seal Grill. Despite the other scars that afflicted me, my enthusiasm for fine dining and drinking seemed to be intact.

By the middle of the following morning, true to his word, George had the bike ready, and I set off for Anchorage with fresh oil and various parts adjusted or tightened. George had showed me the brake pads still had some life, and I was also reassured by the solid, resilient feel of new tires between me and the highway. Just outside Fairbanks, I stopped to look at huge flocks of sandhill cranes feeding in a stretch of open land, gathering for their southward migration, and just after that the bike's odometer ticked off 10,000 kilometres of my own migration, 6,000 miles in two weeks.

Continuing south along that final stretch of the Alaska Highway, the sky seemed full of mountains on every side, dominated by the white peak of Denali, formerly known as Mount McKinley (after a president who never set foot in Alaska). At 20,370 feet, Denali is the highest peak in North America, and the national park that surrounds it had taken a brave step into the future of America's overcrowded parks by closing its roads to tourist traffic and offering shuttle buses to deliver campers and hikers to their trailheads. Compared with the noxious competition between parading vehicles and unspoiled nature in such American national parks as Yellowstone, Yosemite, or Grand Canyon, this was obviously a good thing, but it did mean that the entrance and parking areas were *jammed* with cars, trailers, sport-utes, minivans, campers, and RVs, so I gave up on the idea of making a spontaneous tour of the park.

In any case, Anchorage lay ahead at the end of the Alaska Highway, and that destination had the lure of a name that seemed almost mythical. So I was content to escape the crowds and continue south toward the coast, riding down into a valley of farms and pasturelands, a rare part of Alaska with sufficiently fertile soil and mild weather to permit agriculture. Yet another facet of Alaska's diversity, and while I rode that day I was thinking how diminished the United States would be without Alaska. In the same way the Canadian world-view is profoundly affected by the vast areas of the "True North" which are nearly *unpopulated* — our notion of "home" clearly molded by the places where we *don't* live — most Americans seldom reflect that their mental image of their country includes the prairies, the Rockies, the desert Southwest, the stone-walled fields of New England, the Pacific Northwest, the distant islands of Hawaii, and the wilds of Alaska.

So much of the American character, or at least self-image, was built upon the reality and the ideal of "the frontier," and even for the vast majority of Americans who might never visit "The Last Frontier" (as the licence-plate slogans tout it), the very idea of Alaska must shine as a part of their sense of *possibility,* and a remote outpost in their psychological geography. Just to know there's still a part of their country that isn't all filled up, or all *used* up — though maybe not for long. It should come as no surprise that a creeping industrialization is inexorably devouring that wilderness too, in the guise of oil exploration, drilling, mining, refining, and logging, and the center of that commercial vortex was Anchorage.

With over 200,000 people, it was the metropolis of Alaska, seven or eight times larger than Fairbanks, which in turn is more populous than the state capital of Juneau. Though the "Los Anchorage" sobriquet might be exaggerated by a magnitude of about 15 (despite the "Drive-Thru Espresso" places I began to encounter), everything is relative; after two weeks of riding across the wide prairie, mountain ranges, and the open lands of the Arctic, Anchorage certainly felt like a city as I cruised the busy streets for an hour to get my bearings. However, like Vancouver or Seattle, the urban face of concrete, glass, and steel was softened by the frame of its natural setting: the sparkling blue of the Cook Inlet, and tall mountains all around.

Continuing my inexplicable attraction to the Westmark chain (I think because it was a more-or-less *local* chain), this one a high-rise, I got in just ahead of the bus-tour groups. As I was unpacking in my room, the front-desk attendant called to warn me not to leave my camping gear and sleeping bag on the bike, as I usually did. I asked him, "Do you think anyone would bother stealing *that?*"

"It's Saturday night in Anchorage," he said, "they'll take *everything.*"

Later that night I lay awake in my dark hotel room, listening to the hooting and braying of drunken revellers in the streets, and feeling low. In my journal I once again noted that my thoughts were drawn to Jackie and Selena so much.

> An innocent, smiling memory so often leads that way. Seeing a family travelling together, some old TV show, hearing an old song, or a flute piece that Selena used to play coming over the restaurant's Muzak. So many connections.

Sept 5 Anchorage — Tok
67,792 (550 kms) [344 miles]

Another restless night, and crabby morning. One elevator working, I'm on 10th floor, everybody else here leaving at same time, back to their cruise-ship.

[Later] Stopped for construction on Hwy. 1. Beautiful day, more majestic scenery, road an entertaining slalom course, except for RVs and trucks.

If the word for yesterday was "majestic," today would be "glorious." Scenery, anyway, with the Wrangell Mountains straight ahead on the first stretch, and a winding road through bursts of yellow and orange foliage, snowy peaks almost ethereal, "oneiric," high above. Second stretch, Tok cutoff, no less glorious; maybe more, with that shining glacier sloping down between the forested mountains, and much less traffic.

I remained pretty low, though, never singing, just riding.

[Later] Tok, Fast Eddy's Restaurant, in front of Young's Motel. (Just Say No To Westmark!) Fine, unpretentious place, bread served with plainly marked "margarine" pats, good salad bar, and yet the crab legs dinner was about $25, and many of the other dinners similarly priced; does that pass for margarine-level meal prices here?

Big heavy mug of hot, colored water. Truly the only good coffee I've had was at Telegraph Creek, when I made it myself. Of course I haven't tried the Drive-Thru Espresso places.

Finished reading The Conservationist *by Nadine Gordimer, [brother] Danny's recommendation. Reference to the "man alone" perhaps apt, but plotline hardly uplifting. Man.*

Sept 6 Tok — Haines
68,583 (791 kms) [494 miles]

Rainy this morning, but still looking forward to that moment of "setting off," when the world both contracts and expands at the same time.

There may be nice moments along the way, or periods of pleasant "zen-state," but the best parts of the day are leaving and arriving.

[Later] Lunch in Haines Junction, turnoff for ferry dock at Haines. Today's magic word is "somber." Not gloomy so much as melancholy, I guess. Rain most of the way, but that's okay. Little traffic, and mainly good road. Sense of majestic scenery behind low drapes of cloud, and lovely along big lake in Burwash area. Yellow leaves brighten the roadside. Couple of coyotes crossing. Falcon chasing off raven, hawk with white band on upper tail. [Harrier, or marsh hawk.]

Border-crossing number one, Alaska to Yukon, easy enough: "purchase or receive anything?" "Gas, oil, and tires." Officer a rider himself, and after a bit of "biker chat," he waves me through. Note swans in one of lakes, up in "alpine tundra" area. Then down into coastal rainforest, still green. Little corner of British Columbia, weather so typical: wearing sunglasses and rainsuit.

Another motorcyclist officer at Canada–U.S. border, R100 GS (BMW), another breeze-through. Down past famous Chilkat River Bald Eagle Preserve, only one immature there today.

Still thinking so much of the "lost ones," and often talking to myself.

At least realizing what I'm doing sometimes makes me laugh, and that's okay.

The little port of Haines would prove to be my definitive Alaskan experience. I stopped at a small liquor store to look for a bottle of single-malt whisky, and I overheard a fisherman telling the owner about the 49-pound halibut he'd just caught. On his way out the door he pointed down toward Main Street, a few blocks away, where a black bear was loping across the road.

With a few hours to kill until the ferry sailed, I went to the Lighthouse Restaurant and caught my own halibut — from the menu. A few other travellers seemed to be biding their time there too, mostly older retired couples, and they soon began talking among themselves from table to table, comfortable among strangers so like themselves, from the same generation of friendly, open Americans. I overheard one of the men trying to remember the name of a small town away up north in the Northwest Territories, right on the Arctic Ocean, and I offered, "Tuktoyaktuk?" and soon everyone was exchanging travellers' tales. One younger couple was moving from Anchorage to Reno, and one lady recalled how she and her husband had last been to Las Vegas in 1958, and she imagined it was a lot different now.

One of the men asked the waitress about the local salmon fishing, and she told how she had won the salmon derby the previous year, catching a 44-pounder which had "netted" her $1,600, a three-day trip to Juneau, a $350 fishing rod, and a free dinner in Whitehorse.

After dinner, I took a slow ride around the inlet, and at the top, where the Chilkoot River flowed in, I saw a few people standing on a small bridge. I slowed to see what they were looking at, then stopped and switched off the engine. Straddling the bike, I watched five grizzly bears at the river's edge: a sow with three cubs, and one half-grown — not as big as they get, but big. A young Australian passed me his binoculars, and I got a close-up view of them feeding on the dead salmon. These coastal grizzlies were referred to as brown bears, and as a result of this bountiful diet of salmon, they were considerably larger than their mountain-dwelling cousins.

At the ferry dock I pulled the bike onto the centerstand in the line of waiting vehicles, took out Jack London's *The Sea Wolf*, and relaxed in the saddle, leaning back against my duffel with my legs up on the cylinder heads (a useful feature of the opposed-twin engine design). As darkness fell, the smell of the sea seemed to grow stronger, and a brief glimpse of full moon was overtaken by clouds. Rain began to fall with growing intensity, so I took shelter under the terminal overhang for awhile, or walked around in my rainsuit.

I passed a young woman out walking her little dog, and she looked pretty under the lights of the rain-washed parking lot. She gave me a smile that seemed to go right through me, the way that girls can sometimes do, and I felt suddenly galvanized — dumb, nervous, and afraid. Pretty girls have always tended to have that effect on me, on the rare occasions when I was confronted by one, but I hadn't felt any of those kinds of feelings for a long time.

Perhaps in line with an earlier soliloquy about "unimagined affection," I had never felt I was particularly attractive to women, but something seemed different now. Later, when I was around friends, they would confirm that I seemed suddenly to attract a certain *attentiveness* from women. Even though I still wore my wedding ring (as Jackie and I both had, despite being unsanctioned by church and state), and sure wasn't sending out any conscious "signals," waitresses rested their fingers lightly on my arm, cashiers gave me sympathetic smiles, women on the street sometimes poured their eyes into mine. Taking the Romantic View, I liked to imagine their feminine radar could detect the Air of Tragedy which must surely surround me like an aura. Maybe it was just the more prosaic Air of Availability. Or the line that Tom Robbins translates from Baudelaire as, "Women love these fierce invalids home from hot climates."

This pretty girl on the ferry dock in Haines, Alaska, looked to be travelling alone with her little dog, and if she *was* sending me some kind of signal, what should I do? Was this one of those "opportunities" I should think about, or just an overactive imagination? Whatever it was, I was not ready to deal with it, and when I didn't encounter her again aboard the ship, I put the question out of my mind. Apparently, though, my little baby soul was harboring a spark of response to life other than highways, landscapes, and wildlife.

Sept 7 on board M/V Taku

After long, long wait in steady rain, then the anxiety of riding
onboard over those slippery metal ramps and getting tied down
(pathetic attempt, as usual; must learn proper knot for that), then
a couple slugs of whisky and an exploration of the ship (all excited
by then, by great little cabin with promised window and the thrill
of being at sea, the prop wash surging out behind). Got to sleep
about 1:00, then awake at 4:00 to see Juneau (not — terminal an
island of light in darkness well outside of town), then sleep from
5:00 till about 8:00. Outside to cold wind, rain and "misty fjords"
view of humps receding behind each other in paler grays, and gray,
stormy looking, white-capped water.

Realize that Haines has completely changed my view of Alaska:
black bear on Main Street, bald eagle, and grizzlies eating salmon.
All for real.

[Later] Humpback whales frolicking!

[Later] Lovely lounging day, reading The Sea Wolf *(a "ripping*
yarn," as "elemental" as Conrad). [Also note the ship in the story
was called Ghost*], watching the passing cloud-draped coastline,*
deeply forested, dark and rounded in those hazy layers, and dozing.

Catching a couple of Forest Service interpreter Fran's talks, and
looking at baleen [called "whalebone," flexible, plastic-like plates
used by the whale to filter its food, and by Europeans for such
purposes as corset stays] reflects what London writes of the gory
massacre of the seal hunt: "All that slaughter for the sake of
woman's vanity." Brutality in the service of vanity. Deep.

The ferry docked in Prince Rupert at about nine in the morning, and
I rode off into heavy rain. I had occasional glimpses of high mountains
beside the highway, but my view consisted mainly of slick pavement under
streaming rain and low clouds. The day gradually cleared by around
Prince George, but was never warm. A well-paved road curved gently

through a valley of hay farms and low mountains, the forests noticeably greener now that I was travelling south, back into summer.

By Quesnel I'd covered 882 kilometres (550 miles), and circled the town for a place to stay. The best-looking place had no restaurant, and only two rooms available: a two-bedroom suite or the honeymoon suite, so I rode onward to the Wheel Inn, which I later noted was "cheap — and worth it." Still, it was entirely satisfactory for this undemanding traveller, "clean, good shower, Weather Channel."

A nearby restaurant in an old Hudson's Bay store fed me well with beef stew, red wine, cherry pie, and coffee, and I took a post-prandial walk-about through the dark, empty streets. Quesnel was yet another town that had sprung up in the wake of a prospector's strike — this one from the "Cariboo" gold rush of 1858 — and its downtown area featured an old bridge restored for the use of cyclists and pedestrians, a riverfront park, and tidy landscaping and flowers along the streets.

After a good night's sleep at the Wheel Inn, I was back on the road by six the next morning, clear and sunny, but *bitterly* cold, as I continued south through scrub forest with occasional farms, some large lakes (Williams and La Hache), and small towns. I stopped for breakfast in a town whose name had always intrigued me on the map: 100 Mile House, which had been named by the Hudson's Bay Company trappers for its distance from Vancouver on the fur-trade routes.

And though I was following a less-direct route, Vancouver was my destination that day, to visit my brother Danny, his wife Janette, son Max, and black Labrador retriever, Tara. Danny and Janette had always been more friends than family, and yet more family than friends, and they had come to help look after Jackie and me in Toronto after Selena's accident, then again in London during our "exile," and finally in Barbados, just a few weeks before Jackie's passing. In past years I had often visited them in Vancouver while touring with the band, and after my recent period of solitary rambling, I was looking forward to getting off the road for a few days, and being with people who knew me and my story.

In Jackie's final few weeks of decline she was chained to an oxygen tank most of the time, growing weaker both physically and mentally, less able to endure the heat of the tropical afternoons, but too feeble now to travel anywhere else. She and her sister, Deb, spent hours in the air-conditioned bedroom going over a list of her jewellery, which she wanted to divide among her family and closest friends. On one of my first bicycle trips, from Munich to Venice, I had bought her a pearl bracelet in Zermatt, Switzerland, then carried it over the Alps to Venice on my bicycle, then later bought her a matching necklace. It is said that pearls, being organic, become imbued with the essence of their wearer, and thus are the most *personal* of jewels, so it seemed fitting that they should go to Janette, who both of us liked and admired very much. So I had been carrying those pearls, carefully wrapped, on a delivery mission which now spanned 13,000 kilometres (8,125 miles) and almost three weeks.

But first, my route into Vancouver would delight me with a road I would later rate as one of the great motorcycle roads in the world. Highway 99 began among the dry hills of pine and sage near Marble Canyon, then after Lillooet it went snaking through deep forest, up and down past fast rivers and aquamarine mountain lakes. The sky remained bright, the air cool and delicious, and the sinuous road coming toward me was so challenging and rewarding that I was tempted into the adrenaline zone. Turn by turn my pace increased until I was riding with a complete focus spiced by the ever-present danger and occasional thrill of fear, racing against physics and my own sense of caution in a sublime rhythm of shifting, braking, leaning deep into the tight corners, then accelerating out again and again. I felt a charge of excitement I hadn't known for many months, and found myself whooping out loud with the sheer existential thrill.

From first to last
The peak is never passed
Something always fires the light
That gets in your eyes
MARATHON, 1985

Chapter 5

FİRST CLASS
SADDLETRAMP

I believe in what I see
I believe in what I hear
I believe that what I'm feeling
Changes how the world appears

TOTEM, 1996

At the time of writing those lines, in a time I can only describe as "before," I had in mind the contradiction between a skeptic's dismissal of anything not tangible (true agnosticism) and the entirely subjective way many people tend to view and judge the world, through the filters of their ever-changing emotions and moods. In the days following Selena's death, I had learned for myself how profound and pervasive that syndrome could be, how a sunny day could actually seem *dark*, the sun totally *wrong*, and how the world around me, the busy lives of all those oblivious strangers, could seem so futile and unreal — as futile and unreal as what passed for my own life.

If some of the journal notes I have quoted seem ill-tempered, even misanthropic, this attitude should be understood as a kind of envy, which so often has a bitter aftertaste. In the wake of my devastating losses it was hard for me to accept that fate could be so unjust, that other people's lives should remain unscarred by the kind of evil that had been visited upon *me*. The big question, "why?" was a ceaseless torment, as my brain struggled for meaning (Is this a punishment? A judgement? A curse?), and when I saw other people with their children, or with their lovers and mates, or even just apparently enjoying life, it wasn't so much ill will that moved me, as it was jealousy, resentment, and a sense of cruel injustice.

When it came to those who had cared for me, though, these dark thoughts did not apply, for I felt affection and gratitude not only for their help, but for their *understanding*, for simply knowing what I had endured, feeling for me, and demanding nothing more than that I continue to live. My only contact with those people for three weeks had been by telephone, as I travelled among strangers and carried the weight of that knowledge alone, so I was looking forward to visiting Danny and Janette in their little red house in Kitsilano, just across the bridge from downtown Vancouver.

Their guest room was comfortable, with a good reading light by the bed, and it felt good just to be in their *home*, away from motels, restaurants, and gas stations for a few days. I was hoping that staying in one place would be bearable if I kept myself busy, and if I wasn't *alone*.

The first evening I was there, I fulfilled my mission of delivering the pearls to Janette, and she and Danny tried hard not to show how moved they were (knowing that emotion is contagious and I was still very sensitive, for they had seen enough of my tears in Toronto, London, and Barbados).

When they asked if there was anything I would like to do in Vancouver, I told them I just needed to stay *busy*, and they made sure I did. Danny had a demanding job as a personal fitness trainer and manager of several health clubs, and Janette as an ophthalmologist, and both of them juggled the care of Max, nearly two, and their dog, Tara. With nannies and babysitters to allow them time for work and play, they were the most active people I ever knew, and they included me in their energetic routines.

Danny and I pushed Max in his stroller as we walked fast through the streets on my errands of service and resupply; Janette and I hiked with Tara through the muddy wooded ravines (which the signs glorified as "canyons" and I disparaged as "gullies") near the shore; and the three of us climbed the steep path ("Nature's Stairmaster") to the summit of Grouse Mountain, an ordeal also known as the "Grouse Grind." We went rowing and kayaking in Burrard Inlet amid a rich backdrop of Vancouver's cityscape, the dark woods of Stanley Park, and the high mountains to the north, and I rowed out alone across the heaving saltwater mass among the cargo ships, pleasure craft, and bobbing navigation markers.

A pair of seals seemed to be shadowing me, popping their dog-like heads above the surface on either side several times and just looking at me. I floated with my oars poised above the water, unable to resist the fancy that these two curious, amiable-looking seals were watching over me like two guardian spirits. Being a rational-scientific-skeptic at heart, I had never been one to believe in reincarnation, but in the same way that I found it difficult to dismiss superstitious notions of retribution and evil curses as a "cause" for my late misfortunes, I couldn't avoid feeling somehow comforted by the notion that my lost ones might be still around somewhere. At the same time, I couldn't quite buy the assertions of the "spiritualists," cozy as those fantasies might be for the bereaved, when I pondered such contradictions as how a soul could pass into another life-form and yet still be available for our consultation in a spirit-channel or séance. The rational-scientific-skeptic might settle for such a logical dialectic on the matter, but my primitive spirit often had different desires.

In any case, my little baby soul had been soothed by six active, enjoyable days in Vancouver, and I felt ready to set off again (or maybe I just needed a *rest*). My motorcycle had been thoroughly fettled by a local shop;

I had spent an afternoon giving it a loving clean and polish in Danny and Janette's garage, and all of my baggage and equipment was refreshed and reorganized. With Danny and Janette rising early to wave me off in the pre-dawn darkness, I set off at 6:00 to ride through the empty streets of the glittering city to the ferry dock at Horseshoe Bay.

A short boat-ride across the Strait of Georgia from the city of Vancouver lay the long mass of Vancouver Island, stretching north and west into the Pacific Ocean. The only parts of Vancouver Island I had seen before had been on early Rush tours, when we used to play in British Columbia's capital city of Victoria, which is as quaint and anglophile as its name (with teahouses, cricket pitches, and a newspaper called the *Times-Colonist*), and Nanaimo, another small, less-pretentious city built upon mining, lumbering, and fishing. I had always pictured the rest of that huge, seemingly unpopulated island as a vast park of old-growth forest, and on this journey I decided to explore it more thoroughly.

As usual, my route was anything but direct, beginning with a ferry on the mainland side to Langley, in an area called "The Sunshine Coast" (and it was, with high wispy clouds and views of mountains and ocean I could only describe as "massive"), then a short ride along a winding road to a second ferry from Earls Cove to Saltery Bay, another short bike ride to the pulp-mill town of Powell River (where I found a florist to send a "thank you" bouquet to Danny and Janette), and finally a third ferry across the Strait of Georgia to Comox, on the eastern shore of Vancouver Island.

As I followed the highway north from Comox through Campbell River, where I finally escaped the heavy traffic and had some good riding, my mental picture of Vancouver Island slowly began to erode. The mountains and surrounding ocean made a majestic frame, but the picture within was fairly grim: the island seemed to be nothing more than a big "tree farm," with alternating woodlots of second-growth, third-growth, and no-growth gashes of clear-cut. Signs in front of each plot offered lumber company propaganda, giving the year that a particular stand had been "harvested," "thinned," "replanted" (sometimes overstated as "reforested"), and "fertilized." Every town had a pulp mill belching into the sky, and a closer look at the map showed the spreading network of lumber roads. I passed logging trucks carrying tree trunks so large that a single tree had been cut into three or four pieces, and that one tree made a full load, even for a huge tractor-trailer. As a useful warning, I could always smell the trucks on the road ahead, especially in the rain, for they trailed a sweet perfume of fresh-cut timber, but I still felt sad to see the carcasses of these noble trees.

But when I found myself feeling too self-righteous and sanctimonious about this wholesale strip-logging, I only had to think of my living room in Quebec, with its beams of "B.C. fir." Where did I think *they* came from? I was reminded of the Vermont politician's joke about the difference between an environmentalist and a developer: the environmentalist has his cabin in the woods; the developer hasn't got his yet.

Despite my early start, and what came to feel like a long day, I decided to head for the northern tip of the island and try to stay somewhere up there. This would keep me on the road a little later than I usually preferred (i.e., past cocktail time), and it was 6:00 before I saw the sign for Port Hardy ("Mining, Lumber, Fishing"). My expectations were not overly high, hoping only for a tidy motel room with a hot shower and a plain, nourishing meal, but unfortunately, at the end of that 12-hour day of hard travelling, I was to be disappointed even in these modest expectations.

The town seemed to consist of a handful of strip malls, so bland and characterless I wondered if perhaps the original town had been destroyed by fire, then replaced as cheaply as possible. My reconnaissance didn't take long, and showed little choice of accommodations: one motel looked a little nicer, but the other had location: it was right by the town dock, which was lined with fishing boats and looked to be the "heart" of the town.

Fortuitously (I guess), the Seagate Hotel had one room left, and once again, it was "cheap, and worth it." Furnished with what looked like Holiday Inn castoffs, the room had a nasty smell and a spongy bed with squeaky bedsprings (I couldn't remember the last time I'd heard *that* sound!). When I went downstairs for dinner, the salad bar had a distinctly brownish tinge, and surprisingly typical of many fishing ports on the

Atlantic or Pacific, the only fish available was deep fried. I went with what is often the safest order in such places: steak. Accentuating the positive, I noted that it was "well cooked, with good charcoal taste."

A few of the professional fishermen were gathered around one table, and I noticed that when they talked about the weather, it wasn't in terms of the temperature or precipitation, but the wind: "Nor'west 15." After dinner, I strolled out along the dock and watched the boats being unloaded into refrigerated trucks, and I noted that, "I like to see these places, these people; where they live and *how* they live."

I felt low that night, and not just because of a disappointing reward at the end of a long day's travel. I recognized the symptoms of the "post-visit syndrome," which I had first experienced back in London. During our six months there, Jackie and I had a steady stream of generous visitors from home, friends and family who would come to stay for a few days, and while they were with us we would be entertained and distracted, our spirits would rise, and things would seem better for awhile. Then, all too soon the visitors would go back to their homes and families, while we were left once again with just each other: two sad souls unable to rise above our own bereavement and exile, never mind elevate the other's spirits.

This time, I had left behind a warm family environment in the home of Danny, Janette, Max, and Tara, leaving them to go on with their busy and fulfilling lives, while I was left to go . . . well, back on the highway.

The road led me south again the following morning, through patches of fog in the cool, clear sunrise under stippled pink and purple clouds. Once again, traffic grew heavier further south, and the rest of the day seemed to be dominated by getting through, around, and past other vehicles.

Once I went speeding past an old couple, and smiled as I imagined their conversation: him grumbling about me, and her telling him not to be such an old grouch. Then suddenly I was in tears, thinking, "I'll never get to be a grumpy old grandpa!"

Two-thirds of the way down the island, I turned west to head across to the Pacific side, and I stopped at a rare stand of old-growth cedars called Cathedral Grove. Standing in the muffled gloom under the mighty columns justified the name well enough, for it did feel like a pagan temple to the sanctity and mystery of Nature. But it was sobering to reflect that, as with the dwindling redwoods and sequoias in California, or the white pines in Ontario, the remaining groves were now rare enough that they each had a *name*. It was admirable that these remnants had been preserved, of course, but it was depressing to reflect on what they actually *represented:* all the millions of trees that once shaded the surrounding lands, and most of the continent, and were now gone forever. The ghost forests.

One other remnant of old-growth forest surrounded a set of inlets on the Pacific coast called Clayoquot Sound, the scene of one of Canada's fiercest struggles between environmentalists and the lumber companies. I seemed to recall the protesters had won at least a qualified victory, but once again I was appalled to see what a rear-guard action they — we — were fighting. Not to slow down the destruction to a more controllable pace, but simply to protect the very last specimens of a disappearing forest long enough for it to be appreciated. And missed. On a rock face along the roadside a witty graffiti artist had painted, "TELEPHONE POLES — LAST OF THE OLD GROWTH."

The Wickaninnish Inn in Tofino, a busy little tourist town on the Pacific shore, made a welcome contrast to the Seagate Hotel in Port Hardy. Perched above the waves breaking gently on the beaches of sand and stones, where a foghorn played its two-note tuba part from a thick cloud-bank on the western horizon, the rooms were comfortable and luxurious, and the restaurant was truly superb.

Danny had told me about a mutual friend who had been asking about me, Gay Burgiel, a longtime cycling companion who had also been one of my correspondents in my former life of letter writing (and much else that was "former"). Over dinner I decided to start on a letter to her, the way I used to do sometimes during solitary meals, and see if it would work for me.

Gay and I had first met on a cycling tour of northeast China in 1985, along with Bob and Rosie Boysen, a couple of her fellow members of the New Jersey cycling club, the Western Jersey Wheelmen. In subsequent years I had joined them on their own self-guided bicycle trips, which I christened "BoysenTours," over the Alps a couple of times, across the Pyrenees, and, about 12 years previously, over the Canadian Rockies from Calgary to Vancouver on a route similar to that which I was about to travel in the opposite direction.

Sept. 16, '98
Wickaninnish Inn
Tofino, B.C.

Dear Gay,

It's been a long time since you've heard from me I know, but . . . I've had a bad year (I'm given to understatement lately). It's been even longer since I've had a "dinner guest" like this, but I thought I'd give it a try. Lately my life has consisted of trying things I used to like, and seeing if they're still any good. Starting over, in so many ways, and on such shaky footing. Everything I ever believed has been blown out of the water, even my simple karmic morality of "you do good and you get good." Sadly (*very* sadly), 'taint so.

Anyway, before I get myself (and you) all tied up in abstractions, I'll try my old pattern in these kind of "catch-up" letters: I'll start from now and work backwards, at least as far back as I dare in a public restaurant . . .

"Now" is dinner at the Pointe, in the above-named inn, with its hemi-duodecagonal (I think that's "half of 12"?) view out to Clayoquot Sound, a Japanese watercolor of islands, clouds, and sea. I am most of the way through an extraordinary dinner of oysters, chowder (though far above conventional dishes with that name), and sea bass, with all sorts of delicious little goodies alongside (wild rice, asparagus, crab, salsa, etc), and a dessert I can only describe as "A Symphony in Plum:" sorbet, mousse, confit, accompanied by coffee and Port. You know I've had some good meals in my former life, and this ranks with the best of them. Nice view too.

Sept. 17
Ferry dock, Nanaimo

After a great sleep to the gentle music of the waves outside my room, I set off early this morning across Vancouver Island (what I call an "entertaining" road, with lots of twists and turns of every description), back through the small area of old-growth forest called Cathedral Grove, breakfast in Port Alberni, and to the ferry dock near Nanaimo.

I set off on August 20th, two months after Jackie's death, and one year and 10 days after Selena's, on what I soon came to think of as "The Healing Road" (I'm hoping so, at least). At the time there was no way of knowing if travelling would "work" for me, especially alone, but it has proved to be the best remedy so far. After returning from Barbados, where we had gone for what proved to be a fairly quick, and fairly merciful decline for Jackie (a broken heart works even faster than what the doctors called cancer), I spent a few weeks in Toronto taking care of necessary business and putting that house up for sale, then I went "home" to Quebec.

I spent a month there, which wasn't too bad (despite being surrounded by countless happy family memories), but I knew staying there alone through the fall and winter would not be good. No matter where I go, I have a sense of this very palpable "deep dark hole" right beside me, and there have been times when I've had an almost physical sense of pulling myself back from it. Certainly this is a dangerous time for me, and if I were to fall into a dark bitterness, a bottle of whisky, or a bag of white powder, who would blame me? Early on in this double nightmare, I remember thinking, "How does anyone survive something like this? And if they do, what comes out the other end?"

Well, I don't know, but I am going to find out, for I am armored by one small reflex in my nature: "Something will come up."

Travelling has given me small moments of Truth and Beauty (highways, landscapes, wildlife) and even a few fugitive moments of enjoying life again. There are still tears, and dark moods, and that omnipresent "deep dark hole," but it's always better to be moving.

And now, ferry time approaches . . .

Later that same day . . .
Hope, B.C.

Memories of our stay here on the BoysenTours trip in . . . what? '86? '87? Anyway, I went from a sunny picnic bench at the ferry dock to a cloudy, then rainy two-hour crossing. Putting on my foul weather gear, I rode off into heavy rain, and heavy traffic. Combined with navigating unfamiliar and fairly complicated roads, that makes for demanding motorcycling. I was thinking today that bicycling wouldn't work nearly as well on "The Healing Road," for motorcycling is so much more demanding *mentally* that it helps to keep my thoughts occupied with decision-making, physical execution (not aerobic, but still plenty of work on those "interesting" roads), scanning, defending (as on a bicycle, assume you're *invisible*), navigating, machine-monitoring, and maybe a little sightseeing at the same time.

You and the other Wheelpeople will perhaps be encouraged to know that I got into bicycling in a *big* way in Barbados. To make a brief getaway from the constant vigil over Jackie, I would leave her in the care of her sister, Deb, and go riding every second morning on the grueling and sweltering roads of northern Barbados, eventually covering pretty well every road, lane, and cowpath within two hours of the house we rented. That and bird-watching became my major diversions during two-and-a-half months there, and, combined with a lot of reading, helped to preserve some percentage of my sanity (a quantity yet to be determined!). I also managed to identify all but two of the island's 24 native bird species.

Tonight I settled on a Best Western here in the aptly named (for me) Hope, after a tour of the town's offerings. As a perfect contrast to last night, I dined at the "Home" restaurant, turkey dinner with mashed potatoes, gravy, cauliflower, and a chocolate milkshake. All this trip I've tried to alternate nights of comparative luxury with nights in humbler places: Mom-and-Pop motels and diners. Generally I've resisted reservations, except for the boat from Alaska to Prince Rupert, which was hard to get even six weeks in advance, and last night's inn, which Danny and Janette recommended when I visited them last week. Tonight I tried to book the Chateau Lake Louise for a couple of nights from now, for I've always wanted to stay there, but no luck. I've booked the Banff Springs Hotel instead, which looks similar, but lacks *that* view.

After dinner, I took a walk to look for where we all stayed the previous time [on the BoysenTours ride from Calgary to Vancouver], and though it's now a Quality Inn, I recognized it right off, and the restaurant where that unbearable person [an "entertainer"] was making such a lame racket; a Chinese place now. Wasn't it here where you and Stan went in search of free-wheel parts? Anyway, it seems a nice little town, and changed only in details in 11 or 12 years.

[*Then follows a recap of my travels, leading to this conclusion:*] 14,500 kilometres (9,062 miles) in four weeks, including five "idle" days in Vancouver with the Lindley-Pearts.

Sept. 18
Nelson, B.C.

This morning I spotted the place where all of us bicyclists stopped for lunch near Hedley that time: a big old farmhouse kind of place with a back deck, and, I recall, a very slow waitress. Earlier I took a ride up to Cascade Lookout, in Manning Park, where Bob, Henry, and I did the "optional" eight-mile-long, 2,000-foot-high climb, while the sensible people (like you) reclined on the sloping lawn of the lodge.

From Princeton, I took a different route, staying near the U.S. border through Osoyoos ("Canada's Only Desert," and a pretty town on a big lake), Trail (site of the Winter Olympics some years ago, but basically a mining town), and Castlegar (another one for the name, often seen on Canada's Weather Network). Around there it started to rain hard once more, so I opted for another Best Western in Nelson (a pleasant little town, with lots of "outdoorsy" shops). After a shower and hanging things up to dry, the rain had stopped, and a walkabout led me here to the Heritage Inn, and the General Store restaurant. Good Caesar salad so far, steak to come.

On this trip I've been carrying my little tent and a sleeping bag, just for insurance, and even though I haven't used them yet, I just love *having* them, for I never have to worry about finding a room. Same with my little gallon container of gas; I've only used it once so far, and I love *not* worrying about it. Up in the Yukon and Alaska it was way too cold to think about camping, but I'm hoping to do some once I work my way down to the Mojave, for I think that would have to be fabulous. I didn't bother with cooking supplies, for you can always get *food,* but I'm hoping to meet up with my erstwhile riding companion Brutus for a couple of weeks next month, and we could just take some sandwiches and a bottle of wine and go camp in the desert, and that would be fine.

My long-term sort-of plan (now that I'm daring to *have* one) is to zigzag my way south, staying west of the Mississippi, and maybe end up in Mexico and Belize. If I can stay on the road until after Christmas (that formerly happy family season), that would be best. Then I might store my bike somewhere down there and fly back to Quebec for January and February (primo *snow* season for cross-country skiing and snowshoeing), and after that I could either rejoin my faithful steed and head north, or continue south to South America. From Day One of this Homeric Odyssey (monsters on every side!) I decided to keep it all flexible, with lots of opportunity to change or even bail out if I felt like it. The operative theme is "Whatever Works." No putting *demands* on myself, no commitments, and no goals. Except survival.

Please pass my regards (and/or this letter) to Bob, Rosie, and Henry, and I want you all to know that I'm slowly picking up the pieces of my shattered life. We just have to wait and see what the puzzle reveals!

For now, I'm okay as long as I keep moving . . .

With heartfelt affection,
NEP

Among the few, tiny, yet radiant sparks of hope in my "something will come up" file, those vague imaginings which kept me going down that highway, was a glimmer of fantasy in the back of my mind that I might stumble across my own personal Eden. In my past travels in the world, whenever I came across a place that charmed me I had always been drawn to fantasize about settling down there for awhile: a village in the Bavarian Alps, an island in the Caribbean, the narrow streets of the Île de la Cité in Paris, a tented camp in the Serengeti Plain. Lately, that fantasy had been especially compelling for me, a secret wish of discovering a place of beauty and peace where I could hide away forever.

I had heard stories of people who had suddenly found the place where they wanted to spend the rest of their lives, a home of their *choosing* rather than the accidental background of their upbringing, and I hoped that such an epiphany might happen to me someday, somewhere. Just considering the four wildly disparate examples given above — Alpine village, tropical island, European city, and African savanna — I didn't really imagine that there could be a single place that would satisfy all those desires, but I could still hope, and carry that additional perspective with me when I surveyed a new place.

On this journey, the area around Nelson was the first time I entertained those kind of thoughts. Nelson itself had a hip kind of small-town atmosphere, and it was surrounded by the forested mountains that were the most frequent reflection of my "soulscape." For some people that inner Shangri-La was represented by an ocean shore, for some a desert mesa, for some a bustling city, but for me it was a wooded lake in the mountains — like the house by the lake in the Laurentians, not coincidentally, which I had been away from for a month now, and was already missing whenever I allowed my thoughts to return there. But that didn't satisfy my current fantasy; I was idly looking for a *new* soulscape, one not haunted by the Ghosts of Christmas Past.

Under a heavy overcast, the highway leading north from Nelson ran along the shore of a long arm of Kootenay Lake, and I pictured myself out there rowing for mile after mile under the lowering clouds, my restless spirit soothed by leaning into the oars in a steady, strong rhythm of forgetfulness, then returning to my solitary cabin among the misty evergreens to drowse over a book by the fire.

However, I soon put these fantasies aside, as the road demanded my complete attention. Those lowering clouds began to weep, and after an hour of smooth winding pavement BC 31 led me through 100 kilometres of gradually worsening dirt and gravel, and ultimately dwindled to a one-lane logging road of mud twisting high above long, narrow Trout Lake, surrounded by mountains scarred with the mange of clear-cut logging. As I slowly negotiated the tight, narrow switchbacks, carefully choosing where to place my wheels among the puddles, rocks, ruts, and gravel berms, the rain continued to pour down, and I saw perhaps two other vehicles in that whole distance. I had set out with a vague notion of stopping somewhere for breakfast, but there was nothing along that road, and eventually I gave up on the idea, driven on by the rain, my slow progress along a perilous track of unknown length, and eventually, a feeling of withdrawing into a shell, which made me reluctant to stop anywhere at all.

A ferry carried me and a surprising number of cars and RVs, who had arrived at the same place by a more civilized route (I could tell because they were so *clean,* while my bike and I were mud-spattered and disreputable looking), across Upper Arrow Lake. Riding north to Revelstoke for fuel, I turned onto the rainy, busy Trans-Canada Highway, cautiously guarding my distance from the spray-trailing trucks and sloppily driven RVs. As I climbed toward the invisible summit of Rogers Pass I felt the cold penetrating my leathers and rainsuit, and I turned on the heated vest and grips, grimly contemplated the road ahead, and pondered a song title, "Clouds Hanging on My Handlebars." (Not that I was thinking about songwriting, but I must have retained that built-in reflex to the rhythm of lyrical words.)

In past years, I had crossed Rogers Pass by car and by bicycle. Now it was by motorcycle, and I had yet to see the fabled view of the white summits around it. It looked beautiful in pictures, though. A few elk at the roadside were the only scenic attractions that day.

The charms of Banff were also obscured, though not by clouds and rain. In contrast to Nelson, this once-picturesque small town in the Rockies had been completely *devoured* by tourism, the streets lined with tacky souvenir shops and packed with cars, RVs, and countless tour buses.

The Banff Springs Hotel had an imposing castle-like presence, and indoors, a venerable, even palatial atmosphere on the grand scale, but it felt as impersonal and factory-like as had the bus-tour hotels in Alaska. The lure of "scenic wilderness" had been packaged beyond an inch of its life, until the experience was not only tarnished, but completely hollow.

Walking into the Alberta Dining Room in the hotel, I was first taken aback at its vastness, and then by the throngs of bus-tour groups, with numbered flags on their large round tables, and I noticed that most of them seemed to be Japanese. A trio of guitar, piano, and drums was playing on a low stage, and I laughed out loud when I recognized the song they were plunking out: "Sukiyaki," a hit from the early '60s that I had always presumed to be a *parody* of Japanese music. However, it got a round of apparently genuine applause, and as the band went on to perform renditions of tunes by the Gipsy Kings, Duke Ellington, and Billy Joel, every third song or so was a completely unfamiliar bit of cheesy fluff — apparently Japanese pop hits, judging by the spirited clapping that followed.

After a decent meal of thin chowder, good baked salmon, and a maple chocolate parfait, I escaped to the comfortable chairs of the Rundle Bar for a coffee, a cognac, and a cigarette (ah, those "C" words!), looking out at two rocky cliffs and a forested valley under a low ceiling of clouds. The pianist was arpeggiating melodramatically on the theme, "Memories," from one of those Lloyd Webber barrels of schmaltz, and I heard a great opportunity for him to segue into Debussy's "Scheherazade," my favorite of the cocktail-piano repertoire, but he missed my telepathic request.

I had considered stopping in Banff for two nights, but I was already disenchanted with that idea, and considered my options. I remembered that an artist acquaintance, Dan Hudson, lived in the nearby town of Canmore with his girlfriend Laurie. I'd only met them once before, at a party in Toronto, but for several years I had lived with one of Dan's paintings (a life-size quartet of Canada geese walking over a background collage of actual family photographs, with an overlay of jet fighters drawn in blue lines), and a few years before I had commissioned him to do a cover painting for a Rush retrospective CD (appropriately titled, *Retrospective*).

With the aid of directory assistance I called Dan, and he invited me to visit on the following day, a Sunday. I rode down in the chilly sunshine on the Alberta side of the mountains to the small town of Canmore and parked my mud-spattered bike outside Dan and Laurie's little house on a tree-lined street. Not only would I end up spending an enjoyable day and night with them, but I would carry away several inspirations for my immediate future.

Crowding into the cab of their pickup, we first went to visit Laurie's ailing horse at a nearby stable, then drove up into Banff National Park to the trailhead in Johnston Canyon. Under a clear blue mid-September sky, Laurie took their dog on a more leisurely stroll while Dan and I hiked rapidly up the trail to the waterfalls and the mineral-tinted pools called the Inkpots, talking furiously about Life and Art the whole way. Dan supplemented his unreliable income as a painter by writing and photographing for snowboard magazines, and he told me of his adventures into remote parts of British Columbia and Alaska. His knowledge and taste in art were as accomplished as his execution (one telling moment came when we were driving along in his pickup and trying to remember some artist's name, and Dan told me to open the glove compartment and look it up in his "pocket art encyclopedia" — that kind of thing impresses me). And he could *cook* too. After creating a wonderful meal of mushrooms and oil on bread, pasta with smoked salmon, fruits, and vegetables, and a bottle of Barolo (my humble contribution to the feast), he showed me his garden-shed studio, some of his recent paintings, and slides from his snowboard adventures.

As for the inspirations I took away with me the next morning, chief among them was the realization, glimpsed back at Muncho Lake and in Vancouver on the Grouse Grind, that hiking could be as engrossing and soul-soothing as motorcycling. I began to consider lingering for a day or two sometimes and getting out into the woods on foot, and that tied in with a recommendation from Dan and Laurie that I visit Waterton Lakes National Park, on the border with Montana's Glacier National Park, and stay at the Prince of Wales Hotel. Dan also recommended a back road through the Kananaskis region of the foothills, and it proved to be a perfect ride: some gravel, some paved, and *all* very scenic, with mountains to my right and prairie to my left. I saw a young bull moose, some mule deer, and even a few bison, and when I rode into the streets of the small community of Waterton Park, inside the park, flocks of bighorn sheep were cropping at the lawns. All around was a high, majestic landscape of trees rising steeply in deep green brushstrokes up the sides of gray, craggy peaks, all under a bright sun and blue, blue sky.

The Prince of Wales Hotel was a huge, half-timbered lodge on a treeless promontory above the lake, and I was fortunate to get a room near the top of the building, with a tall, old-fashioned window looking out over the forested shore and glittering expanse of calm water, right down to Montana. At an elevation of 4,000 feet, the air was cool, clear, and delicious, and I opened the window wide, drew up a wooden chair before it, and sat sipping at a glass of The Macallan while drinking in the magnificent view. Before I went to dinner I booked in for a second night, and made some plans to keep me busy and "unreflective" for the following day.

In the morning I rode down to the village wharf and joined a cruise around the lake in a sightseeing boat. The park ranger spoke on the boat's PA system as we cruised slowly along the shore of lodgepole pines, cottonwoods, trembling aspens, and larches (what we in the east called tamaracks, I learned), and she directed our collective gaze to the various scenic attractions, including a 20-foot-wide swath of cleared forest that marked the international boundary, and a slope of tumbled rocks called a "talus," composed of larger rocks than what I had learned to call a "scree." When she pointed out a black bear, the boat tipped as everyone moved to the shoreward side to see it.

Apparently, black bears and the even-more-fearsome grizzlies were plentiful in the twinned parks, and she gave us some tips on how to behave with them. Planning a hike for that afternoon, I paid close attention to her words. First of all, don't feed them ("A fed bear is a dead bear"), and — perhaps obviously — try to stay out of their way. Apparently the thing was not to *surprise* them, so she recommended not hiking alone (which I could hardly avoid) and making lots of noise. I decided to try singing — that should scare them off, judging by the usual *human* response to my attempts at vocalizing.

After a satisfying oil change in the parking area behind "Pat's," perhaps the perfect little gas station, garage, and general store, and a visit to the laundromat across the street (glad to notice that my maintenance concerns gave priority to the machine!), I rode the scenic loop to Cameron Lake, then to the trailhead for a hike to Backiston Falls. Stowing my riding gear in the empty luggage cases, I changed to jeans and walking shoes and headed down the narrow woodland trail along the river. As I walked, I sang every song I could think of, mostly Sinatra-type standards like "I've Got You under My Skin," "Gentle on My Mind," "The Shadow of Your Smile," "I Can't Get Started," and, appropriately, "Old Man River," and it seemed to work: I never saw a bear.

However, another kind of predator was about. I sat on a rock beside the stream and listened to its music, like a whispering crowd, and watched two gray jays in a lodgepole pine, thinking about what a nice rhythm that line had, "*Two gray jays in a lodgepole pine,*" when I saw two women approaching, one in her mid-30s, the other perhaps twice that. I thought idly that they looked like a spinsterish schoolteacher travelling with her mother. When they got closer the younger one chirped, "Hello again!"

Confused, I could only guess that they must have been on the boat trip, and I said, "Um, hello." She moved closer, staring into my eyes, and said with sprightly enthusiasm, "You must be riding that *gorgeous* BMW!"

I liked my faithful steed a lot, but I knew it was anything but pretty, especially to a more "delicate sensibility," and I felt that nervous discomfort again.

"Well, I wouldn't call it *gorgeous,* but it's reliable and trusty."

Had I been quicker of wit and charm I might have added, "Like me," but I am seldom that suave, and I was too rattled by yet another encounter with my seemingly irresistible allure, still uncomfortable with the strange aura I seemed to project, the radiance of my Air of Tragedy. Shrinking away, I gave them a smile and a wave, and slunk back down the trail, singing for the bears. Or perhaps not *for* them, really, but *against* them.

Back in the parking lot, I changed back into my riding gear, and as I searched my crowded belt-pack for the keys, my fingers got caught up on the jumble of wallet, journal, note pad, pen, cigarettes, and lighter. I had a sudden burst of frustration and started *talking* to my things, "Now stop messing around, all of you, or — I'm taking you all home!" When I realized what I was doing, I laughed out loud. There could no longer be any doubt; I was losing it.

Back at the Prince of Wales I decided that instead of drinking alone in my room I'd go to the bar, and while I sipped a Glenfiddich and admired that wonderful view over the lake, I became part of another scene of spontaneous friendliness among strangers. The park ranger on the boat cruise had mentioned that compared with Banff or Lake Louise, Waterton Lakes National Park received only a tenth the visitors, and that definitely helped to increase its appeal for those who did visit, and made it possible for them to appreciate not only the scenery and wildlife, but *each other.* Another positive factor in the prevailing mood of the hotel itself was that it would be closing for the season in two more days, so there was a relaxed atmosphere among the staff, and a kind of camaraderie among the guests about sharing the "Last to Leave" Club.

Seeing my binoculars on the table in front of me, an Englishman pointed out a bear on the meadowy slope of the far shore of this narrow part of the lake, and as he went out, I passed the location to other patrons in the bar, even lending them my binoculars to look at it, and as in the Lighthouse Restaurant back in Haines, Alaska, a wave of shared conversation and mutual appreciation rippled through the crowd.

Back at the bar after dinner (for the "Three Cs"), the bartender poured me a *huge* glass of Remy Martin cognac, smiling as he said, "End of the season." I asked about the music he had been playing that afternoon, and learned that it was the soundtrack from *Swing Kids,* a movie I remembered Selena had liked, and now he was playing another nice CD, a live album by Counting Crows, followed by a more traditional Irish group called Irish Descent. The Prince of Wales Hotel was definitely winning my coveted five-star rating, and the same went for the park itself.

Still, this locale was haunted by ghosts too, even some *new* ones. My brother Danny told me on the phone that night that our old family dog, Nicky, who had been in the care of my parents, had contracted a tumor of some kind and they had decided to "euthanize" him. Under the circumstances, this news didn't strike me too severely, in comparison to my other losses, but still; it was another loss. If I could have felt sadder, I would have.

The previous night I had left my window open to the night air until about 3:00 in the morning, when I had woken up shivering. I dashed out of bed to pull down the window, then huddled back under the covers, noting that my little keychain thermometer read 10°, or about 50 Fahrenheit. The second night, however, it wasn't the cold that woke me in the night, but a strange, loud noise outside my window, a high, raspy kind of *Rhee!* sound.

Suddenly awake, I heard it again and felt a tense shiver that was more than the cold night air. Once again, *Rhee!*, like the scream of a gull. It seemed to be coming from outside, very close by. I had seen ring-billed gulls soaring around the lake that day, but why would a *gull* be outside my room under the high gables of the hotel at one in the morning? My fingers wandered over the bedside lamp until I found the switch, and when I turned it the light shone through the screen and illuminated a large, pale owl sitting upright, the way owls do, right outside my window. (Later, I looked it up in my field guide, and identified it as a short-eared owl.)

The strange thing was that this nocturnal raptor wasn't screaming its challenge and warning to the night air, but right at *me* — like Poe's raven, perhaps — and now it sat calmly regarding me from the railing, just a few feet from the foot of my bed, for perhaps half a minute, and I felt seized by a mixture of wonder and primal fear. Then it turned and disappeared on silent wings.

"*Whoa!*" was the best I could do in terms of a verbal response to such a bizarre apparition, for this apparent messenger from the spirit world was much more unnerving than the two cute seals in Burrard Inlet. I thought of the title, *I Heard the Owl Call My Name*, from the novel by Margaret Craven, and remembered that in that story the call of the owl had symbolized Death approaching for the one who heard it. I felt another involuntary shiver.

Then a wry shake of the head and eyes rotating upward, "This is getting too weird."

We suspend our disbelief
And we are not alone
MYSTIC RHYTHMS, 1985

Chapter 6

THE LOΠELiEST ROAD iΠ AΠERiCA

Try to hold some faith in the goodness of humanity

NOBODY'S HERO, 1993

In my experience, the small, out-of-the-way border crossings between Canada and the United States suffered from a multiple-personality disorder. Most often the officer would ask a couple of questions (Where you from? Where you going?) and send you on your way. Sometimes they would ask about the motorcycle and your travels, just to be friendly, or if they were a little curious. However, on rare occasions the under-employed customs officers in these little nowhere places seemed to go a little "psycho," and decide to make a federal case out of it.

From Waterton Lakes National Park, I was planning to visit Glacier National Park, just over the border in Montana (the other part of what was touted as the "Waterton Glacier International Peace Park"). But as I looked over the map I noticed that Fernie, British Columbia, where my friend and fellow "Rushian," Alex, was born, was just to the west. Wouldn't it be fun to send him a postcard from there? It was only about 500 miles out of my way (a mere scenic diversion), and offered a southerly route back into the Rockies I'd never travelled before, over the Crowsnest Pass. From there, I could follow the meanderings of Highway 3 to the euphoniously named Yahk, cross the border into Idaho, and make my way east again to Glacier.

The Idaho Panhandle was a somewhat infamous corner of the United States, where survivalists and white supremacists were known to gather and live "off the grid." I thought it might be interesting to ride through that region, so I picked a dot on the map with the crossed-flags symbol of an international frontier, and went for it.

Even the most innocent person feels nervous before a border crossing, and the closer I got to this one the more I thought of possible sources of "hassle." Before setting out, I had asked Sheila to get me a set of credit cards under an alias, John Ellwood Taylor (a fine "bluesman" name, I thought, made up of Jackie's last name, my own middle name, and the most ordinary of given names), to help preserve my anonymity in motels, restaurants, and gas stations. To a law-enforcement mentality I imagined those might appear suspicious. Plus I carried a few "emergency sedatives" (in case I got stuck somewhere!) under a prescription Dr. Janette had written for me back in Vancouver, and she had discreetly written it under the alias. So that could be a problem too.

Just before the small building which housed the United States Customs and Immigration facility, I stopped to remove my earplugs, then rode up under the overhang and turned off the engine. A uniform with a hangdog face leaned toward me and asked if I had anything to declare, and when I said, "Two cartons of Canadian cigarettes," he directed me to pull over on the other side of the building.

Inside, a younger, deadly serious officer informed me that they had

had "incidents of hostage-taking," and he ordered me, in a stern, militaristic tone, to remove my jacket slowly and empty all my pockets (he was suspicious of the little plastic tube for my earplugs, and a dry-cleaning receipt).

Then he said, "Pull your shirt tight and turn around to show me that you're not carrying a weapon.

"Okay, sit down over there and don't get up or move around unless instructed by an officer. I am now going to inspect your vehicle."

Intimidated? I guess I was. Ordinarily, when submitting to any such inspection at any border crossing in the world I would demand to be present, but I was so shocked by this level of paranoia I just sat there nervously and worried about what he was going to find. A few minutes later he came in holding my wallet in his white "search gloves," and demanded that I verify its contents. Then, 10 long minutes later, he returned, stripped off the gloves, and charged me $2.40 for "excess cigarettes." Man.

Later I would note, "Nice day until fascist border crossing."

And it had been. Earlier that day, on another cool, sunny September morning, I had travelled west to the Crowsnest Pass, pausing at the site of the Frank Slide, where in 1903 the side of a mountain had roared down in the middle of the night (why do landslides and earthquakes always seem to happen in the middle of the night?) and buried most of the little town of Frank, killing 60 people. I stood on the elevated field of rubble and thought about those people, trying to imagine the enormity of that event, and thought again, "ghost town."

Like Nelson, Fernie was a small mountain community built partly on hard labor (mining and logging) and partly on outdoor recreation, for it was surrounded by mountains and lakes that offered both winter and summer activities. As I cruised the half-quaint, half-prosaic main street (the practicalities of hardware and work clothes, the play-toys of snowboards and bicycles), I decided the best place to find a postcard which said "Fernie" on it would be the drug store. Sure enough, a few minutes later I was sitting on my motorcycle, parked on its centerstand, writing a postcard to Alex.

Concerned only that the name "Fernie" appear on the card, I hadn't really paid attention to the picture, but before I started writing I noticed the caption at the top: "Ghost Rider." Turning it over, I saw a photograph of a lenticular cloud trailing off the peak of Trinity Mountain. Ghost Rider was apparently the local name for this atmospheric phenomenon.

Now, it must be explained that Alex and I shared a particular mode of writing to each other in "Moronese," and with the pen in my left (wrong) hand I started scrawling, "Eye em thuh gost rydur." Then I stopped, my head jerked back, and I thought, "Whoa, yeah! — I *am* the ghost rider!" The phantoms I carried with me, the way the world and other people's lives seemed insubstantial and unreal, and the way I myself felt alienated, disintegrated, and unengaged with life around me. "Oh yes," I thought, "that's me all right. I *am* the ghost rider."

However, even a ghost rider couldn't pass through international borders unmolested by fascists, and after that unpleasantness I felt rattled for the rest of the day. At least the riding was good, following a two-lane through sun-washed forest and mountains. Still curious about the local reputation, I explored a dirt road down through a dot on the map called Moyie Springs, but saw no visible signs of white supremacists and survivalists (though I guess they would hardly *advertise*).

Late in the afternoon I stopped at a motel in Kalispell, Montana, which would give me an early start for a ride across the famous Going to the Sun Highway in Glacier National Park. Dinner added to what was an unpleasant welcome to America, with a "mediocre meal of strange-tasting tortellini and lentil-free lentil soup with a 'hottle' of coffee — haven't seen one of those for . . . not long enough." I also felt compelled to note, I'm not sure why, that the meal had cost 20 U.S. dollars. Maybe because it was both bad *and* overpriced.

I also noted how many older men I had noticed on this trip, Americans and Canadians, who wore their jeans belted and slung *under* their protruding bellies, allowing them to pretend they still wore the same waist size by pushing their belts ever lower down their backsides. The women they accompanied often demonstrated the same oblivious vanity ("vanity without dignity," I decided to define it); they seemed unable to see what they *really* looked like. Women in their 50s and 60s dressing, grooming, and acting like the girls they imagined they still were, though the passing decades might have left them wrinkled, coarsened, jaded, and — all too often — *vast.* (Thoughts of a mean brain in a mean season.)

To complete my "welcome to America" evening, I couldn't even take a walk after dinner, for the motel was located on a busy strip of franchise restaurants, gas stations, stores, and other motels, and there was neither a sidewalk nor even a shoulder to walk on. With traffic speeding by, and whizzing in and out of parking lots, I soon gave it up as a dark, perilous, unrewarding proposition, and retreated to my room to read Jack London's *Martin Eden.*

The motel provided an in-room coffee maker, and I was up early to brew a cup of strong coffee, load the bike, and ride through a cold, cloudy morning to the entrance to Glacier National Park. The Going to the Sun Highway had been built at the urging of Joshua Logan, an early director of the park, to allow people easier access to the park's majestic scenery, and it was considered something of an engineering triumph. Open only in summer, it climbed in narrow, winding loops to Logan Pass, at 6,664 feet, surrounded by peaks approaching 10,000 feet, and as I rode along past sheer drops and switchbacks, I was encouraged to take it easy and enjoy the view. "Not a ride to be aggressive," I noted, "but gorgeous." I saw on the map that, as the short-eared owl flew, at one point I was barely 10 miles from Waterton Lake, where I had been just two days and 570 miles ago, and I pondered the wisdom of my "scenic loop." Still, despite the fascist border crossing and the depressing stay in Kalispell, I had at least learned that I *was* the Ghost Rider.

By noon, I reached the Glacier Park Lodge, a huge log-beamed resort hotel that had been built near the Great Northern Railway station of Glacier East (another imposing log structure, now operated by Amtrak). It had been built in a time before interstate highways and RVs, when tourists with sufficient means and leisure time would arrive by train and take packhorse trips through the park, sometimes as far as the Prince of Wales Hotel across the border.

Once again I arrived at this lodge within a few days of its closing for the season, and thus shared it with fewer people, in a more relaxed atmosphere. The vast interior of the lobby was pillared with giant log columns rising up three floors to the log crossbeams, high above cavernous fireplaces and arrays of comfortable furniture. I was immediately taken with its rustic splendor, so reminiscent of another time, and booked in for a second night, prepared to try some serious hiking. Having skipped breakfast, I was more than ready for a hearty lunch of chili and red wine, then a walk to the neighboring village to buy a day-pack and a water bottle.

On an afternoon "warm-up walk," I set off on a trail with signs warning, "You Are Now Entering Grizzly Country," and once again I was singing all the way, or clapping when I couldn't think of another song quickly enough (the rangers tell you, "just keep making unmistakably *human* noises"). The trail led up through the woods to an overlook, a windswept hilltop of waving grasses and stunted pines, at about 5,000 feet. From that spectacular vantage point I could see the meaning of the slogan of the two parks, "where the mountains meet the prairie," for I looked in one direction across a wooded valley to the green slopes and gray peaks of the Rockies, raising my binoculars to watch a bull elk stroll across a high meadow, and in the other direction over the open prairie undulating in calm golden waves, raising my glasses to watch a distant bird of prey ride the gusty wind.

The next day brought overcast, chilly temperatures, and threatened rain, but during breakfast I pondered the trail maps and ordered a box lunch to carry in my new day-pack. I decided on the trail to Squaw Peak, which looked like about 10 miles return, and stopped at the front desk to ask the staff, mostly young students, if they had any knowledge of that trail. Fortunately, one of them had done that hike about a month previously, and he gave me some valuable tips — especially in telling me he had become lost while returning through one unmarked section, and he'd had to "bushwhack" for awhile. When I reached that part of the trail, where it disappeared into a barrier of scrubby bushes, I decided I would make some strategic blazes with my Swiss Army knife.

A light rain fell as I hiked through the dim woods, but fortunately the soil was gravelly and well drained, so the trail never became too muddy. With a rain hat and waterproof jacket I was warm and dry enough, except for my feet, and I soon fell into a fairly quick rhythm, singing and talking out loud all the way.

A spruce grouse stood at the side of the trail as I approached, and I stopped and turned to sing it a chorus of "Gentle on My Mind": *"But not to where I cannot see you, standin' on the back road, by the river of my memory, ever smilin', ever gentle on my mind."*

The grouse stood there in front of me the whole time, perhaps 10 feet away, seemingly mesmerized by my performance of this classic of lyric poetry in the American language, like "Ode to Billie Joe," "By the Time I Get to Phoenix," or "Little Green Apples" (at least the way Sinatra sang it). Once again, I contemplated the strange behavior of birds and women.

As I climbed above treeline into stretches of sparse meadow and bare rock, I began to see many animal tracks pressed into the soft soil, and piles of scat alongside. By these combinations of spoor I thought I could identify elk, deer, and sheep — and one fresh specimen full of half-digested berries that could only have been left by a bear. In places the earth had been gouged out with sharp claws, a sure mark of the grizzly, and I was sure I could smell a thick, unpleasant musk in the damp air that might be ursine body odor. Feeling exposed and vulnerable, I picked up a pointed, fist-sized rock and carried it with me. Laughable, even at the time, but I wasn't going down without a fight.

I had almost reached the clouds when the trail petered out at a tumble of boulders marking the base of the actual peak, a rough pyramid of bare, wet rocks. Taking shelter from the chill wind behind one of the boulders, I shrugged off my pack and sat down to devour the sandwich, apple, and cookies, all the while clapping my hand against my steaming jeans to keep up the "human" noises, and imagining grizzlies behind every rock.

Bending to keep the rain off my journal, I wrote, "Definitely scary to know they're all around, and unpredictable, and wanting my ham and cheese sandwich!"

Looking out over the sodden view, back toward the tiny lodge five miles distant, and the forest giving way to prairie beyond, I looked up and contemplated the next part of the climb: a long scramble up rain-slick rocks. I realized the view wasn't going to be any wider from up there — if in fact I'd be able to see at all, with the clouds sinking ever lower. What if I got lost in that fog? Or fell and got hurt? The goal-oriented part of me still wanted to go for it, but the survivalist thought better of it, and for once he prevailed.

I headed back down again, an easy downhill ramble, the rain falling heavier all the time. By the time I reached the lodge, Squaw Peak had been swallowed by clouds, and I knew the survivalist had made the right decision. Peeling off my wet clothes for a hot shower, I stuffed my soaked and muddy shoes with newspaper and put them under the steam radiator, which emitted sounds right out of the movie *Eraserhead,* and hung everything else around the room to dry while I went down to the bar for a well-earned drink.

The rain continued for hours, and a TV forecast in the bar even mentioned a chance of snow, so it didn't look as though I would be "going to the sun" the next day. I sat with my map spread on the bar, sipping my whisky, and thought about where to go next. A quote was posted on the wall, attributed to someone named Reggie Leach:

"Success is not the result of spontaneous combustion; you must set yourself on fire."

Nice one, Reggie, whoever you are. (A hockey player back in the '70s, apparently.)

I dashed off a postcard to Gramps at his retirement home in Ontario, telling him about my narrow escape from the grizzlies, and another to a neglected friend, my other colleague (along with the aforementioned Alex) Geddy, Rush's bass player and singer. Like Alex, Geddy had been a compassionate and loyal friend through my troubles, always there at the House of Mourning after Selena's death (he was the first to make Jackie laugh in those terrible days, as Alex was the first to get her to eat something, if only some broth. When she couldn't keep even that down, Alex made her laugh again by saying, "Hey, that's okay — now you can be a supermodel!").

While Jackie and I were in London, Geddy had visited us one evening on his way through town, and while I ("Chef Ellwood") worked in the kitchen, I heard Jackie talking and laughing with him, as he drew her out and raised her spirits. For an evening, anyway.

My partners in Rush through 24 years of professional ups and downs, both Geddy and Alex had proved to be good and caring friends. When I told Geddy I was setting off on this "journey to somewhere," he offered to meet me "anywhere, anytime," if I needed company. I knew he meant it, and promised I would keep it in mind, and try to pick somewhere good, like North Dakota or Iowa, to summon him for a "rescue" visit.

In the postcard to Geddy I also joked about the grizzlies on my hike, telling him that I had "carried a pointed rock, for grizzly punching — yeah right!," and that I was doing as well as can be expected, a line Jackie and I had settled on back in London as a way to answer friends who asked how we were doing. "As well as can be expected."

Though "what could be expected" was arguable, that was still true of how I felt I was doing, and the condition of my little baby soul. My days continued to be woven of strands of light and darkness, hope and despair, though my nights were mostly black and "haunted."

Worst of all, I often awoke at three or four in the morning and lay there for an hour or so, staring into the darkness and thinking bad, bad thoughts. These spells seemed to have been increasing since our stay in London, and the problem seemed to be my stomach — though it was never painful, but only a little uncomfortable, like indigestion. Sometimes I couldn't even figure out why I was awake, and I could never identify what might be causing this distress — rich food, meat, alcohol, or, as I asked my journal, "Was the abuse which caused this insult to my formerly strong constitution self-inflicted, or just the deep and constant aggravations of recent life?" A darn good question.

In any case, lately I defined my overall progress on the Healing Road as, "One step forward, one step back."

Next morning, the clairvoyant combination of weather forecast and map decided I should head back west across Idaho to the Columbia River, and then let the weather tell me where to go from there. Despite the unpromising forecast, I had plenty of sun after all, and that encouraged me to take a couple of side trips to avoid repeating the same route. North from Whitefish to Eureka, through the inevitable forested mountains (my "soulscape," after all), then back south to Libby (on the "excellent 37," as I described it) along the narrow length of Lake Koocanusa (puzzling over the name of this man-made lake which straddled the border, I guessed it was a compound of the nearby Kootenai National Forest and the two country names — similar to those failures-of-imagination found along state borders further south: Texoma, Uvada, Calneva, Mexicali, and so on).

Recrossing the Idaho Panhandle, I turned south at Bonners Ferry (on "busy 95") down through Coeur d'Alene (the source of its name, "heart of an awl," is both strange and unknown) and Moscow. I rode on south through the western corner of Idaho, "stormy seas of wheat" on that bright, windy day, to Lewiston, named for the explorer Meriwether Lewis. His partner, William Clark, was commemorated on the opposite side of the Snake River, in Clarkston, Washington. I paused at a high viewpoint and, with an automatic "wow," looked down 2,000 feet over the two small cities straddling the big river. Where I stood must once have been the post-glacial river bank. A historical signboard indicated an old wagon road winding down its steep slope, and I decided to make my entrance to Lewiston that way, ready to find a motel after nine hours and 473 miles.

From the hotel restaurant, "Meriwether's," I looked back at that view from below, the wrinkled, treeless bluff falling into shadow in the translucent twilight, lights beginning to appear from ranches up along that old wagon road. The restaurant itself was a strange mix of high and low Americana; an elegant dining room decorated with candles, fine linen, twinkling fairy lights and plate-glass windows on that splendid view, a nicely-dressed, well-spoken waiter wearing a tie and a neatly-trimmed beard, and an ambitious menu offering wine suggestions beside each dish (I chose the jambalaya, very spicy, and the accompanying Chardonnay).

However, the "entertainment" at Meriwether's was provided by a muted player piano (complete with a dummy that resembled Harpo Marx) tinkling out honky-tonk ditties, and the few other patrons (only six, on a Saturday night) were dressed in trailer-park chic, with a genderless array of short-long haircuts (a.k.a. "mullets"), baseball caps, shorts and T-shirts bursting with obesity, huge plastic-rimmed eyeglasses, and the inevitable mood-spoiler of a squalling, unkempt child. (Mean once again, perhaps, but note that only one low-life diner at Meriwether's sat alone . . .)

An early start on a Sunday morning often presented me with a world of my own, with the local population sleeping late and their cars and trucks tucked into their driveways and garages. I had another bright, cool morning on empty roads as I crossed to the Washington side of the Snake and into what I described as the "Shar-pei hills," treeless and furrowed with yellow grass. "Righteous riding, 70–75 mph."

In Walla Walla, the "onion capital," as both signs and the perfumed air attested, I bought maps of Oregon and Washington, then stopped for breakfast at an old-time downtown restaurant called the Red Apple. With the weather so fine, I ventured west into the often rain-soaked parts of those two states, for I had heard of a couple of mysterious attractions along the Columbia River: a full-scale replica of Stonehenge, a chateau called Maryhill that had been turned into an art museum in the middle of nowhere, and the Columbia River Scenic Highway.

A Ghost Road.

Only two short stretches remained of the Columbia River Scenic Highway, an engineering marvel opened in 1915, and now mostly replaced by Interstate 84. It was an anomaly in the history of American roads, for it was not built to carry settlers to the frontier or goods to market, but simply to make the spectacular scenery of the Columbia River Gorge accessible to motorists. And although it was paid for by the Oregon taxpayers, it was the vision and dream of one man: Samuel Hill.

As a young attorney for the Great Northern Railway, Sam Hill married the boss's daughter, and thus launched his career as railroad magnate and financier (his death certificate, in 1931, gave his profession as "capitalist"). But, unlike the clichéd "robber baron" driven by greed and power, Sam Hill was the other kind of renaissance American, one whose dreams did not stop at amassing a fortune; they *began* there.

On a remote stretch of the treeless banks of his beloved Columbia River, Sam Hill built a short-lived utopian community called Maryhill (after his already estranged wife, who had moved to Washington D.C.), experimented with irrigated farms and orchards, built the first paved road in Washington State, commissioned a war memorial in the shape of a full-scale replica of Stonehenge (as it would have been when it was "new" — and if the Druids had built their celestial observatories and altars of human sacrifice out of poured concrete). At the Canada–U.S. border, south of Vancouver, he also commissioned a "Peace Arch" in the Roman style (if the Romans had built their triumphal arches out of poured concrete).

On the high rim of the northern bank of the Columbia, Sam Hill built a huge chateau (yes, of poured concrete), again called Maryhill, though Mary was apparently long gone, and never made an appearance there. Sam consoled himself with mistresses, several illegitimate children, and a long relationship with Marie, Queen of Romania, whom he had met while promoting Great Northern stock to European royalty.

The Queen's biographer, Edmond S. Ellerby, described Sam Hill as "a raving American eccentric, a giant aging sheepdog of a man with a cherubic face, a shock of white hair and a penchant for building ramshackle monuments to pipe dreams."

The Queen herself wrote, "Sometimes his ideas come so rapidly and he talks so fast that his friends scarcely understand him. Sometimes the things dreamers do seem incomprehensible to others, and the world wonders why dreamers do not see the world the way others do."

At its completion in 1926, Maryhill became an art museum, and so it remained, exhibiting native arts, a collection of drawings and sculpture by Rodin, and exhibits from the royal family of Romania.

"Sometimes the things dreamers do seem incomprehensible to others." The same might be said for ghost riders. This day, though, I would describe in my journal as a "perfect touring day — weather, scenery changes, 'roadside attractions.'"

From Walla Walla, I drifted west through pretty little farming towns, and as so often in American county seats, I was impressed by the court houses. There ought to be a picture-book on the variety of settings and styles found throughout America. I wondered if any of those small towns had ever saved their taxpayers some money by sharing the same plans for their imposing neoclassical edifice with another county seat — which might be hundreds or thousands of miles away, after all. I decided civic pride would probably preclude that. "We've got to have an imposing neoclassical edifice of our *own!*"

One town name, Irrigon, Oregon, gave me a smile (its setting among irrigated farmland must have inspired that compound), and at a gas station nearby I laughed out loud to see the usual "mechanic on duty" sign changed to "Maniac on Duty — Fully Certified." When I complimented the overalled owner on his sense of humor, he said that not too many people noticed it. Sometimes the things jokers do seem incomprehensible to others.

The Shar-pei hills continued, though on a grander scale along the banks of the Columbia, where I picked up a stretch of Interstate 84 to carry me downriver to Maryhill. Far ahead, the high white dome of Mount Adams glowed in the clear blue sky. I stopped at a rest area for a biological break and a smoke, and as I stood by the bike an old man parked his ancient Mercedes beside me, then struck up a conversation. Admiring the BMW, he told me in a heavy German accent that back in the '30s he had ridden a BMW, then later a Zundapp with a sidecar, which he described as "much better zan zee BMW." Casually, he told of abandoning the Zundapp in Kiev for lack of fuel, then walking *800 miles* home, with nothing but a bottle of vodka and a piece of frozen bread, marching day after day, even in his sleep. Suddenly I realized he was describing Hitler's retreat from Russia in 1943, and that he must have been a German soldier then. Another ghost story.

Near Biggs I saw a sign for Maryhill, and crossed the river on the Sam

Hill Memorial Bridge. After a stop at the visitors' center, where an elderly volunteer filled me in on the whole story, I went off to look at the sunwashed, sharp-edged Stonehenge replica, which had an undeniable presence, even in poured concrete, then high on the Washington bank of the river to the chateau of Maryhill, perched in solitary splendor above the mighty Columbia.

Then back across the river to The Dalles (the only place-name in America with "the" in it, I believe), where the river's high banks created a wind tunnel effect and world-famous boardsailing, and where trees started to appear again. Searching out a remnant nine-mile stretch of the Scenic Highway, I would later express my response in my journal with breathless enthusiasm, "Twisting high and narrow in a most entertaining way. Wow! They sure don't make 'em like they used to."

At Hood River I turned south toward the looming white peak of Mount Hood, without a single cloud to veil its perfection. The winding, well-paved road was shaded by thick old-growth forest, with some stunning views of the mountain's snowfields, and I was riding fast, leaning deep into the corners ("using all those tires today!"), the temperature exactly right for the "minimum dress code" of leathers and T-shirt. "Bliss," I called it. The traffic was fairly heavy, but all seemed to be going the other way, back to Portland after the weekend.

In yet one more complete change of scene, the forest suddenly opened to the dry country of eastern Oregon, the Great Basin desert of sage, grass-lands, and rugged canyon vistas that covers eastern Washington and Oregon, southern Idaho, most of Nevada, and part of Utah. "Unexpectedly spectacular," I noted, as I rode south toward Bend (the home town of a minor character in Kerouac's On the Road, I somehow recalled), where I had decided to stop for the night, after "a long day by choice; just too perfect." It had been a healing day, all right, but balanced, as always, by spells of grieving. One step forward, one step back.

My room at the Riverhouse Motor Inn overlooked a small, fast-moving river, the air scented with tamaracks and pines. In contrast, the lounge and restaurant were bouncing to loud chatter competing with a live big-band and middle-aged female singer, who were surprisingly good, and obviously loved the music they played. I thought how my Dad would have enjoyed their renditions of "Sing, Sing, Sing," "Jumpin' at the Woodside," "Come Rain or Come Shine," "A Foggy Day in London Town," "Little Brown Jug," "I've Heard That Song Before," "Boogie Woogie Bugle Boy from Company B," and "Sentimental Journey." For myself, I wrote down the titles as repertoire suggestions for future hikes in bear country.

Next day the all-seeing, all-knowing map sent me back east toward Idaho, traversing the high plains on long, lonely Highway 20, with the spicy fragrance of sage delicious on a cold, clear morning. Scattered pines and juniper dotted the rangelands at first, then gave way to low scrub and rocky hills. My nostrils flared at the scent of a grassfire, then the rich aroma of irrigation sprinklers near Burns, the most luxurious smell in a dry land. In the irrigated valley near Ontario the perfume of onions returned, surprisingly tantalizing.

I had decided to get to Boise as early as I could, wanting to visit the BMW dealer for an oil change and some small repairs: a new headlight bulb, and fuel gauge, which had quit back in Alberta. Although I was getting along by using the odometer, on these endless, empty desert highways I would need to keep a close eye on my fuel consumption, so I hoped the gauge could be revived.

Unfortunately, it could not be easily fixed, but a stop at Big Twin Motorcycles took care of the other needs, and I rode into the tree-lined streets of Boise (from the French *boisé,* meaning "wooded"), searching for a good central hotel for my other missions: drug store, liquor store, and leather repairs. Parked and unpacked, the friendly woman at the front desk sent me (with sympathetic eyes) to Nick's Shoe Repair, who not only fixed the broken zipper, conditioned two pairs of sun-faded gloves, and cleaned up my walking shoes (doubling as hiking and dress shoes, and still mud-bleached from the Glacier hike) in a couple of hours, but they kindly delivered them to the hotel. A friendly kind of town, I decided.

After a copious meal in the hotel's Gamekeeper Restaurant ("Yes, up there with Wickaninnish: Coquilles St. Jacques, fettuccine with perfect salmon, Cherries Jubilee, Echelon Chardonnay, and good coffee"), I took a long walk through the warm late-September evening, the night air making me think of the word "gentle," and the floodlights glowing on the imposing neoclassical dome of the State Capitol (any of *them* use the same plans?). There were few pedestrians on this Monday night, but many cars murmured by, and I noticed a big record store open late. I was surprised to find myself briefly tempted to go inside, though I quickly put the notion aside, "Almost went in, but what for?" A hopeful urge, I guess, to be at all interested in looking around a record store, but not enough to actually do it. And even if I bought something, I had nothing to play it on.

Setting off early the next day ("gorgeous riding morning, sunny and pleasantly cool"), I saw signs for the Birds of Prey Center, but I had already looked it up in the AAA book and learned that it didn't open until 9:00; I'd be 100 miles away by then. Around Boise, I noticed a lot of espresso bars, often with a line of pickup trucks parked outside, and I pictured these ranchers and cowboys gathered around their decaf lattes and soy-milk frappuccinos. For myself, I chose a classic family restaurant in the small town of Weiser ("wee-zer"), and finally succumbed to the lure of the local onions with a Farmer's Omelette, though its wicked combination of onions and hot peppers would rumble away inside me all day.

It was another day of scenic side trips, first to the Hell's Canyon Dam, at the bottom of the high narrow gorge of the Snake and the Seven Devils Mountains, then another 20-mile climb on a rough road of gravel, dirt, and rocks ("the dry stream-bed effect") edging along a steep slope ("don't look around, instant vertigo"), to the Seven Devils Vista at Heaven's Gate. From the road's end I climbed the last 350 yards on foot, watching a pair of mountain bluebirds frolic together in the last of the conifers (my first sighting of the species), then stood by the small fire lookout on the summit (8,429 feet) and looked out to the Oregon side of Hell's Canyon, and a far gray, green, and blue mountainscape that touched four states. "A serious sidetrip," I noted, "and a hard-won view."

My little red gas can was missing off the back of the bike, and I realized it must have bounced off during the more "entertaining" parts of the ascent. I saw a nice-looking young family, father, mother, and two teenage daughters, just preparing to leave the lookout, squeezing back into their pickup, and I asked the man at the wheel if he would keep an eye out for my gas can, and leave it by the roadside if he found it.

I don't know why I was so taken with this family, but in the few seconds I spoke with them they radiated such openness, friendliness, and health that it melted me inside to look at them. Such a contrast to the bovine trailer-trash the other night in Lewiston (only 50 miles away, as the mountain bluebird flies), they definitely corrected the balance of my personal scales of humanity. Certainly they "weighed" less, in several senses, but *counted* for more, as the good ought to do. Their pickup was a few years old; their outdoor clothes were not made of the latest goretex-cordura-kevlar blend, but they were nice to me, and to each other, and I felt a burning pang of envy. And as I expected, on the way down I found my gas can placed neatly at the roadside.

Riggins, Idaho, was a line of buildings along the two-lane Highway 95, and it seemed to thrive on being a rare point of access for rafters, kayakers, and jet-boat excursions to a bend of the uniquely roadless Salmon River, the "River of No Return." I thought of the old movie with that title, starring Robert Mitchum and Marilyn Monroe, in which they float down a perilous river on a raft, two castaways (three, counting Mitchum's motherless son) set adrift by the vicissitudes of pioneer life, and Marilyn "plays" a guitar and "sings" a metaphorical song by that title, in which *life* is the "river of no return." The movie was nothing special, but the scenery and the metaphor were good.

From my pleasant room at the Riverview Motel, I walked up the dark road to the Seven Devils Steak House and Saloon, and decided to sit at a table outside under the steep valley walls, the surrounding dry mountains, and the rising half moon.

Lately I had been seeing the name "John Day" on maps and signs: a river in Oregon, a nearby town, a dam, and even the John Day Fossil Beds, and I wondered, "Who is John Day?" Was he another visionary westerner, like Sam Hill, who left his name engraved on the landscape as a memorial to the grand scale of his half-forgotten dreams?

Well, no. It appeared John Day was not exactly an American visionary, but more like the butt of a long-running joke. He had been part of John Jacob Astor's 1810 expedition to establish a fur-trading post at the mouth of the Columbia, but his party became divided, and dwindled to two men. At the mouth of what was then called the Mah-hah River, a band of Indians robbed John Day and his companion of everything they carried, including their clothes, and left them naked on the river bank. Fortunately they were rescued by another expedition, but subsequent travellers on the Columbia always pointed out the place where John Day had been robbed and stripped, and by the 1850s the Mah-hah River became known as the John Day River, which also gave us the town of John Day, the John Day Dam, and the John Day Fossil Beds.

And speaking of Americans of dubious achievement . . .

> *Evel Knievel connection lately, around Snake River; wonder where he tried that jump? Also Red Lion [motel] in Bend reminded me of doing the rounds of Red Lions in Northwest tours of old, and his Ferrari Daytona convertible (licence plate "Evel 1") in front of the Red Lion in Yakima. Now he's all fucked up. Like me.*
>
> *How many times a day does the "real situation" invade my brain and threaten to knock me down? So many. Memories of then, and regrets about now. Still unacceptable.*

Sept 30 Riggins — Sun Valley
77,606 (864 kms) [540 miles]

Awake too early. Too dark to leave, so read a bit more Martin Eden *[a semi-autobiographical novel by Jack London], approaching what I already know to be a dark ending. (Given away in the notes to another of his books; I hate that. Stopped reading even the blurbs on back of paperbacks after I saw that it would have ruined the wonder of* The Twyborn Affair *[by Patrick White] for example.)*

Another cold, clear morning, sun on mountain tops to west,
pink and gray. Up long, long White Bird Grade to 4,000 feet.
Breakfast at The Crossroads, Grangeville.
Note how modern-day rednecks are old hippies with white
necks, under long ponytails.
Yesterday I realized that whenever I wonder why a particular
road exists, the formula is simple: There's money at one end, and a
bank at the other. Mine, farm, oil, timber, hydro, etc. True of every
road right up to Interstate, excepting only a few scenic parkways;
usually one man's vision. Going-to-the-Sun, Columbia Gorge:
Joshua Logan and Sam Hill.

In May of 1997, on the *Test For Echo* tour, Rush played a concert at The Gorge, an outdoor amphitheatre overlooking the treeless banks of the Columbia, which rippled westward from the backstage area in muscular bulges of yellow grass. In early evening, the air's perfect clarity played infinite shadings of light over the simple, dramatic landscape, and we took the stage in front of about 20,000 people (one of our largest crowds ever) just as the slow sunset dimmed into the cloudless, transparent twilight — soon overpowered by the colored stage lights, follow spots, and video screens, and overlooked by a rising half moon. It was the most beautiful setting in which I had ever performed.

After the show, as usual, I ran straight to the bus, and driver Dave followed an escort of two security guards on dirt bikes who cleared our way along the lane of deep gravel that led through the parking lot, making sure we didn't run aground on the post-show traffic. In the morning, Brutus and I unloaded the bikes and set off from a rest area in Missoula, Montana, to begin one of our best-ever riding days, south through the Bitterroot River valley between the Sapphire and Bitterroot Mountains, and over the pass to Idaho, then down its length beside the Salmon River and the Sawtooth Mountains, with a side trip to the Lemhi Pass, where Lewis and Clark had crossed the Great Divide from the headwaters of the Missouri.

We stayed overnight in the old Sun Valley Lodge, built by Averell

Harriman in the late 1930s, with gracious, large rooms looking out through tall conifers to the skating rink and mountains. (Another mediocre old movie set in Idaho, *Sun Valley Serenade,* was made in the '40s to publicize the resort, featuring Glenn Miller and Olympic skater Sonja Heinje performing on that skating rink.) At an elevation of almost 6,000 feet, the air was cold and bracing, and I left the window and balcony door open all night, even though the temperature sank to 30°F ("tucked deep into great blankets").

It was another of the many places Brutus and I visited so briefly between shows that we decided were worthy of a longer stop, or at least another visit. But early the next morning, we scraped the frost off our saddles and rode away on another memorable "commute to work," taking the long route to Boise.

In late spring the surrounding mountains and even the roadsides and meadows were still white with snow, and the snowmelt filled the surging rivers like a storm at sea, turbulent whitecaps bursting against the banks. Brutus remarked that for three days we had followed rivers, for there was nowhere else to cut roads in that violent terrain, and I recall him saying that while we were stopped near Banks by a flag lady at a point where a recent landslide covered half the road. We saw evidence of many more slides along that route, and for several miles we rode through the black scar of charred ponderosa pines and mountain sage.

On a sunny day in May, Boise had looked good to us too, with the streets lined with green trees and the domed Capitol building glowing white. Traffic was agreeably light in that small city, and after such a spectacular morning's ride, we arrived at the university auditorium plenty early, and feeling good.

Unfortunately, the show that night was a very *lame* one, by my own standards. After playing so long together, Geddy and Alex and I never played a truly bad show, at least that anyone else would know about, but we had our own inner scale to judge by, and that judge could be stern. My playing felt clumsy and sloppy, and I remember running onto the bus at the end of the show feeling disgusted with myself. As I slouched over the table in the front lounge with a glass of The Macallan and recounted my woes to Brutus, he said, "You're too hard on yourself."

With a shrug, I replied, "That's the job."

In the journal I was keeping of that tour I wrote, "No flow, no groove, mentally or physically. Egregious intro to 'Limbo,' and various other clumsy bits too. Sore elbow again, and legs going downhill. Ah well."

That last comment displayed an unusual measure of philosophical detachment for "the fool I used to be," and I brought more of that quality to Sun Valley this time, a year and a half later.

> *"Fings ain't wot they used to be." Shunted off to low-life Inn [rather than Lodge], but at least I am dining in the Dining Room. Hotel full of conventioneers, but not here; presumably tucking into their free cocktails and buffets. Dining Room is empty (nine people at 8:00; guess who's the odd one?). Oysters Rockefeller and elk* medaillons *with mushrooms, beets, and the locally famous huckleberries (told the waiter to tell the chef, "a great composition," for so it was: with potatoes au gratin and a mélange of vegetables, carrots, green beans, squash).*
>
> *This place is a bleedin' town, once you start exploring a bit. Too much damn shopping for a ski resort. Lots of live music, though, a trio in the Dining Room, another in the bar, and a pianist in the other restaurant too. Nice.*
>
> *A long, but excellent ride today. Cool, sunny, challenging, untrafficked. Wild turkeys, Steller's jays at Lolo, Bighorns at Lost Trail Pass.*
>
> *Getting spoiled, not appreciating that I sometimes ride for hours without stopping at all. Except maybe for a cattle drive! (As today.)*
>
> *I'm spoiled also by weather. Saw a single cloud today and thought, "What's that, a snowy peak?"*
>
> *Had to stop to photograph that sign, "WARNING — WINDING ROAD FOR 77 MILES." Oh no!*

*Meant to note that after the second time I saw an antique shop
called "Thistle Dew," I started to wonder why. Then I got it:
"This'll do." (I guess?)*

*Two 8,000-foot summits today, and darn cool they were too
(in both senses). Snowy peaks of May a year ago [just over a year;
seems impossible!] all bare now except for few small patches on
north faces.*

*Passed 20,000 kms [12,500 miles] of this journey today, after
41 days.*

After another night interrupted by a stomach "interval," an hour of
wakefulness and dark thoughts, I got up early and decided to try a hike
along a trail which traversed the ski trails to the summit of Mount Baldy,
just the other side of Ketchum from Sun Valley. Parking the bike at the ski
lodge, I began the long, relentless ascent of a constant-grade trail which
led steadily up through forest and open ski runs, a two-and-a-half hour
slog from the trailhead at 5,700 feet and climbing to 9,150 feet at the
summit, called The Lookout, where I stopped to eat the lunch I had
brought from the hotel.

From the deck of a cabin at the top of a ski-lift I sat and looked around
at the valley over half a mile below, and the cutting edge of the aptly
named Sawtooth Mountains under dramatic cumulus clouds. A sudden
roll of thunder rumbled in the distance, sounding like dynamite at first,
and I watched a storm pass to the north, trailing veils of dark rain. When
I felt the wind around the cabin begin to pick up in chilly gusts, I was
smugly glad I had brought my rain jacket, but when I reached into my
pack I discovered I had left it at the hotel. Fortunately I was able to make
the hour-and-a-half descent to the motorcycle and the short ride back to
the hotel before two sharp peals of thunder heralded a sudden, brief
shower outside my room.

Next morning I started out riding eastward on the Sun Valley Road,
pausing for a moment at the Hemingway Memorial, a bronze bust in a
grove of trees by Trail Creek. Ernest Hemingway ended his life in 1961 with
a shotgun blast to the head in the front hall of his home in Ketchum,

Idaho, near Sun Valley. He is buried under a plain stone slab in the local cemetery, beside his fourth wife, Mary. At the end he was ill, feeble, and suffering from paranoia and the effects of electroshock therapy. Earlier that year, he had spent *days* trying to write a simple reply to an invitation to John F. Kennedy's inauguration, and perhaps he decided that if he couldn't write anymore, he couldn't live anymore.

A Rush song called "Losing It," from 1982, opens with a verse inspired by Hemingway's sad end, attempting to express the frustration of being unable to do something which, to him, was more important than life itself: *"Sadder still to watch it die, than never to have known it."*

The memorial itself displayed an inscription Hemingway had written as a eulogy for a local friend.

> *Most of all he loved the fall*
> *The leaves yellow on the cottonwoods*
> *Leaves floating in the trout streams*
> *And above the hills, the high, blue, windless skies*
> *Now he will be a part of them forever*

On my solitary travels I often found myself tracing, and even searching out, the ghostly footsteps of deceased writers: Hemingway, Steinbeck, Jack London, Mark Twain, Ezra Pound (born in Boise, of all places), Edward Abbey, Sinclair Lewis, Wallace Stegner, Willa Cather, Mary Austin, Ernie Pyle, Jack Kerouac, Truman Capote (around Garden City, Kansas, where he had researched *In Cold Blood*), and, down Mexico way, B. Traven and Malcolm Lowry. All greats, and all gone. Ghost Writers. I felt the presence of a few living writers too, in the places they had "illumined:" Annie Proulx, William Least Heat Moon, Robert Pirsig, Cormac McCarthy.

The quasi-nostalgic pang I sensed while travelling through these haunted locales was akin to something I sometimes felt in historical settings I meandered into on my travels, places that marked the passing of other ghosts — the Oregon Trail, the Pony Express Trail, Lewis and Clark's path to the Pacific, scenes of tragedy like Wounded Knee, or beside the Pacific Coast Highway in Oregon, a more personal memorial to a young man who had been swept off the rocks and out to sea by a rogue wave. Sad, sad, sad.

After my pilgrimage to the Hemingway Memorial I had intended to try an unpaved road leading east over the Pioneer Mountains, but it didn't look good. A steady rain began to fall, and the sign, "Not Maintained for Passenger Vehicles" meant what it said; the dirt surface was soon awash, and fist-sized rocks rolled down the bank and across the road in front of me. I turned around, riding back through Ketchum and down through Hailey.

The rain tapered off into a cool, windy morning, though my mood remained dark. At Craters of the Moon National Park, I paused briefly to smoke a cigarette and look over the black fields of rippling lava, then turned westward again, with another pause to look at what the sign claimed to be the highest sand dunes in North America. Like a mirage among the sage and grasslands, the sharp-edged, pale brown pyramids of the Bruneau Dunes rose to 700-foot peaks against the gray sky. Then onward, out of Idaho into a corner of Oregon, past areas of irrigated farmland and eroded canyons, under clouds high and low.

Turning south on the two-lane blacktop of Highway 95, I rode for hours on a straight, empty desert road with hardly another vehicle in sight. Despite the perfect conditions to make time, I tried to keep my speed down, for the state of Oregon had found it prudent to post a 55 mph limit, though as soon as I hit the Nevada line, it rose to a more reasonable 70.

Oregon could be maddeningly paternalistic that way. Sam Hill, lobbying for his highway back in 1912, had come up against the same "bewildering mix of conservative and liberal," and Oregon's governor had described his citizens to Sam as "fine, but damned peculiar." (However, the governor also assured him, "they will follow you because you smell of money and have held the Queen of Romania's hand.")

Although modern-day Oregon's progressiveness was often admirable, that same liberal-conservative (or conservative-liberal) mindset could also tend toward the presumption that its citizens (and visitors) weren't ready for too much freedom. The unreasonably low speed limits were one example; another was the statewide ban on self-service gas stations, presumably because people were not responsible enough to fuel their own vehicles without the risk of spilling fossil fuel and causing fires and environmental degradation. Or maybe it was designed to increase employment at the minimum-wage level.

Like most motorcyclists, I prefer to pump my own gas, so I can fill the tank as full as possible without overfilling it until gas spills down the side of the hot engine — risking fires and environmental degradation. A fill-up was also an opportunity to look over the machine, check the oil level in the sight glass, inspect the tires, have what pilots call a "walkaround." So, in the spirit of Thoreau's tradition of civil disobedience, when I pulled into Oregon gas stations I tended to take matters into my own hands: unhook the nozzle, turn on the pump, and do it myself. (You've got to resist oppression!)

And on a road like Highway 95, I kept a careful eye on my fuel level, and took advantage of gas stations when I found them; they could be scarce. Just after a fuel stop at the Nevada border town of McDermitt, I pulled to the roadside for a break beside a "historic site" sign, and read that the nearby Owyhee River had been named as a corruption of "Hawaii" by Hudson's Bay Company trapper Peter Skene Ogden, who had sent two Hawaiian trappers (?) there to hunt, where they were promptly killed by Indians. Another ghost story.

My destination, partly by design and partly by default (for there were few other choices in sparsely populated northern Nevada), was the little town of Winnemucca. The "design" part of this choice was inspired by a song Brutus had introduced me to called "I've Been Everywhere," as performed by Canada's Hank Snow. Perhaps the ultimate hobo song, maybe even the ultimate road song, it opens with the lines, *I was totin' my pack, along the dusty Winnemucca road.* (Brutus and I canvassed truck drivers and the road atlas for *days* before we discovered Winnemucca was in Nevada.) Then it builds to a rapid-fire recitation of cleverly linked place names:

Reno, Chicago, Fargo, Minnesota
Buffalo, Toronto, Winslow, Sarasota

Wichita, Tulsa, Ottawa, Oklahoma
Tampa, Panama, Mattawa, La Paloma
Bangor, Baltimore, Salvador, Amarillo
Tocopilla, Baranquilla, and Padilla — I'm a killer

I've been everywhere, man, I've been everywhere, man
Breathed the mountain air, man
Crossed the deserts bare, man
Of travel I've done my share, man
I've been everywhere

And on for another three or four verses. It took me awhile to get even one verse planted in my head, and to deliver it in one breath, but it was a great number for in-helmet "recitation" (not to dignify my vocalizations as "singing"), especially on an empty two-lane leading endlessly across the wide open spaces of the Great Basin desert — to Winnemucca.

The "dusty Winnemucca road" lived up to the song's description, with a stretch of modest sand dunes spilling onto the pavement. But my destination, after all, was just a dull little town on the Interstate, and a Red Lion motel built, like nearly every hotel in Nevada, onto a big casino. Despite my continuing mood of doom and gloom, I had come to appreciate the long open stretches of two-lane highway across the sagey sea and mountain-studded plateau of the Great Basin, but the towns and cities were another thing. I liked the *natural* face of Nevada, but was not as impressed by the *human* face.

At the Red Lion in Winnemucca I stood in line waiting to get into the hotel restaurant beside a hyperactive young brat harassing his mother for coins, while she ignored him and mechanically fed the "Wheel of Fortune" slot machine. When I finally got a table, I noted,

Amazing quantities of flab here — big guts and big butts. (And big
mouths, behind me.) All must die. Foul mood all day, not helped
by this scene.
    572 miles for this? Well yeah. Had to really. (Never mind why.)

From Winnemucca, I decided to head in the vague direction of Salt Lake City to get some service done on the motorcycle. But it was the weekend now, so there was no reason to hurry there. On the map I saw the Bonneville Salt Flats, and decided to have a look at that attraction, and to aim to spend the night in the nearby little town of Wendover.

My route was far from direct, however, describing a big circle through central Nevada by heading south from Battle Mountain through Austin Summit, then east to Ely on a long stretch of Highway 50, then north on long, long Highway 93. The day was another schizophrenic Nevada experience, 436 miles of empty roads through the elegantly bleak high desert, only to arrive at another destination of shabby glitter, electronic buzzers and bells, and lifeless humanity.

West Wendover, Nevada, sprawled across the state line from Wendover, Utah, but the "action" was all on the Nevada side, of course — flashing lights atop a row of casinos, some with massive hotels attached. On a Saturday night, the huge parking lots were filled with pickups with Utah license plates, as the sin-deprived "jack" (lapsed) Mormons flocked to this podunk Las Vegas for a weekend of (presumably) guilty pleasures.

Many of the hotels were completely full, and I settled for a Super 8 motel — mediocre, though I joined their special club (as John Ellwood Taylor) and received a 10 per cent discount that night, and for every stay thereafter — then was drawn by curiosity to walk over to the Rainbow Casino next door. The giant lighted sign out front advertised performances by the veteran San Francisco band Starship (formerly "Jefferson"), and the '60s revivals of Jan and Dean and the Lovin' Spoonful.

Hoping to find some dinner, I walked into a loud, bright casino the size of several warehouses, filled with flashing neon and mirrors and thousands of blaring slot machines, blackjack tables, and a couple of shiny plastic restaurants tucked into a corner, like the afterthought they surely were.

I was powerfully tempted to escape this madness for the comparatively normal Burger King across the street, but I waited in line for a bad dinner at a plastic lunch counter, then hung around to hear the Lovin' Spoonful perform in a small bar open to the vast casino, their mid-'60s hits punc-tuated by the bells and buzzers of slot machines and P.A. announcements.

The band consisted of the original bass player and drummer, who was now the singer, autoharpist, and tambourine player (and quite good in all capacities), augmented by a younger drummer inside a plastic box (for sound isolation), a female guitarist who doubled on keyboards, and a guy who had apparently replaced Zal Yanofsky, the original guitarist, back in their heyday. Their best-known member and original lead singer, John Sebastian, was conspicuously absent, but they played competent versions of all their hits, plus a few others by contemporaries like The Association ("Cherish"), and the Left Banke ("Walk Away Renée"). Despite the distractions of glaring white lights and electronic machines and voices, the older musicians seemed to be enjoying themselves, the younger ones worked hard, and the crowd of maybe 200 middle-aged listeners seemed to appreciate hearing "Summer in the City," "You Didn't Have To Be So Nice," "Nashville Cats," "Do You Believe in Magic," and "Jug Band Music."

Essentially, I was seeing a bunch of regular people out for a fun weekend, I guessed, but the whole atmosphere felt so strange to me. Either all *this* was alien, or I was. Restless and downhearted, for three long weeks I had been travelling alone, covering thousands of pointless miles from the Rocky Mountains of Montana and Idaho into the sagebrush desert of the Great Basin in eastern Oregon and a large circle of Nevada. The Ghost Rider, speeding through a land of sparse vegetation and bony mountain spines under vacant skies, searching for the Healing Road.

Earlier that day, I had spent several hours riding east on Highway 50, which meanders across the width of Nevada, and that evening, I made a note about its nickname, then added a sad reflection.

"Highway 50 called 'The Loneliest Road in America.' I know."

Next morning, I set out to see the Bonneville Salt Flats, where every year, the Land Speed Trials attracted a host of outlandish machines attempting to set new records in various classes — from jet-turbine cars to streamlined motorcycles. All that sort of thing had fascinated me as a boy, and I thought I would indulge this nostalgia by having a look.

But when I rode up the narrow, raised access road to a large sign marking the spot, I found myself surrounded by *water*. The sign informed me that the speed events ran in summer, "before the rains," and even though in such an arid region the rain might only come twice a year, when it *did* fall it tended to collect on the hard surface for days and weeks, even if only a few inches deep.

A late-model sedan with rental-company stickers parked beside me, and a middle-aged man with a heavy German accent looked around, then said to me, with a Teutonic frown, "It's a speedway for *ships*."

Backtracking into Nevada to the crossroads of Oasis, I picked up a lonely little road running northeast to Utah again, blasting along through threadbare, rugged rangeland on a cold and breezy day. I fell into a great mental groove, "drifting away into the zone, thoughts far away while 'main brain' handles the road — until wind demands total focus."

Intermittent rain harried me down the Interstate to Salt Lake City, where I checked into the Marriot early enough to catch up on my laundry and phone calls. Brutus assured me he was still going to meet me, and said he just had to "take care of some business first." I also talked to my Mom, and tried to sound cheerier than I felt.

The Weather Channel outlook was ominous for the next few days, with snow in the mountains and most everywhere to the north and east, so I had some thinking to do about my immediate future. I had thought about heading back into Montana, and maybe to Yellowstone National Park, but it appeared that for at least a few days, the high passes in between would be more welcoming to a snowmobile than a motorcycle.

The hotel was under invasion from an army of mutual-funds brokers having a "convention" (translated, as usual, as "party"), and I had been placed right next to one of their "hospitality suites." Booming voices and forced hearty laughter rattled the walls, and I pulled out my handy motor-cycling earplugs and carried on reading Jack London's *Northland Stories*. In the hotel restaurant, I had overheard one of these broker-jokers at the next table going on and on to his dinner companions about the details of his running: his best times, his heart rate, his endorphins, and so on until he bored me as much as he must have bored his tablemates. Then he started going on about his daughter, Rhiannon, and I sneered to myself, "You named your kid after a Stevie Nicks song? Say no more." (Jealous, jealous.)

Eventually the mutual funds "hospitality" in the next room ran down, and the partiers — I mean *conventioneers* — went off to drain another bar, so I was able to get to sleep and rise early to head to the BMW dealer for an oil change, new tires, and a loose exhaust system repair. Brutus and I had stopped at BMW of Salt Lake during the Rush tour, and of all the dealerships we visited we found them among the most friendly and knowledgeable, so I was glad to return.

A long séance with the map and the Weather Channel had told me to head back west again, away from the snow, and in early afternoon I rode out of Salt Lake to Nephi and picked up Highway 6, The Grand Army of the Republic Highway, and then Highway 50, The Loneliest Highway in America, this time to take it all the way across Nevada. A sign warned, "No Services for 88 Miles," and true enough, there was nothing until the Nevada border (predictably, a casino). The wind was bitterly cold on the high Great Basin desert, driving through every pore of my multi-layered clothing, and the forecast was even colder overnight, well below freezing everywhere in the Intermountain West.

Parking for the night in Ely (pronounced "Elee," I learned from one of the BMW guys), I walked up the street to the Hotel Nevada, a 1920s relic that had survived by turning its once-elegant lobby into the inevitable casino, jammed with the flashing lights and incessant whirr and trill and ring and beep of the slot machines. Off to one side, the restaurant retained its vintage charm, with half-round booths and an old-fashioned lunch counter, the walls lined with historic mining photos. But it was open to all that noise, and the food was indifferent. I had observed back in Wendover that "People don't go to a casino, or to Nevada, to *eat*, I guess," and this place was no exception, though the cherry pie was pretty good.

The Loneliest Highway in America was having its effect on me, and that night I called several friends for solace and company, but I still felt lost and very alone. When I awoke at the Best Western "Parkvue," the temperature was 22°F, so I decided I might as well stay for breakfast and hope it warmed up a little. Back at the Hotel Nevada, the whirr and trill and ring and beep continued, and I noted, "the fun never stops in Nevada."

Despite the bitter cold, I did enjoy my long crossing of The Loneliest Highway in America, past sagebrush plains, juniper mountains, salt pans, dust devils, and occasional sand dunes, all unfolding before me under a crystal sky. At one point I was riding through a wide valley, a shallow concavity stretching to distant brown teeth at either end, where I could see at least 20 miles ahead of me and as far behind, and there was not another vehicle in sight. Feeling the call of nature, for some reason I was inspired to simply park the bike on its centerstand in the middle of the road, switch it off, then wander off to the side and relieve myself. Still nothing in sight, I stretched my arms and legs, my neck and back, lit a cigarette, and walked around a little, stretching and smoking.

Pulling out my camera, I took a photograph from behind the bike so that it appeared to be riding down the road by itself: the ghost rider. From then on, this setup became a "device" for me, and a source of entertainment, as every day I watched for a suitable location to take a Ghost Rider photograph, trying to capture the perfect background and, of course, an empty stretch of road.

After several peaceful, contemplative hours of steady desert riding I reached the junction town of Fallon, and suddenly Highway 50 was anything *but* lonely, for heavy traffic surrounded me all the way to the Interstate, and into Reno: "The Biggest Little Town in the West," as the famous sign has it. Though always overshadowed by Las Vegas (playing, say, a tough and scrappy Jean Harlow to the flamboyant extravaganza of Mae West), Reno had a busy strip of its own, a carnival midway of flashing lights, blaring speakers, garish casinos, and dense traffic, and after the tranquility of that day's ride it seemed like madness.

I made a pilgrimage to the National Automobile Museum, which I had visited every time the band had played in Reno, right back to the late '70s. Back then, it had still been the personal collection of Bill Harrah, a gambling tycoon who could well afford to be whimsically acquisitive (it

has been said before that gambling only pays if you own the casino).
Harrah eventually filled three huge warehouses in the suburb of Sparks
with something like 3,000 cars, sometimes buying them from other collec-
tors by the train-car load, while his own restoration shop refurbished
them to jewel-like perfection. His collection grew to include such whims
as one of every Ford model for a span of almost 50 years, some racing cars
and outrageous customs, many examples of the opulent classics from the
'20s and '30s (both European and American), and a few celebrity cars, like
John Wayne's Corvette, Joan Crawford's Cadillac limousine, Carroll
O'Connor's Maserati, and Howard Hughes's Plymouth sedan from the
early '50s (another tycoon who could afford to indulge his whims, because
of his phobia against airborne "germs" the car had been fitted with an
elaborate air-filtration system filling most of the trunk).

After Harrah's death, the Holiday Inn Corporation bought his whole
enterprise of casinos and hotels, including the car collection, then
auctioned off about 90 per cent of them — including two of my favorites,
a Bugatti Type 57 Atalante with its swoopy body in a gorgeous two-tone
finish of cream and caramel, and a red Ferrari 166 MM Barchetta (the
"hero" of an old Rush song, "Red Barchetta"). Those treasures were gone
to somebody's private garage somewhere, probably, like so many of
Harrah's unique classics, which at least he had shared with others.

The 300–400 cars the corporation retained were manipulated into a
tax credit by making them the *National* Automobile Museum, and the
ones on display tended more toward the crowd-pleasers, the celebrity cars.
Still, a representative selection was presented from different eras in full-
size dioramas and street scenes, showrooms, and garages filled with
period detail. Well done, and always worth a visit, but I lamented the loss
of what it had been. (The ghost cars.)

> *Too bad he didn't ensure its survival; but maybe he didn't care. I*
> *understand about that. But too bad all the same. I remember the*
> *missing ones.*

Yes, that last line pierced me as soon as I wrote it down.

I remember the missing ones, all right, every minute of every day. Only the previous morning I had been on the phone with the landscape architect who was designing a memorial for Jackie and Selena to be placed in the cemetery plot I had bought in Toronto. None of that had been a cheery mission. I didn't know if such a monument would mean anything to me, or if I would ever want to go there, but I knew it had to be done, for myself and for the other grievers. To remember the missing ones.

In Reno there would be yet another poignant reminder of all I had lost. Deciding that if I was going to stop in a town like that, I would stay in the most ridiculous of its many follies, so I checked into Circus Circus, a massive high-rise with live circus acts performing among the incessant whirr and trill and ring and beep of the slot machines. Amid the din in and around Art Gecko's Southwest Grill, an older couple at the neighboring table made friendly conversation with me, and said they were celebrating their 60th anniversary. Couples were always a torment to me, especially those who had grown old together, but I swallowed the stab of sorrow and wished them a happy anniversary.

The following morning's ride I called "Escape from Reno," as I wheeled out on a cold, clear day and followed a twisting little road high up to the picturesque showplace of Virginia City, quiet in the early morning, before the tourists arrived. Then I swung down around Lake Tahoe, the deep blue lake high in the forests of the Sierra Nevada, and another area that had always appealed to my inner, ideal "soulscape" of lake and forested mountains. Unfortunately, I found myself trapped in a frustrating series of construction delays, alternately crawling and walking — or shuffling along — in a line of trucks and cars.

As I straddled the bike beside one of the asphalt trucks lining the shoulder, the driver leaned out of his cab and talked for awhile about my motorcycle, and about one he was going to buy, then told me about another road I could take over the mountains that wouldn't be so busy. Glad to escape, I turned off on Highway 89 to the Luther Pass, then on 88 to the Carson Pass, at 8,573 feet, where I climbed into thin air, glacier-scraped granite, small lakes, and tall pines. Once my nostrils flared at a tantalizing, delicious fragrance I couldn't identify in that context, then smiled when I caught up to a line of slowly climbing hay trucks — the scent of my farming heritage.

Descending on the California side, I felt the air becoming warm at last (for the first time since riding into Vancouver nearly a month previous), and soon I was hot enough to stop and remove a few layers of clothing from under and over my leathers. The price of that comfort, however, was *traffic;* it seemed I had to share this more temperate and fertile state with a lot of other humans and their vehicles, all the way across the dry yellow foothills and irrigated farmlands of the northern Central Valley.

Another smell teasing the air turned out to be a truck full of garlic (probably from nearby Gilroy, the "Garlic Capital"), and when I reached the even busier Napa Valley I was surrounded by green vineyards and fragrant eucalyptus. Turkey vultures circled high, looking for roadkill, and I reflected that, despite many cartoons of desert desolation, I had rarely seen vultures in the *real* desert. Of course, these scavengers of carrion would gather where they were more likely to find food, and a land with more life inevitably means more death. (Alas.)

The Inn at South Bridge in St. Helena, right in the heart of the Napa Valley, was many levels up from my recent accommodations, and I had a bright, luxurious suite that immediately invited me to stay for another night. After several nights of "humble" restaurants, I was in search of a good meal, and the lady behind the front desk suggested a neighboring restaurant of some repute, Tra Vigne. Unable to get a reservation by phone, I tried waiting at the bar, but after my desert sojourn, I was also unused to crowds — and "attitudes."

> *This place very "modern California," and jammed full of . . .*
> *modern Californians. Question: Do some lesbians dress like men*
> *just so they won't have to dress like women? Just wondering . . .*

One of the small bar tables was free, so I sat there, feeling hemmed in by people, and had a drink while I looked over the menu. I asked the bartender if I could order something, and he informed me, with a certain lofty disdain, that I could only eat at the *bar*, not at a bar table, because there was "no server for that area." When I asked if I could pick up my food at the bar and eat it at my table, his nose elevated even higher, and he sniffed, "A *cafeteria* we're *not!*"

I dismissed him as a "Californicator," got out of there and walked down the street to the main part of St. Helena, where I found a modest-but-excellent bistro and had a fine meal right at the counter. Back at the hotel, I tried to call Brutus, for I hadn't been able to get hold of him for a few days and was hoping to finalize our plans to meet up sometime soon. When he didn't answer his cell phone, I left a message for him at home. I was starting to worry about him.

There were things about Brutus's life I didn't *want* to know, but I was aware in a general way that our entrepreneurial Brutus occasionally involved himself in the import/export logistics of certain herbal remedies frowned upon by federal authorities, and I knew he was staying at a motel near Buffalo working on some deal. So when he didn't answer the cell phone, and the hotel receptionist told me he was "gone," I feared the worst.

The next morning, I set off on a narrow, winding road through the wooded hills between the Napa and Sonoma Valleys, on another literary pilgrimage, to Jack London State Park. London had called his beloved Sonoma Valley "The Valley of the Moon," and the park preserved a part of his "Beauty Ranch," where he had experimented with modern farming methods in a landscape of yellow grass and live oaks. The park also contained the ruins of his dream home, Wolf House, which had been only days away from completion when it burned down mysteriously. London was deeply affected by its destruction, and by the possibility that arson might have been the cause, for he counted himself a friend to all people, and the loss is thought to have contributed to his death a few months later, in 1916.

It was the end of a life fully lived, but sadly all too brief, for he was only 40 when he was brought down by liver failure, apparently caused by years of alcoholism, overwork, and a recent addiction to laudanum and other opiates, still widely prescribed in those days. Scott Fitzgerald's famous quote about "no second acts in American lives" might have been coined for Jack London as much as for himself, another "ghost writer" who burned himself out and died young.

Jack London's published credo:

> *I would rather be ashes than dust!*
> *I would rather that my spark should burn out in a brilliant blaze*
> *Than it should be stifled by dryrot.*
> *I would rather be a superb meteor,*
> *Every atom of me in magnificent glow,*
> *Than a sleepy and permanent planet.*
> *The proper function of man is to live, not to exist.*
> *I shall not waste my days in trying to prolong them.*
> *I shall use my time.*

Born to an impoverished, unwed mother in Oakland, California, in 1876, London's youth had been harsh but adventurous: an oyster pirate around San Francisco Bay, a cannery worker, a sailor on a seal-hunting voyage across the Pacific, a temporary student, an ardent socialist, and even a hobo riding the rails across America, before travelling north to the Yukon in 1897, when he was barely 20. While prospecting unsuccessfully for gold, and suffering through an endless winter of frostbite and malnutrition in the one-room cabin (the one I had seen reassembled back in Dawson), he couldn't know he was mining the material which would provide him with dozens of stories and several novels, and unimagined fame and fortune. His first book, *Son of the Wolf*, was published in 1900, and he soon became the most publicized writer in the world, outshining even Mark Twain or Charles Dickens. (Commenting on London's youthful affiliation with socialism, Twain remarked, "I hope that fellow London gets his wish for socialism — then he can send out the militia to collect his royalties!")

Having achieved this success, however, London was too generous, and perhaps too profligate, and had to work incessantly to afford his lifestyle, which included ambitious indulgences like the building of the sailing ship *The Snark,* in which he and his second wife, Charmian, set out to sail around the world in 1906, a tale endearingly recounted in *The Cruise of the Snark.*

Even during that difficult voyage across the Pacific (ultimately abandoned due to London's ill-health), he kept up his output of 1000 words, as he did every day of his writing life. In truth, he *had* to keep producing magazine stories and articles, to pay for the ship, the voyage, the construction of Wolf House, the upkeep of Beauty Ranch, the support of his first wife and two daughters, and the vast sums he gave away to friends, relations, and even strangers who wrote to ask him for money.

As to how London could maintain his fund of *ideas* for the dozens of magazine stories he churned out, I found an interesting clue during a later "ghost writer" pilgrimage (often an excuse for a spurious destination on my aimless wanderings). In Sauk Centre, Minnesota, the home town of America's first Nobel laureate in literature, Sinclair Lewis, I stopped at the museum devoted to him, and saw a letter from London to a young Lewis thanking him for his latest batch of story plots, for which London was paying Lewis $50 each. To me, this was a surprising insight as to how London could keep up such a prolific output, but still — just as Shakespeare's masterful language was often woven around second-hand plots, it did not detract from the effortless artistry with which London wrote his finest stories and novels, like *The Sea Wolf* and *Martin Eden.*

By all accounts, Jack and Charmian had been deeply in love, and had shared life in a way uncommonly egalitarian for their time. The house she lived in after his death was not far from the ruins of Wolf House, and not far from London's grave (under a boulder in the woods, where he had asked to be buried), and she had called this stone mansion "The House of Happy Walls." Now a museum, it was filled with souvenirs of London's writing career, and of their travels and life together. Seeing all those relics of their vanished lives made me sad and tearful, and once again made me rail not at the futility of life, but at the futility of death.

> *They loved each other, did cool stuff together, but that didn't keep him alive. Or her either, for that matter, though she lived on alone for many years (ach!).*

On that weekday afternoon in early October I saw only a handful of people on the paths in the park, and the air of melancholy stayed with me as I strolled through the woods and ate my lunch beside the crumbling stone remains of Wolf House. I hiked up to see the little lake and boathouse farther up the hillside, and the small cabin where Jack and Charmian had been living when he died. Despite the somber atmosphere, in the same way that my sad time in Barbados had been brightened by birdlife, the live oak trees flickered with a wonderful variety of birds, and I trained my binoculars on eight or nine different species, from the acorn woodpecker to the elusive hermit thrush, which has perhaps the most beautiful song of any bird, a tumble of liquid notes sometimes heard in the evening stillness.

When I got back to the Inn at South Bridge, I saw the message light blinking on my telephone, and a little alarm went off in my head, because only one person knew where I was: Brutus. When I picked up the voice-mail message, though, it wasn't him, it was his wife, Georgia. Her voice sounded distraught, and the message was brief. "I'm at my Mom's. I *really* need to talk to you."

When I called her, her voice shook as she told me Brutus had been arrested, and "It's bad." I told her I would do whatever I could, and she gave me the number of a lawyer in Toronto who somebody had arranged to be involved from that end. I tried calling him, and then my own lawyer, but it was 8:00 at night back east, and I couldn't reach anyone.

> *Sad, sad, sad. Now my best friend is in jail. No details, but Georgia says, "it's bad," and I'm sure it is.*
>
> *Do everything I can, of course, but not hopeful, and this has not*

*only darkened my day, but my life. We were supposed to meet up
and ride together soon — now what? Don't know what to do.
Carry on for now, I suppose. But what little spark I had keeping
me going is . . . flickering. Ach.*

*Also talked to Dr. Earl on the phone this morning; he figures I
have an ulcer, and says take four Zantacs every night for a month.
Life gets better and better. Ach.*

At that point, I realized my existence had reached its absolute nadir,
and my own personal hell, fittingly, was a really bad country song:

*My baby died, my wife died, my dog died,
And my best friend went to jail
So I'm ridin' down that long, lonesome road*

With an ulcer.

Anyway, there was little I could do about any of that, except perhaps to
help the friend in jail, so Brutus became one of my few "missions" in life.
Early next morning, I called the Toronto lawyer, Mr. Bloomenfeld, who told
me Brutus had been arrested with a "truckful" of a controlled substance of
a leafy green nature, and that with his two prior convictions in the U.S. for
similar "lapses" (my friend and colleague Geddy once defined jail as "The
House of Bad Decisions"), Brutus was in serious trouble.

Then the lawyer added, "If we lose control of this case, he could end up
with life without parole." Chilled by these thoughts, I chased down my
own lawyer in Florida by telephone and asked him to find "the best
criminal lawyer in Buffalo," and called Sheila at our Toronto office to
arrange for Brutus's family to be covered financially for awhile, so at least
he wouldn't have to be worried about them too.

Not knowing what else to do, and feeling restless, agitated, and very
low, I packed up and kept riding, following a route Brutus and I had
taken, ironically, a year and a half earlier. North through the Napa Valley
to Calistoga, through the humid woodlands of Robert Louis Stevenson

State Park (another Ghost Writer) to the arid country around Clear Lake, then the little road, State Highway 16, that Brutus and I had followed to get to the show in Sacramento, and where we had nearly run out of gas, and had to buy a couple of gallons from a little repair shop in a ramshackle farm building.

When I rode past the Arco Arena, a great hump of concrete just outside Sacramento, I was reminded of playing concerts there in years past, and my imagining of the inside of that arena alive with a crowd of thousands of screaming fans at a concert of blaring music and flashing lights, with *me* at the heart of it, seemed as remote and unreal as a remembered movie scene.

That last time I had arrived at the Arco Arena by motorcycle, with Brutus (alas!), and an earlier time I had ridden through the streets of Sacramento alone on my bicycle, from the hotel to the arena. That day, back in the late '80s, I had seen two women standing on a street corner with their children, holding up a sign that said, "Will Work for Food." At that time, such pitiful indications of despair had not yet become commonplace, and as I passed them on my bicycle I was shocked and moved. Circling back, I gave one of the surprised women a $100 bill and rode away again, shaking my head with sadness.

Oh, it was a sad world, and it seemed to only get sadder. As I pushed on through central California I kept thinking about all the lost ones of the world, all the ghosts, and my little baby soul was dark and cold as I rode down what I'd truly come to feel was The Loneliest Road in America.

When I heard that you were gone
I felt a shadow cross my heart
NOBODY'S HERO, 1993

Chapter 7

DESERT SOLITAIRE

We travel on the road to adventure
On a desert highway straight to the heart of the sun
Like lovers and heroes, and the restless part of everyone
We're only at home when we're on the run
On the run

DREAMLINE, 1991

If forested mountains reflected my personal "soulscape," there were other
kinds of landscapes that appealed to me as well, and to different *parts* of
me. The more I travelled in the four great deserts of the American West,
the more I came to love them too, each in its own character: the sagebrush
and juniper shrubs of the Great Basin, the creosote bushes and Joshua
trees of the Mojave, the agave and smoke trees of the Colorado, and the
ocotillo, palo verde, and saguaro cactus of the Sonora. I came to think of

all these desert vistas as my "dreamscape," for the awesome scale of sheer *space* in these arid lands of mystery, subtlety, and harsh beauty reflected a setting that was surreal, and yet familiar; foreboding, yet full of grace.

The word "desert" refers only to the desertion of *humans*, of course, for the plant and animal life in these regions is rich and enchanting, and perfectly adapted to what Mary Austin called "The Land of Little Rain." Consider the humble creosote bush, a raggedy dark-green shrub which dotted the high Mojave desert by the billions, all evenly spaced (its roots were thought by some scientists to emit toxins which prevented any other plant growing too near), and giving off a pungent scent that filled the air after a rainstorm (the source of their name). Taken all together, the count-less creosote bushes not only represented the largest biomass of any life-form in the West, but certain colonies of creosote were also thought to be the *oldest* living things on Earth, spreading from the same rhizome roots for 10 or 12 thousand years.

The more you studied the desert, the more you saw how *alive* it was, seen and unseen. Coyotes, tarantulas, crows, gila woodpeckers, horned larks, rabbit-brush, burro-weed, all the different cacti, and sometimes even flowers — the roadside occasionally glowing with the white lily-like trumpets of the sacred datura, or the delicate red blossoms of the tall, slender ocotillo. Because these apparitions were rare, sometimes occur-ring only once a year, their presence was felt more deeply than a meadow of wildflowers in the prairies or eastern woodlands.

Riding a motorcycle on an empty desert two-lane also had a dream-like quality. No traffic to threaten or distract, no tight, blind corners through the trees, no worries about gravel on the pavement or stalled trucks hidden around a fast bend. Everything was *open*, every source of danger was, literally, miles away, and so was any source of beauty. The landscape unfolded in a slow tableau as I rode toward the next rise in the road, or the next jagged range of mountains, and there was plenty of time to look around at the big picture as well as the details, resting my legs on the cylinder heads and letting it all come toward me.

On the run from overcrowded California, and full of worry about

Brutus sitting in some hell-hole of a jail in Buffalo, I headed east again, toward the mountains and the desert. Since I wouldn't be meeting up with Brutus for awhile, I had decided to make a rendezvous with Jackie's sister, Deb, her partner, Mark, their two-year-old son Rudy, and bull terrier Dexter, who were also travelling through the West in a big rented RV.

In the past year and two months Deb too had been trying to live through her grief over Jackie and Selena, and in some ways her loss was as great as my own. She had lived with our family for about 10 years in Toronto, after all, so she had been very close to both her sister and her niece, and at the end, it had been Deb and me who had held each of Jackie's hands and watched her take her last breath in the hospital in Barbados. So she and I *understood* each other.

I had been calling her often on my own travels, both at her home and on their cell phone in the RV, and we had agreed that we would meet up as soon as they got out to my "neighborhood," anywhere in the West. When I had been feeling crowded and aimless in California, I decided I didn't have anything more important to do than get back to the desert dreamscape and ride 1,000 miles across Nevada and Utah to visit them. A mission as good as any for the Ghost Rider.

After a couple of hours I made it back to the Sierra Nevada, and on the long climb up Highway 108 I stopped for breakfast in the town of Sonora (during the California gold rush after 1849, one of the wildest, most lawless places in the West, but now a sleepy little mountain town). I was reminded again of Brutus when I saw a group of motorcyclists walking away from their parked bikes, obviously out for a Sunday ride together. One of them invited me to join them for breakfast, but I declined, a little wary of their "colors" — their vests and jackets advertised one of the Christian motorcycle clubs (of which there are several). As wary as I have always been of proselytizers, in the wake of what "the gods" had put me through, I was even less open to theological discussion. Whatever deity people tried to hold up as a metaphysical explanation, justification, or consolation, as far as I was concerned *none* of them had been very good to me. Lacking the patience or blind faith of Job (or having failed the "test of faith"), I had no use for Him, or Her, or Them.

Before leaving the restaurant, I put on my long underwear under the leathers, and dug out my heavy winter gloves and plastic rainsuit, for I was heading up to the Sonora Pass, one of the higher passes in the Sierras, at 9,624 feet. It would be cold up there now, in early October, and in just a few weeks, when the snow started to fly, the pass would be closed for the winter. The ride up (through Harte Twain, a doppelganger ghost-writer town named after Bret Harte and Mark Twain, who had both written famously of the gold rush days) carried me into my mountain soulscape on a glorious day, clear and cold, the road winding endlessly up to the high pass and down again. On the far side of the Sierras, I looked down over the blue expanse of Mono Lake, eventually picking out the sculptural peaks of the tufa formations along the south shore, and beyond, the dreamscape of the high desert.

Mono Lake was a rare example of a unique, desolate area that had *escaped* being destroyed by thoughtless exploitation, if only narrowly. In the '70s the lake had been rapidly dwindling, siphoned away to the voracious thirst of the ever-expanding megalopolis of Los Angeles. However, a campaign to save the lake had gained enough publicity and support to sway public opinion, and Los Angeles had been obliged to stop its "piracy," and even return the streams that fed the lake.

In the late 1800s, Mark Twain had written a prescient observation about the place of water in the West, "Whiskey is for drinking; water is for fighting over." So it has been throughout the 20th century, with virtually every western river dammed and distributed among different states (and sometimes into Canada and Mexico), every aquifer pumped up from ever deeper underground, until it seems as though every single drop of the most precious commodity in the dry western states has been gathered, rerouted, argued over, and, ultimately, subsidized by the federal government.

If Mono Lake had been saved for the present, Owens Lake, just to the south, hadn't been so lucky — in fact, it was no longer a *lake* at all, but a white, mineralized *playa*. The whole Owens River system had quite literally been stolen by the City of Los Angeles at the turn of the century, when the city's phenomenal expansion had far outgrown the tiny Los Angeles River beside which it had first grown (as the "Pueblo de Nuestra Señora de La Reina de Los Angeles," or "town of our lady of the queen of the angels"). The city's first water commissioner, William Mulholland, was charged with finding a new supply, and he set out in a horse-drawn wagon across the Mojave to the Owens Valley. The Owens River delivered water from the Sierra Nevada snowmelt and the White Mountains in Nevada, and emptied into Owens Lake, which was surrounded by irrigated farms and orchards, and even plied by steamboats serving the nearby mining areas of Death Valley and the Panamint Valley.

Within a few years, the majority of the land surrounding the river and lake had been bought up, surreptitiously and even fraudulently, by representatives of Los Angeles, and a vast aqueduct was built to carry its water across the desert to the thirsty city. By all accounts, Mulholland himself was a dedicated civil servant, from humble beginnings as a ditch-digger to ultimately holding the whole Los Angeles water system in his head, and he did not profit from the schemes that grew around his public works. When he opened the aqueduct, he gave perhaps the shortest dedication speech ever, pointing to the water and saying, "There it is. Take it."

Others were less civic-minded, however, including the mayor at the time, who bought the only land in the Owens Valley suitable for a dam site, and the Otis and Chandler families, owners of the *Los Angeles Times* (which had campaigned loudly for the bond issue to pay for the project). Together with other admittedly far-sighted capitalists, they bought the dry, worthless land of the San Fernando Valley, then used the "excess" water from the aqueduct to irrigate what would become the most lucrative citrus groves, and later, real estate, in the West.

Mulholland, meanwhile, ended his life in disgrace, after a dam built under his supervision, in San Francisquito Canyon, collapsed one night during a flash flood and caused huge destruction and loss of life. In modern times, he is chiefly memorialized by the famous Mulholland Highway, a scenic two-lane winding along the crest of the Hollywood Hills and the Santa Monica Mountains.

In the main town of the Owens Valley, Bishop, I stopped at a gas station and removed a few inner and outer layers, then rode south to Big Pine and turned east on California 168, a little road that Brutus and I had taken on our first trip to Death Valley, during the *Test For Echo* tour. Twisting and climbing on an almost empty two-lane of perfect pavement, squeezing down to one lane between the boulders at Westgard Pass, then two more 7,000-foot passes at Gilbert Summit and Lido Summit, I came down into the high desert of creosote and Joshua trees, cool and sunny, and across the line to Nevada.

At the junction with 95 I came upon the Cottontail Ranch ("Always Open"), which was actually a brothel, with a big gravel parking lot out front where a couple of semis and a few cars were the only business that afternoon. ("Didn't stop," I noted.) Heading north through the near-ghost-town of Goldfield to the junction with the Grand Army of the Republic Highway, I decided to look for a room in the little town of Tonopah (the "pah" suffix means "water" in Shoshone, and thus shows up regularly in place names in the arid regions of the Great Basin, like Ivanpah, and Pahrump — which must be the Shoshone equivalent of Soggy Bottom).

Tonopah was a little town, but big enough to have a decent Best Western motel and a cozy little Mexican restaurant, Su Casa — recently opened in a time-honored location that had obviously served "good basic food" under several names before, with the same decor and fittings of naugahyde, formica, chrome, paper napkins, and plastic water glasses.

Tonopah was big enough to have street crime too, for I noticed two boys, 10 or 11 years of age, playing around the parking lot that evening, and the next morning when I went to check my tire pressures I saw that the valve caps were missing. An exotic souvenir for these small-town boys no doubt, a harmless prank, but I was forced to keep my speed down on those wide-open desert highways in fear of the unsecured valves suddenly letting go from centrifugal force. Not until Utah did I encounter a garage big enough to sell me a couple of valve caps (for fifty cents), and then I felt I could speed *safely*.

From my journal for that day, October 10ᵗʰ.

Cold morning, but clear and bright, with beautiful landscapes of vast high desert and rugged, folded peaks, their features shadowed in morning sun. Swallow-like birds [horned larks] all over the road, flitting up ahead of me, often missing by inches. Few cows on the road too.

I couldn't resist stopping for breakfast in Rachel, Nevada, a tiny cluster of prefab buildings and mobile homes on the "Extraterrestrial Highway." Rachel announced itself by a sign reading, "America's UFO Capital: Aliens Welcome," and the souvenir stand in the restaurant was filled with such related merchandising as alien-shaped guitar picks and UFO bumper stickers and coffee mugs. Rachel's proximity to the Nellis Air Force Range (including the legendary, perhaps mythical, "Area 51") and the Nevada Test Site attracted a certain fame based on reports of strange flying objects which might have been "reverse engineered" from captured space ships, such as the one allegedly collected at a crash site near Roswell, New Mexico. Whether or not you "want to believe," it's all interesting stuff.

Equally interesting to me was observing the kind of people such myths attracted. The walls of the restaurant, called the "Little Ale'Inn" (ouch), were lined with cartoons and slogans disparaging the government, the president, his wife, the Bureau of Land Management, gun control advocates, and anyone else seen to be interfering with western "freedom." (The so-called fierce independence of the ranchers of the western states toward the federal government, upon which they depend for subsidies and free rights to over-graze federal lands, has been described as, "Leave me alone, and give me more money.")

Sign above bar: "Thank you for holding your breath while I smoke." Like the bed and breakfast owner I read about in Alaska: "Sure there's a non-smoking area — outside!"

Passed Warm Springs (stream steaming) and Five Mile Ranch,
where Brutus and I "rustled" gas that time.

That reference goes back to the Rush tour again, in the spring of '97, when Brutus and I were riding across the United States on our second cross-country blitz (coast to coast in five days). Apparently we still hadn't learned to apply a little healthy skepticism when looking at maps of the American West — not only might a name on the map not represent a gas station; it might not represent *anything*.

So when Brutus and I pulled out of Rachel, Nevada, that morning, we decided not to bother refueling yet. We figured we had another 60 miles worth, and could easily make the next town on the map, Warm Springs. However, the next stretch of highway was straight, deserted two-lane, and we were lured into opening our throttles wider and wider, until we were cruising in formation at 100 miles an hour. High speed meant high fuel consumption, and our gas gauges sank almost visibly, until I glanced down to see the bright yellow light of the reserve indicator glowing.

Then suddenly my eyes froze on the road ahead, and widened in disbelief. An instant fear-response made me back off the throttle without even thinking about it, and I stared ahead at a huge black shape materializing from behind a rise in the road. It was a jet fighter, from the nearby Air Force base, and its menacing shape seemed to hover in front of us, then bank sharply and speed off to the south. The pilot must have decided to have a little fun and throw a scare into us; and he succeeded. (I realized later that my precognitive alarm at this sudden apparition was the conditioned response to "cop!")

When we got to Warm Springs, of course there was no one there. We pulled into a gravel parking lot beside a couple of deserted buildings, and when we shut down our engines, we heard only the wind. We looked at each other, then climbed off the bikes, took off our helmets, and had a smoke break. Now what?

Brutus spotted a payphone on a wall, and leafed through the phone book for a gas station we might be able to pay to bring us gas, but none of them answered. A pickup with a horse trailer pulled into the parking lot beside us, and a rancher in late middle-age, a younger woman, and an adolescent girl climbed out and opened the trailer to release their four horses, giving them some air and water on the shady side of the trailer. While Brutus worked the phone, I went over to ask the rancher if he knew of any gas stations nearby. The woman was spreading a foil-wrapped tray of fried chicken on the hood of the pickup, and as we talked it became clear that she was his daughter, and the girl was her daughter.

The two of them agreed that the nearest gas was in Ely, 100 miles to the north, or Tonopah, 50 miles south. When I explained our predicament, the rancher said, "I wish I could help," then pointed at the truck with a chicken leg, "but I'm runnin' diesel."

With fine western hospitality, he offered us a piece of the chicken too, but I politely declined; I was still full from a bad breakfast we'd had back in Panaca, and I was also too worried about what we were going to do about this situation. The daughter suggested that we might be able to buy some gas from a rancher, and said they'd passed a sizeable ranch about five miles back.

The Five Mile Ranch, it was called, with its brand of five chevrons on a sign over the gate. We drove up the laneway and stopped in the yard, but didn't see anyone. The compound included a house, several outbuildings, and a couple of mobile homes, while a new mid-size Chrysler and a couple of "respectable-looking" pickups and tractors were parked in the yard. So the place looked inhabited, but still no one appeared. A tiny sprinkler dribbled on a fenced patch of lawn. The front door of the house was padlocked (!), but the workshop doors were wide open, tools and hardware visible inside.

I walked nervously back to the mobile homes and a farther outbuilding in a grove of cottonwoods, calling "Hello" as I went, but there was no reply. When I returned to the bikes, Brutus was poking around the big steel fuel tank, perched high on a wooden cradle.

"Can you tell the difference between gas and diesel?" he asked.

"By the smell I can."

He handed me the nozzle, I smelled it, and told him it was gasoline.

"Well, I'm going to take some. We can leave some money."

I don't mind confessing I was terrified, but I didn't have a better idea. Except one thing:

"Let's leave the money first," I said, already imagining a door slamming open, the click-click of a chamber being filled, and a voice drawling, "Wudda you boys think yer doin'?"

Later that day I wrote, "I can't remember when I've been so afraid," and I couldn't wait to get out of there. In the old days, they used to hang horse thieves because by stealing a man's horse, you virtually condemned him to death. Might they not attach the same seriousness to gasoline rustling? Anyway, we took two gallons each, and Brutus left a $20 bill (probably 20 times the at-the-pump price, in those times) with a note explaining our predicament.

Thanks to Brutus's fearless resourcefulness (and where had that got him now?), we had been rescued from a bad situation, but I felt guilty about it, and even a year and a half later I felt nervous when I rode by that ranch on my way to breakfast in Rachel, and more memories of travelling with Brutus.

I carried on east on the Extraterrestrial Highway, noting the red pavement near Panaca (probably a signal to outer space), then onward to the Utah border, as the regularly spaced Joshua trees (named by Mormon settlers for their alleged resemblance to the upraised arms of a prophet) gave way to scrub juniper, then larger junipers and rocky, pillared canyons.

That night Deb and Mark and family planned to make it to an RV park in Springville, Utah, near Provo, and I covered over 500 miles that day before I checked into the Best Western motel across the street from the RV park, made a series of phone calls regarding the Brutus Situation (gave myself "phone ear," I noted), then had a quick dinner at the "Flying J" truck stop while I waited for them to arrive.

It was then I realized that I hadn't seen a familiar face for nearly a month, since Vancouver, and I was excited about the idea of being with people I knew, and especially, people who knew me. A break from always having to be on guard, or avoiding certain topics of conversation with strangers (for example, how I dreaded having someone ask me an obvious pleasantry like, "So, do you have any family?"). I could just be at ease with them, and share feelings silently, or make familiar jokes that might evoke the past — but in ways Deb and I found *comforting* rather than wrenching. We kept Jackie and Selena alive for each other, and we also shared the feeling that we were the only ones who really knew what had been lost.

Another reason for our rendezvous was that we were all on our way to Las Vegas. After all Mark had endured trying to care for an inconsolable partner and a newborn son, Deb had wanted to do something nice for him, and had latched onto a plan dreamed up by Brutus — who had been planning to meet up with me in Las Vegas and take a motorcycle riding course at the local racetrack with three-time world champion Freddie Spencer. Mark had been a keen motorcyclist for many years, and Deb had signed him up for the riding school as part of their family getaway. Obviously Brutus wouldn't be joining us, but at least I'd have Mark to share the experience with.

The next day, we made our separate ways down to Las Vegas, their RV to the park at Circus Circus, and me to the riding school's designated hotel, Excalibur, a huge showplace of pseudo-Arthurian style built on, of course, a vast casino. There I finally acquired an address where I could write to Brutus, and I told him all about my experiences in Las Vegas in a letter from Zion National Park in Utah, the first of many long, handwritten letters I would be writing to him during our mutual exiles. It would prove to be good therapy for me, and it didn't seem to hurt him either.

The opening comparison to being in Zion as opposed to Babylon is from a Rush song called "Digital Man," in which I borrowed the dichotomy from the Rastafarians — though Bob Marley seemed to refer to Zion as a "promised land" located in Ethiopia, while his evil Babylon (as in the live album title, *Babylon By Bus*) seemed to be the United States. Some might say he got it exactly backwards.

Oct. 16, '98
Zion Lodge

Hey Buddy,

About 15 years ago, this jerk I used to know put these words in a rock song:

"He'd like to spend the night in Zion,

He's been a long while in Babylon"

That's pretty darn true for me today, after four nights in the howling chaos and annoying low-life society of Las Vegas! Man, I was not in the mood for that place. In the past, I've always found it moderately amusing (or at least that other guy did), but the traffic, the incessant jangling and ringing of slot machines, the crowds of fat ugly people, the lousy food, lousy service, and cheesy hotel room just drove me *nuts*. I was awful glad to escape from there this morning.

It also occurs to me that *you* wouldn't mind spending a night in Zion too. Another line that prescient jerk might have written for you: "Where would you rather be? Anywhere but here." I'm sure that's true enough, no? This time it's *my* turn not to know what to say or do, but I hope I can be as good a friend to you through this bad time as you were through my bad times. I've told you before, but it bears repeating: *nobody* was as devoted to being *my* friend as you were, and I'm glad to have the opportunity to repay some of that dedication. So before I get away from this maudlin seriousness, just let me say that not only will I do anything I can to help you get out of, or through, this ignorant situation, but your family will be looked after for as long as it takes. Just don't you be worrying about that. As long as I'm around, they'll be okay.

Now stop your blubbering, or I'll give you something to cry about.

The Freddie Spencer course went pretty well — meaning that I didn't crash! I didn't get my knee down, but I got "hanging off" pretty well, and definitely learned one or two things about getting around quickly on a scooter. As we suspected, Freddie himself was quite a character, though he just "dropped in" from time to time to tell a few anecdotes from his racing days, or to give occasional demonstrations of sublime riding skill. During the second day, we each had the opportunity to follow him on the "racing line" around the track, and that alone was worth the trip. Humbling, to say the least.

Nick Ienatsch (former editor of *Sport Rider* magazine) did most of the actual teaching, articulating Freddie's principles of smoothness, bike-handling, and body motions in ways we mortals could understand. There were only seven of us in the class, so everybody got lots of individual attention and substantial track time (though never enough!).

Mark had a good time too (and also didn't crash), and it was nice hanging out with them at the RV park, watching "South Park" episodes and eating "trailer trash" food at the Circus Circus and Excalibur buffets. Yum. And that reminds me: the same day I found out about your "misadventure," I had finally broken down and called Dr. Earl to ask him why I was waking up in the middle of the night exactly six hours after I ate, and he said "that's a pretty classic symptom of an *ulcer*." ****! (Not sure if you're allowed to read bad words where you are — ha ha.) So now I have to take a bunch of Zantacs every night for a *month*, and hope it clears up; especially before I hit Mexico.

And just so you don't get the idea that I'm having too much fun, I couldn't get a table for dinner here until *8:30*. Man! Babylon may have been jam-packed with wall-to-wall human waste, but Zion is pretty crowded too. (Though I did notice a big difference between the kind of Americans who frequent the national parks, compared with the ones in Vegas: these people are half the size, with twice the vitality.)

You'll remember our brief-but-unforgettable overlook of this area from up by Cedar Breaks, and it's just as spectacular up close. The Lodge is nestled between the walls of the canyon, higher than it is wide, all reddish sandstone with cottonwoods and pines along the Virgin River at the bottom. I was lucky enough to get a cabin, though it's one of those "fourplex" deals, and the stone fireplace is only a fake gas one. I guess you're probably crying for me. This afternoon I took a hike up the canyon wall to the Emerald Pools, and sometime I'll send you the photos I took from there. Sometime when I really hate you and want to torture you . . .

Okay, yeah, it was beautiful, but there are a surprising number of other people who seem to think they have the right to, like, *share* it with me, you know?

The same thing happened in California. After I talked to you from Salt Lake City, and there was *snow* blocking my way to Wyoming and Montana, I headed west through Reno, and from then on I was trapped in outrageous traffic. Getting through Lake Tahoe was already like L.A., with construction all over the place, and from there to Napa seemed like being in a bleedin' *parade.* (Maybe I was a little spoiled after weeks of the Yukon, Alaska, B.C., Idaho, and Nevada.) I spent a couple of days in St. Helena (where, alas, I was freaked to learn about *you*), and did a nice hike in Jack London State Park over in the Sonoma Valley (by the way, Deb wanted to write to you as well, so I asked her to send you a couple of his books that I have enjoyed lately). I realized as I came down out of the Sierras that I was actually warm for the first time in a month. The morning after I talked to you from Ely, it was 22°F, so it was nice to be riding through California in just leathers and a T-shirt.

But the price of that was all these vehicles around me, so I ran right away from there, back to Nevada by way of a great ride over the 9,500-foot Sonora Pass to Big Pine, where I picked up that fabulous road we took in the other direction, through Westgard Pass. After a night in Tonopah, and breakfast in Rachel (pausing to genuflect before the Five Mile Ranch, our unknowing saviors), I rode across to Springville, Utah, to meet up with Deb and Mark.

And that pretty much brings us up to *now*. I could only get one night here, so tomorrow I'll move on to Bryce Canyon, and generally bum around this area as long as the weather holds. It was pleasantly warm in Las Vegas, but darn chilly again back up here, though no snow at least.

But I don't know; it feels like there's somebody *missing*, you know? (Actually, there are a *few* people missing.)

I don't know if I want to try the Hole-in-the-Wall road on my own, or the North Rim, but maybe I'll head up towards Moab and see what's shaking there. On November 3rd, I'll be meeting Alex and Liam at Alex's place in Santa Fe, and that will be nice, but sometimes I admit I feel a little "lost." Being a "saddletramp" suits me in many ways, but some mornings I'd just like to be in Quebec, making my *own* food and bumming around the house, instead of bumming around America.

But no. This is the best thing for me, at least until Christmas, and when I have those moments of weakness, the only thing to do is keep *moving*.

I miss you man, and wish like hell you were here with me in Zion, instead of there in Babylon. We'd *both* be having a lot more fun!

(Early next morning . . .)

I was going to keep this going awhile longer, but since they've got a post office right here in the lodge, I decided to get it sent off, and that way you'll get it sooner. I know from experience with my English friend and his periods of "holiday at Her Majesty's pleasure" that a "bit o' dosh" can be handy, and I was also able to get a money order here, so I'll send you a couple hundred simoleons for any "necessaries" you might be able to acquire.

If you're up to it, I'd love to hear from you, and I get semi-regular mail infusions from Sheila, through the office, if you wanted to drop me a line. If there's anything else I can do for you and yours, just ask; I'm here for you. (Maybe not *here* exactly, but I'll be *somewhere* for you!)

Here's hoping that the bail thing comes together, and that your loyal supporters (like me) will be able to raise the "King's Ransom" to get you the gosh-darn-heck *out* of there!

"I loves you some lot."

"What?"

"Nutting."

Your friendly neighborhood
Ghost Rider

While I was buying the money order and mailing the letter to Brutus, I learned that my little cabin would be available for another night, so I took it. During breakfast I asked the waitress about the lodge building itself, for I knew it had been another destination from the old train-travel days (Union Pacific in this case), but nothing seemed to remain from that time. She told me the original lodge had burned down in the '60s, and had been rebuilt in 90 days. "And they've been trying to fix it ever since." The chairs and tables had been made by the grandson of the original maker, in "branch and canework" construction.

On the wall of the restaurant, I noticed Utah's version of the warning against alcohol, similar to the one that was posted in restaurants and bars in California.

"WARNING — THE CONSUMPTION OF ALCOHOLIC BEVERAGES PURCHASED IN THIS ESTABLISHMENT MAY BE HAZARDOUS TO YOUR HEALTH AND THE SAFETY OF OTHERS."

I had little patience with this kind of overstated "father-knows-best" paternalism, and to my journal I editorialized, "Oh, fuck off."

Later that day I editorialized further about everything on my mind in yet another letter to a distant friend. It seemed I had entered a period of deep reflection, and as always, I seemed to do my best reflecting on paper. This letter was written to Mendelson Joe, a Canadian painter, musician, political activist, environmentalist, motorcyclist, writer of wonderfully idiosyncratic letters, and dweller in the north woods. A man of size and scale, physically and philosophically, Joe was possessed of (and by) a fierce intelligence, inflexible integrity, boiler-plate opinions, razor-sharp humor, and blistering contempt for most of humanity. We agreed on many things, disagreed on some, and enjoyed a stimulating, if sporadic, correspondence.

Oct. 17, '98
Zion National Park

Dear Joe,

You'll be my guest for dinner tonight, in one of the most beautiful places you, or I, have ever seen. We're dining at the Lodge, where I've been staying the past two nights, and I'll be having artichokes, vegetable beef soup, Ruby Red trout, and Kendall Jackson Chardonnay. You can have whatever you like!

On both sides of us, the red sandstone canyon walls rise up 2,000 feet, and the floor of the canyon is barely that wide, so the cottonwoods and lush vegetation along the Virgin River only see the sun in the middle of the day. Last night, on my way back from the restaurant to my little cabin, I stopped to watch the tamest herd of mule deer cropping at the lawn, one of them an antlered stag, then looked up to the brightest stars I've seen since . . . I don't know when.

Today we (that's you and me) went on a 10-mile hike, climbing those 2,000-foot walls in the first four miles, up to Observation Point on the canyon rim, where we paused for a picnic lunch overlooking the eroded walls, some angular and fortress-like, others rounded in swoops and swirls by the action of water and the stones it hurled along. Higher up, the rock is white, while lower down the iron and other minerals have stained it various shades of red and brown. In short, gorgeous.

The Great White Throne, The Three Patriarchs, The Weeping Wall, Angels' Landing, The Emerald Pools, The Temple of Sinawava, all these have we feasted our eyes, binoculars, and cameras upon. And Joe, you're probably breathing a little hard, for the canyon floor is at 4,500 feet, taking us up to 6,500 feet on the rim, so it was a breathtaking walk, in both senses.

And this is how I've been getting along lately, as a modern-day saddletramp. I discovered up in northern B.C. that hiking is a suitable alternative to motorcycling — to keep me "moving" — so whenever I come to a place like this I try to pause and take in the scenery and the birds.

The exercise is good, and it also slows down my pace a little. Moments of Truth and Beauty had been sorely lacking in my life lately, and it was the motorcycle which first delivered me to some sublime encounters with highways, landscapes, and wildlife. Pausing along the way, mainly in the national parks, and getting into the woods has been equally . . . if not uplifting, at least *stabilizing*.

You can imagine that I have been rocked to the very foundations by the unbelievable and unacceptable tragedies of the past 14 months. You know as well as anyone the way I tried to live my life — if I did well, I would try to do good, believing in some basic karmic principle that "if you do good, you get good." Well, it ain't true at all, for that is also the way Jackie lived, and the way we taught Selena to be, and her whole focus in life, even at 19, was to go out and fight *injustice*. Now she never will, and the world is the poorer for it.

And me, I've got to start all over. Not only build a new life, but construct a new *person*. I call my old self "that other guy," for I share nothing but his memories, and everything he ever liked I've had to discover all over again, one by one, so that I've held on to, for example, reading, motorcycling, and birdwatching, but I'm not yet sure about art or music (I can look at it or listen to it, but not with the same "engagement" I used to), and I have no interest in work, charity, world events, or anybody I don't know. In my present gypsy life, I encounter a lot of people every day, and some of them I instinctively like and respond to in a brief encounter at a gas station or small-town diner, but for the most part I look around at ugly and mean-spirited people and think, "Why are you *alive?*"

And more: sometimes I have a strong urge to take a machine gun and mow all the bastards down. (Sure, I've got a little anger!)

This was brought home to me sharply last week, when I was in Las Vegas for a few days. In the past I've always found the place moderately amusing (or at least that other guy did), but this time it was unbearable: Pigs! Scum! Cows! Low-life beasts! Die, die, die!

However, I was there for a good reason: Freddie Spencer's school at the Las Vegas International Racetrack. Months ago, Brutus and I booked that, and although he didn't make it, for reasons which I'll get to in a moment, I did meet up with Jackie's sister Deb, who was making her own trip down the "Healing Road" in an RV with her little family. Her partner Mark, a CBR 600 rider from way back, also took the two-day course.

I recall writing to you when I was taking the Jim Russell course in Formula Ford cars at the racetrack at Mont Tremblant, in Quebec, and while that was pretty exciting, this seemed way more *serious,* in the same way that riding a motorcycle on the street is more serious than driving a car can ever be. The main pressure, of course, was not to *crash,* and I was happy enough to succeed on that level, but I also had some highly adrenalized *fun* (rare and welcome in my recent life), and learned a thing or three about bike-handling. Even riding away from there on my way up here, I felt more comfortable and confident on my old GS than I had coming down that same road a few days before.

That R1100 GS has just passed 84,000 kilometres (52,500 miles) of which 27,000 (16,875) have been covered in the past two months, and it's still the most comfortable, versatile, and *fun* bike I can imagine. From 1,000 miles of dirt, gravel, and mud up to Inuvik and back, to the endless twisties of the roads of Idaho, to the long, desolate stretches of Nevada's Highway 50 ("The Loneliest Road in America"), it's been my faithful steed and companion. A few oil changes, a couple sets of tires, new brake pads, and a 10,000-kilometre service in Vancouver, and again in Vegas, and on we go. My very loose "plan/no plan" is to drift south through these western states (I've already been driven out of Wyoming and Montana by early snow in the mountains, and have endured morning temperatures in the 20s in these higher elevations), and down into Mexico, and maybe Belize, until I get through Christmas — that formerly happy family season in Quebec. Then I'm thinking of storing the bike in San Diego, and flying back for January and February, the prime winter months, in hopes that cross-country skiing and snowshoeing will "work" for me in the way that hiking is on days like today, or on other days in Glacier Park, Montana, Sun Valley, Idaho, or Jack London State Park, in California.

There have been those who have actually said they *envy* me, though mostly strangers, and I doubt you'd be that short-sighted or self-absorbed. This is way more freedom than anyone should ever desire, and carries way more baggage than "freedom" can ever sustain. This is more like "desperate flight," and another name I have for myself is "The Ghost Rider." I'm a ghost, I carry a few ghosts with me, and I'm riding through a world that isn't quite *real*. But I'm okay as long as I keep moving . . .

So — Brutus. *[Summary of his story.]*

Man. It's awful for him, and for his wife and son, and I've taken it pretty hard too. First my daughter, then my wife, then my dog (my parents had been looking after him, but he had to be put down a month ago), and now my best friend. It's tough to be philosophical, you know?

But I'll help look after his family (I said I've lost my charity, but not my generosity to those I care about), and see if I can help get him out on bail for awhile, at least, but it's pretty sure that it will be a long time before we ride together again. Of course, he knew the score (can't-do-the-time, don't-do-the-crime and all that), but still — it's a blow.

And that same day I found out I have an *ulcer*. (Wonder why?)

But tomorrow I'll move on to Bryce Canyon National Park, then Capitol Reef, Canyonlands, and The Arches (Utah's pretty rich in incredible scenery), and just keep moving. Nothing else to do.

Ruby's Best Western Inn,
Bryce Canyon National Park,
Utah

Well, here we are in a new scene; and one even more spectacular than yesterday's. At 9,000 feet, looking south toward the Grand Canyon, and surrounded by unbelievable rock formations that form spires, pinnacles, arches, towers, and Gothic battlements. It's named after an early Mormon settler, Ebenezer Bryce, who reportedly said, "It's a hell of a place to lose a cow!" No doubt. (Interesting to note that the Utah state park guidebook changes that bad word to "heck.")

Today, I just did the scenic drive around the park, stopping at the various viewpoints to look and photograph (I've taken more photos in the last two days than I usually take in two *weeks*), and tomorrow I'll get out and do some hiking. They've already had a good fall of snow here, just a few days ago, so I'm glad the roads (and sky) are clear at the moment.

Anyway, I wanted to get this finished up and sent off to you, so I'll shut up now. I hope things are not-too-bad with you, Joe, and now that I'm putting pieces of my new life together this way, I'm sure I'll be more in touch in the months, and years, to come.

Over and out from the "Healing Road," Highway 12 in Utah,

Your friend,

NEP

On a long hike through a part of Bryce Canyon National Park called Fairyland Canyon, I walked down into the eroded sandstone walls and towers, between the sculptured pinnacles called "hoodoos," all of them etched in a horizontal symmetry of colored strata. These individual elements of the scenery seemed more like works of art than of nature, and the landscape felt more like a *museum*. Among the comparisons that came to mind were Gaudí's splendidly organic works in Barcelona, like the Sagrada Familia cathedral; the mud-mosques I had seen along the Niger River in Mali; the crumbling Greek ruins in Ephesus or the Parthenon; the Anasazi pueblos of New Mexico; the Foreign Legion fort in *Beau Geste;* the Valley of the Kings in Egypt; or perhaps something equally monumental, but unearthly, like a vision of Atlantis.

In a national park visitors center I had picked up a book called *Desert Solitaire,* by Edward Abbey, who had been a park ranger at Arches National Park in Utah during the '50s, and I was deeply impressed by his essays and stories set in the high desert and canyon country of Utah and northern Arizona. He wrote of rafting and hiking through Glen Canyon on the Colorado just before it was flooded to become Lake Powell, and I began to understand some of what had been *lost* in the course of building the great dams. Then there were some of his *human* insights, such as this, "By the age of 40, a man is responsible for his face. And his fate." Wanting to share this discovery with one friend who would surely understand, I immediately mailed Brutus a copy of *Desert Solitaire,* along with an anthology by various writers called *A Desert Reader.*

Abbey referred often to Moab, a small town in eastern Utah located between two national parks, Arches and Canyonlands, and I decided to head up that way, passing through an amazing variety of landscapes in southeastern Utah, from prairie to lunar to redrock to high forest (9,400 feet) to sage and juniper, then up through Hanksville and around the Henry Mountains (the last-named in the U.S., I learned from a book about Major Powell's exploration of the Colorado River I was reading, *Beyond the Hundredth Meridian,* by Wallace Stegner), to Moab, Utah.

Moab proved to be the perfect small town, at least by the Ghost Rider's exacting criteria — those being that a town should have a decent motel, a good restaurant, a small museum of local history, a friendly post office, and a well-stocked liquor store. St. Helena, California, in the Napa Valley, had been my previous favorite, but Moab trumped it for its isolated and spectacular setting, its lack of crowds, traffic, and "Californicator" attitudes, and its feeling of being an oasis of culture in the middle of thousands of square miles of forbidding wilderness.

The Center Café, for example, was a totally unexpected treat to the palate of a jaded traveller, with its unpretentious elegance, sophisticated menu, and at least 20 different wines available by the glass. Then there was a fine little museum, open until eight at night, with displays of the area's aboriginal life, geology, natural history, and pioneer and mining tales, and the nearby library too (with a display of first editions of Abbey's books), which was open until nine.

Edward Abbey was obviously something of a local hero in Moab, for the local bookshop was called "Back of Beyond," after a company owned by a character in his novel *The Monkey Wrench Gang,* in which (with typical humor and irreverence) Abbey introduced the concept of eco-terrorism, thought to have inspired real-life practitioners such as Earth First! Like many of the shops on the main street of Moab, which catered to visitors to the nearby national parks as well as world-renowned mountain bike trails and off-road vehicle tracks, Back of Beyond was open in the evening, and I enjoyed a leisurely after-dinner browse in its shelves. One whole rack of books was labeled "Abbey and Friends," and I couldn't resist buying a whole boxful of treasures to mail home from the friendly post office.

During my travels, I had often seen the chrome-plated plastic "fish," a Christian emblem, affixed to the back of cars, and a few times I had been amused by a clever "evolutionist" variant in which the fish had little legs, with "Darwin" spelled out inside. (There were other variations in which a shark labeled "Jesus" was swallowing the Darwinian amphibian, with levels of irony perhaps unintended, and once I laughed out loud at the sight of one with "Gefilte" spelled out inside the fish.) I was mildly excited to finally find the Darwin ones for sale at Back of Beyond, and though tempted to stick one on the back of my luggage cases, I decided I didn't want to give offense to any believers by trumpeting my "non-belief," even though they might not show me the same courtesy.

The following morning I set out for a hike in Arches National Park under a steady, light rain. Sheltering under Navajo Arch for lunch, I put on my rain jacket and carried on. (Though I noted the melancholy atmosphere conveyed in the simple words, "rain in the desert.")

The next day I rode the "scenic drive" around the Island in the Sky section of Canyonlands National Park, and the twisty road in was worth the trip alone. Still overcast, the prospect from Grand View Point was a little diminished, but never mind: there was the confluence of the Green and Colorado rivers, the beginning of Cataract Canyon and the far-off, legendary Maze.

Mark and Deb were passing through Moab on their way north, and that night I visited them at the RV park, then agreed to meet up with them down in Monument Valley the following day. I was still waiting to hear what was going on with Brutus, staying in contact with his lawyer about the upcoming bail hearing, but there had been no news.

During a break in the *Test For Echo* tour, in the spring of '97, Jackie and her long-time friend, Georgia, flew down to meet Brutus and me in Durango, Colorado, and we spent a few days travelling together through the Four Corners region: Brutus and me on our bikes, and the girls in a rented minivan. For the next few days I would be travelling some of those same roads, with the inevitable poignant memories.

Oct 24 Mexican Hat, Utah

Long way around yesterday, via Monticello, Dolores, Mexican Water, Bluff, Kayenta, and Monument Valley. Cloudy most of the way, even one brief shower. Tooth getting worse: infection, I now suspect, but of course it's the weekend, in Mexican Hat!

Few drops of rain north of Blanding, where we four had breakfast that previous time, and just past the turnoff from Mexican Hat, where Brutus and I waited for the "lost minivan." Gave me a pang, all along that road we had travelled together, feeling very sad approaching the San Juan Inn, and tears to find I'm in the same room Jackie and I stayed in. Ach.

Dinner last night at Goulding's (mediocre) in Monument Valley with Deb and Mark, then nervous ride back. So dark out there. Awake until 2:00 a.m., finishing The Monkey Wrench Gang (excellent), then starting Desert Anarchist. Bufferins finally bring relief, and again this morning. Maybe head to Flagstaff, get treatment. Antibiotics, no doubt.

"Somewhere Down That Crazy River." The San Juan River, in this case, hiking along the rimrock of the "Goosenecks" [high, meandering canyon], trackless but for occasional 4WD, ATV, or boot tracks. Trying to watch for rattlesnakes, and not walk on "cryptobiotic soil" (these National Park Service ranger signs and Abbey are having their effect on me).

Sitting here on canyon rim, in Goosenecks, silent but for whispering brown river far below (and the usual ringing in my drum-deafened ears!). Light breeze, pleasantly cool, few washes of white cloud here and there.

Hiking back with silhouettes of "monuments" above canyon, through quarry, old dump, gravel pit in distance. Came out from hike on cliff above hotel: scary. Crumbly red sandstone, and no *apparent way down. But as usual, no going back!*

If tooth remains quiescent, maybe try Page tomorrow. Rent a boat and look around Lake Powell, and the Glen Canyon that used to be there, before it was flooded. The Ghost Canyon.

Halloween decorations up here and last night. Second most "celebrated" event in America, Mark heard on the radio. After Super Bowl, I guess.

On a gloomy day of heavy rain I rode down into northern Arizona, then west through Black Mesa and the electric railroad which features in Edward Abbey's *The Monkey Wrench Gang,* along with the huge coal power plant (called Navajo Scrubber Plant, or some such) right by Page, Arizona ("Shithead Capital of Coconino County," according to Abbey). Circling the little town, which had grown up around the dam construction, I rode down the "Jesus Row" of big churches, then across the dam, where I parked to look at the lake and imagine the canyon as it must have been.

Discouraged by the continuing heavy rain and my nagging toothache, I thought I would head down to Flagstaff. The rain became biblical, the streets of the town were deeply awash, and I took refuge in a Hampton Inn by the Interstate, watching on the Weather Channel as they kept returning to "Stormwatch" and the big story of heavy rains in Flagstaff. (Yes, I know.)

A big wet blanket covered the whole Southwest, but Yuma showed sunny and 80°F. So, leaving early next morning, even as the rain turned gelid on my face shield and slushy gray on I-40, I headed *down* (elevation-wise) as fast as I could. A long stretch of old Route 66 had been bypassed by the interstate, thereby cutting off and effectively killing a series of towns from Seligman to Topock (the ultimate "Ghost Road"), and I turned onto that long loop, as lonely, scenic, and "entertaining" as I remembered it being when Brutus and I went that way in the spring of '97.

The Sitgreaves Pass stretch was steep, winding, narrow, and rough, and I remembered reading that in the westward migration of the Great Depression, the *Grapes of Wrath* Okies had sometimes paid locals to drive their overloaded vehicles over that section, and some of the grades were so steep they had to be climbed in *reverse.*

Then down past Lake Havasu, where I stopped near the "ghost bridge" — the original, actual London Bridge, bought, disassembled, shipped across the Atlantic, and reassembled in the Arizona desert by Robert McCullough, of the chainsaw family (who claimed the lake had been created to test his outboard motors).

After finally shedding my rain gear and under-layers, I rode south past scattered RVs parked in gravel washes, and "settlements" of them near the Interstate at Quartzsite, down and down to Yuma, Arizona, through stretches of farmland irrigated by the dregs of the Colorado (pretty much all of it siphoned off to the cities and irrigation projects of California, Arizona, and Nevada by that point).

Yuma had a nicely renovated old-town area, and I checked into a classic charter-member Best Western motel, the Coronado, built in the '30s, with drive-up units under red tile roof, flowering bougainvillea, and open-air laundry machines under a breezeway. It seemed like a good place to stay an extra day, and take care of some chores.

Oct 27 Yuma

Busy day. Started with phone calls to Sheila, my "central liaison," then Brutus's lawyer (faxed "character reference" and "offer of employment"), then out to find oil change venue. Not easy! Couple of refusals, then bike shop reluctantly allows it: if I'm "time-efficient." Man, what's the big deal? Anyway, done.

Then visit museum in Territorial Prison (no prizes for guessing who I thought of there), send more finished books from post office, wander the main street area (still pretty dead), and the Century House museum. Lady there gives me more info than I could take in, but learned that Laguna Dam near here was first on Colorado, and that lettuce is flooded to keep soil cool, always planted in north-south rows, and fields are leveled with laser-guided machines. Also grow cabbage, broccoli, and cauliflower.

About 40 bikes from "Iron Horse Tours" in parking lot, mostly cruisers: Harleys, Hondas, one [BMW] R1200C. Am I jealous of their companionship? On reflection, no. Prefer being solo saddletramp.

Oh yeah — tooth got better, by itself! Life is good . . .

[Letter to Brutus]

Oct. 30, '98
Bisbee, AZ

Hey Puddle-Jumper!

For a week now I've been putting off this letter, having heard there was a bail hearing coming up. Well, I called Bloomenfeld [the Toronto lawyer] from a payphone in the middle of Organ Pipe Cactus National Monument yesterday, only to hear that the judge had "suspended judgement." Well, that's enough: I'm going to write you a ding-dong letter, and see what happens *later!* Wouldn't want you to feel neglected . . .

In any case, I guess that's good news (from what I've learned from "Law and Order" anyway). Basically, "I'll think about it," no? Today I was thinking that you usually have enough bad luck to get *into* bad situations, but enough good luck to get *out* of them. So far, anyway. My hopes are with you this time.

So, what brings me to the bustling burg of Bisbee? I thought you'd never ask . . .

[Recap of my travels as far as Yuma]

Heading east from Yuma on I-8, this half-familiar motorcycle appeared behind me, black with protruding hard bags, headlight on bright, and riding in proper, staggered formation for 100 miles to Gila Bend. It reminded me of someone I used to ride with, but alas, I wasn't fooled. Just another Ghost Rider.

South of Why, and just west of Gunsight (the day before I passed Nothing, Arizona — love it!), I decided to check out Organ Pipe Cactus National Monument, and ended up camping for two nights there. After two months of carrying tent and sleeping bag, it was finally *warm* enough, for one thing, and there was a general store and café five miles down the road in Lukeville, on the Mexican border (otherwise known — and signed — as Gringo Pass), so I went for it. I nabbed one of the few *shady* sites, under a mesquite and a palo verde tree, and set myself up among the saguaro, organ pipe, cholla, ocotillo, prickly pear, and creosote. I rode the 20-mile scenic loop around the eastern section of the park, on a classic desert road (gravel, sand, rocky wash), picked up bread, cold meat, and cheese in Gringo Pass, walked the trail around the campground as the sun went down to leave a bright half moon, stars, planets, a passing satellite, and a few lingering jets from the Air Force base (the Barry M. Goldwater Range).

Up for the sunrise next morning, I rode down to Gringo Pass for breakfast (past about 100 border-patrol suvs), then did an eight-mile hike to the abandoned Victoria mine, walking along and naming all the newly learned cacti and shrubs. Great bird-watching too, with many found only in that part of the Sonora desert.

Early Next Morning
Still Bisbee

So, having used up my on-hand oil filter in Yuma, I noted the address of the bmw dealer in Tucson, thinking to stop by if it "crossed my path." Fortunately it did, for I got to talking to a couple of the guys there, and when I told them I was thinking of heading north to Canyon de Chelly, one guy says it's snowing up there, everywhere above 7,000 feet, and raining everywhere else.

Nothing if not flexible, I said, "Well, maybe I'll go to Tombstone instead," and the other guy offered, "Yeah, go down through Tombstone to Bisbee and stay at the Copper Queen." So I did.

You can imagine that Tombstone is pretty much a "theme park," with regularly scheduled "Gunfights at the OK Corral" and people dressed as cowboys and music-hall girls standing around the covered boardwalks. But still, stuff actually *happened* there, so it carries a certain amount of conviction, especially on a cool, overcast day with a gusty wind blowing dust through the street. And what do I hear just as I'm parking my bike in front of the saloon? "Ghost Riders in the Sky."

I don't know if I told you or not, but that's been the title of my [imaginary] "book" lately — and me. "Ghost Rider." Literally and metaphorically, I feel a bit of a ghost drifting around the West; I sure carry some ghosts *with* me (you among them; no offence!), and so often I find myself following the ghostly trails of Jack London, Hemingway, Edward Abbey, Major Powell, or even places like Telegraph Creek: a real live (or dead) ghost town. Sometimes it's *me* who's not real; sometimes it's the rest of the world, but either way I always feel a sense of "alienation" toward everybody and everything.

Even this place fits. Bisbee was once the largest mining town in the *world*, with 20,000 people, and the Copper Queen hotel, built around 1903, was its centerpiece. Now I might compare it to that Hotel La Fonda we stayed at in Taos, slightly funky and clinging to a faded past, like the town (like me!). Set in a narrow valley at 5,000 feet, it's supposed to have the best year-round climate in Arizona, and so attracts enough visitors, along with some retirees and the kiss-of-death "artists' community" (that would be aged hippies, I imagine), to keep it going. A ghost town for a ghost rider.

What's that line from "Aquarius," "mystic crystal revelations"? Yeah man, that's it . . .

If I can ever do as Jonny Bealby did [in *Running With the*

Moon, the tale of a motorcycle journey across Africa as a kind of desperate therapy following the death of his fiancée], and crystallize these mystic revelations into a book, that title would make a fine sequel to *The Masked Rider*. But we'll see about that. More and more often these days I feel pangs of homesickness, and would love to be sitting at my computer and looking out at late autumn on Lac St. Brutus, but . . . not yet. I'm still determined to hang in until Christmas (or hang out, or hang on), and another good thing which emerged from my visit to "Iron Horse" in Tucson (BMW, Triumph, and MZ) was learning that it would be no problem to store my bike there, which might make a good "gateway" from Mexico.

And maybe by that time I'll be able to see *your* ugly mug. I really don't want to see you *there* (in several senses), though of course if this nonsense stretches out too long I'll come visit, but I don't think it will be nice. The last time we got together in Quebec makes a better memory to hang onto, for me anyway.

But we'll see what comes down, and of course I will visit the great El Cuervo anywhere, if he wishes it. Even . . . there . . .

Same with the phone; if you want to talk to me on that cursèd instrument (an angelic *harp* to you!), just say the word. For now I'm okay talking to you this way, and I wouldn't want our conversation to be warped or stilted by "circumstances," or surroundings. But as people had to do for me during my tribulations, I'll follow *your* lead, Buddy-boy.

I'd certainly like to hear from *you*, if you've got the time (ha-ha), but that too is up to you. I read once that Thomas Jefferson received a letter from a friend complaining that he had nothing interesting to report, and old Tom told him, "Just tell me about the events passing daily under your eyes." So yeah, I'd like to hear about what you do in a day, what you can do, any characters you've encountered, what you're reading (Georgia told me about you hanging around the law books — good idea! You could probably get a lawyerin' job in Tarawnna!), and all like that. Sheila gets mail to me fairly regularly, and I would love to hear from you. Or maybe when the judge is finished "reserving judgement," we'll be able to get you out of there, and I can talk to you like a "normal" person. Whatever, I'm here for you, buddy!

Oct. 31

Socorro, NM

Or I'm *here* for you. Or somewhere. Anyway, I'm *there* for you.

And a Happy Halloween to you. Hey, what you going out as? Ha.

Early today I passed a place in eastern Arizona called Skeleton Canyon, and a sign pointed out that Geronimo, "the last of the hostiles," had surrendered there. Stories and more stories, everywhere I go, and most of them "ghost stories," fittingly.

I was thinking today that it's impossible to really write about these areas, or to *know* them, without a *lot* of study. The West is so darn *complicated*, you know — with interwoven political conflicts over water, mining, logging, rangeland, and Indian reserves.

This afternoon, threatened by thunderstorms and hail, I made it here to the Super 8 Motel, next door to K-Bob's Steakhouse, after a nice long ride of 703 kms (439 miles). (Odometer now at 88928 [55,580], for 31821 [19,888] on this odyssey.)

At 6,000 and 7,000 feet most of the way, it was also darn *cold*, but some splendid scenery through the Gila National Forest, and the Very Large Array [radiotelescope dishes] just west of here. Tomorrow I hope to check out the Trinity Site, if I can get in there, then mosey over toward Roswell, to tie together the Outer Space connection with Rachel and the Extraterrestrial Highway.

The next day, I'll be heading for Santa Fe to meet up with Alex and Liam for a few days, and I'm looking forward to that; not least to being in somebody's *home* for the first time since Vancouver, six weeks ago. (Deb and Mark's RV doesn't count.) Not that I'm not at home in the Super 8, you understand, but . . . you understand.

Anyway, time to wind this epistle to a close. I'm sure you've got better things to do than read *my* drivel all the ding-dong day! And if not, why, I'll write again soon! I've got a copy of *The Monkey Wrench Gang* to send you, and as soon as I get to another bookstore, I'll send you some other good stuff. Santa Fe should have something. Meanwhile, I'll enclose another couple hundred *cruzeiros* for your dining and dancing pleasure, and just let me know if there's anything else I can send for you, or do for you. I remain,

Your obedient servant
The Ghost Rider . . .

Before setting out on this journey, and along the way, I had jotted down the names of any places I might like to see — whether a geographical feature like Devil's Tower, Wyoming (never did get there), Bonneville Salt Flats, a car museum, the Grand Coulee Dam, or Jack London State Park — and in my map case I carried that list of various places of "Americana" which might cross my path — or come within 1000 miles, realistically.

The Very Large Array of radio telescopes was on that list, and as I rode across the high plateau of the Plains of San Agustin in New Mexico, the miles of white dishes, angled symmetrically to the storm-clouded sky, were a dramatic sight.

Roswell, New Mexico, was on that list too, as the alleged scene of a UFO crash in the late '40s which gave birth to the UFO craze, as well as a series of conspiracy-theory books and made-for-TV movies about the incident. Since adolescence, I had been attracted by the romance of such tales of the mysterious and supernatural, but the museum, a former cinema, was ultimately disappointing to a would-be convert; it only documented the history of the *story*, and there wasn't a single piece of real evidence. (I know, I know — the *government* stole it all . . .)

Another scenic attraction on my list was White Sands National Monument, and its dunes of pure white gypsum powder were spectacular under the desert sun. Riding along the blinding white roads, with banks plowed to the side, I couldn't escape the illusion that I was riding on a snowy road in Quebec: most disconcerting on a two-wheeler.

A fitting end to my travels on the high desert, and indeed to this phase of my solitary quest, was a stay in Santa Fe. Alex and his wife, Charlene, had a house there, and he and I had arranged to meet for a few days in early November. It also happened that our long-time friend and tour manager, Liam, was on his way home from a tour of Japan with another band, so he agreed to stop off there too.

Liam's professional relationship with Rush was difficult to define, for it was so wide-ranging and *crucial*. Formally, he was the band's tour manager, as well as the executive producer of our recording projects (both jobs might be simply stated as the responsibility for getting everyone and everything in the right place at the right time — with all *that* can entail), and he was also a close friend to all of us. (In fact, he was married to Sharyn, Jackie's friend since her teens.)

Liam had actually been with the band longer than *I* had (before I joined, Geddy and Alex had played together for six years as Rush, with another drummer), and over the years of our ascent from nowhere to somewhere, success-wise, he had worked his way up from second-in-a-crew-of-two to the quiet, but absolute, president of an on-the-road crew that numbered more than 50 stage technicians, sound mixers, light-show electricians, rear-screen projection operators, riggers, and truck and bus drivers.

Along with Sheila, Liam had perhaps done the most to hold my life together through the past 14 months of hell, for he was so knowledgeable about "how to work the world." When I needed flights to England and hotel rooms for Jackie and me and Brad and Rita, it was Liam I called. When I needed to find grief counselling for Jackie in London, it was Liam I called. And more; he was also one of those I called when I was just feeling lost and lonely.

In every way, it was so nice to be in someone's *home* again, for the first time since my stay with Danny and Janette in Vancouver. After another two months of motels, gas stations, and restaurants in a world full of strangers, I was able to relax with two of my best friends, a real fireplace to play with, Alex's legendary cooking, shared stories from our respective adventures, a few excursions around Santa Fe and up to the Anasazi ruins at Bandelier National Monument, and sleeping in a lovely guest room with good sheets and pillows.

Inevitably, I would have to pay for this interlude by suffering yet another attack of the "visitor syndrome," after I left there to ride on alone while Alex and Liam flew home to rejoin their lives and families. But while it lasted, I surrendered to the warmth of companionship and the feeling of being cared for by good friends.

I turn my back to the wind
To catch my breath, before I start off again
Driven on, without a moment to spend
To pass an evening with a drink and a friend

I let my skin get too thin
I'd like to pause, no matter what I pretend
Like some pilgrim, who learns to transcend
Learns to live as if each step was the end

TIME STAND STILL, 1987

LETTERS TO BRUTUS

We are islands to each other
Building hopeful bridges on the troubled sea

ENTRE NOUS, 1979

One evening in Santa Fe when Liam, Alex, and I were sitting around the kitchen table drinking and telling stories, the telephone rang. I had been trying to reach Brutus's lawyer all afternoon, and when Alex handed me the phone I hoped it would be Mr. Bloomenfeld with some good news. But what I heard coming out of that receiver was the voice of the man himself, and the familiar salutation, "Hey, buddy, how ya doin'?"

Surprised, delighted, tongue-tied, and moved, I let him talk for a few minutes, then was able to ask him a few questions about how he was getting along (surprisingly well), his legal situation (unclear as yet), and if there was anything else I could do for him (send more books). He was definitely the same old Brutus, cheerful and optimistic (at least for those few minutes on the phone), and just speaking to him, hearing his voice, made me feel better, and much closer to him again.

After I said goodbye to Alex and Liam on a rainy morning in Santa Fe, heading vaguely west again, I passed through three dark, lonely days. The only thing that seemed to keep my spirits up enough to keep me moving forward (if that could be said to be my actual *direction*) was that more and more I began to see the journey through the eyes of *Brutus*. Despite the grimness of his situation, somehow things still looked brighter through his eyes than through mine (at least the way *I* saw it; he might not have agreed).

On the phone in Santa Fe, Brutus had said something like, "You just get out there and ride for me," and I told him I would, but if it was true that Brutus was living vicariously through me, in a way I was doing the same with him — riding along every day, thinking about what I was seeing and feeling and how I was going to write it to him. From then on, much of my story would be told to Brutus, in a series of letters that I thought about all day while I rode across the West, then wrote down while I sat drinking a glass of The Macallan in my motel room, or the bar, or at a table for one in a restaurant. My whole life became a letter to Brutus.

Nov. 13, '98
Furnace Creek Inn
Death Valley, CA

Hey Fender Bender!

If that dateline isn't torture enough for you, I'll add that I'm having a frozen margarita on the upper terrace, facing the salt pans, the chocolate-colored Panamints and their mocha-colored alluvial fans, and the setting sun in a wispy-clouded sky.

Should I shut up now? Hell, no. I'm alone and fairly miserable, and it's all your fault! Well, maybe not *all*, but you know what I mean. You're supposed to *be* here, making me have fun, instead of languishing there with all your *new* friends.

Anyway, I'm glad to be here for a couple of nights, for I've been having some pretty nasty days lately. The week in Santa Fe was nice all right, but as Jackie and I used to find in London, it was great having friends visit, but *worse* when they were gone. I pulled out of there on Monday morning feeling low, fragile, and dispirited, and was immediately hit by cold rain, fog, nasty cross-winds, construction through Albuquerque, and even heavy flakes of wet snow, blinding and worrisome "under-wheel." Down I-25 (getting *south* as fast as I could!) the snow went away, but the crosswinds were *deadly*, especially while passing trucks, and where I bypassed old Las Cruces to Deming, the cold rain grew ever worse. I hunkered down in Lordsburg for the night, weepy and lost (at an exceedingly mediocre Best Western and neigh-boring restaurant, "Kranberry's"), and carried on next morning (sunny at least, though still cold and fiercely windy) to Tucson for an oil change with my buddies there.

I had a route carefully mapped to miss the sprawl of stinky Phoenix (Abbey's "the blob that ate Arizona"), but 50 miles out of Tucson my speedometer died. Hating to turn back, I carried on north to the dealer in Phoenix and convinced a reluctant service manager to fix it ("can't get to it today," "everybody's booked up," "haven't got one in stock," the usual). In my usual shy and retiring way, I settled in to wait him out, and suggested he might have a GS around he could take one off. (Why doesn't this ever occur to these guys *first?* You can tell they've never been parts manager for a farm equipment dealer, like I was for my Dad, where you have to get your customers going *now!*) So, a few hours later, I was again hunkered down in a mediocre Best Western, just west of Phoenix (had to get *out*, at least). Next day, rain and cold again, as I headed into that mysterious part of southeastern California (the

Colorado Desert, officially), with irrigated farmland almost from the Colorado to the Imperial Valley, and an impressive stretch of sand dunes, the Algodones Dunes.

Clouds and rain increased as I rode up the east side of the Salton Sea (or *sewer*, according to the nice old lady at the museum in Yuma), and I could just see that the scenery was *probably* nice, on nearly every other day of the year. Ach. I tried going east on I-10 to Joshua Tree, but the cold and wet even put a "damper" on that. I'd planned to stop at Roy's Motel that night, but it was still so early that if I went straight there I'd arrive by about 2:30 — too early. (For me, the corollary to the Scooter Trash rule about not drinking until I'm parked, is that as soon as I'm parked, I start drinking!)

So I thought I'd go east a ways on that 29 Palms highway, 62, where a road was shown leading up northwest to Cadiz, not far from Amboy. Nothing promising (or paved) appeared (nor *existed*, I learned later; how is it that with only maybe five roads and 10 towns in the whole Mojave, they can't get it straight on the *maps?*), so on I went, meeting up with that road we took across from Parker and Havasu when *we* went to Joshua Tree (and Roy's), then north on truck-filled 95. And the skies darkened, and it *rained*. (I've now delivered rain to all of America's deserts, from the Great Basin to the Mojave to the Colorado to the Sonora; shouldn't they be paying me?)

(Pause to watch sun sink behind Telescope Peak, and savor second margarita. You with me here?)

Nice, although sunset at 4:20 is a bit harsh.

As it was the day before yesterday, riding in heavy rain on a narrow desert highway, mud and sand flying up behind the trucks in long dense clouds, all over me and my bike (which had left Santa Fe *gleaming;* for about a minute), and I was wiping frantically at my face shield and trying to get by those trucks. Perilous, nasty, and *miserable*. As that early darkness came on, I crawled once again into a mediocre Best Western, in Needles, its restaurant, the "California Pantry," rendered even *more* mediocre because of course I couldn't smoke after my glutinous fettuccine and syrupy cabernet. (You with me here?)

But, yesterday morning the sun came slinking out of the clouds, slowly and reluctantly (ashamed of itself, no doubt), and I took old 66 all the way to Roy's Motel. Walt [the owner] and I sat out front for an hour or so, and I just told him you "couldn't make it this time" (true enough), for of course he asked. I had been tracing those old alphabetical ghost towns at the water stops [from the Santa Fe railroad], but couldn't find "F" and "B," which he filled in, and he hadn't known about "H," and was glad to learn it. So: it was Amboy, Bolo, Cadiz, Danby, Essex, Fenner, Goffs, and Homer.

Roy's seemed much the same in its "funky splendor," though he's had to install those "retractable foreskin" nozzles on the old gas pumps, and a tornado came through last summer and tore up his double-wide out back, and the "CAFE" sign off the roof of the portico. This weekend, he's got some "money-men" coming in from New York and Vegas to talk about putting in a swimming pool, a golf course (!), and fixing up the row of motel-type rooms in back. He seems to think it could happen. But *we* knew it when . . .

From there, after setting up a "Ghost Rider" shot with the bike on its centerstand facing down the road, with Roy's and the Amboy Crater in the distance, I turned north up the Kelbaker Road to Kelso. Thanks to all the rain I've been bringing to the Southwest, the Mojave is like a green *sea* of creosote bushes. The doors and windows of the Kelso Depot are sealed with plexiglass sheets, with a sign out front announcing that they're "studying the possibility" of making it the headquarters for the Mojave National Preserve. Seems like a good idea. Then through Baker, home of the Giant Thermometer (only registering about 65°F) and the Mad Greek restaurant, and right about there, life started to get a *little* better. From my journal:

Started to feel better looking at those Mojave vistas: sloping
speckled sea with tawny, rocky islands, stretching far and wide.
Missed turnoff for Dante's View, but turned around and went
back. Wasn't going to miss that overlook to start my visit. Cold up
there, but not down here! Caught last glow of sunset over
Panamint Range from terrace. Yesss . . .

And what a treat it is to be here. Just finished spicy corn/crab
chowder, in elegant dining room, and have my cozy little room to
go back to. Especially appreciate this after three Best Westerns, and
three rough days.

Outside for coffee, cognac, and smoke. Stars brilliant.
Remember seeing Hale-Bopp [comet] from this very table, only a
year and a half ago. So much has changed . . .

Are you with me here? I know you are.

Unfortunately it's a bit busy around here: some kind of a
"49ers Days" convention in Furnace Creek, with about a gigajil-
lion RVs packed around the ranch. I went to the Visitors Center to
get the "passport stamp" for the front of my journal (I noticed the
stamp and pad back at Zion, and started collecting them from the
National Parks and Monuments — or "Money-mints," as Abbey
says — and I've got nine of them now), but ran away from there
pretty fast. Rows of booths selling "Western Art," live old-time
music (scraping fiddles), and crowds of silver-haired, tight-
jeaned, cowboy-booted, big-bellied RV people.

Fortunately, not much of that penetrates up here, though I was
greeted by a trio of guitar, upright bass, and sawing fiddle in the
lobby, and I could hear distant waves of noise carrying up the hill
last night from the RV park, as I sat by the *outdoor fireplace* down
by the pool (how'd we miss that?) poking away at my own personal
fire (smelled like mesquite, too) and looked up at the smoke
drifting across the stars. Then, as usual, I was asleep by nine.

After a month in Mountain Time, that's understandable, and would be alright, except that I'm awake at *five*. When I'm riding, there's no point in setting off too early in the morning freeze (not when I don't have some lunatic's insanely complicated and impossibly long itinerary to an unreachably far destination!), but on the other hand, that's a bad time of the day to be laying there *thinking*. (I imagine you're with me here too.)

So, one reads, doesn't one? Today I finished the *Best of Abbey*, which I'll send you soon. Lots of great stuff in it, but I was especially blown away by his riff on Death Valley, which seems untoppable, and it's immediately followed by another on New York, believe it or not, in which he captures all the beauty and horror of *that* place. I hope you have received *The Monkey Wrench Gang* and the Stegner book by now. Abbey's *The Brave Cowboy* was another great read, but I was unsure about sending it to you, as most of it takes place in *jail!* The movie version of that, *Lonely are the Brave* (hey, that's us, right?), was for sale in that excellent Moab bookstore (called "Back of Beyond," after Seldom Seen's company, and apparently opened by some of Abbey's friends), and I think I'll get it when I mail-order a bunch of stuff from there.

Anyway, I was finding all the jailhouse minutiae a little harsh, but maybe you'd just find it, I don't know — well-researched?

On that subject, I was sure surprised to hear your voice on the phone last week. Alex had said it was your lawyer calling me back, which I'd been expecting, but when I heard your dulcet tones, well, the old "could have knocked me down with a feather" cliché seems apt. I hope I wasn't too "jingled" (to use Jack London's excellent word), for the three of us had started to get into it about then, but it sure seemed like a good conversation to me. Definitely set at rest all the questions I'd raised in my last letter, anyway, and gave me a better sense of where you're "at" (man). (Besides with me here, I mean.) I feel a little bad that I haven't been in touch with Mr. Bloomenfeld this week (being wrapped in my own miseries as well as the three-hour time difference) so I don't know the latest on the "reserved judgement."

Out of guilt for not having called my Mom in about a week, I called her the other night, but I must call again and let her know that I'm a *little* better than that now. A little. Otherwise, I've pretty much done the turtle thing and crawled into my shell, for protection.

Today I went for a hike up Golden Canyon to Zabriskie Point, from -190 feet to +710 feet, then down through Gower's Gulch, with a picnic lunch on a shady rock along the way. You'll remember the lifeless and surreal vista from that overlook, and that's what I was hiking through. It worked for me . . .

Tomorrow, alas, I'm off to L.A., there to get the bike looked after (new tires and major pre-Mexico service) as well as sorting out the Mexican "insurance" and such, and I've booked in for four nights at the old Sunset Marquis in Hollywood to get all *that* stuff done. After that, I don't know. Truth to tell, I'm in no hurry to head down to Mexico. Everything will get just a little more *difficult,* you know, and I'm not exactly up for that right now. In Tucson, I picked up Clement Salvadori's book on motorcycling in Baja, and all of the great-sounding roads are treacherous dirt, of course, and I don't think I want to try those on my own. (Yes, it's all *your* fault again; because you're not with me here!) However, my "arena of operations" is ever-shrinking, weather-wise, so I'll be more-or-less *forced* to get adventurous pretty soon. And I'm sure I will. I can't stay lost and flailing like this *forever.* (Can I?)

When my speedometer broke the other day, it became one of those "turning points." I pulled over and "took a meeting" with myself — should I just head back to Tucson and *park* it, "put on my parachute," and *bail?* No, I decided. Not ready to hole up in Quebec, and especially, to face *Christmas* there. So, onward. Walt suggested I come back to Roy's Motel and stay there for a day or two, "we'll get some wine and sit and watch the cars go by" (like you and I did), and I wouldn't mind coming back here for a longer stay (once the "49ers" are gone; I was just reading in the lobby that they've been having an "Encampment" here every year since 1949, and next year, the 50th, will be *really* big. Don't miss it).

There are sure lots more hiking possibilities around here, and it's a great place to stay. But I guess I'll decide when I get to L.A. At least I'm getting used to not knowing where I'm *going,* even on a given day, and I can live with that. My Standard Operating Procedure these days: "Something will come up."

There's a nice phrase Salvadori uses in giving directions, "Just follow your front wheel." So I will.

All this has taken us right through another excellent meal (on days when I hike I'm allowed to have dessert), coffee and smoke outside at "our table," cognac at the bar (better light for writing) and back to my room after a look at the stars. Now, my "captive audience," it's getting late (almost *nine*), and time for me to plot a route into The Big Smoke (oh joy). I'll try to call your "special number" there and leave the number for you. (I'm sure I'll have exciting Hollywood Tales for you, which you will have heard before you get this letter. It's all getting too confusing.)

You with me here?

I know you are.

> Follow your front wheel . . .
> *Ghost Rider*

The band's long-time photographer, and our personal assistant during two tours in the early '90s (*Presto* and *Roll The Bones),* Andrew MacNaughtan, had recently moved from Toronto to Los Angeles, and he sent me a message through Sheila at the office inviting me to call him if I travelled that way. I hadn't much desire to deal with the sprawling madness of Los Angeles, but if I was going to Mexico (still uncertain), I needed to sort out some insurance, get the bike serviced, and generally prepare myself for further adventures, so I decided I might as well do it there.

When my motorcycle was parked in the garage below the Sunset Marquis hotel, where I had so often stayed with the band on tours going back to our first one in 1974, I sat by the pool and ordered a margarita, drinking to what I hoped would be a tolerable few days.

I strolled around Hollywood and along Sunset Boulevard on various errands, while the bike went into the BMW shop. I left my number at Brutus's "residence," for he could only make outgoing calls, and he was able to call me for another good conversation. I bought a few more books to mail to him, now that I knew he was allowed to receive them (though no more than four at a time, and no hardcovers — apparently drugs or razor blades could be hidden in those).

Andrew drove me to the AAA offices to arrange my Mexican insurance, and as another loyal, caring friend, he also made me get "out of myself" a little bit, introducing me to a group of Canadian ex-patriates he'd met up with, including Dave Foley from the comedy troupe "Kids in the Hall," easy-going, boyish, and dry-witted; the amiable, dreadlocked musician John Kastner; his friend Rob, a young actor and writer who also had interesting hair and good conversation; and their friend, Tim, who ran an independent record company, and with quiet awareness, often seemed to be our "tour manager" when we were out on the town.

The bunch of us spent some long, memorable nights around the kitchen table of Dave's house in the Hollywood Hills, and I met some other good characters, like Matt Stone, one of the creators of the cartoon series "South Park." I was glad to tell him that his work had helped to sustain me, and even make me laugh, during some very dark times, and his funny stories of dealing with the corporate world were so reminiscent of my own conflicts with the "business" side of the music world that I felt an instant empathy for him and his partner, Trey. Like me and my own partners, they were just a couple of more-or-less goofy guys from the suburbs (of Denver in their case) who had made it big with something they loved to do, and were now running up against people who did not really understand them at all.

One night, Andrew and I attended a live taping of Dave's TV show,

"News Radio," and another night Dave invited us to a stand-up comedy show at Club Largo. Both of those gave me some rare laughter, and reminded me of how much more "accessible" live comedy is (like live music), and of how seldom a man alone laughs out loud. Especially a man who is alone with a lot of ghosts.

Dave was dating a pretty young Canadian girl at the time, Gabrielle, and Andrew and I met the two of them for dinner before the comedy show. Later, Andrew told me she had called me "a hottie," and he laughed and teased me about that. I just blushed (no one had ever called *me* "a hottie" before — must be that Air of Tragedy again) and thought no more about it.

In the end, I stayed in Los Angeles for a whole week, which I certainly hadn't expected to do — much less mostly *enjoy* — but by the last day I was feeling restless and a little shaky. Walking around West Hollywood on a few last errands, I saw a BMW convertible that was exactly the same as Jackie's, then a movie poster of Drew Barrymore, who looked a bit like Selena, and suddenly the tears were pouring down my face.

Early the next morning, I got myself back on the road and headed down to Mexico, still thinking about everything I saw and did as a "letter to Brutus."

Nov. 25, '98
Loreto, Baja California Sur

¡Hola! Paddle-Wheeler —

As a matter of fact, it was *Walt* who recommended this town, and so far it's pretty nice. The Hotel Oasis, almost empty, and right on the beach of the Sea of Cortez, which is also almost empty. This being the week of American Thanksgiving, I thought things might start getting a bit crazy, but no sign of it so far. Not here, anyway. I've been trying to pace myself to stay away from the

"Cabos" until after the weekend, so hopefully that will work out.

Mainly I've been following Clement Salvadori's advice so far, and I'm so glad I picked up his *Motorcycle Adventures in Baja* back in Tucson. It's been a great help, and has taken me to places I wouldn't have found, and on roads I *definitely* wouldn't have found.

From L.A., I headed east on I-10, and cut south on that mountain road you and I took to San Diego, up through those high forests, meadows, and ranchlands, and down into the Anza-Borrego desert. Once again, it was nice taking it *slow*, poking around the state park and the weird RV oasis of Borrego Springs, the west side of the Salton Sea, then through El Centro and the massive irrigations of the Imperial Valley. Salvadori's recommendation in Calexico, the De Anza, looked nice, but unfortunately was no longer a *hotel*, but an apartment building, so I ended up in the heinous "El Rancho," which was not even worth its $30 tariff. I had wanted to be *central*, as usual, but for no good reason. The "town," such as it was, catered strictly to "cross-border shoppers," and there was nowhere to eat but suspect-looking Chinese and franchise burger joints. I ended up at some name-brand pizza place eating lousy spaghetti with Pepsi. And getting depressed. As it was I'd spent one too many days in L.A., just as I'd done in Santa Fe; I'd go along thinking, "this is alright, this is alright," until suddenly, it *wasn't* alright, and I was freaking!

Here's how I told it to my journal (your "alter ego" in some ways) that night in Calexico.

This should be the last entry in this U.S. journal, covering almost two months. Ups and downs. Have thought of so much that didn't get written, as usual, but one recurring reflection is the feeling of being hurt. Beyond grief, sorrow, pain, and usual, expected responses, it's a state of feeling tender, wounded, as if betrayed (ah yes — by life), and scarred beyond even my present understanding.

This must be the nadir of the whole journey (three months long as of yesterday; hard to believe. Or . . . not).

*Often thinking of home now, and hope to make it there —
whole — by New Year's. So much can happen, as we know too
well, but I would like to survive to be there this winter, see how it
goes, if I can put together some kind of life. Without sliding into
that deep, dark hole . . .*

Anyway, the border crossing was easy. In about an hour I had
my little "holográfica" sticker, for $11 instead of our three days and
who-knows-what in brokerage fees [when Brutus and I flew our
bikes into Mexico City], and I was in the dusty streets of Mexicali
— where I *immediately* got lost. Of course: it was Mexico, and a
sign was missing somewhere at a *glorieta* [traffic circle]. Eventually,
I found the road west to Tecate, through smoking, crawling
trucks, ancient, speeding buses, oil-burning pickups, cringing,
tongue-dragging dogs, sudden, unmarked *topes* [speedbumps],
army checkpoints with well-armed teenaged soldiers who spoke
no English, dusty roadsides strewn with garbage, potholes,
oncoming drivers weaving to miss them and heading straight for
me. All the good stuff.

As our friend Mills would say, "Time to fear!"

Bypassing Tijuana, I cut west and south to Ensenada (busy
and built-up, but fairly nice, with the biggest Mexican flag imaginable billowing above the waterfront), then back eastward to . . .
Mike's Sky Rancho! Mecca for dirt-bikers and Baja racers, but
Salvadori warns "it can be a rough 22 miles," and indeed it was.
Dirt, sand, rocks, stones, streams, ruts, and all that. But, he assures
you, "a well-ridden Gold Wing [heavy luxury-touring bike] can
make it, much to the disgust of the dirt riders," and sure enough,
when I finally pulled in (after having a good, long look at the last
20-foot-wide stream crossing, full of sand and stones) a bunch of
guys were standing there beside their one-cylinder, unladen dirt
bikes, and one of them started shouting, "How did you do that?"

"How did you *do* that?"

I just said, "With great fear."

They all gathered around, and he said, "You came up the same road we did?" I said, "I guess so," and he blurted out, "But you're not even *dirty!*" True, I did look quite smashing: the mechanic at Hollywood BMW had shined up the bike; I had on my relatively new Vansons [summer leathers] for the first time, and I'd even had my boots cleaned up nice in L.A. "Well," I said, "I guess it's 'cause I wasn't following anybody."

Really, it was because I'd been going so *slow!*

Anyway, it sure looked funny to see my big red GS lined up with about 30 dirt bikes and a couple of ATVs in the courtyard that night. I was their total hero (except for the ones that *ignored* me, in their "disgust"). Nearly everybody there was on organized Baja tours, so at the communal dinner I was put with the other "oddballs:" two older guys who'd come in by pickup — one an ornithologist, Jim, who'd been flying his private plane into Baja for 20 years, the other a botanist, Norm, who *lived* in southern Baja. Great dinner companions, and I picked their brains about the flora and fauna I'd been seeing in the southwestern U.S. (it was Jim who confirmed that the swallow-like birds I'd been seeing in the high desert were horned larks), and they told me about the birds and plants I would be seeing further south in Baja. (Here in Loreto, I bought Norm's book, *Plants and Trees of Baja California*, so I can learn more of their names.)

As Salvadori describes Mike's, "it ain't fancy, but it's fun," and at 4,000 feet it was also darn cold that night (low 30s) and I slept with all my clothes on under the blankets. Since the generator went off at 9:00, and those Petzl headlamps aren't much good for reading, I was asleep pretty early, and in no hurry to get moving in the morning. And despite my impact on the dirt riders, I wasn't feeling too cocky, because I still had to make it *out* those 22 obstacle-ridden miles.

Of course, it's often easier that second time, and so it was; especially without the sun in my face, so I could tell the difference between dirt, sand, rock, and stones before I was *on* it (or *in* it).

Then I took another "short cut," 50 kilometres [31 miles] of decently graded dirt back to the main north-south road; after the ornithologist, the botanist, and Mike himself (son of the original Mike, apparently) had assured me there would be no *deep sand*. And sure enough, other than some washboard and some deadly switchbacks (Hunter Mountain-like, once more), that was a pretty nice piece o' dirt.

Then it was back to diesel cheese and oil-burning pickups for awhile, and I stopped that night at what Salvadori described as a "must stop;" "if you wouldn't be fazed by the road conditions," that being three miles of *heinous* sand on top of a washboard-ridged surface (yikes!) to a place on the Pacific shore called The Old Mill, site of a former mineral refinery and fish cannery, now a pleasant little motel ($25), restaurant, and bar. (The peso is now at 10 to one, so things are *cheap*.)

One group of the "dirt-dudes" was staying there too, and it seems they had a bet going among themselves about which route the "street bike" had taken, and some of them were shaking their heads in disbelief when I said "that lovely dirt road going west out of Valle de Trinidad." Ha-ha-ha! Scooter Trash *rules!*

Sort of. Or at least, we *used* to. Some rival gang done put a double-whammy, heebie, jeebie, triple-gainer, tri-square quad-ruple, jim-jammer *curse* on us, that's what *I* think. There ain't no other way to account for all this, less'n we been *hexed*.

The last few days have been almost comical in that respect too. Somehow I twisted my back on the way down from L.A. (best I can recall, while looking back at one of those 45° V-intersections), and it's been giving me fits of pain, stiffness, and impeded motion (familiar to you, I know), then, after 38,000 trouble-free kilome-tres, my GS has developed a disconcerting "lurch" when I downshift to third (though not when I upshift?) in the last couple of days. In L.A., I bought a spare headlight and taillight bulb to carry with me, and today an *indicator* bulb went out (of course). I was able to find one here, but while I was installing it, I unlocked the steering to test it and knocked my helmet off the handlebar, scratching the face-shield to hell. Of course I've got a spare, but it's my old bug-and-gravel-pitted veteran of the whole last tour. None of these things would have been a problem a week ago, but now it's like, well, maybe I can get it sorted out in a couple of weeks, in Mexico City: along with whatever *else* goes wrong before then. And then there's my fargin' *ulcer*. Yesterday I tried having huevos rancheros for breakfast, and suffered all day, and today I couldn't resist an omelette "con chorizo y chesa," and felt like I'd eaten a goddam jumping-cholla cactus!

What the hell is going *on* here, you know what I'm saying?

And of course, as predicted, all the basic functions have become just a little more difficult here: gas, food, water, lodging, riding, navigating, telephones, mail, that sort of thing. (My Baja-expert dinner companions at Mike's warned me against trying to send anything home by Mexican mail, so I can only hope this letter will even *get* to you.) One of the dirt-bike guides also tipped me off about filling up in El Rosario yesterday, for even though my map showed a Pemex in Cataviña, apparently it's always either out of gas or the pumps aren't working, and sure enough I had to go over 200 *miles* before there was another one, keeping the speed around 110 kph [69 mph], and making 370 kilometres [231 miles] on a tankful, and the day before I'd had to use my spare can to make it to another of those widely scattered "Magna Sin" Pemexes. The one I stopped at today had only *one* of its four pumps working.

But, to quote the English expression Brad and I love so much, "Still . . . mustn't grumble." (Which must always follow an extended rant of grumbling, as this does!)

Yesterday I did a long stretch, 600 kilometres [375 miles], down through the Vizcaino Desert (can't think what sets it apart, for all of Baja is desert, I'm learning), passing the famous "boojum" trees, organ pipe and cardón cactus, cholla, some agaves that resembled Joshua trees, ocotillo, barrel cactus, and fat-trunked baobab-like trees (called elephant trees), palo verde, and mesquite, then into a long stretch of low scrub after Guerrero Negro.

It was a good road overall, narrow, but not too many potholes. I stopped for the night at the date-palm oasis of San Ignacio, which Salvadori rates as "the most charming town in Baja." So far I would agree — a laurel-shaded zócalo [main square] walled in by ancient shops and a 17ᵗʰ century Spanish mission, silent but for barking dogs and crowing roosters and kids playing soccer, nestled in a lush valley of date palms amid miles of surrounding cactus desert. At sunset, hundreds of turkey vultures circled in to roost in the date palms and the communication tower.

The six-unit motel there was $20 (cash in hand, never mind registering or anything "official" like that) and was apparently built by a German sailor who jumped ship in Santa Rosalia (the port just down the road where I had breakfast this morning), back around the turn of the century, and his descendants still run it. So many *stories*, everywhere I go. Santa Rosalia was developed by the *French*, as a copper-mining center, and the church there was designed by Gustav Eiffel, all of metal gridwork and riveted panels, for the Paris Exposition in 1886 or so, then disassembled and brought *here*, to Baja California. Wild. (It looks like a Quonset hut combined with Captain Nemo's *Nautilus* from *20,000 Leagues Under the Sea.* In a *nice* way.)

Today's opening journal entry is fairly "illustrative," I think:

Nov. 25 San Ignacio — Loreto
95,037 (303 kilometres) [189 miles]

Sparkling morning riding out through palms, to desert and volcanoes.

Rare breakfast stop, here on sunny terrace of Hotel Frances in Santa Rosalia, old mining town with locomotive and rusted train cars on display. Nice. Quiet.

Gila woodpecker on pole, hummingbirds in laurel tree, vulture spreads wings, back to sun, on utility pole across street.

Eiffel pre-fab church a sight. So many stories everywhere.

First sight of Sea of Cortez also, blue and calm. Island on horizon. Slept well, back a little better. Blazing through Cadillac Desert — better not run out of books!

Thinking today as I rode that my survival remains an act of pure will. Holding myself together like a soldier wounded in battle, and feel that I could collapse from within at any time. No peace anywhere, no redemption imaginable. Just sense of waiting, killing time. Waiting for what? For time to pass, I guess. Can there be healing? Don't think so. Only strive to minimize scars. Not get too twisted, too crippled inside.

(Still, mustn't grumble . . .)

Nov. 26, '98
Loreto

Alright, alright, let's try to lighten this thing up a little. Don't want to get *you* all depressed too (oh no!). Obviously, I'm hanging around for another day, and I may stay tomorrow too. I'm tempted, but I'll wait and decide in the morning. Whatever happens, I'm bound to stay one day too long again.

Yesterday, I was wading in the ocean a little, and a local started yelling something at me and pointing at the soles of his feet. I was thinking he meant sharp stones, coral, or maybe sea urchins, but I asked at the front desk, and the guy told me he had been warning me about *stingrays,* and said it wasn't a good idea to go in barefoot. So I went out and bought some chic black rubber sandals, which will come in handy for walking around in too, now that I'm getting down into the true *tropics.*

(Are you getting bored yet, hearing about my *shopping?* Well, too bad, you big fargin' loser; what are you, too *busy?* Ha-ha-ha!)

As I was saying in a postcard to my grandfather today, "get down here right away; it's hot, it's sunny, it's cheap, and you can lay in a hammock under the palms and read all day!" That's what I did, other than walk around the pleasant town, visit the old mission and its well-done museum, and go bird-watching along the "malecón" (seawall), the beach, and small lagoon.

Now I'm going to have the "Thanksgiving Special" dinner here at the Oasis. Not exactly "local cuisine," but my stupid stomach will probably like it better (though Baja is pretty much "seafood central" anyway, and that hasn't been a problem). We'll see what happens when I head over to the "mainland" (as it seems to be called around here), which I'm planning to do by the ferry between La Paz and Mazatlán. I haven't yet looked at the map beyond there. Maybe I'll head for Oaxaca, for a start. Just for you.

Because of course it's written between all these lines that you are sorely missed on this trip, but be assured that there are several roads and interesting places that Salvadori goes into positive *raptures* about, especially some particularly tempting dirt side-trips, that I'm going to pass up. And not only because I'm "un pollo" [chicken] (just ask the guys at Mike's Sky Rancho, man!), but I've got to save a few things for us to explore, right?

(By the way, I forgot to wish you a Happy Thanksgiving. Since you're an "American Resident" these days, did they give you a special dinner? Also, if you have to hang around there for a while, do you think they'll give you a green card? Probably . . .)

Anyway, it's about time to bring this exciting episode to a close, in hopes that maybe I can get it *mailed* tomorrow. (And then *its* adventure will begin: here to La Paz to Mazatlán to Mexico City to who-knows-where, and hopefully, to *you*.) Our last phone conversation left me feeling that you had a pretty good grip on your situation, with realistic expectations (hardly "hopes") for your immediate future, and I sure hope it works out in some more-or-less "tolerable" fashion.

I'm sure you're not exactly a happy camper these days, and I imagine you're looking forward to Christmas about as much as *I* am. And like me, at best you can only feel resigned: "just sense of waiting, killing time. Waiting for what? For time to pass, I guess."

Still, mustn't grumble . . .

Your,
Ghost Rider

After a longish march through the pretty little town of Loreto to the post office, I walked back along the *malecón* to watch the boys fishing off the pier. They were pulling them in as fast as they could. One rangy-looking young man came over to my perch on a big rock and tried to engage me in conversation. He said he was from Sinaloa, the state directly across the Sea of Cortez from Baja California, and when I told him I was from Toronto, he nodded sagely and said, "Blue Yays," which stumped me for a moment, until I realized he must be a baseball fan.

He asked me if I wanted to go to a "Mexican party," with "lots of ladies," and when I declined, he asked if I wanted some "mota." I didn't know that word, but he translated it as "weed" (apparently from *la motivador*, "motivator," curiously). When I said no thanks, he said, "You prefer smoking 'skunkweed,' like the Americanos?" I shook my head no again, and said "too many police."

Cryptically, he said, "I forgot about that."

I continued ignoring him as much as I could, watching the fish and the birds, but he persisted, telling me in a confiding way, "I'm shy too."

I nodded and shook his hand, then walked back to the Oasis motel and went for a swim in the warm, shallow sea, then lay in the hammock for awhile. I finished *Cadillac Desert* and went on to Mark Twain's *Roughing It*, an account of his travels from Missouri to gold-rush country during the 1850s.

In the evening, I walked back up the *malecón* to a restaurant with the unfortunate name of El Chile Willie's. I ordered a chowder, which never came, and I waited so long for my skewered shrimp and lobster that I wrote six pages of a letter to my friend Gay, bringing her up to date on my latest travels, inner and outer.

Back along the water again, I stopped at the hotel bar, thinking I would sit outside with a cognac and continue writing the letter to Gay. There were only two other customers, a very drunk, though pleasant, English couple. The man could hardly talk, his face all slack as he intently tried to pour the contents of his saucer into his cup. The "Englishman's wife," on the other hand, started talking and couldn't seem to *stop*.

In an accent that is called "Estuary English," as spoken by educated people in the general area of the Thames estuary, everything she said seemed to end with an exclamation mark. "You're so *quiet!*," she said, "I've been *watching* you!"

"You must be on *sabbatical*, aren't you? Is that it? Always reading and keeping to yourself, aren't you? You want *nothing* to do with humanity, do you? What are you reading so seriously, anyway?"

I just blushed and mumbled something about Mark Twain, looking down at my feet, and she kept going.

"You want nothing to do with humanity, I can see it! Oh yes! I've been watching you!"

I blushed and mumbled again.

"You're a *striking*-looking gentleman, *you* are!" (Me?)

"I call you the gentle giant!" (What?)

"You're *my* gentle giant!" (Me?)

"Really, you're just *it* with me — you and my husband!"

That worthy looked up with a drunken laugh and said, "You can try *that* role for 24 hours if you like, mate."

I blushed and mumbled some more, and he motioned to the bartender to bring me another cognac, on him. Thanking him, and nodding quickly to his wife, I went outside to sit and write, eventually confiding to my journal, "must admit she got me all 'kerfuffled.'"

From Loreto, I continued south along the narrow Baja peninsula to La Paz, taking a scenic route recommended by Clement Salvadori in *Motorcycle Adventures in Baja,* on 40 miles of smooth dirt through rugged cactus desert to a paved stretch of what *used* to be the main road, the so-called "West Side Highway."

La Paz, the capital of Baja California Sur, was a good-sized city (100,000 people), a fishing-boat harbor with a nice waterfront and an imposing stone cathedral on the zócalo of trees and gardens. Checking into the hotel right on the harbor, the first thing I did, while fishing for a tip for the bellman, was drop my wallet down the elevator shaft. Passport, credit cards, cash, traveller's cheques — everything. It took two maintenance guys about half an hour to get it out of there, between two sticks poking down through the doorframe.

One of my main reasons for stopping in La Paz was to book passage on the ferry to Mazatlán, and once my "essentials" were safely recovered, I hustled over to the ferry office, only to learn that I could only book *one* day before, not two or three. Oh. However, I learned that I could book my cabin at the company's office in Cabo San Lucas, so I decided to take care of it there.

On the way back to the hotel I passed the cathedral, and felt drawn inside. In the Catholic fashion, the interior was vast, ornate, and silent, filled with gilded, colorful statues of the Virgin, various saints, gory crucifixes, the Stations of the Cross around the walls, votive candles burning at the altars, and the afternoon light filtering through the tall stained-glass windows across a few bowing figures, mostly women. I chose an empty pew in the middle and sat down to enjoy a moment of stillness and peace. Not prayer, exactly, but perhaps "a step outside myself."

In a Catholic church I often felt a connection to Selena, though not in a *religious* way, but because of a memory of her response to the church of Sacre-Coeur, in Paris. Near the end of Rush's most recent tour of Europe, part of the *Roll The Bones* tour in 1993, Jackie, Selena, and Deb had met me in Paris for a few days. After one day off together, Selena drove with me and my driver, Peter (an old friend from my younger days in London), to Amsterdam for a show, then back to Paris, where we spent another few days walking the streets of that beautiful city. It was Selena's first visit to Paris, and she was powerfully impressed.

One day, the four of us climbed the high stairs to the church of Sacre-Coeur, perched in white splendor atop the Butte de Montmartre. Like her parents, Selena would never "get" religion, but we all understood spirituality, and at age 15, Selena was suddenly and completely entranced by the devotional atmosphere inside that church, the nuns singing softly, the respectful hush, the incense and candles. Wanting to light one of the votive candles herself, she decided to light it for the only Catholic she could think of, her cousin Sean.

As we walked quietly through the church, and up around the dome to admire the view over all of Paris, Selena was wide-eyed and filled with the *spirit* of the place, the awesome scale, the stillness, the grandeur and the grace — exactly the effect churches were designed to have, but religion too often degraded. After that day, Selena had been forever impressed by the spell cast by that church, and now that she was gone, I discovered that visiting the Catholic churches in Mexico helped me to connect with her, as she was then, and to the good memories of that time in Paris.

The trip home from Paris had been memorable, too. Deb flew back to Toronto, while Peter drove Jackie, Selena, and me to Southampton in England, where we boarded the QE2 for a five-day voyage to New York City. Truth to tell, the girls were a little bored sometimes, but I had just *loved* that crossing — reading together in our cabin with its private deck and sliding glass door looking out on the open ocean, roaming the deserted decks on cold, foggy afternoons, playing deck games together, wonderful food and drink, and formal dress for dinner every night — that part Selena had loved, for she always loved to get dressed up. I was glad to have those memories, at least, but they still burned me. The tears came as I sat in a pew in a Mexican church and thought about all that had been. One step forward, one step back.

The next day I continued on to Cabo San Lucas, and over dinner that night in the open-air restaurant I noted my impressions of that fabled resort town.

Nov. 29 La Paz — Cabo San Lucas
95,779 (243 kilometres) [152 miles]

Well. About as expected. No, not as bad, so far. Can't swim in ocean, because of riptide. Sound of surf from room is nice, though, and the air is noticeably warmer since crossing Tropic of Cancer today.

Solmar Suites hotel, swim-up bars (three pools), massive, manicured beach (empty), beautiful rocks and cliffs behind, real little poinsettias on bar tables, real fan-palm palapa (shelter), romantic Mexican pop music (sentimental, anyway), good margarita. Cactus wrens, English sparrows, American "yackers."

Thinking how my opinion softened toward that loudly self-amused, fat American with brutish face and cigar. Three of them caught marlins today, he fought his for 45 minutes, and said (or shouted), "I'll never forget today! I'll never forget today!" Had to forgive boorishness for that boyish excitement. A little, anyway . . .

[Later] Dinner. Weird to be in resort atmosphere like this, alone.

And now — here come the mariachis! I put my 20 pesos in the big guitar and asked for "Guadalajara," which was . . . perfunctory, I guess. Maybe I'm spoiled by Mariachi Cobre [an excellent "progressive mariachi" group whose CDs Brutus and I had bought in Mexico City]. Or Oaxaca [where we had first heard real *mariachi music].*

(Another half-baked theory, this one on the roots of the mariachi style: combination of flamenco, gypsy, folk, opera, Moorish. Name comes from French "mariage," as they were hired for weddings during French occupation in 1800s.)

Been in Mexico one week now. Half in Loreto, I realize. That seems to be the place. If I had any brains, I wouldn't tell anyone about it.

But I don't, and I will.

[Later] Big ring around moon, three or four days from full. Rain coming? Big wave every 10 seconds, sometimes like distant explosion, booming sub-bass.

After lengthy struggle with phone (for reasons too stupid to go into, to quote Mark Riebling), finally got through to Steven, who seemed exasperated not to have heard from me, to know what I wanted to do; when I had thought it was understood, and had been waiting to hear from him, back in L.A. Oh well. Guess he's got his problems too . . .

Jackie's brother Steven was a semi-retired diving instructor and "old salt," and he had also been hit very hard by the family tragedies and the waves they sent through the whole web of relationships, and by the sudden, shared shock that everyone around us felt — that such things *can* happen to us. Steven had been part of my life and one of my best friends (in every sense of the phrase) since my teenage years, when he and his brother Keith (now the majordomo of my Quebec home) had worked at the local record store, Sam the Record Man, in my hometown of St. Catharines, Ontario. The record store was the second-favorite hangout for a young musician, after the musical instrument store, Ostanek's, where we would stand around among the guitars and drums for hours, talking and dreaming of our golden futures.

During our early 20s Keith, Steven, and I had lived together in a house in the country with another friend, Wayne, just before I started going out with Jackie. In fact, I ended up moving out of that house to move in with *her*, and I remember being nervous about telling them, afraid they would be upset about me "living in sin" with their little sister. But Steven had actually steered the two of us together in a way, sometimes asking me to give Jackie a ride home from the record store if I was hanging around at closing time, so I needn't have worried; the two brothers were happy for us both.

Through the unimaginable twists and cuts of fate, everything had changed for all of us, and like me, Steven found it a heavy weight to bear. He was the kind of man who felt responsible for everyone in his family, all the time, and perhaps deep inside he felt these losses as a kind of "failure" — as if his loved ones had died "on his watch," when it had been *his* job to keep them alive. I understood that feeling, because of course I *shared* it. Perhaps the first responsibility of a husband and father is to protect his wife and child, and deep inside myself I felt that I had failed at that, too. For anyone who knew and cared about Jackie and Selena, there were so many shades of darkness in those tragedies.

I have already described Steven's leading role in that long-running nightmare, visiting us in London and helping us get situated, moving into the Toronto house and to Barbados with us, supervising Jackie's treatments and care (he was also a trained paramedic), and playing "gatekeeper" when the number of concerned friends at our door became overwhelming.

His wife Shelly, an emergency room doctor, became another tireless and invaluable friend, lending her medical expertise and sharing the late-night watches during Jackie's decline, and I hadn't seen either of them since Barbados. They were planning a visit to Belize in December, and I had promised to meet them there, and was still intending to do so. I guess Steven had forgotten that when I say I'm going to do something, I generally do it, and had been waiting for some more formal plans to be made. He didn't understand my loose travelling style, by which I had been gradually making my way toward one spurious goal after another — to Vancouver to visit Danny and Janette, to Las Vegas for the racing school, to Belize to meet up with Steven and Shelly. It all made sense to me somehow, but perhaps not to anyone else.

From Cabo San Lucas I made my way back to La Paz for the ferry crossing, then started working my way across the "mainland" of Mexico, a story taken up in a letter to Brutus written a few days later, with journal entries as I included them to him.

Dec. 5, '98
Hotel Camino Real
Oaxaca

¡Hola, Pollo Loco!

Once again, this is a place I don't need to describe to you, but don't go running away (ha ha); I've got some stories to tell about *getting* here.

When last we spoke, I was "lounging in Loreto" (for I'm hoping you received that letter — and this one, for that matter!), which I did for another day after that. It joins my select list of excellent small towns, along with St. Helena, California, and Moab, Utah. Maybe I'll take you there sometime.

[Recap of ride from there to La Paz to Cabo San Lucas]

With everything I had read and heard about Cabo San Lucas, I was prepared to *hate* it, but it really wasn't that bad. I stayed at a resort-type place out toward Land's End ("Finisterre"), which was fairly empty (continuing my progress as "Mr. Out-of-Season"), and walked into town several times taking care of business, and even for dinner and a stroll around at night. And you know, despite the Hard Rock Café and Planet Hollywood, and even KFC and Domino's and Burger King, it remains a Mexican town at heart, in so many subtle but unmistakable ways. That character is pretty hard to kill, and it ends up that the *franchises* look out of place, while the town survives despite all. If you're looking for it, anyway.

From Cabo I followed the "loop" back to La Paz, with the blue Pacific on one side and miles of green cardón cactus (similar to saguaro) on the other, stopping in a charming little town called Todos Santos for breakfast, at the Hotel California (since 1928, and claimed by some to be the inspiration for the Eagles' song), which would have been worth a stay, I think.

Maybe I'll take you there sometime.

Back in La Paz nice and early, I stopped in at a small motorcycle shop recommended by the invaluable Mr. Salvadori, bought some good 20-50 oil, and performed an *epic* oil change right out front. "No problemo," a big contrast to places like Yuma, or even Whitehorse, where I got turned down all over the place. Never understood why.

The helpful travel agent in Cabo, Eduardo, assured me that I needed to be at the ferry dock by noon (for a three o'clock sailing), and so I was: only to sit and swelter for three hours, and be the last one loaded on, along with three California dudes on incredibly loaded dirt bikes, carrying huge packs, surfboards, and even a *guitar.* They admitted they didn't have much advantage over me, and had been having some trouble getting through sand. I guess so!

The ferry turned out to be one of the nicest I've ever been on. Though fairly old (built in 1974, and a veteran of the long-discontinued Cabo-Puerto Vallarta run), I had a nice cabin with two berths separated by a little settee and table, and there was a proper restaurant, like on the Naples-Tunis ferry. People were friendly, and music played *everywhere:* a live band in the bar, a "CD jukebox" in the open-air bar at the stern, and even when I wandered up by the bridge, I heard music playing from there. In the restaurant they were playing a Madonna anthology, and that got a bit weepy for me when things like "La Isla Bonita" came on, and reminded me of Selena and me driving in the Porsche from

Lac Echo, with the top down and that song turned way up loud. Everything else I heard, however, was *Mexican* music, in Spanish, which again testifies to the strength of their excellent culture.

The moon was almost full, and the Sea of Cortez was calm, with enough of a tailwind behind us to make the air on deck seem still. Altogether it was a very enjoyable crossing, getting into Mazatlán about 8:00 the following morning.

Dec. 6, '98
Cuernavaca

Okay, it's a new scene now: I hope you're keeping up with the program. We're staying at the very excellent "Las Mañanitas" here, one of those Relais and Chateaux joints, I noticed by the front entrance when I arrived; after touring around for a while looking for it! Cuernavaca remains as difficult to navigate in daylight as it was when we arrived in the dark.

Apparently this place has been ranked among the best hotels in the world, and I can believe it, with lush lawns and gardens in a peaceful walled courtyard, decorated with peacocks, crowned cranes, flamingoes, and parrots, and an elegant suite with a private terrace. And yes, I chose it from the Lonely Planet guide. I can't imagine how we ended up in that lowlife "posada" last time, unless you were going through the Rough Guide in what's-her-name's Volkswagen, on the way from the airport!

Anyway, we're getting ahead of our story, aren't we? Getting off the ferry in Mazatlán, around eight in the morning, I had been powerfully tempted to head straight for the old "Devil's Backbone" up to Durango and the "silver cities," but adding up days, subtracting Sundays (for "practical purposes," i.e., Mexico City service and resupply), and planning toward meeting up with Steven in a week or so, way over in Belize, plus not wanting to

repeat the same route *exactly*, I decided to head south for a bit.
Now we join my journal entry from later that day:

Restaurant Cuiza on island in river, mid Puerto Vallarta, nice jazz
playing. Feet and eyes worn out from sticker-hunting, of all things,
but it keeps me off — er, on the streets.

In a tourist-o-rama town like this, you'd think it would be easy.
But you'd be wrong. Must have looked in 25 or 30 stores (the tackier
the better) all along the malecón, all through the old town, and
found one cheesy little sticker in the far corner of the funky old-
town, by Playa des Arcos. But it's good to have a quest, however
cheap and meaningless. Or maybe especially so.

Nice hotel, though a bit messed up with pre-season renovations;
that's what I get for being "Mr. Out-of-Season" again. Restaurant
pleasant too, right beside river, lights in trees, candles on tables,
good music. Shame to be alone. (No tears tonight please.)

Such lush greenery today. Was trying to remember when I last
rode in the shade. Truly can't remember. Tunnels of trees and
palms hung with ivy, tall grasses, cliffs and mountains, some great
twisty bits, winding up and down through trees.

This place, hotel just across river, and back streets of town (cool
church, e.g.) proof that there's always a real town behind the
schlock. Maybe even in Acapulco. Though probably not in "Canned
Coon" and "Cozusmell."

Good meal too, blue corn and crab chowder, "three ravioli"
combo with crab, shrimp, and fish in cream sauce. Now cheesecake
with fruit, and coffee.

Strange feeling riding away from Mazatlán. Felt less remote,
somehow; maybe because at least partly "familiar." Though didn't
really recognize anything, possibly because when Brutus and I went
up that way, from Manzanillo, we were pretty tense: after the big
crash and all. [As mentioned, in our first trip through central
Mexico, Brutus had gone off the road in this area, cracked a couple

of ribs, and messed up his bike pretty badly.] Yet I had a stronger sense of "foreign." Maybe because it's not *desert! Tropical green, all around, until sight of the bay (thick haze all day too), which is thought to be an old crater.*

So much passing today, constant trucks and buses, especially before Tepic, turnoff to Guadalajara and Mexico City. Diesel cheese!

Jovial Mexican on street says to me, "Señor! Where is your wife?" Ach.

Dec. 3 Puerto Vallarta — Zihuatanejo
97,200 (752 kilometres) [470 miles]

Handful to spell, this town, but not to sing! ["Zee-what-an-ay-ho!"] Passed by here with Brutus on way to breakfast stop in Ixtapa, before his mighty crash. Experienced that whole day today, but in reverse.

Passed 40,000 kilometres [25,000 miles] today, during this long, long ride. Very tough, with either lots of trucks and buses, or relatively empty and ceaselessly narrow and winding along coast. No Pemex [gas station] for long way; we must have been lucky, for I had to use extra can at about 340 kilometres [213 miles], after filling up near Manzanillo. Had thought of aiming for Acapulco, but this was plenty far enough. In about 4:30, after nine long hours; and with no breakfast. My first sort-of plan for today was to stop at Las Hadas for two or three days, but started looking at map and adding up days, and decided to "do" Oaxaca now, and maybe get to Palenque or something after Mexico City.

Different "wave sound" here, more "white noise" and constant. Got up last night to see big waves coming in, like a storm. This morning passed "John Huston's Restaurant," Playa La Blanca, I think it is, with original sets from Night of the Iguana. *Like Las*

*Hadas, next time. So beautifully green and lush around there, with
palm-furred mountainsides, and the same all the way. Occasionally
bits slightly drier, more scrubby, but always green.*

*Too late and too far away (and too tired) to check out this town
for "realness," but last night's live music at the waterfront
amphitheatre was almost all locals. Seems to be generally true that
if there was a town, there is a town. Just have to look for it.
Mexican culture is strong: "You cain't stop it." And glad I am.*

Well, hadn't meant to give you such a *long* extract there, but it
all seemed to be stuff that might interest you. Sorry about all the
talk of nice meals and that; probably a bit of a torment compared
to the fare you're receiving at *that* Relais and Chateaux joint!

From the map (that lying Mexican map!), I decided that
Zihuatanejo to Oaxaca ought to be "doable," so off I went. The first
obstacle was our old nemesis, Acapulco; if there was a way *around*
it, I sure couldn't find it, and no helpful sign appeared to guide me
(surprise, surprise), so right through *miles* of busy, sweltering,
smoky, dusty, and frustrating Pie de la Cuesta, "downtown"
Acapulco and out along the coast by Las Brisas, the "pink palace."
As I noted in my journal about Acapulco, "I'm really getting to
hate that place!" Though I can't deny there's lots of *Mexico* in it —
just none of the good parts.

Then I had to stop for at least four roadblocks today, mostly
army, but one with the notoriously corrupt "Judiciales." I don't
remember *any* last time, do you? Result of Zapatistas, or rising
crime from failed economy? Pressure from the U.S. to *appear* to
combat illegal immigration and drugs? Or make-work project for
the military, to keep them out of the "coup" business? Could be.

Anyway, with all that, it was already about 3:00 before I turned
off into the mountains, taking a different road than we did, but I
still thought I might make it by, say, 7:00. Fool that I am. Washed-
out and potholed, endless second- and third-gear twists and turns

with patches of loose gravel, villages with *thousands* of topes [speedbumps], often unmarked, trucks and buses to get around, dodging pigs, dogs, chickens, cows, horses, and burros. All the good stuff.

And soon, it started to get dark . . .

Oh man, was I *freaking!* The first time on this whole long journey I've travelled at night, and of all places: in the mountains of Oaxaca. In addition to the obvious hazards to life and limb, apparently the "bandido" threat is very active these days on the roads of Oaxaca, even along the coast, and Lonely Planet warns, "the best defence is not to travel at night." But I didn't know what else to do; there wasn't a Best Western anywhere to be seen, and camping at the roadside didn't seem a particularly clever option either. Being in such a weakened state anyway, regarding internal strength and resilience, I was nearly in tears trying to face up to this crisis. Nothing to do but ride onward, though slowly, carefully, and fearfully.

It was 9:30 before I made it to the Camino Real Hotel in Oaxaca, 918 kilometres [574 miles] and 14 hours from Zihuatanejo. I guess you could call that "doable." Saw one hotel, on the dusty main street of Tlaxiaco (once called "Paris Chiquita" — ?), which seemed to be the happening town out there, but by then I'd had an hour or so to get used to the darkness, the moon was coming up, and — truth to tell — the place looked pretty scary. I wasn't *that* desperate by then, even after getting lost there (no signs at main junction), and was actually glad, just after that, to see a sign saying "Oaxaca 144."

"Oh, that's not so bad," I thought.

At least the last 65 kilometres were "Cuota" [toll road], fast, safe, and lightly trafficked. But dark! First time I've ridden at night this whole trip; hope it's the last. Not as horrible as I'd thought it was going to be, when I realized it was going to happen, but bad enough. And carries the potential for *so* much worse: a flat tire, a breakdown, a crash, *bandidos.*

Never a dull moment, that's for sure, and I never had a moment of feeling really tired, either, in the sense of being *drowsy.* Yesterday and today, fired up with a sense of mission, commitment, and 100% alertness. Ready for anything, all the time.

Plenty tired *now,* though.

However, next morning, I was sitting at a sunny café in the zócalo having "huevos oaxaqueños," watching the strongly "indígena"-looking people go by, and thinking, "was it worth it?"

Hell, no. I was exhausted, sore, bleary-eyed, stiff all over, with blisters on my hands and a *very* tender ass! I felt *awful.* But at least I was in Oaxaca, and with a whole day to spend. I didn't feel like doing anything major, like the ruins of Monte Alban, but there was an excellent new museum in the convent beside the church of Santo Domingo, and a collection of pre-Hispanic art in the Rufino Tamaya museum, and of course, sticker-hunting (fruitless, alas).

Unfortunately I couldn't get a table overlooking the zócalo at El Asador Vasco (Saturday night, after all), but it worked out okay. The "pollo en mole negro" *was* worth all the trouble of getting there (and had been a main inspiration). There wasn't much happening in the zócalo yet, and this time they had an excellent group, "Les Romanceros de México," playing right in the restaurant, with three of those 12-string mandolin-type players, two guitarists, and a young guy on tambourine and maracas (good too). After dinner, I strolled around, things just getting going at 9:00, and had my scuffed old Rockports painstakingly shined. Marimba music seems to be very "in" this year in Oaxaca, for there were two groups working the square, but only one mariachi group. It wasn't quite as happening as when we were there, or perhaps not that early, for there were certainly lots of *people* around, but I was still too tired to hang around much later. And no complaints, it's still a most *excellent* city. Maybe I'll take you there *again* sometime!

The streets were thronged with hawkers (lots of mylar balloons), families, and a fair number of police. Despite all my protests, I must admit that does make me feel more secure in a crowded street situation, especially after reading the latest reports on Mexico City's current crime situation — whoa! It seems to be a *lot* worse than when we were here, since the economy took that big dive. After reading that stuff, I got more serious about security, and was working off three separate wallets — leg, belt pack, and another one hidden with my good watches in the pocket of my rolled-up day-pack in the duffel bag. I should come out with *something* remaining. Also, there are tales of hijackers on the Oaxaca roads at night; kept me alert last night too!

Anyway, it's the next morning now, in Cuernavaca, and I had a nice walk around yesterday, to the Jardín Borda, summer home of our old buddies Mad Maximilian and the lovely Carlota [Emperor and Empress of Mexico for three years, in the 1860s, which resulted in him being executed by a firing squad in Querétaro, and Carlota going insane and living as a ward of the Vatican for another 30 years, still thinking she was the empress of Mexico], the Palacio de Cortés, and through the busy streets of this rather *frantic* city, in which this hotel and its beautiful gardens make a lovely oasis.

So much *life*, talk and laughter and music, buying and selling, shoe-shining, politicizing, and birds squawking in the treetops so loud I was sure they were *toys* or something (long-tailed grackles). The city is a bit grungy, it's true, and there's too much traffic in those small streets, but as many cities know, here and in Europe, that's hard to fix. I also noted the stoplight merchants: gum, candy, Santa hats, lottery tickets, newspapers, but best of all, a *fire-eater*.

Today I'm off to visit our pals at Grupo Bavaria [the BMW dealership in Mexico City we had visited on our journey], Pablo, Rodolfo, and Miguel (I think that was the little mechanic's name, no?), hoping they're still at the same place on Calzada Tlalpan. If not, I'm in trouble, for it's my "no-drive day" in Mexico City. [To combat air pollution the city only allows vehicles whose licence numbers end with certain digits to drive on particular weekdays]. But I've written down old Martín's number ["ambassador" from BMW club], just in case I need some help.

Interesting that the ride up from Oaxaca to here didn't seem nearly as dramatic as it did going the other way, a few years back. I asked myself in my journal, "more experienced, or just *spoiled?* Well, I still *liked* it, just wasn't *fazed!*"

Anyway, it's me off to "Make-sicko" City [courtesy of Mexican writer Octavio Paz], where I'll get this mailed, and send you a couple more books too. The next exciting installment of this story, the journey to Belize, is sure to follow soon. For now, know that I think of you every day, and that there are lots of great places just waiting for you.

Maybe you can take me there sometime!

El viajero fantomo

[Journal notes]

Four Seasons Hotel, Mexico City,
December 9th

In El Restaurante, with excellent guitar duo playing from balcony in courtyard. Wish they'd lay off the Christmas stuff though. No one else here, at 7:00, but I'll just drink champagne by myself. I'll show them!

And write myself a letter.

Earlier today, while riding, I was thinking of how missing my girls was so often like a physical ache, and just now, that connected with the Ghost Rider — "phantom pain." Hurting for a piece of you that's been torn away.

Everything well organized to leave here. Laundry done, "dress up" clothes dry-cleaned, box of stuff sent home, so luggage a little lighter, books and letter to Brutus, business taken care of, all that, and hope bike will be happy too. On the "last leg" now.

Nice talk with waiter about different parts of Mexico. Such good staff in this place, in every capacity. Expensive, and worth it. Going all out, with Oscietra caviar and huachinango with purees of tomato and huitlacoche. Waiter surprised I can even pronounce that last one [a kind of fungus, like truffles, considered a delicacy], but I just told him, "Well, I've travelled here before, and once you learn to say Teotihuacán, or huachinango, you get the idea."

Oh man, what a meal. Devoured in about three minutes, but couldn't help it. Too good.

Suddenly at 8:00, everybody shows up. More beautiful women. (Not that I care.) Toying with notion that, in terms of what I expressed in The Masked Rider, *Mexico offers both Africa and Paris. Soul and sophistication.*

Just looked around to see if I was the only one here alone. No, there's one other loser. I mean loner. Oh joy.

Also just had glimpse into future (a wishful one, anyway). For example, transcribing these notes, and even expanding on them — maybe make a book out of all this, after all. Hope that happens, in a way, and yet . . . what a long, mysterious road the future seems like from here. Can't even picture it, really, except in limited terms of maybe two months. Too scary. Still, right now two months is plenty to think about. That's, like, next year!

Maybe it will be okay . . .

After dinner, strolled out into courtyard, fountain playing, guitars playing, big crowd on open terrace upstairs, lots of people in bar, couldn't go back to room.

One more cognac.

And goodnight.

After a little confusion at the BMW dealer, and a little confusion with the busy streets and misleading signs, I didn't get free of Mexico City until early afternoon, then made my way to Veracruz, on the Gulf of Mexico. Brutus and I had hoped to visit Veracruz on our previous visit to Mexico, but after spending three days in Manzanillo while he recovered from his injuries and had his motorcycle fixed up enough to ride again, we didn't have time to get to Veracruz. Thus, as with many places, I stopped there with Brutus in mind.

In fact, most of the time I *rode* with him in mind, for Brutus was very much with me on this journey now. So often I was riding along and thinking of what I would write to him, and how I would describe it, and saving up all the details in my head and my journal notes to convey them to him in a letter, once I got to Belize and had time to write again.

For now, I was trying to make some time, for I had agreed to meet Steven and Shelly in a few days at a small town called Corozal, just across the Belize border, and along the way there was another place I knew Brutus would want me to take the time to visit. Palenque was the name of a vast, ruined Mayan city in the troubled state of Chiapas, and at the time of our previous visit the rebel "Zapatistas" were frequently holding up vehicles and robbing tourists, and travel there was "not recommended." As far as I had been able to learn, things were a little calmer in the area lately, so I was going to try to visit it, for Brutus.

According to the Lonely Planet guidebook, the Palenque area was the rainiest part of Mexico (also "always sweltering, and rarely a breeze"), and my experience confirmed those observations. I arrived at a small resort in blinding rain, and checked into a spare, cozy cabin on the bank of a muddy stream, overhung with lush tropical trees and vines. Heavy rain fell most of the night, and in the morning I noted in my journal that this was a tropical *rainforest*, after all, and I reflected on a less-obvious contrast to the deserts where I had been travelling so much: "In the desert all foliage is designed to *conserve* moisture; here leaves are *huge* and many, to lap up as much as they can. Lush life, *large* life. Every stone with moss or mould, but not so different in desert, where simply more *modest.*"

I was reading a book called *Remembering Babylon,* by David Malouf, and his thoughts on the essential quality of "endurance" made me think of the ponderosa pine seeds that germinate only after a fire, or certain desert plants that germinate only if their husks are worn away by stones in a flash flood, thereby ensuring they will have enough moisture to grow. I also remembered reading about certain fruit seeds which would only germinate if they were *excreted* by birds or animals. In Darwinian terms, this apparently helped to assure their dispersion, but the metaphor that occurred to me concerned the ordeals of new growth — that in order for a little baby seed (or soul) to grow, it would have to pass through fire, flood, or . . . shit.

During those long days of riding across Mexico, my thoughts turned ever more strongly toward home, or at least the *idea* of home. I still had to get through two more weeks of travel, and the dark day on the horizon called Christmas, but all I seemed to be thinking about as I rode was making the trip back to Mexico City. The long trip *home,* it seemed like.

> *Getting ahead of myself or what? Feelings of anticipation bring back that childhood sense of Time; its incomprehensible linearity, how unreal there seems from here, in either direction.*
> *Still, four months as an exile, a drifter, a saddletramp, a ghost rider. Enough already!*

In Palenque I seemed to be "Mr. Out-of-Season" again, for I sat alone at the resort bar ("enduring — or ignoring — Christmas music"), and at dinner the tables were empty but for a couple of American families. I had been in Mexico long enough to be able to order my meals in Spanish, at least, which I tried to do as a matter of principle, and that day I noted my favorite word-of-the-day, *mantequilla* (butter), and remarked that at first I thought their butter was "flavored," with herbs or something, but then decided that no, it was simply a little rancid.

That night I started *The Orchard Keeper,* by Cormac McCarthy, and noted that it was, "typically beautiful but grim, McCarthy's own special oxymoronic style. Written in '65 or so; his first?"

The rain tapered off in the morning, and I rode up to the ruins and spent a few hours exploring the huge complex of pyramids, the tumbled stones which had been partly reassembled once they had been cut out of the surrounding jungle, so dense and green. I remembered reading Graham Greene's *The Lawless Roads,* about his travels in Mexico in the late '30s, where he had described visiting these ruins when they were just overgrown mounds, and it was easy to see that if they were neglected again they would soon be absorbed by that prolific, relentless tropical growth.

On a gloomy, overcast day, only a few groups of Mexican students wandered through the wet grass between the temples. "Far from crowded," I noted, "except with ghosts." Flocks of melodious blackbirds flew overhead, and another bird that at first I took for an African hornbill, because of its shape and rhythm of flight, but finally identified from my *Birds of Mexico* as a toucan. In the nearby woods I also spotted a yellow-billed cacique, which the book described as "elusive."

I climbed the 69 steep, narrow steps of the largest pyramid, the *Templo de Los Inscriptiones,* and then followed the claustrophobic passageway that led down inside it to the crypt. A triangular stone door and huge carved slab surrounded the small room where the sarcophagus had been, though it and all the other recovered treasures were in the museum in Mexico City — except for a jewelled death mask, which had been stolen in 1985 and never recovered. "Yet another ghost story," I noted, and was also intrigued by the tale associated with a smaller temple, the *Pyramide del Conde,* named for an eccentric German, Count Walbeck, who had lived inside the pyramid for two years in the 1800s, with a companion who was only described as "his lady friend." I tried to imagine how they would have lived there, buying food from nearby villages and collecting rainwater, though at the time I never thought to wonder *why.*

The next morning, I made my way to the border, then across to Belize and the seaside village of Corozal. Tony's Inn and Resort was a small hotel right on the shore of the Gulf of Mexico, with palms and Norfolk Island pines above a curve of beach and the sea of blue and green. Steven and Shelly and I hadn't seen each other since Barbados, so it was an emotional meeting, but a welcome one. As we sat together at the outdoor bar and drank margaritas, I realized that I was talking a mile a minute. Other than Andrew in Los Angeles, who was only *starting* to become a truly close friend, I hadn't seen anyone who really knew me for more than a month, since Alex and Liam in Santa Fe, and it was so good to be with people I felt comfortable around.

Steven and Shelly had rented a Jeep at the airport in Belize City, and as we travelled on together they offered to carry my bags with them, so I enjoyed the luxury of riding an unladen motorcycle for a few days. I also enjoyed having someone to talk with in the evenings, and thus didn't do much writing in my journal, until one sunrise, when I sat in the dew-wet grass on a pyramid-shaped mound, an unexcavated Mayan site in the resort of Chan Chich, where I described the early morning wildlife:

> *Up at 6:00, standing atop mound to west, jungles of Guatemala behind. Spooky howler monkeys around, "stentorian (or stertorous?) breathing" sound. Little blue heron, bat falcon, couple of vultures, parrots, sound of melodious blackbirds and loud drumming of woodpecker on hollow tree, "chortle" of Montezuma's oropendola (my favorite of the local birds for sight and sound). Two flocks of ocellated turkeys, tall tree hung with oropendola ("yellow-tail") nests, many birds heard but not seen. Parrots' raucous chatter. Turkeys not pretty, but beautiful, their bare blue heads with red warts and spectacular plumage.*
>
> *[And how about some of these bird names? Ivory-billed woodcreeper, red-crowned ant tanager, buff-throated foliage gleaner, slaty-tailed trogon.]*
>
> *Talking with Steven last night about whole "Gallon Jug" [plantation] scene around Chan Chich (drinking their coffee again this morning), all of it part of the Bowen family "fiefdom," 250,000 acres or something, and no doubt there's lots more around the*

country. Family also owns Coca-Cola bottling rights for the country,
and have been here in Belize for seven or eight generations appar-
ently, so must be descended from British planters, or lumber barons.

Resort here in Belize that was taken over and robbed by
Guatemalan baddies, also bus hijacked and soldier killed. Stories
and more stories.

Chipping away at a letter to Brutus last couple of days, bringing
him "up to date" since Cuernavaca.

Dec. 17, '98
Chan Chich Lodge
Belize

¡Hola Chupacabra!

Two miles from the Guatemalan border, in the middle of
hundreds of miles of jungle, at the end of 80 miles of dirt road, 12
cabañas in the center of an unrestored Mayan site, grassy mounds
covering ruined pyramids and temples around a plaza of tropical
gardens, palms, ceiba trees, and tropical hardwoods. This
morning's guided nature walk gave me a page-full of bird sightings, and after dinner tonight Steven, Shelly, and I are signed up
for the night walk. After looking at the photos from the lodge's
infrared-triggered camera on the path nearby, of jaguars, ocelots,
and that sort of thing, I'm hoping we see, oh, maybe some leaf-
cutter ants . . .

So yeah, this is a pretty special place, and we came here from
the Lamanai Outpost Lodge, which is set on a wide part of the
New River, beside some *restored* Mayan ruins, and also offered
great bird-watching (including two kinds of toucans — say that
fast! — and lots of parrots), the spooky-monster sounds of
howler monkeys in the trees, and though not quite as upscale-

luxurious as this place, still very beautiful and friendly. My thoughts run along the lines that Jackie and Selena would love these places, and *you* would love *getting here.*

And speaking of getting here . . . when last we spoke (I sure hope you've been getting my Mexican letters; my Mom reported that none of the postcards to my grandfather had arrived, after three weeks), I was just about to head for Mexico City. Well. I made a smooth exit from Cuernavaca, taking the "cuota" way up high through surprisingly thick forests of mixed pines and deciduous trees (which we didn't see in the darkness of our passage), as high as three-thousand-something meters, then winding down to the Calzada Tlalpan. You'll remember that I had to get turned around and on to the side part of that, which wasn't an easy manoeuvre, and when I did, I found no Grupo Bavaria.

Thinking I must have come in too low, I circled around again, up to the Periférico and through the usual madness, all the while painfully aware of the "6" at the end of my licence plate, and every time I passed a cop sure that there was a flashing light above my head saying "arrest me." Anyway, sure enough, the BMW shop was gone. (The night before I had entertained that thought, and laughed at myself for worrying so much: made a journal note, "No wonder I've got a freakin' ulcer!")

Next morning now, and before I continue with that riveting tale, I must tell you about our night walk. Shelly begged off, so it was just Steven and me, with our guide Luis. We each had bright flashlights, while Luis had a big trigger-operated spotlight over his shoulder for when we *found* things. And we did too, creeping along the dark forest trails and playing our beams in the undergrowth and up into the canopy, occasionally stopping and turning off the lights to stand in the absolute dark and listen. Creepy! Luis found us a white-eared possum, a kinkajou (possum-like tree critter), a pauraque (a nighthawk or "goatsucker" — see your salutation above!), and best of all, an *ocelot*. Trés cool. (And would make a lovely collar for my Vansons, I couldn't help thinking, ha!)

So anyway . . . there I was, lost on the Calzada Tlalpan, in the mid-morning Monday madness of Mexico City, on my "No-Drive Day." Now what? Well, I parked the bike, hailed a Beetle taxi, wrote down the name "Grupo Bavaria," and between us, worked out that it was "cambio," was now "un domicilio," and that the new place was "un poco largo" [they've moved; it was now a house; the new place is a little far away], but that I would follow him there; still feeling like a "moving target" on the road, with that number 6 just screaming at the world. Or at least at the cops.

The new dealer is in San Angel, next to Coyoacán, and is a slick, brand-new, motorcycles-only operation, owned by a nice young English-speaking dude named Erik. (There was also a uniformed paramilitary-looking security guard out front, with a tightly leashed Alsatian, which hints at the current social climate of Mexico City.) So there I was; yet I was not *there*. The service department was in a separate location, right back near the intersection of the Periférico and the Calzada Tlalpan. Oh man!

Armed with map and directions, I flailed my way over there, unapprehended (Erik suggested that I would have been better off *removing* the offending plate, but said they didn't pay too much attention to motorcycles anyway), and met Pedro, the 62-year-old service manager who was cast in a similar mold to our old friend Martín. A prime character, and I just had to surrender and listen to everything he had to say about what was wrong with my transmission, where I was going next, how I should get there, and all like that.

Another indicator of life in Mexico City these days is that it's not safe to hail a *taxi:* an epidemic of robberies, especially against foreigners, and people beaten up until they surrendered the PIN numbers for their ATM cards. *¡Jesu Christo!* So Pedro got me a Beetle, spoke to the driver and showed him some police badge which he possessed (for some reason I didn't quite catch), and I was off to the Four Seasons. A couple of good days there, taking care of business, sending *you* a letter and a couple of books, visiting a dentist to have a couple of crowns glued back in, working phone, fax, and Fedex, eating well, and looking at all those beautiful women that seem to adorn that hotel (as you'll remember — and not that *we* care).

(Later that same day, in Belize City.)

As you know, it's hard to get much letter-writing or journal-izing done when there are *other* people around, expecting you to pay them attention and that. And me so used to being the "lone saddletramp," the Ghost Rider, but of course it's nice having some company. Shelly flew out of Chan Chich at noon today, bound for home, and Steven in his Jeep Wrangler followed me back out through the jungle and Mennonite farming communities (*lots* of them in this country) to the main road, and south through drier savanna to this place, a nice inn in what is, by all accounts, a pretty nasty city. However, it was a destination we could reach in daylight, and will set us up to head into the Maya Mountains tomorrow, for a night at Francis Ford Coppola's joint, the Blancaneaux Lodge. If it's anywhere near as nice as where we've been, it will be alright.

(I have just been adding up all my bird sightings of the past few days — because I'm a very boring guy! — and came up with more than *40*, most of which I'd never seen before. The best thing, of course, is that all this nature-watching keeps my little brain occupied in healthier directions than it tends to wander into on its own.)

And after that lengthy parenthesis, back to Mexico City . . .

So I show up at the Altavista BMW service department at 7:30 on Thursday morning, for that is when Pedro says he'll be there, but no one shows up until 9:00, when I learn that Pedro has *quit* (some disagreement with the owner, who reminded me of that pony-tailed guy from the Logística company, while Pedro, as I said, reminded me of Martín, so you could imagine certain "personality conflicts").

The air pressure in my rear tire had been down 10 pounds when I left Oaxaca, and I had topped it up along the way, asking Pedro to check it out and replace the tire if it was punctured. When I showed up that morning, the tire and wheel were off the bike, with a mark showing a big nail in it, but the *new* service manager, a young German-Mexican named Kurt, hadn't known what I wanted done, or how to get hold of me, and now he said, "*Maybe* we can get a new tire by tomorrow . . ."

Oh man.

So I notice a couple of GSes in the shop belonging to the Edelweiss tour company, and one of them has a fairly new Bridgestone on the back. And you can guess the rest . . .

A little past noon, I'm heading around the Periférico to the west (the way we went with Luis that time), then across the city on a central expressway called the Viaducto, toward the airport and, hopefully, Puebla and the east. After various confusions, missing signs, and flailing circles, I escape, and head to Veracruz.

As you had surmised, it was a very happening town, with a colorful zócalo under a lighted clock tower and palms wrapped in beaded lights. Marimba bands, mariachis, acrobat on a slack wire, a dance orchestra, hundreds of people on a humid evening, a funky waterfront arcade of souvenir stands (no *stickers* once again, though at least I learned the word to ask for: "calcomanías").

Dec. 22, '98
Placencia, Belize

Well, Mr. Stinky Pants, sorry to leave you hanging like that for so long, but I've been . . . busy. Yeah, that's it. Anyway, here we are at the end of the road (and *what* a road, but I'll get to that) and from here it's all back-tracking for me — back across to Mexico City, and home, home, home!

I'm not sure which direction to take *you* in, at this point, in terms of catching you up, for once again, there's a *lot* to tell. For now, I'll pick up the story from Veracruz, and try to get you from there to here (and I can tell you right now, you almost can't *get* here from there). I'm also a bit out of the loop regarding your status, for I called the elusive Mr. Bloomenfeld *twice* from Mexico City, but he didn't call back. Must have thought it was you calling. Ha ha . . .

Anyway, aiming for Palenque that day, I didn't think I had too far to go (that lying map again!), so I started out on a scenic route along the coast; until the rain came pouring down, when I defected back to the "cuota" [toll road].

A journal excerpt:

Just thinking, would really like a day of more-or-less peaceful travel. Haven't had since Baja.

[Later] And won't get today. 144 pesos ($40) in tolls once again, including a couple of small bridges on the initial "scenic route." Probably balances what I would have paid, if I'd stuck to the "cuota," like a sensible person. ("It looked nice on the map." Classic Mexican mistake!) Another long day, though I guess any day in which I "arrive alive" is a good day. Sort of.

It all started . . . with a fairly easy exit from Veracruz, then some flailing around for the right road. So often the number is wrong, or the one destination given isn't even on the map, or is so remote and seemingly wrong (like Oaxaca from Mexico City) that you think it can't be right.

On the numbers, can the map be wrong? Was thinking today that I love the idea of a country that can put up wrong or, at best, imprecise signs, but the reality is something else. Call it hell.

Then the rain, heavy enough to stop for rainsuit. (Watched by curious locals the whole time.) Now the "scenic route" seemed pointless, so took "escape route," 175 I think, which did provide one amazing little town along river, with nice plaza and church, and buildings in every shade of pink, yellow, blue, and green. Then circled entrance to cuota a few times; again, none of the entrances looked right. Once on, I had a nice long stretch of four-lane, then construction at Lazaro Cárdenas. No signs, just dust and chaos and tons of traffic. From then on, trucks and buses to pass, and again through Villahermosa, no agreement with signs and map, just keep going and hope it's right. As I wrote after first Mexican trip, "even when you're on the right road, you have no way of knowing."

Hawkers today selling pineapples, oranges, bananas, and parrots (sure sign of climate change). Especially prevalent at toll booths. Always soldiers there too: don't even think about toll-jumping!

Begin to be more daunted by the journey back to Mexico City. Could be long, and tough. Looks wide open on the map. The map . . .

Anyway, Palenque was all you thought it would be. I spent an extra day there, and went hiking around the ruins, and up and down the pyramids (my legs ached for *days* after all the steep, narrow descents), and was again pretty much "Mr. Out-of-Season" there, scoring a nice little cabaña in the forest, beside a brown stream hung with trees and vines, and the constant sound of sawing insects, and at night, fireflies in the rain. Very nice. Remind me to take you there sometime. If we're in the area . . .

Then it was time to dash for the Belize border, during which journey I was struck by a black *vulture!* They seem to be a little more sluggish in lifting off their roadkill than the turkey vultures we're used to, and this fat fucker flapped straight ahead of me instead of to the side. When I saw impact was unavoidable, I just ducked and held on, and it hit heavily, tearing my left front signal light right off, and leaving vulture-tidbits all over my gauges, handlebar, mirror, tank, and leathers. Like, *yuck!*

Cleaning up as best I could with some roadside leaves (with a glance back down the road at the black lump of dead vulture — lunch for his brothers), I carried on, got through the border with minimal nonsense, and brought you to the beginning of this letter.

Well . . . for a start, Mr. Coppola's place was overpriced, and the staff was, for the most part, none-too-swift. The setting, beside the fast-flowing Rio Frio amid young (probably third-growth) pines, was nice, but that was about it. I probably won't take you there sometime.

(Incidentally, Chan Chich has rather fallen in our estimation now, with the discovery of about 50 angry red bites, presumably bedbugs, on hips, thighs, back of knees, and other tender areas.)

Next morning, Steven and I were tempted by a 35-mile trip to the Mayan ruins at Caracol (and the end of the road), but the weather threatened, and we were already 20 miles up a fairly "dynamic" mountain dirt road, so we decided to get out and head south. Probably wise, for no sooner had we turned down the "Hummingbird Highway" than it started to rain *hard:* tropical-style. Looking for a place to stop for rain gear, and wiping at my face shield every few seconds, I headed across one of those wooden-plank bridges: the base laid diagonally, with two "tracks" of lengthwise planks. Usually I took those in the middle, to avoid the wheels getting caught on the planks, but this time it was a mistake, for that was where all the trucks and buses had dripped their oil and grease, and with the sudden heavy rain, and the *heat,* it was hopelessly slick.

The bike went out from under me, sliding all the way to the end of the bridge and tearing up the whole front end on the side-railings. Fender ripped off, headlight smashed, oil cooler twisted up and in, instrument binnacle mashed back into the forks, side trim-bits torn off, engine guard crushed, and the *other* front signal light demolished. As for me, I took a pretty good fall too, bruising my ribs (not as well as *you* did, of course) and banging my forearm against one of the railing uprights as I slid by (I had time to think, "broken arm for sure," but just a nasty bruise — oh yeah, and some pain). The Vansons saved me from splinters and worse damage, and one of my boots was torn up a little, but that's certainly acceptable.

Steven was right behind me, and fortunately carrying all my bags, so we determined that I seemed to be in one piece, picked up the bike (which *wasn't*) from under the guard rail (many of these bogus "temporary" bridges don't even have them, which would probably have put the bike *and* me in the river), and bungeed and strapped the binnacle away from the forks, then tossed the rest of the wreckage in the Jeep. Otherwise, the bike ran and steered fine, and a friendly maintenance guy at the hotel made me a plexiglas cover for the headlight. It and the instruments sit at a crazy angle, but they all *work*. What a machine.

And now we faced the *worst* road known to man. And of course, it rained like hell. (At least, if it rains in hell, it's like that, and this road goes there. Or comes from there — 40 miles of muddy washboard, potholes, and sloppy mush.)

You can imagine that I was feeling pretty sore and stiff, my ribs taking a nasty pounding and my bruised throttle-arm soon in moderate agony, plus of course I was still fairly freaked at having *crashed*. So near the *end* too, after exactly four months, and 44,000 kilometres [27,500 miles]; oh yeah, I turned over 100,000 coming out of Palenque, and stopped to photograph that exciting event on the odometer. At one point, we even stopped and took shelter under a roadside "palapa" for a while, hoping the rain would let up. It didn't. Three-and-a-half hours to go 40 miles, all in first gear, and often with my feet down in the slop, as "outriggers." Steven was in 4WD the whole time, and couldn't have gone much faster even on his own. You'd have *loved* it!

However, this place is spectacular: the Luba Hati, "house of the moon," where Jackie and I were *supposed* to have spent a month last March, when we came back from London, as a beginning to putting together some kind of a new life. Well, it didn't quite work out that way, did it?

Anyway, that's about enough out of me, eh? (Every letter seems to get longer, but then more seems to *happen* as I travel south.) Now I just want to get through the next few days, make it back to Mexico City, dump the poor smashed-up "El Rojo," and fly away home. From there I'll be able to call you, and we'll talk.

But if you start laughing about my crash, I shall just hang up. It's all your fault, after all, that I have to do my own stunts!

Later dude,
El Bridge-Buster

One afternoon, the owner of the Luba Hati gave me a note from a local hardware and lumber merchant, Steve Christensen, who wrote that he had seen my smashed-up motorcycle parked there, and wondered if I might be "fed up" and want to sell it. I thought about it, briefly, but decided that our travels together were not over yet.

Steven and I did stop at Mr. Christensen's lumber yard to talk to him, and I learned that he was an American (in his 40s, I would guess) who had been in Belize for 13 years; he said he couldn't take the "political correctness" in the United States. Once again I wished I were a more *inquisitive* reporter, for I would like to have known what that meant to him.

Although disappointed I didn't want to sell my bike, he invited me to drop by his home and have a look at an older R100GS that he had completely rebuilt, and he also let me change my oil under his lean-to garage.

Another interesting character Steven and I talked with in the town of Placencia was Larry, a dreadlocked local, who told us the story of his "lady" who lived near Toronto, in Scarborough, and how he had flown up there and driven her car all the way down to Belize, even though he had no driver's licence. Hard to imagine how he pulled that off.

Then there was Alva, the young black waitress at the Luba Hati who had been cheerfully bantering with us the previous evening, but when I saw her at the bar that afternoon she was in a *foul* mood, and said she wanted to "shoot somebody." I told her, "If you're not careful I'll tell you all *my* troubles!"

She was overworked and underpaid, no doubt, and seemed mad at everybody, but especially at some man — the one she wanted to shoot. I told her, "It's not worth going to jail for some stupid man," and she said maybe she would go out and kick a dog instead. I said, "Yeah, how about you kick all the dogs, and I'll kick all the cats?"

Then Alva got her back up at the manager, Lynne, who wanted her to set the tables for dinner as well as tend the bar, and she huffed and puffed as she bustled around, grumbling and mocking Lynne's cheery chatter to some arriving guests. When I told her that Steven and I would be leaving the following morning, Christmas Eve day, because there was "no room at the inn," she snapped back, "Well, at least you're not *pregnant.*"

Good one, Alva.

The next morning Steven followed me back up that horrible muddy road again, and we spent a cheerless Christmas Eve at a rundown little resort in Dangriga called the Pelican Reef Beach Club. Then we travelled hard all through Christmas Day, keeping ourselves distracted by being on the move, riding and driving up through Belize City and back to Tony's Inn and Resort in Corozal, where our travels had begun.

Early the following morning, Steven and I said an emotional goodbye, having survived yet another bad time together. Steven was driving the Jeep back to the airport in Belize City to fly home to Ohio, and I was on my own again, crossing the Mexican border and riding with a desperate urgency for Mexico City.

Now that Christmas was behind me I could not wait to be *home* again, back at the house on the lake, and I thought of nothing else. By the afternoon of the second day I had made it all the way to Mexico City, dropped the poor smashed-up bike at the BMW dealer, and checked into a room at the

Four Seasons. I felt excited just to have made it *that* far, even though my flight was not until the following night, but this time luck was with me. There was a seat available on a flight that night to Toronto, with a connection to Montreal. So after a couple of celebratory drinks and a fine room-service dinner, I checked out around midnight and taxied to the airport.

Home. I wondered how much snow there would be outside. I thought about the rooms in the house, and how they would look. I thought about the photographs of Jackie and Selena everywhere, and wondered what it would be like to look at them now. I thought about all the memories, and wondered how they would feel, up close again like that.

I had been away for four months and one week, and I had travelled 46,239 kilometres, 30,748 miles. It had been a long journey, in every way. Had I changed? Had I "healed" at all?

Part of me was certainly excited about the idea of being in that house again, but there was a ghost of a doubt there too. I was certainly carrying a homesick *fantasy* with me about how it was going to be to be back in that house again, but I couldn't be sure the real-life experience would end up being a *good* one. Thinking about what I had said earlier about the fantasy of "travelling," I could just as well have been talking about the fantasy of "home." As always, I couldn't tell how I was going to feel until I *felt* it.

At that point in my odyssey, all that mattered to me was to feel that I was still moving forward, still willing to try, still finding the strength to face the shadows and the ghosts, every morning and every night, on the Healing Road. Still believing that "something will come up."

The evening plane rises up from the runway
Over constellations of light
I look down into a million houses
And wonder what you're doing tonight
If I could wave my magic wand
I'd make everything all right

PRESTO, 1990

Book 2

HOMEWARD ANGEL,
ON THE FLY

I had a dream of a winter garden
a midnight rendezvous
silver blue and frozen silence
what a fool I was for you

PRESTO, 1990

Chapter 9

WINTERLUDE

play of light — a photograph
the way I used to be
some half-forgotten stranger
doesn't mean that much to me
trick of light — moving picture
moments caught in flight
make the shadows darker
or the colors shine too bright

AVAILABLE LIGHT, 1990

Photographs and memories. After nearly 20 years of family life, a long row of photo albums filled the shelf of the hall closet in the house by the lake. I couldn't imagine *ever* wanting to browse through the pages of those books again, unless I really wanted to torture myself, but among the many framed photos that filled the house, there were three that I especially loved — and hated.

One of them was a black-and-white shot taken by Deb, from the Tuileries Gardens of Paris, of Jackie, Selena, and me sitting on a bench. Taken from behind, it showed me in the middle with my arms spread across the back of the bench, enclosing both of "my girls," and Selena's face in profile, looking toward the two of us.

Another was a color shot taken on the very last morning, August 10, 1997, by Jackie's Uncle Harry, just before Selena set out to drive to Toronto. It shows the three of us standing on the deck, with trees and lake behind, and the white, furry mass of Nicky laying in front of us. On one side is a smiling man with a shaved head (my pattern used to be to shave it on the first of July and let it grow the rest of the year), and an "Area 51" T-shirt and shorts. Jackie is also summer-casual, barefoot in shorts and T-shirt, hair a little wild from sun, wind, and water, and Selena in the middle, looking young, strong, and beautiful. She had exercised hard all that summer, swimming, walking, taking golf lessons, and pounding the tread-mill while she watched reruns of "Perry Mason" and "Green Acres," and it had paid off; as she headed back to Toronto to start university and take on the world, she looked *great*.

The third love/hate photo was another black-and-white shot, this one of Jackie and me, taken by Andrew (the Los Angeles Andrew) on the occasion of the three members of Rush receiving the Order of Canada (Canada's highest civilian honor, something like a "good citizenship" award) in 1997. Me in my Armani tuxedo, sporting my Order of Canada medal with a proud smile, and Jackie in black dress and elegantly groomed, leaning toward the camera with a wide smile and shining eyes.

Photographs and memories.

When I flew back from Mexico City, arriving on the morning of December 28th, 1998, after four months of travelling across Canada, the western United States, the width of Mexico and the length of Belize, I knew I was flying back to face those photos again, and everything else that filled that haunted house.

Keith picked me up at the airport and delivered me to the house on the lake — though by now that lake was frozen over and buried under the same deepening blanket of snow that covered the house and the trees all around. It all looked so wonderful to me. My soulscape, in my soul's season of winter.

Keith had been busy during my absence, not just keeping the place up to his usual standard of perfection, but working with his friend Pierre, a fine carpenter who had helped build the house back in 1992, to remake Selena's bedroom into the Selena Memorial Library. Just before I left in August, I had met with the two of them and drawn some pencil marks on the walls, and now those hieroglyphics had been translated into a three-dimensional realization of maple bookshelves, a glass-fronted cabinet opening through the wall into the hall, and upstairs in the loft, an arched doorway to connect with the loft of my office. They had done a beautiful job.

Over the summer and fall, Keith had also been ferrying occasional pickup-loads of treasures from the Toronto house. Sister Deb and I had already gone through the personal stuff there, boxing up what we thought ought to be saved (hard to guess about that, for you tend not to care about *things* too much, so you end up saving whatever seems significant or relevant to the lost one — or *ones*, in our case). Other than that, there were only a few paintings from the Toronto house I knew I wanted to keep, and the books — the *hundreds* of books that had once filled the high shelves in the family room there. So that would help to keep my restless mind busy for the first few days, emptying the pile of boxes on the floor of the Selena Memorial Library and filling all those brand new, empty bookshelves.

During my stay in the summer, I had told Keith about my plan of making the house a kind of statement of "rebellion," an expression of my new persona as "bachelor with a vengeance." I mimed this attitude for him with a fist raised to the sky, and the defiant shout of, *"I'll show you."* Meaning Jackie and Selena, of course, for "abandoning" me.

Beside the photographs of each of them on display all over the house, I often placed one of my fine model cars or motorcycles, or something "manly" like that, and I also deliberately violated Jackie's taste for uncluttered spaces by filling the living-room shelves with art books and African carvings, and every stretch of wall with a painting or two, even hanging them salon-style, on two levels, on the high walls.

Keith lived in a small town nearby, and while I was home I tended to have him come by every few days to do the chores, and to help me with my "redecorating." As a rule, he tended to share Jackie's more austere taste in interior decoration (or call it more "tasteful" taste), and one day while I had him up on the ladder hanging pictures, I said to him, "You know, Jackie would just *hate* this. She'd say it was *cluttered*."

Without looking my way, Keith muttered, "That's one word she might use."

"Ha," I laughed, raising my fist and my eyes to heaven again, "I'll show *you* what happens when you leave me all alone!"

In truth, I think Keith kind of sympathized with my bachelor-with-a-vengeance stance, for I had half-jokingly mentioned that I was thinking of putting my Ducati 916 (one of the most beautiful of motorcycles) in the living room, and when I got back from Mexico, I laughed to see it sitting in the front window, flagrantly shiny, red, and *so* unfeminine.

My brother Danny, Janette, and Max had spent their Christmas with Janette's family in New Brunswick, and after visiting some friends in Montreal, they drove up to visit for a few days after New Year's. Danny and Janette had often visited that house, in happier times, and they seemed to feel the weight of the "ghosts" pretty heavily. Danny wrote me later that he felt I was "a little farther along in the grieving process" than they were.

At first, I felt a twinge of offence at that comment, for I sure didn't feel all that "far along," but then I realized that, in a way, it was true. To a degree (which varied every day), I had grown *used* to the idea of being alone, and part of me had simply *accepted* that this was how it was going to be now. Thinking about my relative stage in the grieving process, I realized that I had been a full-time, professional griever for a year and four months by then. Focused entirely on loss, survival, and the state of my little baby soul through every minute of every day and night, I actually did seem to have made some degrees of progress, regained a little strength.

Perhaps the Healing Road had done its job, after all. Maybe all along my motion had actually been *two* steps forward, and one step back.

Now that I was giving up the gypsy mode for awhile and returning to the hermit mode, I knew that I still had to protect myself from the pitfalls of too much solitude, too much "reflection." The first thing I decided was to take advantage of my friends and family by making them come and visit me, maybe every week or two, so I wouldn't be in danger of falling too deep inside myself.

Another protection I prescribed (griever, heal thyself) was to continue my "writing therapy." Just as writing letters had proved to be a good sounding board during my travels, I resolved to spend some time at my desk each day telling *someone* how I felt, what I had done, what I hoped to do. Ventilating.

Brutus would still be my main "audience" (and I his "house band"), but there were also a few other friends I wanted to reach out to — those who had fallen out of touch during my recent troubles, but who had written along the way to let me know they were thinking of me.

I can see in retrospect that this was another measure of my modest healing and tentative return to life, that I wanted to open myself up to a wider circle of friends again. Certainly not as wide as it used to be, for in past years I had kept up a fairly steady and fairly prolific (if sporadic, during tours and travels) series of letters to distant friends, but I didn't have the "enthusiasm" for all that anymore.

At this fresh juncture in my life, with its *tabula rasa* (for good and ill), I would choose those people I was sure I still *wanted* in my life, and invite them back in. If they were willing.

And able. For obviously it wasn't that easy to be the friend of an all-time loser like me, to be willing to share the reality of such awful tragedies, and I wasn't blind to that either. Still, some good people seemed able to put up with all that, to my constant surprise, and I was certainly grateful to them for that true magnanimity — greatness of soul.

Inevitably, my first letter from the house on the lake would be written to my poor imprisoned friend Brutus, whose request for bail had finally been denied, and who was now waiting until an acceptable plea-bargain could be negotiated. The federal authorities were offering him a deal if he was willing to "spill a few names," but he knew that idea would not be good for his health, or his family's.

The house on the lake had always been a special place for Brutus too, in fact, he had been the one to *discover* that beautiful area, and to show it to me. Back around 1990 he and Georgia had been visiting us at our log cabin on Lac Echo, about 10 miles away, and every day Brutus went driving around the southern Laurentians looking for a piece of property to buy. One day, he came back telling me about a lake he had found which was just being opened up to development, with only three houses built on its thickly wooded shore, with water so clean you could drink it right out of the lake.

The next day, we loaded a canoe onto the roof of his Jeep, and Selena and I drove with him to have a look at this paradise. The owner of the land around several lakes in the area, Louie (later my neighbor and woodland mentor), was also selling a few islands on this lake, and Brutus, Selena, and I paddled around for half the day going ashore to explore the islands as well as we could (we had to "bushwhack" through the dense underbrush to try to see the lay of the land), and cruising along the shore to look at various lots that were available.

The islands were small, none of them larger than an acre, and they would not be practical to build upon (given the autumn freezeup and winter thaw, for a start), but they were still tempting from the point of view of our "inner child" — how exciting to have your very own island! We decided to be sensible, however, and within a week we had each bought a piece of land along the lakeshore — *and* an island.

Unfortunately, with everything else that was gone from there, Brutus's land had been sold back to Louie a few months ago to pay some of his lawyer bills. But just as Brutus was the one who could best understand my feelings about motorcycling and travelling, he could also best understand my feelings about the house on the lake.

Jan. 7, '99
Lac St. Brutus, Que.

Hey there Blunderbuss!

It's a bee-yoo-ti-ful winter morning here, sun just clearing the trees behind Louie's house, with a crisp -12° [10°F], and about 10 inches of fresh powder overnight. A fair blizzard was blowing last night, and before I went to bed I turned off the inside lights and sat up for awhile to watch the ever-popular "snowglobe effect" in the outdoor lights.

The winter fantasy I have been carrying around with me day and night on the road all these months has come true, just the way I imagined it, and I have sure been digging it. (Well, actually Keith's been digging it — I just admire it and play in it.)

As I told you on the phone, I spent the first few days here happily indoors, wallowing in simply *being here* (for so long all I wanted was this: to be alive and here, and I'm not taking it for granted yet). With the Selena Memorial Library successfully organized and somewhat decorated, and the living-room shelves filled with all the books on art, cars, motorcycles, and birds (a most righteous combination, I think), I gradually started to reintroduce my scooter-softened physique to outdoor activities once again — not that I had a choice, with the ever-active Danny and Janette visiting. One day I was snowshoeing with Danny in the morning, then cross-country skiing with Janette in the afternoon, so I've been getting some "fresh air and exercise" alright.

There's nearly two feet of snow on the ground now, which is just perfect for snowshoeing, and at least enough for cross-country skiing on the Aerobic Corridor, so I've been exploring my woods pretty widely on the 'shoes, and driving down to the village once a day to ski on the Corridor, going a little longer every day.

And speaking of winter in these parts, don't it *look* fine out there? You know it does, with snow all over the trees and all, and it's interesting to reflect that all the places I've seen in the past four months, however beautiful, have only served to make this look *better*. It's "The Place," you know? I know you do.

Amid all the excitement I felt about getting back here, one little black doubt kept nagging at me: what would it be like to face it all *emotionally* again? To look at all the photographs around here, the stuff that fills this place, and the place itself; to see their faces all the time, wherever I looked, in frames as well as in memories. (I may have told you all this on the phone, but it bears recounting, for my own sake, if not yours. And you're my captive audience, after all, so you have to read whatever I write. And whatever my brother writes too!)

Well, what seems to have happened during this longish interval of time and distance is that I've reached one of those stages along the "Grieving Road." There is a pretty well-defined series of "phases" you go through (I used to know all this stuff in detail, from reading all them Grief Books over in London, but I've wisely let much of it flow out of my head), with various steps through dominant Shock, Disbelief, Denial, Anger, and that. Finally, you're supposed to reach Acceptance. (Not to be confused with Happiness, Peace, or Resignation.)

Anyway, "Acceptance" seems to be where I'm at now, for when I first came into this house and looked around at the photos of Jackie and Selena, the words that came into my head were, "I know." That's all. Not that I can really "accept" it, or necessarily live with it, but at least, "I know."

That's something, I guess, and to that degree, I suppose the "Healing Road" did its job. I've just started to look over some of my journal entries from early in the trip, and find myself, at that time, just *hoping* I'd be able to wander around until Xmas, and maybe wander down through Mexico and Belize, and, in what was then the far-distant future, get back here for the prime of winter. That plan actually worked out, I can say now, in both an outer and an inner sense, and now I've just got to work my way through Phase Two.

As with Phase One, I'm not sure exactly how it's all going to work, but I'll use the same *modus operandus:* no pressure, no obligations, but just try to get myself through the days as divertingly and healthily as I can. Now is another "Danger Time," of course, when I could easily slip into Evil Ways, so I'm keeping an eye on myself. That's why I've been keen to get out on the snowshoes and skis, and I hope to get into some kind of a regime with cross-country skiing, working up to a good long ski at least three times a week. Not only would it keep me busy, but my "level of fitness" could use some picking up too.

Anyway, I'll be trying to keep myself occupied in non-destructive activities, and hopefully I can get interested in doing something around here, like getting back to the writing thing. But again, no pressure, no obligation. I'll just start typing up my notes and sorting out the material I've collected, and see how it goes. Up to now, I've been spending an hour or so in the morning here in my office, just sort of dabbling at things, and I'll see where the keyboard takes me.

That's another thing to get used to — typing again, after being "Mr. Freehand" in my journalizing and letter-writing for such a long time. But I do like it. My typing is not only neater than my printing (forget about writing), but I also find that I do communicate much more *spontaneously* like this, for I know anything that comes out too stupid can be fixed up later! But both are good, I guess. Depends on yer soy-cum-stances, don't it?

But yeah, lots to do, alright. The guest room and the front hall are still stacked with boxes, with more yet to come from Toronto, so there's always plenty of that kind of sorting-out to do. My old office here, which is now "annexed" to the upstairs loft of the Selena Memorial Library, is a terrible mess. I've only begun to nibble at the accumulated mail and stuff, though I did find a good letter from you after I spoke with you, and that was nice.

I was distressed to hear you've had to forego the companionship of that amiable young African-American chap, Reginald, for I'm sure it had been frightfully jolly to converse with him in the "colorful" manner you describe. Really breaking down those cross-cultural borders, what?

Why, one might discourse at great length and depth about such common enthusiasms as those great old minstrel shows. So charming, with all the humorous characters in blackface, singing and dancing so winningly. Or that Sammy Davis Jr; such a great entertainer. And the toe-tapping music of those nicely dressed Motown singing groups from the wonderful '60s. Indeed, in moments of candor such as might well overcome two such soul mates in their shared incarceration, one might even be tempted to share one's own experiences of "getting down" in the "neighborhood" with the "brothers."

And I say! No doubt in the natural manner of this verbal intercourse you would even find occasion to utilize such delightful verbs and adjectives as "boogie" and "jive!" Ripping good fun, I'm sure, and it is to be regretted that you have lost such a quaint and diverting companion.

[Later that same day . . .]

Well, I'm just back from a long bushwhack on snowshoes, way back in the woods across the road. I remember that you and I once snowshoed around the perimeter of the "Hunderd Aker Wood," but I don't think I ever dragged you farther back into the bush, from the northeast corner, into the timber concessions and Crown land. A few winters back, I was able to get through there and connect with some logging roads, used only by occasional snowmobilers in winter and hunters in the fall, and make my way all the way to the Aerobic Corridor. However, a few summers' growth since then, and, especially, last year's famous Ice Storm, have pretty well blocked that trail, so today I took a pair of twig-clippers out there and had a go. In a couple of hours of plodding, bending, and fierce snipping, I cut perhaps two million sumac sprouts, plus countless other "whippy" bits of growth, but I'm still mired in a dense thicket back there. Next time I'll have to take the handsaw with me, for there are a number of fair-sized trees bent right over the trail.

But that kept me harmlessly occupied for a couple of hours, and on the way back I cut across the land, over the frozen surface of Stinky Lake, where Danny and I had blazed a trail a few days ago (our tracks all but obliterated by last night's heavy fall), following the siren song of a distant chainsaw. Pierre and Keith were working on the other trail, clearing the largest deadfall from the property line at the far end. We never got to it last summer, for just clearing the main trail across the road took four of us a whole day, but I asked them at least to get rid of the biggest trees on the trail, so a guy could get through without having to go over, under, and around them.

And so homeward, to heat up a can of delicious pork 'n' beans, then another short session at the desk. I'll just finish up this letter and get it sent off to you today, which will be a good excuse to go out. One thing I've already learned about trying to start the cross-country ski program is that having an errand to run is a good excuse to go for a ski, and going for a ski is a good excuse to get an errand done. This may work!

Anyway, that's all today's big news. Be advised that yesterday I sent a package to you with two books, a money order for a couple hundred *huitlacoches*, and two photos I thought you might like (since they feature you, of course). I'm not sure if you have any place to keep things like that where you are now, but I thought I'd send 'em along anyway, in case you did.

Otherwise, you know what to do, I don't have to tell you. Just

like on the ski lift, "Keep Your Tips Up!" Or, as your lamented
former friend and "Funky Home-Boy," Reginald, no doubt
advised you, "One must accept these quotidian events in a refrigerated manner, my consanguinary brother, do you understand
what it is that I am saying?"

Fight the Power, Brother
The Ghost Rider

[Letter to Lesley Choyce, a prolific author and the founder of the
company, Pottersfield Press, which published my first book, *The Masked
Rider*]

Jan. 15, '99
Lac St. Brutus, Que.

Dear Lesley,

Well, here I am, back home in the woods again, where I surely
belong, and I'm glad to say that it's just the way I'd been dreaming
about it, day and night, for about the last two months of my self-
imposed "exile." A true and righteous blizzard is raging outside,
the air so thick with snow you can't see across the lake, and it's
drifting around in whipped-cream peaks on top of the more than
two feet which has already fallen since my arrival (Dec. 28th). The
temperature has stayed around my "winter optimum" (-10°C)
[14°F], though it got down near -30°C [-22°F] a couple of nights,
which gave me a good excuse to fire up the old woodstove.

Sure, I've got a furnace and everything, but the woodstove is
part of my "emergency preparedness" program. CBC-TV in
Montreal, whence I get my daily weather info, won't let anyone
forget that exactly one year ago was the big Ice Storm, and though

this area wasn't the worst hit (and though we were in London at the time), the power was out here for about 12 frigid days. That's why I have a woodstove. And a generator. And a four-wheel-drive car. And snowshoes.

And that's why every Quebecker knows you must always be well supplied with emergency supplies of booze and smokes!

So, I'm slowly easing into whatever kind of a life I'm going to have here. A guy can't take off and spend four months as an irresponsible saddletramp without arriving home to a certain amount of *chaos,* but of course there's a certain amount of chaos inside me too, so it . . . balances.

[A recap of my travels and the "acceptance" theory]

. . . so, after four months and 46,000 kilometres [28,750 miles], four countries, six provinces, two territories, 11 American and 17 Mexican states, maybe it took all that just to say, "I know." That's enough for what's behind me, I guess, but I just hope it's enough for what's *ahead* of me, you know?

Well, in the immortal words of The Brain [in the cartoon show "Pinky And The Brain"], when he clobbered Pinky and Pinky asked him "What'd you do that for, Brain?"

The Brain answered sagely, "Time will tell, Pinky. Time will tell."

Selena and I used to love those guys.

I did quite a bit of reading in my travels, which included a lot of background on where I was travelling, especially books about the American deserts, but that led me some interesting places. Do you know of the American writer Edward Abbey? I discovered his *Desert Solitaire* in a National Park Visitor Center, and became a total fan immediately. *The Monkey Wrench Gang, The Brave Cowboy,* and many more of his fictions and nonfictions were soon riding along in my bags, as I travelled through the West he writes about with such love and understanding.

My interest in Jack London has also grown into a complete

admiration for masterpieces like *The Sea Wolf, Martin Eden,* and so many great short stories.

[The tale of my visit to Jack London State Park, and about London's sad end]

He and his wife Charmian seem to have loved each other well, and had many adventures together, and he certainly had an interesting and successful life, and yet none of it was enough to keep him *alive.* Or her either, for that matter. It made me sad. A lot of stuff does.

But as I may have intimated in my postcards (which I'm glad you received; along the way I wanted to let a few people know that they were alive in my thoughts, and that I was still alive in *theirs!*), out there on the Healing Road I did stumble across some important moments of Truth and Beauty.

It was the simple things: a sunrise ride across Saskatchewan from Neepawa, Manitoba, where I'd taken shelter the previous night from a late-August thunderstorm, and now the Sunday-morning road was empty and endless and still shiny-wet, reflecting the clear sky and the rising sun behind me. Or riding past the lakes and forested mountains along the Alaska Highway, and passing a family of caribou, a black bear, or a bald eagle. Gyrfalcons above the tundra on the Dempster Highway to Inuvik, grizzlies in Alaska, whales cavorting beside the ferry which carried me down to Prince Rupert. Highways, landscapes, wildlife. Once again, concentrate on the essentials.

Another important process which had to go forward during this journey was that of *reconstructing* myself. I expect that job will continue for awhile. Needless to say, my foundation has been shaken so profoundly that even now I have no idea about such rudimentary notions as "who am I?" and "what is life?" I used to know these things, or feel that I did, but at the bottom of my soul there's a sense of rejection toward whatever was.

The elemental "faith" in life I used to possess is completely gone, to the extent that I now carry the built-in assumption that whatever I used to do was probably wrong (it didn't "work," after all), and thus every little element of my former life, behavior, interests, and habits, was up for re-examination.

So, I came back to reading, bicycling, motorcycling, rowing, and bird-watching, and found them good. Now I can add snow-shoeing and cross-country skiing to that list. And watching it snow. Oh yeah — and letter-writing.

During the journey I kept a pretty good journal going (like reading, it's useful when you're travelling alone, especially in bars and restaurants) and I've ended up with three volumes of "Ghost Rider" notes (Canada, U.S., and Mexico/Belize), though I haven't started transcribing them yet.

Anyway, thanks again for your good wishes along the way, and know that I am now ensconced in my snowy domain (yahoo, just look at it snow!), feeling my way through the days. For now I plan to be here for the next couple of months, at least, save for one reluctant trip to Toronto which I'll have to make at some point, to deal with matters medical, dental, financial, legal, and all fun things like that.

Let's both look for an opportunity to get together sometime soon; I'd like that. Maybe you'll be in Montreal (just an hour from here), or we'll both be in Toronto, or, come Springtime, maybe one day you'll look down the road and see a distant apparition of red paint and black leather, as the one-and-only Ghost Rider comes a-riding your way . . .

Bye for now,

Your friend,

NEP

[Letter to Mendelson Joe]

Jan. 19, 1999
Lac St. Brutus, Que.

Dear Joe,

Well, I'm here, and I'm alive.

(Let's start with the essentials.)

For at least the last month of my self-imposed exile, that's all I
wanted — to be here and to be alive. It was a long journey down
that ol' Healing Road, and of course, it ain't over yet. Not hardly.
In fact, I guess it begins again every day. Well, I'm here and I'm
alive. Start with the essentials.

For a couple of weeks in early December, I travelled around
Baja California, which I did enjoy a lot, then took a ferry over to
"mainland" Mexico, to some of the places where Brutus and I had
ridden a few years back. Despite the inevitable frustrations of
travelling in a "struggling" country, I do like Mexico, especially the
people.

For one thing, they understand about *music*. Aboard that
overnight ferry I took from La Paz to Mazatlán, I noticed there
was taped music playing in the dining room, a live band in the
bar, a "CD jukebox" blaring at the stern, and even when I stood up
by the bow to look at the moon rising above the still waters of the
Sea of Cortez, there was rhythmic Latin music floating out from
the bridge. Music is everywhere, all the time, and very often in the
towns my spirits were lifted by live music. In the main squares,
mariachi bands, marimba bands, dance bands, and solo violinists
and guitarists roam around, entertaining the people and receiving
their willing contributions.

And also, nearly all the music is *Mexican*, even the pop music,
and considering Mexico's status and location (a former Mexican
president once remarked, "Poor Mexico: so far from God, and so

close to the United States"), it's remarkable that the youth in particular have escaped the pervasive reach of that Amerikan-Disney-ghetto influence.

In the "native" communities of the western U.S. and Canada, and even in the far north, I would see the local youths out "cruising," packed into a tarted-up old car with the doors breathing in and out to the booming bass of inner-city rap music. Probably the big beats and angry rhymes of the "ghetto gangstas" do express the universal frustrations of "disaffected youth," but for the Inuit kids as much as for the Mexicans, the imported stuff is certainly in a "foreign language."

How great for the Mexican people that they've got their own music, and that it's part of such a strong culture. Even in the most heinously overdeveloped resort towns, with their Hard Rock Cafés and Planet Hollywoods, I've found there always remains a *Mexican* town, if you know what to look for. Even in Puerto Vallarta, one of the most "ravaged" of all the Pacific Coast beach resorts, I was able to find the narrow, uneven backstreets, the quirky old church on the open square lined with street peddlers' tables, and right in the middle of the tourist strip of souvenir shops and bars along the seawall, a live-music show, full of joy and life, entirely performed and attended by *locals*.

I probably mentioned in my previous letter that Nature has been an important source of Truth and Beauty for me lately, and throughout my travels I've been especially drawn to the birds. It worked great on my hikes, of course, carrying a little field guide and binoculars, but even as I rode along on the motorcycle, I learned to glance at, say, a hawk on a roadside post, and memorize the field marks: medium-size, yellow-billed, body barred in brown-and-white, tail white-edged, black primaries. Then I'd look it up later, and be able to identify it, scientifically, as "some kind of hawk." As a kid of seven or eight, my ambition in life was to be a "professional bird-watcher," and I may finally have reached that goal.

Last summer, when I set out on my journey, I was driven by a sense, or a hope, that motion would be a good "diversion" for me, especially compared to sitting here and stewing in my own bile, but I had no idea just how important it would be. Some mornings I would wake up freaking and sad and lonely and desperate, but as soon as I got on the bike, the world would first *contract*, to the size of the machine which carried me and everything I needed, and then it would *expand*, to the wide new world of highway, landscape, and wildlife coming at me.

Once I started getting out and hiking in the woods and mountains, I found the same benefits applied. It wasn't about the beautiful scenery or the peace and serenity of Nature; it wasn't the *looking* that mattered, it was the *moving*. To be on the road, or on the march, that was the thing.

Up here, I've found the same "therapy" in snowshoeing and skiing. It's not like I'm taking much joy from the beauty of the winter woods, for often I find myself staring down at the *ground* as I plod along, but my mind gets into that "movin' groove," and at some point I'll think, "Hey — where have I been for the past 10 minutes?"

Then maybe I'll stop and look around at the scenery, with a freshly smoothed-out brain.

And that's my profession these days (apart from "bird-watcher"); taking care of my "little baby soul." That's the way I've come to define my life, for now. The expression "a soul in peril" came into my head the other day, and I think it's apt, for I sure face a whole lot of dangers right now. So far, it has been some help just knowing that, forewarned and forearmed, and I've been able to gently "guide" myself along less-destructive paths. (Again, keep *moving*.)

So far it's been working okay, but I'm not out of the woods yet, not by a long way. What I really lack is my former power of *enthusiasm*, of getting fired up about doing a particular thing, or learning about it, so that it became more important than anything else in the whole world. It used to be so easy and automatic to summon that dedication and sense-of-mission to activities like long-distance bicycling, telemark skiing, motorcycling, swimming, learning about art, history, and even the "big stuff," like music and writing.

These days, there's nothing I really *want* to do, in the way that I used to be driven, and there's nothing I really *have* to do, in the sense of keeping myself housed and fed. You might agree with a friend of mine in England who has also spent most of his life in poverty, that I'm luckier than some who have lost everything and are *poor* too. I can partly get my mind around that, but not totally. I don't feel luckier than nobody, really.

But yeah, it's true that I don't *have* to do anything (for now, anyway), but when you add that against the "double negative" that I don't *want* to do anything, then you see the danger.

I mean, I'm pretty wary of the "Why?" question these days, for I daren't apply it to what has happened to my daughter, my wife, my dog, or my best friend. Far as I'm concerned, ain't no "why," ain't no "fair." So why get up in the morning? Why pretend to "carry on"?

A writer friend of mine, Lesley Choyce, put the question to me in a letter just yesterday, saying that he was glad I'd found something to keep me going, but wondered, "what was it?"

Well, to tell him (and you) the truth, I don't know what it was, or is; maybe I'll figure it out later. It seems I have a little reflex in my brain which, through all the dark times I've experienced before this darkest of all possible times, has seemed to hold onto the thought, "Something will come up." Good enough for now. I'll just try to "guide" myself gently along reasonably healthy paths, and try to avoid as many of the dangers and poisons as I can. Just hang out, basically, and wait for that ol' "something" to come up.

At least the snow is back, whipping around in the air today

and giving some motion and brightness to a gray day. The snow on the ground remains pretty soppy after yesterday's rain, so forget skiing, and I think even the snowshoes would become a slushy, heavy mess pretty quickly. So I'll try a walk down the road. There are only five other houses on my dead-end road, usually only occupied by weekenders from Montreal, so it's a quiet place to walk on a midweek day.

Joe, thanks again for your letters along the way, and for your genuine concern for me, and I can only report, as usual, that I'm doing "as well as can be expected."

And as usual, I hope you are too.

Your friend,

NEP

[Letter to Steven, who lived near Columbus, Ohio, where his wife Shelly was an emergency-room doctor. I had asked him to let me know how he was *really* feeling.]

Jan. 26, '99
Lac St. Brutus

Hey there, Ugly American!

I say: good venting there!

Seriously, well done. I asked you to try it, and you obviously gave it a sincere shot. I could feel the fire and vitriol in those words, right through the cold medium of the fax machine's digital reproduction.

"How was it for you?" (He asked her politely.) I hope that putting it down like that did you a teensy bit of good, as I have sometimes found it does (at least "on the day"), and I also hope you understand that in any case, it can't do any harm, nor ever be taken "out of context." Not when it's addressed to this particular audience.

For a start, you can appreciate that reading stuff like that doesn't hurt me a bit. Like I was describing to you before, these mundane things are annoying and unnecessary all right, for everyone and especially for us "walking wounded," but such pests and parasites in life are not really *real,* after all. Not like that groin-sucking *Cimex lectularius* [the bedbugs of Belize] whose depredations are still fully evident upon my epidermis. Now *that's* real!

In contrast to the picayune things, certainly I am moved and concerned when I hear about your serious complaints, like matters of health and mental wellness. And that's as it should be, for I care about you. But when it comes to the other stuff in our lives, I'm glad to know about it, just to be more in touch with your life, but it doesn't *affect* me, you know?

Like the way it's been working lately with Deb and me: we already know we share the big hurt, the massive, fundamental, existential, world-shattering Loss, so that remains understood and unspoken when we talk on the phone. So, like a couple of housewives, we tell each other about the small stuff that's bugging us that day. It's just a chance to unload, or download, and often speaking it aloud breaks the "spell" of such troubles.

But another thing that comes through all too clearly is that you're still feeling so isolated and directionless, and though I understand that, there are some things I've learned that I think you might profit from, and in a minute I will tell you about them.

I think it's safe to say that I have been left even more "bereft" than you, and not only in the loss of my family, but in the loss of absolutely *everything* that I thought made up my life. My life and "self" were reduced to absolute zero, and even now I think of my previous self as "that other guy," and feel we share nothing but the same set of memories.

Maybe the only difference between you and me at this remove

is that I have known for quite awhile now that everything was gone, and that I had to completely start over. In the past six months or so, my response to that realization has been to try everything that I *used* to like, and see if it still "worked" for me, even if in a totally different way. Thus I came back to, for example, reading and walking in England, cycling and bird-watching in Barbados, and since then, motorcycling, snowshoeing, and cross-country skiing.

Some things from the "old life" still have no interest, or are too dangerous to mess with, like the emotional power of music, for example. That was a problem, for I can hardly imagine life without music as some part of it, but I had to find a new way to use that power.

Right now, I don't want or need the emotional engagement of music, and certainly I don't need the memory-associations of the music that was part of our "family life." So I started with "neutral" stuff, instrumental music and old standards, like Big Frank, that would "transport" me in the way that music has the power to do, but not take me bad places.

For example, lately I'm listening to all kinds of old cassettes that have reappeared from the basement in Toronto, as boxes of old things get moved up here, and most of that stuff is music I used to listen to, say, 15 years ago; music that engages me on a more personal basis, and can be listened to purely as a *sensory* pleasure, rather than just reminding me of better times.

Interesting that whenever I try to listen to music that I have been part of in the past, like when Geddy gave me the CDs of the live Rush album they were working on, it just doesn't register in a personal way. It's always "that other guy," and though the "new guy" I'm trying to construct out of these fragments, John Ellwood, might appreciate the work "the other guy" did, it's just not me, you know? I can't even imagine the dedication and single-minded effort he put into that stuff. I still admire the accomplishment, and respect the hard work that made it possible for him to play the drums at that level, but it's just not *me*.

I watched my instructional video the other night, just as an "experiment," and the same thing happened. It was like the guy talking and playing on the screen wasn't me. I could appreciate what he was doing, and what it had cost him to be able to do that, and it's not like I considered it all a waste of time or anything. It just didn't have any relation to the "me" I'm living inside now.

So okay, that's the way it is. Same thing with movies; any kind of emotional dramas are right out, again because I don't *need* that. What Aristotle called the purpose of art, the "catharsis" of releasing your pent-up feelings, is just not *relevant* to my current station in life. My feelings are fully evident, and fully expressed!

Thus, I watch stupid, unemotional stuff, like Speedvision: the Dakar rally, last summer's motorcycle races, or even classic car auctions. Or, the other night, I laughed at myself for watching the NHL All-Star game, but just as you've found with football, it may be *stupid*, but that's okay. It keeps the stupid part of your brain occupied, and that's the important thing. For whatever you call that "stupid part" — subconscious, unconscious, left-hemisphere — it's always the troublemaker.

So, here follow some "directives," some "instructions" which reflect the more useful things I have learned. The proper way to look at these observations is that they are necessarily *adaptations*. I have found that it's meaningless to talk in terms of "dealing with it," or of "working through it." No. This particular *It* is not something to be dealt with, or worked through. This kind of It simply changes everything, and there's no coming to terms with it. No deal to be made, no compromise. (I think Ayn Rand once wrote, "You can't compromise with evil.")

Here and now it's about starting all over again, from the ground up, and as Darwinian organisms, we are expected to adapt to these new circumstances. Adapt or perish. We can't change what is, or its effects on us and our view of life. That is all done. If we truly want to try to carry on from this dark crossroads, we can only try to guide the inevitable changes in *ourselves*. We would not be who we are if this was something we could "get over," or simply carry on from where we left off. Once I expressed the way I see my future this way, "I know I'm *scarred* by these experiences, I just don't want to be too *crippled* by them."

If there is any point in carrying on, it is not in simply *existing*, in cluttering up the world with another bitter and nasty old man, or a joyless hermit, or a suffering martyr forever living in the past, and punishing everyone else for what life has done to *me*.

I don't like the feel of the word "Acceptance," the technical term which is applied by the "griefologists" to the stage of the process in which I presently find myself. I found on my return from the Healing Road that after all that time and distance, I had at least transcended "Denial." But to me, knowing that these things are true doesn't mean I *accept* that truth. Far from it. As far as I can see, I will *never* accept that life is supposed to turn out this way. Especially *our* lives. It's not the way I lived, or Jackie lived, or the way we taught Selena.

This is not at all the way I thought the world worked, and after all, it is not "acceptable" that Selena and Jackie had to die. No way. Not in my world. So that world, or that world-view, is gone. Some well-meaning people have tried to offer me what they perceive to be a "comforting" thought of the "everything must happen for a reason" kind, but I shut them up right away (as politely as I can). Somehow they don't see that it's absolutely no consolation to look at it that way, and more, it brings up some terrible questions in your head: "There's some kind of *reason*? What? They *deserved* to die? I deserved to *lose* them? The world didn't *need* people like Jackie and Selena?"

Bullshit. Then sometimes my thoughts wander in paranoid directions, or perhaps primal superstitions. "Was it something I *did?* Did someone who hates me put a *curse* on me?"

The rational mind can easily dismiss such "voodoo," but after all, it's not the rational mind we have to deal with here. It's the "stupid mind." And of course, it's not a *strong* mind that lies awake in the darkness and ponders these deadly questions.

So, those of us on the "inside," like you and me, are left trying to "accept the unacceptable." We're expected to pull ourselves together and carry on (expectations sometimes from others, sometimes just from an unextinguishable part of ourselves), but we face a pretty desperate battle, after all, for there's nothing to pull together!

Everything that we were, everything we based our lives upon, everything that we believed is gone. In my journal one time, I expressed the feeling of *hurt* that I carry around, so similar to the feeling of being betrayed, and I concluded that I *had* been betrayed, by Life itself, and that's pretty deep. So, the betrayed ones, like you and me, have to start all over again, from Absolute Zero, and construct some new version of "Life," one that we can "live with." No way we can hold onto what we used to believe, and no way we can forget what has actually happened in our lives, and in our worlds. We will never *trust* Life again.

However, once again, we've got to adapt, even to that unbearable reality, or one way or another, we will perish. Period.

So, the list of directives. These theories are sometimes developed from insights I gained from all the "grief books" I read back in London, but that academic basis (which is, after all, only the collected experiences of other human beings, sometimes "interpreted" by those who have studied this dark area) and those insights were only valuable because I applied them to my own experience — what has worked for me, what gets me through these long, joyless days and nights in a non-destructive way.

Again, if it's true that only Time is the proven healing agent, then it is necessary to adapt to *that* reality, and it becomes paramount just to "hang on," to survive, so that the supposed magic powers of passing Time have a chance to do their thing. As I told you, that process does seem to have been at work during my four-month odyssey. Though there's still far to go down that "Healing Road," and no end in sight.

One of Napoleon's generals, Marechal Ney I think, had the motto *D'abord, durer* (at first, to last). This admirable "first principle" was also adopted by Ernest Hemingway, both as a personal and professional keystone. Same for us. If Time is going to be any use to us as a healing agent, then we've got to be around for it to *happen,* you know?

So, the directives. Here we go:

1/ KEEP MOVING. The best, simplest, and most important thing. In the way that marching around the park worked for me in London, or bicycling worked for me in Barbados, I was gratified to find that on my "very large journey," motorcycling worked for me, and later, hiking.

If your "little baby soul" is cranky and restless, you've got to take your little baby soul out for a ride and calm it down. Sometimes it seems to go to sleep in about a minute, but that's okay too, of course (you just want it to be *quiet,* right?), and sometimes I seem to go into a trance-like state, and I'll "come to" and think, "Hey, where have I been for the past 10 minutes?" "Far away," is the answer, and that's sometimes a good place to be. I use cross-country skiing as an excuse to get out; go do an errand, and have a ski on the way. Or go for a ski, and do an errand on the way.

Either way, it gets me moving, and gets things done. Which is another important directive:

2/ KICK YOUR OWN ASS, GENTLY. I've been trying to set a few modest goals, both daily and weekly. In the course of a day, it's good to get some stupid things accomplished, and off your "list."

I guess because it leaves you feeling that you and the "rest of the world" still have something to do with each other!

Like today, for example, I can think back on sending a fax to my brother on his birthday, leaving a phone message for Brutus at his "hotel" on his birthday, phoning my Dad on his birthday (yep, all on the same day), then driving to Morin Heights to the ATM machine, to St. Sauveur for grocery shopping, and planning all that so I'd still have enough daylight left to go snowshoeing in the woods. And *then* I could drink.

Not a high-pressure day, and hardly earth-shaking activities, but I laid them out for myself and did them (even though tempted to "not bother" with each of them at one point or another). I gave myself a gentle kick in the ass when necessary, or cursed myself out for a lazy fool, and because of all that, I consider today a satisfactory day. Everything that needed to be done got done. And by "needs" I certainly include taking my little baby soul out for a ride. And drinking.

And there are little side benefits from such activities, like when the cashier in the grocery store wished me a genuinely-pleasant *"Bonjour,"* and I forced myself to look at her and return the greeting. The world still seems unreal to me, but I try not to purposely avoid contact with pleasant strangers. It wouldn't be polite!

Another "little goal" for me right now is spending an hour or two at the desk every morning, writing a letter or a fax to someone like you, or Brutus, or Danny, who I want to reach out to, or conversely, to someone I've been out of touch with for a long while, maybe for a year-and-a-half or two years. These are friends that I've decided I still value, and that I want as part of my "new life," whatever it may be.

It doesn't really matter what, but just so you can say that you changed *something* in the course of your day: a neglected friend is no longer neglected; an errand that ought to be dealt with has been dealt with.

3/ ALLOW OTHERS THE PLEASURE OF HELPING YOU. Good
for them; good for you. I have certainly learned to "lean" during
these times, and I have found many people eminently worth
leaning upon; yourself chief among them. However, I know that
you don't have such people around you, in your "exile," and I am
also aware that there is more sympathy and help offered to me, as
the "chief victim," or "central bereaved."

But, take advantage of whatever you can, as I have been doing
lately, for example, with Keith. Pushing ever more of the "chores"
of life in his direction, and I must say that he's been doing a great
job for me. And not only in the sense of "doing the job," but he is
doing everything he can to make life *easier* for me. Refreshingly
discreet, and careful not to "intrude," but following up on the
smallest hint of something he could take care of. I hope it
continues.

4/ THE "REPLAY" SYNDROME. Oh man, that is torture. From
the very beginning, that August night when Chief Ernie pulled up
here with the terrible news, I have been tormented by an endless
loop of Selena's accident, different "imaginings" of it, all horrible.
That's bad enough, and it continues, and it's neither worse nor
better than the *real* memories of Jackie at the end.

Lately, when I feel one of those "replays" starting up, I try to
stop it: get up, move around, literally tell myself "fuck off," "stop
it right now." (Yes, I talk to myself a lot lately, but I think I give
myself good advice!)

Again, motion: move your thoughts elsewhere, physically if
necessary.

5/ MAKE PEACE WITH OTHERS WHERE YOU CAN. And where
it's worth it. You and I have been through the direst extremes of

human experience, perhaps comparable only to soldiers at war. It was tense and intense. We all did everything we could, all focused on Jackie. Feelings ran high, and any friction or tension was a direct result of the situation, and ended with it.

I hope that is true between you and me. We may have been alienated temporarily by our ways of handling such horror: you isolating yourself, which has the effect of alienating others. Nothing permanent, nothing important. Put it behind us. No discussion necessary, no "forgiveness." No wrong done, nobody hurt. Just how we individually handled "the heat of battle." Surprised to find *myself* more open to others through that time, probably because of experience with Selena's death and looking after Jackie. Had to depend on others, and had plenty of others I could depend on.

Back in February of '98 when we came back from England with Jackie's "death sentence," it was only because *you* were there that I could (or felt I could) let go of myself, after six months of holding Jackie up, of trying so hard to be strong and "good" in the face of what I must have known was a losing cause, one way or another. At that point, it all became *too much*, and I just wanted to be *numb* for awhile. I had known its value before, in Britain, but knew it wasn't good for Jackie, and that I couldn't get "out of it" and still look after Jackie, keep her *alive*.

It was a heavy weight, and for a very long time, so when we came back to Toronto and you came riding to our rescue (or at least relief), I was glad to turn it over to you for awhile. Being "out of it" was a very desirable place for me (still is) and to anyone who dared criticize me, I would have said, "Sure I'm fucked up — how *should* I be?"

No argument there. I'm not proud of all that, but I "pulled myself together" when the time came, and I know that Jackie never *really* blamed me for choosing "out of it" for awhile. In fact,

I think she was reassured to know that I took it that hard, and I was glad to notice that when anyone dared criticize me, she came out on my side.

(Somebody stop me! This machine is out of control! Use what you can, and "recycle" the rest.)

NEP

[Letter to Lesley Choyce]

Feb. 5, '99
Lac St. Brutus, Que.

Dear Lesley,

Here I am again, just back from the dreaded trip to Toronto I mentioned "looking forward to" in my previous letter. Cramming all the unpleasantness into two days kept me busy there, and got all the crap taken care of, while I also had a couple of more enjoyable engagements, like dinners with my erstwhile partners.

But I was sure glad to get away from there. Too many memories, for one thing, and a lot of them come out of nowhere: a mental "flinch" as I drive along and glance at the Gap on the corner of Bay and Bloor where I once met Selena to take her shopping; or the restaurant where Jackie and I once had dinner with Louie Bellson and some other "drum guys"; even just the streets Jackie and Selena once used to walk and drive on.

It's all too much, really.

And not only was I glad to get away from *there*, I was glad to get back *here*. In these past weeks it has become clear to me that I love this house, and in a different way, I also love my land, "The 100 Aker Wood." It's good to have something to love, after all (reminds me of the movie of *The Grapes of Wrath:* "It's not much.

Just dirt. But it's my dirt"). And this house full of all the art and treasures that Jackie and I collected, and all the memories of Selena and our three lives together, has begun to evolve into a good thing. Protective and private, soothing and beautiful. I always said I wanted to live in a "comfortable museum," and that's what I'm building here.

With the Toronto house up for sale (lo, these many months), I've gradually been moving all the "art-stuff" from there and "folding" it into this house, so now I have an environment that Jackie surely would have described as "cluttered," but it suits my cluttered soul, and provides diversion for the eyes.

"Bachelor with a vengeance," that's me. A decorative Ducati in the living room, canoe hanging artfully from the ceiling, car models displayed here and there, and a painting to decorate every expanse of wall. Now that I have all my books installed in the "Selena Memorial Library," it is once again a "living" room, and to me it kind of represents the "heart" of the house. With mementos of Jackie and Selena on display there, that notion is somehow . . . apt.

I still get blind-sided sometimes by a sudden stab of painful memory, triggered by a photo or an object, but that's not surprising. Perhaps I'll get over those things, one by one, so that the only memories that cross my mind are *good* ones. In any case, escape is at hand, no farther away than across the road, and it's so therapeutic to head into the woods on my snowshoes or cross-country skis, losing myself in the motion, the dance of forgetfulness. For you, "the coastline of forgetting," for me, the Forest of Lethe!

One good thing that emerged from my trip to Toronto was the opportunity to read your latest, *World Enough,* and what a fine piece of work it is. The highest tribute is the way it "hooked" me, and here's a perfect illustration: On my way back from dinner with my friends one night, I was thinking, "good, now I can get back to my *book*." That's the greatest spell a writer can cast, of course, and I can tell you that I was well and truly *rapt*.

Well done sir. Another masterpiece, in my opinion, right up there with *The Republic of Nothing*. Great characters, truly "living landscapes" (you are perhaps the first writer ever to wax lyrical over an industrial park), vivid weather (loved the King and the Lords and Ladies, for they added both your "trademark" magic, and poignant metaphors), and the narrative is so skillfully woven.

In the reading of it, some of those old storytelling metaphors occurred to me, like to "spin a yarn," or to "weave a tale," and I was also thinking that maybe there are two basic approaches to telling a story: to spin it out, thread by thread, in the classic narrative way, or to unravel it, like a curtain, to reveal the action on the stage behind. Like Faulkner, say, or Patrick White. I guess you have used both of these techniques in *World Enough*, making the reader wait, for example, as Karen's fate is gradually revealed. Of course, it is also important that the technique is *invisible*, so that I only noticed these things when I thought back, "How did he do that?"

Same with the politics, so astute, so compassionate, so germane to the story, and yet always in the "show, don't tell" mode. Either the action reveals the injustice, or the characters voice it, but the "omniscient author" is never called upon to preach. (Let that be a lesson to me!)

I don't know if the title was drawn from the text, or woven into it so deftly, but either way, it works beautifully, especially to include the whole phrase, "world enough and time." (Where's that from? Wordsworth maybe?) I also loved the juxtaposition of Whitman and Eliot, "Leaves of Grass" and "Prufrock." This applies very deeply to me these days, for I certainly feel as if I've moved from Whitman's existential and physical ecstasies to Eliot's "thoughts of a dry brain in a dry season." (That's "Gerontion," but it will serve.) It may have been prophetic that a few years ago I had to come up with a corporate name, and chose "Prufrock Interests." Though at the time I intended quite a different sort of irony!

One question you raised in your letter that's been rattling around in my (dry) brain is about the mysterious "thing" that has kept me going these past months. The answer is, I don't know. Not yet, anyway. I've been so busy figuring out *how* to survive that I've given no thought to the *why*, and right now I don't have the brain-power, or perhaps the need, to go there. No doubt one day it will "crystallize," as such knowledge seems to do.

My guess is that the prime mover is instinctive, biological. The trouble with thinking about why I chose to live, is that I can't avoid thinking about why Jackie chose to *die*. (For there's no doubt it was a matter of choice, and will.) Though thinking of pure Darwinism, and the cellular drives to survive and reproduce, the answer to both questions might be as simple as that. Either way, I hate it. And it's not fair. Though as I wrote to my friend Mendelson Joe, "Ain't no 'why;' ain't no 'fair.'"

Buen viaje, amigo

Why are we here?
Because we're here —
Roll the bones
Why does it happen?
Because it happens —
Roll the bones

ROLL THE BONES, 1993

Chapter 10

SEASONAL AFFECTIVE DISORDER

Scars of pleasure
Scars of pain
Atmospheric changes
Make them sensitive again

SCARS, 1990

[Letter to Brutus]
roi-de-neige des Laurentides

Feb. 8–9, '99
Lac St. Brutus, Que.

Hey there Mangeur-de-Merde!

A brand-new Monday morning for me here, and the pattern continues. A little "desk-piloting" in the morning, then out in the woods for the afternoon. Over in the "100 Aker Wood" on my snowshoes yesterday, I made it around the perimeter (the first circumambulation since you and I did it, I think), and used up the last of my orange trail-ribbon marking the boundary lines and potential trail routes.

The day before, I made it all the way through the Crown land and the old logging roads up to the Aerobic Corridor. After the days of trail-clearing and sumac-snipping I was telling you about, finally I could just walk there, and it makes a nice "march."

For the first time I noticed the hunters back there have set up feeding troughs opposite their tree stands, and no doubt they feed the deer there for *weeks* before hunting season, then just set up and wait to knock 'em down. Man, just like I saw in Alaska, that ain't huntin' — that's just *shootin'!*

The animal tracks in the snow have become a real source of fascination too, checking them out and learning to read them. Of course I've got a couple of field guides for that, but there are some I've been seeing a lot that have me wondering, for they sure look like wolves. Bigger than fox tracks, often travelling in twos and threes, and keeping a relatively straight line, as foxes, coyotes, and wolves do, and domestic dogs *don't;* rambling around and sniffing everything. Besides, there aren't any dogs around here, that I know of.

Yesterday, when I was out in the woods I was pretty sure a pack of those hungry wolves was on my trail, watching me from behind the rocks and trees, and just waiting for their chance to creep up silently and tear me to pieces. But I got away.

In all these ways, my woods have become so important to me lately — so therapeutic — and I want more trails! The important note about the trail thing is that it involves the *future,* and thus has me thinking ahead, even "looking forward" to something. Most days I don't have much of that feeling. As I told you, I usually wake up and almost immediately utter an ancient Anglo-Saxon word. So I'm diggin' the woods.

Last week, I had to spend a couple of days in (cue thunder and lightning) Toronto. Didn't like it. Too many memories smacking me from every side, and too many goddamn people. Into two busy days I crammed all the necessary business: dental, medical, financial, and funereal (a most enjoyable visit and "delivery" to Mount Pleasant Cemetery — ach!), and had dinner one night with Ray [Rush's manager], and the next with Geddy, Alex, and Liam. It was great to be around those guys once again, for they always get me laughing, and their friendship is all about *support,* and no pressure about anything professional.

So that part was nice enough, though on the drive back here I couldn't help thinking "bummer thoughts." Like what a drag it is for other people to have to hang around with *me.* Throughout this long nightmare, all of my friends have come through for me in such a righteous and big-time way, but after all, at this point it can't be much fun to be around me: thinking of what to say, worried about a flagging conversation, a tactless remark, feeling awkward and sad and helpless to do anything for "poor old me." I don't know. All I can say is, *I* wouldn't want to be my friend. ("And I'm *not* either." "Shut up." "No *you* shut up." "You're the one who's sick you know." "Just shut up!")

One of my Toronto meetings was with my broker, and I asked

him for an estimate of what my "fixed income" might be, if I considered myself retired and living on my investments. Then I asked Sheila for an overview of my annual expenses. And guess what? Sheila's number was more than *twice* the broker's number. I'm no mathemagician, that's for sure, but I know that's not good.

So I agonized over that for a few days (something else to worry about — great!), then decided just to live the way I do, and when my money's all gone, I'll *die!* Poof! Simple, no? I don't know why no one else ever thought of that. Maybe I'll pick up some extra income on the side working as a financial planner for other people. "Well, Mr. and Mrs. Gluck, weighing your assets and liabilities, I think you should sell everything, spend all your money, then *die.*"

Enough grumping — something good to talk about, something good to talk about . . .

Well, the Selena Memorial Library is now a complete A/V center. Deb picked me up a good slide projector and a wall-mount screen, so I've been spending some time going through all my "Ghost Rider" slides and arranging them in carousels. Now I've got those done, I'll start going back through the Scooter Trash stuff too.

And now I can give slide-shows! Just think, next time you visit me you'll be able to sit, spellbound, and look at all my slides, for *hours.*

Or maybe you'd rather stay where you are . . .

Today I'm going for a ski, probably just a nice, easy glide along the Aerobic Corridor. When David Mills was up here [another long-time friend who, with his wife Karen, had been very supportive through "everything"] we did the Triangle, a 10-kilometre loop (marked "difficult" on the maps) which offers a lot of ups-and-downs, some of them steep and narrow. I fell at least *12* times (though often just "bailing out" when careening downhill, out-of-control), while that suave son-of-a-gun didn't fall once.

Not even a token tumble, just to make a clumsy friend feel a little better. You believe that?

Why, once I even drew *blood,* planting my face in the snow and slicing my nose on the icy crust. I said a lot of bad words that day. However, as I said to David on the way back, I wouldn't have chosen to do anything else, and I'll certainly do it again, another day. (Useless to protest about the difficult conditions, for my so-called friend had no apparent trouble.)

But I'm still finding that getting out on the 'shoes or the "skinny sticks" diverts and calms the mind — the soul — so well. Good thing too, for this little baby soul has been doing a *lot* of mewling lately. Probably got colic or something. Teething, maybe. Yeah, that's it — my little baby soul is starting to grow teeth!

I like that.

Anyway, today the trails will be clear of the weekend riff-raff, so I'm looking forward to a bit of inner peace-and-quiet. Rock that little baby to sleep . . .

I like that too.

Anyway (yet another "anyway"), while I'm out I'll check the post-office box and see if it doesn't contain some kind of scribbling from you, then continue with this later.

Feb. 9, '99

So . . . I had a great ski yesterday afternoon. A cold, sunny day, a scrawl of green wax, and perfect snow conditions. Parking by the mail boxes at the top of Chemin des Blageurs, I started off on the Corridor, then wandered off on a side-trail above Lac Cochon, breaking away from the easy-peasy and into the woods for some more natural terrain, with some challenging ups and downs, and — without falling once — grooved my way over to the junction with the Viking Ski Club trails.

By the trail map it looks as if there's a good little loop I could do on the Viking trail, and maybe today I'll try that. (Navigating ski trails can be like figuring out Mexican roads, so if you don't hear from me in a week or so, call somebody.)

Oh yeah: I'm glad you liked *Islands in the Stream*. It was made into a beautiful movie too, with George C. Scott, Claire Bloom, and David Hemming as the "rummy." (Maybe the boys would like to rent it one night, hmm?) In the movie version, they did a great job with that last line: "You never understand about anybody that loves you."

Haven't my last couple of letters been talking about just that kind of stuff?

Deep, man.

Later, baby,

NEP

[Letter to Hugh Syme, my partner in the art direction of Rush album covers since 1975, as well as the cover of *The Masked Rider* book, the instructional video on drumming, *A Work in Progress,* and the two Buddy Rich tribute albums which I had produced]

Feb. 11, '99
Lac St. Brutus, Que.

Dear Hugh,

Sorry I've been out of touch for so long, but . . . I've been having a bad year. (I've also developed a certain gift for understatement.) However, I'm sure I'll get over all this, and get back to some kind of a life, in, oh, about 10,000 years. Until then, I'll just try to stay active. That's it — just look busy. (Like the bumper sticker, "Jesus is Coming/ Look Busy.")

I've been back here in Quebec for about six weeks now, after a four-month motorcycle odyssey on what I came to call the "Healing Road." That road doesn't really have a destination, of course, but there are some nice views along the way, and that's what did me good. You can imagine that coming back from Barbados, after losing Jackie too, I was pretty much shot down. I didn't like anything, didn't care about anything, and didn't want to do anything. A dangerous time.

So, in the process of trying to rebuild something, I tried things I used to like, to see if they were any good. A few of life's "consolations" crept back to me; though nothing was ever how it *used* to be. During the six months Jackie and I spent in London, I started to be able to read again, and then started walking: for *miles* around London, Regents Park Canal and Primrose Hill in the north, along the river to St. Paul's in the east, west through Hyde Park and Kensington Gardens to Holland Park, or south through Kensington and Chelsea to Hammersmith Bridge. March, march, march . . .

In Barbados, it was bird-watching, which has continued to divert me on my recent travels, and in Barbados I also took up bicycling again. With Jackie's blessing (as the one, after all, who had bought me my first grown-up bicycle, which really started something, and then my first motorcycle, which started a whole *other* something), I bought a mountain bike, and every second morning got out and lost myself in the hills and the heat of the northern part of the island.

Rowing came back to me last summer, and out on the lake I hauled furiously at the oars of my sleek little rowboat, venting some energy, and some anger. (Yep, I carry around a fair amount of that useless commodity, and say lots of bad words in the course of a day.)

During my long, dark teatime of the soul, dragged under by that maëlstrom of unending nightmare and horror, I could only cling to family and close, family-type friends, and fortunately they came through for me in a life-changing way.

From experience and the reading of many "grief books" (now there's a cheerful area of study), I know that it's up to me to re-establish contact with the people I want to continue to have in my "new life." (Them that's willing, anyway.)

These days, I'm slowly starting to reach out to other old friends, a letter at a time, and I do still enjoy this process of putting words together, of trying to express things. However, at the moment my ambition ends there. Or *here*. Letter-writing is sufficient for now, and I'm certainly not about to push myself too hard. It's enough for me to do a little "communicating" every day, and to take my little baby soul out for a ride. With a few other bits and pieces of daily chores, that's my job.

Sure I know there's probably a powerful book to be woven out of my life, out of my recent "travels," both existential and geographical, and even including strands from the Rush tour, but I also know that making a book like that would be perishing hard work. I'm not ready for that yet. As the Kilimanjaro guides advise you on making the ascent, *pole, pole*. Slowly, slowly.

My previous enthusiasm for life and work has taken a serious blow too. Now it's hard to imagine that anything *matters* very much, and of course that's just the opposite of the mindset it takes to get obsessed with doing something. So I just keep moving.

Out on the road, I started calling myself "The Ghost Rider," for I felt so alienated and isolated from all the normal life around me, I carried so many "ghosts" with me (in my "baggage" as it were) and was often travelling in the "vapor trails" left by older ghosts too, as I visited landscapes reminiscent of Jack London, Ernest Hemingway, Lewis and Clark, pioneers, prospectors (even some "ghost towns," which made for a deep metaphor), Pony Express riders, Mormons, Lakotas, Apaches, Aztecs, and all the lost souls of the past.

I started a series of "Ghost Rider" photographs, where I would stop in the middle of an empty road, park my bike on the center-stand so it looked as if it was riding along, then run back down the road to take a photo from behind, of bike, diminishing highway, and surrounding landscape. Once I hit on that idea, it became my "device," and I've got some great shots like that taken in the sagebrush desert of the Great Basin, the creosote desert of the Mojave, the massive stone monoliths of Monument Valley, the cactus deserts of Arizona and Baja California, and even on muddy roads through the rainforest in Central America.

Long ago, Geddy told me that he was working with you on the packaging for a live album, but I've neither heard the music nor seen the artwork. That's another area where I feel seriously divided, for all of that kind of work came out of the old me, and I feel especially alienated from "the guy that was in the band." (Some serious personality breakdown here; I could be doing a "Sybil" in reverse, fragmenting from one into many. Cool!)

But whenever I've tried to listen to Rush music, or even watch my instructional video, it just doesn't feel like *me*. Hard to explain, but even harder to live with, so I stay away from that area. In fact, music in general is weird for me. I can hardly imagine life without some kind of music in it, but I have to be careful of its emotional power. You'll remember from your art history that Aristotle defined the purpose of art as catharsis, the vicarious trigger and release of emotion. Well, I don't need none of that Greek stuff; I've got plenty of emotion being triggered and released all the time, and it ain't *vicarious*.

Also, if you think of music as "the soundtrack of your life," then perhaps you'll understand that these days, that's the kind of music I don't need reminding of. (It was a bad movie, man, at least the *ending* was, even if the music was good.) And I'm no longer interested in exploring new music, or keeping "current," and don't listen to the radio.

So I've been listening to neutral sorts of things, like Big Frank (Sinatra, of course, the "swinging" stuff more than the sad songs), and a lot of '80s music: stuff I can listen to for entertainment without none of that darn catharsis stuff.

And now Brutus is "away" too. Fuck. (My favorite word lately.) I'm supposed to carry on without my daughter, my wife, my dog, and now my best friend. What kind of a test is this? And who signed me up for it?

Well, I can only cling to the "Roll The Bones" philosophy, and not torment myself with questions of "why" and "fair." It happened 'cause it happened; I'm here 'cause I'm here, and I'll try to make the best of that shitty information.

Otherwise, I'm doing "as well as can be expected." I hope you are too.

Your much-embattled friend,

NEP

[Letter to Mendelson Joe]

Feb. 26, '99
Lac St. Brutus, Que.

Dear Joe,

First, a heartfelt "thank you." That's one of the most thoughtful things anyone's done for me in a long time. The day I received your package [of acrylic paints, brushes, and artboards] I happened to be having a particularly bad day, so the beauty of your offering shone even brighter.

I haven't yet "squeezed any pigment," but I notice that just the idea has already affected the pattern of my *thoughts*. For example,

I find myself looking at the paintings in my house with different eyes — not just admiring the *effects,* but thinking about how they were done.

One winter landscape of yours (lozengy yellow full moon over a frozen lake with ice-fishing hut) is one that I've always liked to "drift into," but the other day I found myself thinking about those cunning shadows in the snow, "Hmm . . . how would I go about getting that effect with paint and brush . . ."

Or I sit looking at my Ducati in the living room, watching the way light plays across its curvaceous shape in different tones of red, and think how I might mix the paints to capture a shape like that in pure color, rather than outline. These are "adventurous" thoughts, and you can see that your gift has already given my brain an interesting workout. We'll see where it takes me from there.

This week's crisis for me has been the reverse of Spring Fever: the thaw is definitely coming, and I'm scared. Although we still have plenty of snow, and last week I went cross-country skiing every single day in perfect conditions, this week it's already noticeable that the days are getting longer, the sun is getting stronger, and it will soon be over. Rain and mud and gloom are on the horizon, and my little baby soul doesn't want to go out and play in *that.*

Through January and February, I have been able to assemble a reasonably tolerable way of getting through the days and nights, as I've described to you before, but it's time now to start thinking of new alternatives. You can be sure I'll try squeezing pigment, for one thing, and there's always my GS in Mexico City, if I need to find a way to *move.*

I was mentioning in a letter to Brutus lately that since I've been back from my journey, I don't miss the travelling so much, but I do miss the *riding.* Even when I go into the village here to the post office or grocery store, I wish I could take a motorcycle, and earlier this month I had to make a quick trip to Toronto, for business, medical, and dental reasons, and I would actually have enjoyed it if I could have made the journey on two wheels. Same with any invitations to visit friends or family: "Wait 'til motorcycle season." (Up here, that can be as late as *May*, with all the sand, gravel, and broken pavement winter leaves behind on the local roads.)

Geddy gave me a book recently called *The Perfect Vehicle* ("What It Is About Motorcycles"), by Melissa Holbrook Pierson, and I highly recommend it to you. This woman is a fine writer and a serious motorcyclist (Moto Guzzi, of all makes), and I've been joking lately that I may have to marry her — if she's got any money.

She writes movingly about the romance of motorcycles, and makes the same connection I have about the natural human yearning for *motion*. "We quiet our babies with cyclic movement, and we quiet ourselves by going."

Obviously, this woman understands my little baby soul . . .

Funny you mentioned the ice on the lake. That's something I've always been *very* cautious about, and have never liked to cross frozen water alone even when I know it's safe (like now, when it's been good and cold for months, and the ice is several feet thick). Sometimes I'll go out there if I'm *with* someone, on snowshoes or skis, but I make them walk 40 or 50 feet away to the side, and carry ski poles as well. Just in case.

Well, I got tired of guessing how thick the ice might be, especially early in the season, so just last week I bought an ice auger, like ice fishermen use, so that I can drill down and see for myself. Haven't tried it yet, but it will be interesting to do some exploratory drilling here and there.

Otherwise, I'll hold onto these last few days of perfect winter, try to use them well, and know that they also give me something to look forward to next year — and that's pretty important for me right now. Some days I don't feel I've got all that much to look forward to (or perhaps much that I *care* to look forward to), so when I can think of cutting new trails next summer, or skiing and snowshoeing on them next winter, then that's good for me.

My little feathered friends have also offered another distraction, which is *feeding* them, and now I have three differerent kinds of bird feeders outside the kitchen window, offering mixed seeds, sunflower seeds, and a suet ball. So far I've only managed to attract a few chickadees, but they're cute enough, and there are blue jays and lots of woodpeckers around here that should pick up the "free food" message, plus the spring migration will soon start (ach!) and bring in the "travellers."

Did you ever hear anyone lament the coming of spring so much? Well, of course it's a matter of *circumstance* with me; I've got a tenuous balance going in my life right now, and the changing season is enough to disrupt it. Plus I think there are certain ways winter's moods *suit* my little baby soul: the bleakness and cold austerity of the white landscape, the dormant woods, and the way my house, my sanctuary, is enclosed and protected by high banks of snow. Right now I'm more-or-less comfortable as a "winter soul," and can't really imagine being a "springtime soul."

I was reading somewhere lately that the chickadee might be considered the quintessential Canadian bird, for even on the bitterest winter day they're cheerful and chirpy and active. Chickadees are winter souls too.

However, they too must follow the seasons — adapt — and that's the name of my game these days. Adapt or perish. So I shall carefully guide my little chickadee-soul into the grave new world of Spring.

I remember you once describing the order in which you put together a landscape painting, starting with "what was there first," and I've found that my own process of world-building has had to start with the *land*. The first things I began to appreciate were landscapes, highways, and wildlife, and of course they were the elements I needed to start building a world — from the ground up. Quite the task I have ahead of me: build a world, a person, and a life.

Well, things are tough all over.

Thanks again for your thoughtful present, Joe, and know that it's already given me the great gift of "something nice to think about." That's pretty precious stuff to me these days, on the roller coaster ride of my so-called life.

Last week I had a few days when I felt pretty good in the here-and-now; but this week I've had a few days when I felt pretty bad about *everything*. After the good days I actually suffered a twinge of *guilt* over whether I was maybe "getting over it" too easily, but I needn't have troubled myself — the crash soon came. Those are the kinds of cycles I will also have to adapt to, I suppose, for which Dog give me the strength!

(Or chickadees, anyway.)

Yours,
NEP

[Letter to Brutus]
le petit oiseau d'hiver

Mar. 1, '99
Lac St. Brutus, Que.

Hey Fahrvergnügen!

A new day, a new week, a new month, and almost a new season too. Me, I'm not too happy about any of that, and this week I've had a bad attack of "reverse Spring Fever." I sense the change coming, and it makes me feel cold and afraid.

Hell, I was just getting some kind of grip on the idea of being a *winter* soul! I've come to realize that it's not just the snowy activities that have been good for me and my little baby soul; it's also as pervasive and elemental as the way the world around me *looks* — the austere and light-filled landscape. (When you think about it that way, to the visual cortex, summer is actually darker than winter.) In all these ways, the winter season suits my mood, and I also like that closed-in feeling, my sanctuary tucked away behind the deep snow and high snowbanks. Cozy, like.

Though it's not over yet, of course, for the snow is still deep and winter is most definitely still heavy upon the land, but last week the first signs of change started to appear. The days are longer, and the sun is stronger, so that even when the temperature rises only one or two degrees above freezing, everything starts melting. Dripping off the eaves, pooling in the driveway, and gurgling in the eavestroughs.

Yesterday was a particularly gloomy day of rain and sleet, though at least it turned to snow in the evening, and by this morning a few inches had "refreshed" the landscape nicely. The trees had been bare, the roads reverting to brown, and the snowbanks were pock-marked like that Athabasca Glacier we walked on in the rain up in the Columbia Icefields.

However . . . I'm pleased to report that my bird-feeding station is becoming a big success in the neighborhood, at least with the chickadees, and I also had a couple of purple finches the other day. As the migration season approaches (alas!), I'm sure I'll get more "exotics" passing through. It's nice to have the little birdies to look at from my kitchen window. A bit of life out there.

From *The Birds of Canada:*

> *Whoever saw a dejected chickadee? Even on the greyest day of midwinter, when the thermometer remains below zero and the snow lies deep over the land, the chickadee is the personification of cheerfulness and good nature.*

Right on. So now my soul is a chickadee (though I don't know about the "personification of cheerfulness and good nature," but we'll work on that). Trouble is, the robins are coming, and I can't really picture my little chickadee as a "springtime soul." So this past week has been a difficult one for me. "Transitional," I suppose I could call it, to put the best possible gloss on it, but it felt more like . . . oh, let's say "miserable." This pathetic little question keeps rising to the scum on the surface of my brain: "What am I going to do?"

Don't know yet, but I'm thinking about it . . .

This week I have it in mind to have a go at typing up my Ghost Rider journals, which might be the kind of "project" I could undertake with the limited mental resources presently available. Not *writing*, just typing. (As Truman Capote said about Jack Kerouac.) But of course the main problem facing me in the next month or two, as snow turns to mud, is how will I be able to take my little baby soul out for a ride?

So I'm also trying to kick my ass a little bit to get in touch with my buddies in Mexico City this week, and get them to work on putting my poor old GS back into riding shape. Get my parachute packed, as it were, in case I have to bail out. I don't have any plans for that at the moment, or even any particular wish to go a-rambling again, but I suppose I have to consider the possibility.

When Mark Riebling visited a couple of weeks ago, he brought me a biography of Keith Moon, the total hero of my teenage years, and I was reading that last week. His life and times brought back so much of my life in the '60s and '70s: playing in bands, going to my first Who concert, living in London, all of that. But here's the guy's real actual life, and it wasn't very pretty. Increasingly out of it all the time, on anything, in and out of health farms, rehab, and even a psychiatric hospital, broke all the time, screwing up all the time, letting friends down and embarrassing them instead of entertaining them, insecure, unhappy, and often pathetic. Pretty much washed-up before he was 30, and dead at 32. A nice life to reflect on, and reflect against my own, during a week of existential crisis! But it just happened that way . . .

[Then follows a long recitation of woes: family health crises, a huge tax bill, Brutus's legal and financial situation, septic-tank troubles, and general existential sorrow.]

There's only one word for all of this, and for once there's no need to spell it out. But I will. FUCK!

There, that's better. I realize that all this "dumping" could be straining even *your* unlimited resources of resilience and good cheer, and I'm sorry for that. (Say, I think you're the real chickadee around here, "the personification of cheerfulness and good nature." Yeah, that's you all right.) Anyway, sorry about shoveling all this darkness your way. It just happened that way.

Now don't you go over-reacting just because I decide to "vent" a little. It's probably good for me (must be; it doesn't "taste" very good), and hopefully it won't do you any harm either. I presume that you feel somewhat as I do, that I've got enough troubles of my own that Other People's Troubles just don't hit me that hard.

Well all right, yours do; but that's just because, like William Jefferson Clinton, "I feel your pain." But don't you go feeling mine, or I'll kill ya.

Got that? Don't you lay a finger on my pain, man!

On the bright side . . . the week before last I had such a *great* run of days, skiing every day like the *roi-de-neige* I am, in perfect conditions of bright sun and fresh snow, and leading up to an *epic* circuit of the Viking trails, at least 25 kilometres [16 miles] and over four hours, to return limp, exhausted, but triumphant. That was all great, but those were the "good old days." Just a bit of light between tunnels, as it were, for the darkness came crashing down again.

Yesterday I was going to shave my beard, in some gesture of change and renewal (a scene right out of *Islands in the Stream*, I realize now), but I decided I had to save it until Brad and Rita arrive — I can't deny her the opportunity to express her disdain for the world's stupidest beard. (I haven't even trimmed it since last July, so if you imagine Major Powell with a goatee, that will give you some idea. It's ug-*leee*. Same with my hair, but I'm going to let it go for awhile; it's good to wake up looking like a certified maniac after electroshock therapy!)

So I hope you're doing about the same as I am (no better, no worse), so we can both be miserable together. Whenever I start thinking, "Jeez, I'm the world's biggest loser," I think again, and go, "No I'm not — I know somebody who's a bigger loser than me!"

Then I feel loads better.

Hope you do too.

Your little chickadee

[Letter to Brutus]
la neige est mon dieu

Mar. 4, '99
Lac St. Brutus, Que.

Hey there, Sissymary Pantywaist,

How you doin' today? Here we gots us a dark, wet day going on, with rain, lots of dripping, and soggy snow sitting around looking as gray and puffy as your face after an all-nighter. We had about eight inches of new snow yesterday, descending in the thickest, heaviest fall you can imagine. The flakes were just pouring down, like a dense white curtain, and as I skied along (*plodded* really, for of course the snow on the trails was deep and untracked), the scene around me seemed positively surreal.

I was crusted from head to toe in a skin of snow and ice, and the world's stupidest beard was so weighted down I could shake it like a pendulum. (So of course I did, and it felt cool!) By the time I got back to the car, it was buried under a good four inches of new snow, though I'd only been gone for an hour and a half.

It snowed steadily like that into the night, and then a warm front invaded from down your way, and brought warmer temperatures and rain overnight. That's pretty much what's going on now, though the barometer is the lowest I've ever seen it (I made a mark with my Sharpie to commemorate the event), and it's dark out there. Wind fitful from the east and northeast too; that's never good. The CBC forecast has it that later today a cold front from the west will bring back the snow, and give me a nice day tomorrow. Amen.

And that makes a day like this, as gloomy as it is, easier for my little chickadee-soul to endure, for I had a good ski yesterday, and this morning's ultra-low barometric pressure has me feeling pleasantly stiff and sore from today's exertion of shuffling through 10 kilometres like a snowplow.

Anyway, it's time for this little chickadee to get on with his day, and maybe also get this letter mailed. Though I just sent you one on Monday, I have a feeling this one's a little more cheerful. My Mom called last night and asked if I was getting the blizzard she "wished" for me; after talking to me the other day (under the strained circumstances I told you about), she decided that what I needed was a good blizzard, so she used a mother's power to wish it up. She wasn't wrong.

Despite the gloom of the morning here, I "know" the snow's coming back, and again on Saturday, so that's okay. Well done, Ma!

The other night I got a fax from Liam which stirred up the black soup of my brain pretty badly. It was innocent enough in intention: he only said that he'd met with Geddy and Alex to discuss ways of cutting our collective expenses with no income, um, coming in, and that they'd talked about all the gear at the warehouse, and what to do about it. So I guess poor old Liam was assigned to ask me for my thoughts on that "simple" question, which of course opens up a completely massive set of *other* questions, and the answer to one has to contain the answer to all the others. Man!

He must have known what he was asking of me (or at least, he *will!*) and that fax spooked me so much that for a couple of days I didn't even come up here to my office, just so I wouldn't have to look at it on my desk.

Bad enough I should have to even *contemplate* such a decision, in my present state, just as it affects myself, but how much worse to know that the "right" answer would make so many *other* people happy? (And I ain't talkin' about strangers.)

So it's a question with a certain "weight" to it, you might say.

Then there's the fact I haven't touched a drumstick in 18 months, nor wanted to; in fact when I go into the furnace room I've noticed that I avoid even *looking* at the little drumset in there. Drumming was so central to my whole life before, and perhaps as a consequence of that it remains the farthest away from my "interests" right now. For me, even the abstract notion of playing the drums remains way beyond even thinking about, and I've told you before how remote I feel from "that guy." So for now, I've been able to follow the wise course: I'm ignoring the question completely.

Actually, while I was skiing yesterday I was thinking up all the "conditions" I could demand in return for going back to work. "I'll only go on tour if *Brutus* is riding with me again, so you'll have to get him out of jail and get him a green card."

Well, I don't know if anybody's got *that* kind of power. But, like the beautiful closing line of *The Sun Also Rises,* "Isn't it pretty to think so?"

Anyway, I shall continue *not* thinking about the question (for it is truly unthinkable to me right now) and I will try to find a way to let everyone know that I'm not thinking about it (really hard).

So tell me, my little captive chickadee, do you find that now you're able to understand Maya Angelou's title, *I Know Why the Caged Bird Sings?*

Keep on chirpin'

[Letter to Gay Burgiel, my bicycling friend from New Jersey]

Mar. 24, '99
Lac St. Brutus, Que.

Dear Gay,

[Recap of the winter's activities]

Over the winter I've also had a good "rhythm" of visitors, pretty much planned to alternate a week or two on my own with a visit from relatives or friends. For these visitors from Toronto, or Vancouver, or New York, who want to discover the "true woods," I've been a great advocate of snowshoeing. Anyone can learn to do it easily ("if you can walk," etc.), and it allows them to get out in the woods and appreciate the beauty of "the great white silence."

Last week, Jackie's brother Steven was here (the same one who was in Barbados with us looking after Jackie, and who met me in Belize to travel through the dark days of the Pagan Midwinter Festival). As another soul that's been damaged by our recent tragedies, he was able to find the same "sanctuary" that I have in that combination of motion and setting. We marched through the woods and across the frozen lakes to remote parts of the surrounding bush *I* hadn't even explored before, and as a semi-retired diver and all-round nature lover, Steve also took to my recent interest in animal tracking; trying to identify and interpret the marks in the snow left by "ghost animals."

Porcupine, moose, deer, rabbit, snowshoe hare, squirrel, fox, mouse, weasel, grouse, and a surprising number of otter tracks have been spotted and identified, but mysteries remain. Some large canine tracks measure out as either eastern coyotes or gray wolves, but the locals don't seem to know of coyotes around here, and though wolves were known in former years, they were mercilessly trapped and poisoned (by deer hunters) even as the area has become more settled, so it seems unlikely that any remain. The field guides include this area as both coyote and wolf ranges, so I'm listing either as "possible." But until I have better evidence, I'm unwilling to say, "There be wolves here." Research continues . . .

My elaborate birdfeeder is a constant source of entertainment too, with woodpeckers and nuthatches at the suet blocks on top, chickadees and finches eating seeds in the middle feeders, and redpolls, siskins, and juncos on the ground. Even at night I am often visited by a flying squirrel swooping down from a neighboring tree, and mice dart in and out of their snow tunnels to pick up the leavings.

And that's the shape o' my days up here. Soon to undergo some seasonal changes, but I'll keep "adapting" as best I can. It takes a lot of will, I don't mind admitting, but I'm equally glad that at least I can devote myself to it full time. What Freud called "grief work" is something every griever has to go through, and though it's certainly possible to distract yourself from that task with other jobs, willing or not, it only means the grief work remains to be done.

Better if you can simply concentrate on the matter at hand, do the work you have to do as best you can, and find occasional diversion in something therapeutic, like moving, which also yields other benefits: fitness, stimulation, temporary distraction, something to plan, and even some small things to look forward to. That's important to hold onto as well: something to look forward to.

Well, for now I'm looking forward to summer, for cycling, motorcycling, swimming, rowing, and trail cutting — which makes me look forward to next winter, when I can snowshoe and ski on those trails. It's not much of a life, but it'll have to do for now.

Maybe I'll get more "serious" as time goes on. Or maybe I won't. In any case, that's got nothing to do with grief work, and nothing to do with "The Care and Feeding of a Little Baby Soul." Different priorities, these days.

Your friend,

NEP

[Letter to Lesley Choyce]

Mar. 30, '99
Lac St. Brutus, Que.

Dear Lesley,

[Recap of the winter's activities]

Unfortunately, the season for snow sports has taken a heavy hit in the last few days, for it's been in the "tens" every day, bright and sunny, and when you stand outside all you hear is a symphony of water-music, dripping from the roof, gurgling in the eavestroughs, and splashing into puddles of ice on the ground.

Now comes the season of mud up here, a time I've been dreading. My need for "physical therapy" could be filled by, say, cycling, or even motorcycling, but for the next month or so the roads around here will be a mess of sand, gravel, ice, mud, and flowing water. Rowing would also be okay, but it will also take a few weeks to melt several feet of ice off the lake. As for swimming . . . well, that will be awhile too.

Comes the season of Limbo.

"How low

Can you go . . ."

Well, not too far, I hope. I've got my "parachute packed," if I need to bail out. A couple of weeks back I smelled change in the wind (more like, felt it in the sun on my face), and contacted the

BMW dealer in Mexico City to have my bike ready to ride by mid-April or so.

I have no particular desire to go a-ramblin' at the moment, but it might be good to fly down there and ride the bike back home (via a suitably scenic and winding route, of course), and get back here sometime in June, all ready for summer sports. A plan like that might see me through to the end of summer, anyway, and that will certainly do.

Have I ever mentioned an American writer named James David Duncan? I may have, for to this reader he seems like a natural kindred-spirit to you. Though his "song" is of the Pacific Northwest, like you, he manages to show his love not only for the place, but for his characters, and he can plumb their depths, and their fates, without using too much "lead." Like, he gets deep without getting too "heavy," man.

The River Why is the book I had read previously, and lately I read *The Brothers K,* which is one of the best novelizations of the '60s I can think of, embracing baseball, Buddhism, drugs, Vietnam, religion, and, of course, sex and love. And a nice job he did of it, too.

However, I have decided to impose a personal ban on all novels based on baseball or World War I. I realize baseball makes a nice demotic setting for any number of themes, and that WWI has a romantic distance and the fragrance of tragic youth and all that, but enough already.

Got that, world of modern fiction writers?

Well, glad I got *that* off my skinny chest. (It's important for me to vent my anger. Everybody says so.)

Another recent reading treat was Hunter S. Thompson's *Hell's Angels,* and I've come to think he's a very underrated writer. He's at least the Kerouac of his generation. I've only read this and *Fear and Loathing in Las Vegas,* but in both cases he was able to tell an outrageous story and at the same time transcend it, offering moments of genuine Truth and Beauty. I'd say he's the real thing.

It seems to me that he became so sensationalized as a character that he became underrated as a writer.

And his insights about the Angels were astonishingly sharp — that they didn't represent the end of something old, like "the last of the outlaws," or "cowboys on iron horses," as the rest of the popular press insisted, but rather they represented the beginning of a *new* kind of "uncivil disobedience," which has continued to this day.

Thompson's book was written in 1966, when the hippies were just taking over from the beatniks, and the race riots were sweeping the States, and now I think we can see that he was right, and amazingly prescient. The Angels were the first of the punks, the gangs, the "gangstas," all the other still-extant biker syndicates, and even the incredible marketing success of Harley-Davidson among the middle-aged "wannabes" of today.

These present-day executives and family men with a touch of gray grew up seeing *Life* magazine pictorials of wild parties and motorcycle processions at an Angel's funeral, or *Time* magazine articles on a biker's life of power, violence, speed, and sex, and hey — they can still "identify" with being a rebel, man. Or at least the image.

Perhaps to some extent, today's right-wing extremists and militias are inspired partly by the KKK, and partly by the Angels. It's significant that in the mid-'60s the Angels used to go up to Berkeley and beat up the peace protesters. Also, they said they only picked up the Nazi regalia to outrage the "straights," but it's not hard to read more than that into it.

And now it's time for me to take a walk down the muddy road in my rubber boots. It's not much, but it will get me outdoors for awhile. As my mother used to say when she sent me outside, "Just get out there — it'll blow the stink off ya!"

Later,

NEP

[Letter to Martin Deller, a long-time friend and fellow drummer who had also been very helpful during the early days of my troubles]

Mar. 31, '99
Lac St. Brutus, Que.

Dear Marty,

[Recap of the winter's activities]

On weekends, or just for a change, I march around the woods on my snowshoes, and I've done a lot of good exploring around this area. I also started paying attention to the animal tracks in the snow, then studying the field guides on the subject back home in front of the fire, with Macallan in hand. Lately I've been carrying a tape measure with me to measure size of prints, length of stride, and width of track — all the stuff you have to know to be a "tracker." Next year, my very own trapline . . .

However, now comes the season of Limbo for me, and I'm not sure what will happen. Though I spend a couple of hours at my desk in the morning, I've only been writing letters or faxes, or taking care of necessary business; no drive to take on "serious work." I haven't even gotten around to typing up the notes from my journey, and if I read over stuff I was working on "before," I just lose interest. Back in August of '97, I had been halfway through writing a book about my adventures with Brutus on the *Test For Echo* tour, but now — I just don't *care.*

It has become clear to me that whatever was most central to my life before is now the most remote. That means drumming and writing, whether lyrics or "serious" prose. In the "scavenger hunt" of putting together some kind of a new life, I've been able to pick around the edges of former enthusiasms, and once again fit in, say, reading, motorcycling, bird-watching, and cross-country skiing, but my mind, my soul, simply shies away from any thought of drumming or writing. At this point, the lack of a "creative urge" is neither a good nor bad thing, for it is certainly a luxury anyway, and has nothing to do with my present mission of *survival.*

In time, it may become clear that the "urge," the "soul," whatever you want to call that "central zone," is simply closed for renovations. Someday we'll have a grand reopening and be ready to go to work again. On the other hand, it may be that the source of these things has been battered beyond recovery.

Either way, there's nothing I can do about it but try to survive, for if Time is supposed to do its healing thing, it's up to me to let it pass. As gently as possible.

In that spirit, I have tried to stretch this ski season as far as I can, and it's driven me into new areas of waxing. I even tried klister once, but it was a sticky, gooey nightmare. It seemed to start working just after I gave up and turned around to go back . . .

However, I have had some great ski-days when it's been right around 0°C [32°F] (purple wax), especially when it's cloudy. By March the sun is so strong that it affects the snow regardless of the temperature, so that it's hot and slippery in the sun, and cool and "grippy" in the shadows. But I've definitely expanded my knowledge in that area of alchemy. Why, today I actually redid the pine-tar surface on my skis, burning it in with the torch and all that manly stuff, then put on a couple of coats of glider wax — smoothed out with the *electric iron.*

Just another one of my acts of defiance, as "bachelor with a vengeance." I shall certainly never use an iron on *my* wardrobe, so what better use than to melt ski wax? None, I submit.

I also like to thumb my nose at convention (and especially *wimmen*) with a motorcycle in the living room, wearing my cowboy hat at the dinner table while watching "Inside Nascar" on Speedvision, and leaving all my dishes on the counter until morning. (I don't really mind doing them then, half-awake and watching the birds at the feeder, but right after dinner it seems silly not to go sit down in front of the fire and relax.)

I had also been flying my freak flag by growing the world's stupidest beard — a goatee which hadn't been trimmed since last July. It finally got too stupid even for me, and once Brad and Rita arrived a few weeks back, and she got a chance to tell me "you look like a Mormon," I knew that it had done its job as a symbol of that-which-all-women-hate, and I was able to get rid of it.

Now I'm letting my hair grow, but only as long as it maintains the "electroshock in the morning" look. Once it gets too long, of course, girls will start to like it. That will never do.

I hope everything is good with you and yours, my friend, and maybe we can get together sometime and do some skiing.

Bye for now,
NEP

[Letter to Mark Riebling, a writer friend who was living in his own "rural isolation," in upstate New York]

CAMP ELLWOOD®
For the Care and Feeding of Little Baby Souls™

Apr. 5, '99
Lac St. Brutus, Que.

Hail, Marcus Magnanimus,

Your fax from the Central Market (how quaint) came over the wires awhile back, but unfortunately, given the antediluvian technology, somehow all the pages overlapped into *one* page, then were divided into paper-size by my machine. Thus the last paragraph of every page is missing. Man — the troubles we have in simple *communication,* eh?

The Song of the Age, I guess. The *zeitgeist.*

Hey — I had previously figured that I was *El viajero fantomo* in Spanish, and *Le cavalier fantôme* in French, so it occurs to me now that in the language of Goethe (and your antecedents), I am *die Geist Reiter.*

It would be cool to be the *Zeitgeist Rider,* but I don't think I'm up to it.

Anyway, I wanted to let you know about that technical glitch (what we scientists call "a fuckup"), and ask if you could maybe snail-mail the hard copy to me, so I can read the rest of what seemed like a really good letter. I'm so pleased that you enjoyed the instructional video, *A Jerk in Progress,* and yes, I am proud of it. "That other guy" did some good work, and as you pointed out, he truly tried hard.

Winter is giving way to spring around here, though reluctantly (so it seems to me, anyway, in a classic pathetic fallacy), for even after more than a week of above-zero temperatures, there's still a couple of feet of snow in the woods and on the lake. With all the snow we've had, especially in March, this thaw is like trying to melt a *glacier.* Now that I think of it, the roadside snowbanks have the appropriate dirty look of glacial moraines, and the lake too is wrinkled and waved like the surface of an ancient icefield.

And it's sure been an epic winter for *my* purposes. I was cross-country skiing until the last week of March, and snowshoe season still isn't over; I am planning to head across the road to the 100 Aker Wood later today, for it's gloriously sunny and mild. There's also some good downhill skiing still to be had, and I'm planning to give that a shot tomorrow (after a week-long search to locate my telemark boots).

Overall, the same mantra continues to apply: *keep moving.*

This need has caused me some anxiety as the season changes, for now comes the Season of Mud, followed closely by the Season of Blackfly, and I've been concerned about how I would get any outdoor action for the next month or so. Cycling might be possible, though hardly *inviting*, with the roads strewn with mud and leftover sand and gravel, cold spring rains, and the aforementioned flies, which tend to cluster around your head in maddening clouds, especially when you're, say, grinding slowly uphill.

So with this "difficult time" ahead, I've experienced the interesting phenomenon of observing my brain as it operates on two separate levels, and often at cross-purposes. One part of me — the conscious part — is appreciating the day-to-day life here, watching nature and the weather, and not wanting to stir anywhere at all.

At the same time, another part of my so-called brain is busy contacting the BMW dealer in Mexico City to get the bike ready to ride, making lists of things that would need to be done before I take off, and even starting the usual pre-trip "staging area" in the bedroom. (A corner where things are assembled as they're thought of, over the course of a week or two before leaving. It's a good system — you have time to remember everything, and "edit out" the unworthy.)

But the weird thing is I don't even know what that Jung-brain, Freud-brain, Ur-brain of mine is goddam *doing*. Where is it taking me? When are we going? I can honestly tell you, from the mundane-brain, quotidian-brain, stupid-brain part of me, I don't know.

Yesterday I was digging in my "Ghost Rider" box of maps, and I found myself pulling things out and setting them aside: the Lonely Planet Mexico guide, but *not* the Baja one; the Western States and Provinces map, but *not* the Eastern one — though as far as I knew I was still thinking about taking a ferry that runs from the Yucatán to Florida. See what I mean, though? There are decisions being made here of which I have no part!

Needless to say, I'm a little bemused by this process.

Also in the news: Lately I've been waging a most enjoyable war with a neighborhood squirrel (good title, no? "A Most Enjoyable War"), who keeps jumping from the wall of the house onto my bird-feeder, then hanging there impudently while he fills his rodent face with my finest sunflower seeds. First I tried chucking snowballs at him, but as a pitcher, I am hardly big-league material — even in a fantasy league. Jackie's sister Deb, who had been visiting for a few days, suggested a squirt gun, and this ignited the proverbial animated light bulb.

Digging in the furnace room, I found my old nerf-arrow bow, and a Super Soaker gun, and the hunt began. It's developing into a regular *Caddyshack* scene, with me in the Bill Murray role, as I go spying out of windows and stalking around with my "weapons," then cranking open the kitchen window to fire off a few rounds.

"Ha ha, squirrel — your ass is mine!"

The Super Soaker is the most effective counter-offensive weapon, but the nerf arrows are more fun. The other morning I laughed out loud, seeing myself as anyone else might have: a lunatic in a cowboy hat and lumberjack shirt hanging out the kitchen window and firing bright yellow nerf arrows with extreme prejudice.

It's good to have a mission, and it's good to have a laugh.

In fact, I see him out there now, patroling the trees of No Man's Land, at 12:00, obviously on a pre-attack recon. Time to go secure the perimeter.

God, I really do have to wonder about myself sometimes. I just peeked out the window from upstairs here and saw the squirrel hanging on my feeder, ran down three flights, grabbed the Super Soaker from the kitchen (no time to mess with nerf arrows this time), and raced out into the snow in T-shirt, jeans, and slippers, and started firing madly.

The key word is "madly" . . .

However, it does keep me entertained. Along with bird-watching, animal-tracking, letter-typing, and Speedvision-watching, defending the birdfeeder against squirrels is among the few pursuits that are both harmless (even to the squirrels) and diverting (possibly ditto). Diversion is good too.

Just at sunrise this morning I was standing at the kitchen window (Dawn Patrol for Operation Squirrel), and saw a good-sized fox (one of the red-gray hybrids they call a "cross" fox) trot slowly across the edge of the woods, right across my field of vision, so that I could watch it for several long seconds. The snow was crusted by an overnight freeze, and the fox moved over it so lightly that later I couldn't find even one of its tracks.

That was a nice vision to start my day.

I hadn't heard of *The Pagan Book of Days*, but it sounds like a great thing to live by. If you can get me a copy, I'd love to have it. By the by, either name is fine to send stuff to up here, for anonymity is no problem in a post office box. They know me as both N.P. and John Ellwood Taylor — well, I don't think they actually know who John Ellwood is. But then, neither do I!

And I guess that's about enough for today, from one Walden to another, and from one Henry David to another (you're going to live there *without running water?* — ho ho!). Though I've always heard that Thoreau's much-vaunted self-sufficiency used to include regular visits to Ralph Waldo's for meals, laundry, and to "get his end away" with Mrs. E.

Well, that sounds okay. Add a few other bucolic necessities, like single-malt whisky and herbal remedies, and I'll stay here by the Pond. Who needs water, after all, except for rowing and swimming.

Okay, and making ice . . .

Unfortunately, I don't think I'll be staying by my Pond much longer. That secret-strategist inside my tiny little brain seems to have the notion that travel would "broaden" me or something, and is obviously preparing to kick me out into the cold, cruel world of strangers and their hell-bent vehicles.

Well, what can I do? Best just do as I'm told.

Anyway, I hope you and your work are going well, and that you'll get *one* of your books finished, say, this year?

Your friend,

NEP

[Letter to Steven, who had recently visited]

Apr. 9, '99
Lac St. Brutus, Que.

Greetings from Camp Ellwood, a four-season, full-service retreat specializing in the techniques of aerobic grief therapy pioneered by our founder, John Ellwood Taylor. We offer outdoor activities and nature-watching until you're really, really tired, followed by delicious and nutritious meals prepared by Chef Ellwood (trained in Europe at the famous Marks & Spencer institute), and complimentary alcoholic beverages. Evening entertainment includes slide shows by your host, and whatever's on CBC or Speedvision.

Recent client testimonials:

"Do we have to go snowshoeing in the rain?"
"Is this how muskrat is supposed to taste?"
"When are you going to get the satellite dish fixed?"
"Can I go home now?"

[Letter to Brutus]
le fou au bout d'hiver

Apr. 15, '99
Lac St. Brutus, Que.

Bonjour, Pierre Concassée,

Say, there's a good manly nom-de-plume for you, eh? I saw it
on a sign in front of a local quarry and gravel pit, and thought of
you right away. "Smashed-up stone," yeah.

Another thing made me think of you lately. It seems to me that
when you last visited here (long-ago-last-summer) you brought
me a hardback copy of *Cold Mountain*. I had been reading about
that one for awhile in the newspaper reviews (why, even in
Britain, I think), and had the impression it would be a book I
would enjoy. But when I took off from here after that, of course I
didn't want to carry any hardcovers with me.

So, it wasn't until this week that I finally got around to reading
it, and yes, it's a good one, alright. Real good. The more I think
about it the more impressed I am with what he accomplished in
that book, on levels of history, folk wisdom, character-drawing,
and — especially — painting a landscape so brilliantly.

I'm presuming you read it before giving it to me, because in
various places throughout the book were the pieces of a torn-up
ticket to the movies. It's always interesting to run across things
like that in a book, old or new. Though this one was less than a
year old, it still made a little "time capsule." When pieced together,
it revealed the following information: "Eglinton Theatre, July 18,
'98, 3:30, Armageddon, $6.50."

Tell any tales to you?

All this winter I've been keeping a Post-It pad and pen beside
my bed, but I hadn't used them at all until last week, when I had

to write down the word Edward Abbey used (in *Black Sun;* that's a nice book too, as I think you noted) for those showers you see falling high over the desert, but which evaporate before they reach the ground: "virgas," he called them. A lovely word for a lovely sight.

There were a couple of passages in *Cold Mountain* I felt compelled to stick a note on, and I copied them out today:

There was fact in what the dark voice said. You could become so lost in bitterness and anger that you could not find your way back. No map or guidebook for such journey. One part of Inman knew that. But he knew too that there were footsteps in the snow, and that if he awoke one more day he would follow them to wherever they led as long as he could put one foot in front of the other.

You could grieve endlessly for the loss of time and for the damage done therein. For the dead, and for your own lost self. But what the wisdom of the ages says is that we do well not to grieve on and on. And those old ones knew a thing or two and had some truth to tell, Inman said, for you can grieve your heart out and in the end you are still where you were. All your grief hasn't changed a thing. What you have lost will not be returned to you. It will always be lost. You're left with only your scars to mark the void. All you can choose to do is go on or not. But if you go on, it's knowing you carry your scars with you.

Yeah, well, shut up, eh? I don't need no smarty-pants writers telling *me* about how life is ignorant and all. Nary a one of them knows it better than *I* do.

Last night I started Jonny Bealby's other one, *For a Pagan Song,* and though so far it's a good tale well-told, the copy editor should be *shot*. There are so many typos in this book it's positively *alarming*, starting right on the first god-damned page! As you know, such solecisms leap off the page and hit me like a smack in the face and set my brain vibrating in outrage and confusion; it's such a disservice to any reader to have to stop and figure out what it's *supposed* to say. As the egregious typos piled up, it was rattling me so much I almost sent the book flying across the room. But I'm persevering.

I have just made a list to order some of the books you mentioned, especially the *Sand County Almanac,* which I keep hearing about. Just last night I was watching the *Cadillac Desert* video that Steven got for me, and the author, Marc Reisner, mentioned that book.

Like you, I kept running into Barry Lopez's name, and in that Back of Beyond bookstore in Moab they had a special section titled "Abbey and Friends," with a bunch of his books. I bought *Desert Notes/River Notes,* and when I started reading it, at first I was interested, as he waxed poetic about the desert, the plants, and the animals.

Then I realized that what he was saying was not *true.* I mean, literally. For poetic effect he was changing and inventing the "nature of Nature." I'm sure he felt entitled to do this in the pursuit of some "higher purpose" — a new and important kind of "myth-making," I'm sure his admirers would say. All full of "powerful images," and "visions," and "poignant poesy," like. But it's one of the few books in my life I have ever given up on in disgust, and I almost tossed it right in the trash.

And it illustrates the gap that often separates people who *apparently* like the same things: like what I felt in Belize, for instance, at the nature lodges. One night, I was looking around at all the other guests, in their Tilley Endurables and soft-looking, yet pinched-up faces, and said to Steve and Shelly, "Does this mean *we're* eco-tourists too?"

Shelly said, "No way; we smoke and drink and swear too much."

Right on. Good thing, too.

You've probably run into references to Abbey being considered an "embarrassment" to the Cause by the usual run of self-styled environmentalists ("No way, man — he's not one of *us*"), because he liked to chase women, drink booze, smoke cigars, shoot guns, and kill snakes. (Somewhere I read that he used to throw beer cans out of his pickup onto the highway, as he explained, "Because it's a *highway*.")

Another thing made me think of you today. As you know, I've been having trouble being decisive about what to do now; and I do mean *now*. Until yesterday, I hadn't even left the house for three days (I feel like a *prisoner*, ha ha), and was starting to get a little . . . dark. Heavy. Dispirited.

Today I was really trying to kick my ass to start making some phone calls and doing some serious organizing, but first I kicked that droopy butt o' mine out the door, and made it go for a long walk. The rest of me went along too, to keep an eye on it. (Not easy, as you know.)

The snow's getting patchy on the exposed ridges hereabouts, islands of rock and brown leaves showing through, but where the snow is, it's still deep. So I did the lap around Lac St. Ellwood once again, which, since Deb and I walked it a couple of weeks ago, I have measured with the car odometer and found to be slightly over 10K. It was sunny and about +5°C [42°F] but the wind had a real "cut" to it. Even so, with all those hills, I managed to work up a modest sweat, and most important, to "lose myself" for awhile. (I couldn't get away from myself *completely*, because I kept catching up to myself. Just think about that.)

It being a Wednesday afternoon in mid-April, I didn't see another soul. Only two or three cars in driveways, wood smoke from one chimney, and the sound of somebody hammering. The walk actually worked pretty well in inducing the "vacuum-brain" trance, but of course it didn't produce any decisions, or get any organizing done.

Later in the afternoon, I drove into town for flowers, groceries, and post office (just to show I could get *something* done), and what made me think of you was that, just past the village, a utility truck was blocking one lane as they worked on the lines. And what do you think? They had *flag babes* out there! [The signal workers, often female, who control the flow of traffic past a construction site.]

Man, no one else I know would understand the effect that sight had on me, but you know there is nothing more evocative of the open road, at least *our* kind of roads, than flag babes. I laughed out loud at the strangeness of that notion, and all it conjured in me, and I knew right then it was a sign. Time to go.

By the time you read this, I will be gone. (Sounds like one of those melodramatic letters from a dame or something.) Brad is driving up tomorrow to hang for a couple of days, then give me a lift to Tarannaw, where I'll spend two or three days (oh joy) taking care of beeswax, collecting last-minute supplies, and like that.

Last night, I called Andrew in L.A. to get the number of the Automobile Club of Southern California, so I can renew the insurance I bought from them, which expired on January 1st. He is urging me to stop by there and "rage" with him, and he was teasing me about Dave Foley's girlfriend (apparently they're not dating anymore) wanting me to come back there too — the one who said I was "a hottie." (Me?) Well, I don't know about any of *that*, but I had been thinking about riding that way; I wouldn't mind seeing Freddie [my drum teacher, who lived in the San Fernando Valley], and maybe the Rich family [Buddy's widow, Marie, daughter Cathy, her son Nick, and husband Steve, who I had become good friends with during the making of the Buddy Rich tribute records] in Palm Desert. But I don't think I'll know where I'm heading until

I get there. (Now there's an existential manifesto.)

That's the way it was last fall, and it worked okay; the decisions of routes and destination always seem clear on the day, so I'll follow the *laissez-faire* approach.

Might be I'll just want to get back *here* as quick as I can.

To add to the stuff that I have to deal with before I can fly away, the Toronto house appears to be sold. Given the family real-estate curse, I hesitate to believe it until it's a done deal (closing May 28th) but it looks good, and of course, it would be a relief. After Jackie's bequests to her family are taken care of, the remainder will at least help to pay my taxes this year. Oh joy.

I'll just be glad to have it all done, done, done.

And now I'm gone, gone, gone, baby. It's time for me to quit messing around, close this letter, and get on the phone. There's a lot to do. I'll write you from somewhere, of course, and hopefully it won't be long before I'm right back here — where you know where to find me!

Later, Chimichanga,
Ghost Rider

Though we live in trying times —
We're the ones who have to try
Though we know that time has wings —
We're the ones who have to fly

EVERYDAY GLORY, 1993

Chapter 11

BACK IN THE SADDLE

Too many hands on my time
Too many feelings —
Too many things on my mind
When I leave I don't know
What I'm hoping to find
When I leave I don't know
What I'm leaving behind . . .

THE ANALOG KID, 1982

As the first part of my escape plan for mid-April, my good friend Brad
drove up from his home in St. Catharines to spend a couple of days at the
house by the lake. Of all my friends, I had known Brad the longest — since
childhood — and with his wife, Rita, he had shared so profoundly in my
bad times (Toronto, London, Barbados) that there was no one who was so

comfortable for me to be with, or so comforting. I rode back with Brad as far as Toronto, where he dropped me at a hotel, for I needed to take care of some business before I flew out to Mexico City.

Toronto had become a "ghost city" to me. I had lived there with Jackie and Selena for almost 15 years, and I still didn't like spending time there. On those familiar streets, sudden memories could leap out and *grab* me.

In a controlled environment like the house by the lake I had learned that I could arm myself against those memories, so that looking at the photos of Jackie and Selena everywhere, for example, became a part of something I was *used* to, and to which I had somehow adapted or accepted, maybe. Even in that house I would sometimes chance to look over my shoulder and get an unexpected glimpse of one of those photos, and feel a physical stab of unguarded pain.

Thus, when I did have to spend some time in Toronto — where most of the "business of my life" was, after all, my doctor, dentist, accountant, lawyer, all that, as well as many of my friends — I would arrive in town wearing my "armor," prepared to keep a close guard on where I went, what I looked at, and what I let myself feel.

I had begun to develop the thinnest of skins around my little baby soul, and could sometimes steer my thoughts away from certain directions, and even actively *prevent* myself from feeling sad or despondent. Sometimes I could do that . . . but not all the time.

One day it might even feel alright to be driving down Avenue Road and to look over at Brown School, where Selena had gone from kindergarten to Grade Six, while on another day it might make me crumble. One day I might be able to visit the cemetery plot and picture how the monument to the two of them was going to look when it was finished; other days just the *idea* of going there was unbearable.

The cycle of grieving still felt to me like "one step forward, one step back," though the progress I had measured since the summer might indicate it was "one step forward, one step back — less an inch." My little baby soul moving in baby steps. Sometimes it seemed I was getting a little stronger, others it just felt like I was putting on a better performance, and if I was fooling anybody, I wasn't fooling myself.

I also noticed that I had started to grow different "masks" to go with that armor, and in retrospect I could see this process had begun back in August, when I first set out to go travelling. Because I still felt so raw, vulnerable, and alienated, it had been necessary for me to find a way to cope with the world, a "stance" from which I could face strangers every day — to make the normal small talk while checking into a motel, say, or during a chance encounter with a friendly stranger.

My first defensive persona was John Ellwood Taylor, after the alias I had created for my credit cards (and my new Super 8 discount card), and the name went with the need for a character who was pragmatic, stoic, and quietly courteous. A travelling man, he kept to himself, looking after the motorcycle, reading maps and road signs, choosing motels, and giving strangers a shy smile.

The Ghost Rider was another fairly separate facet of my personality, a more romantic, reflective character; the one who gave me the restless urge to keep wandering, who responded to the highways, landscapes, and wildlife; who chose the roads and scenery through which John Ellwood would navigate us.

As time went on, I would notice more of these "adaptive personalities" emerging to fill necessary roles in my ongoing drama, all of them amplifications of some facet of the real me (whoever he was) which I could hide behind when I needed their protection, as it were. My ghostly bodyguards.

However, I always felt centered as an entity, however amorphous (or polymorphous), and I thought of myself simply as a man made up of the remains of "the fool I used to be." I was learning to face the world in all its guises, and I was starting to feel more comfortable with people, whatever mask and armor they might wear.

Another factor driving me away was Selena's approaching birthday, on April 22nd, and I knew I didn't want to spend that day in Toronto. One thing I had learned from the books on grief and bereavement was that it was better to make a "ceremony" out of those kind of days — to find a way to memorialize the lost one in an appropriate fashion, and not think you could just glide by such a heavy date on the calendar. Like the memories, if you didn't find a way to face up to them, they would ambush you.

Thinking of what I had felt in the church in La Paz, down in Mexico, I thought the ancient cathedral in Mexico City might make a suitable setting for a private memorial service for Selena, so as haphazard as the rest of my life might be, I had carefully made my plans to get to Mexico City before that date.

On April 21ˢᵗ I caught the overnight flight to Mexico City, and once again began to document the story of my life in "letters to Brutus."

> Apr. 26, '99
> Creel, Chihuahua
> (*Barranca del Cobre*)
> [Copper Canyon]

¡El Cuervo Fantasma!

It all started badly. At about one in the morning I arrived at the Four Seasons in Mexico City to find they were overbooked. So I got shunted over to the Marriott for a night. (Free, though!) Next morning, I allowed them to bow before me. Especially that sweet thing Monica, at the front desk. Man, they got some pretty *señoritas* around that place, as I'm sure you remember. (Not that *we* care.)

That first day in Mexico was Selena's birthday, and I had made careful plans on how to "memorialize" that day. Early in the morning, I walked to the big cathedral in the Zócalo, went inside and bought two princess-sized votive candles (the biggest they had, of course) and lit them in front of the chapel for "Nuestra Señora de Guadalupe" (because of a plaque about "mujere et niño," so I substituted "niña"). I sat there awhile, and cried some (well, a lot), amid the pious old ladies, tourists, and construction workers.

(From *Cadillac Desert*, I learned that the cathedral is sinking *one foot* a year, because of over-pumping the groundwater. Seems like that city just don't have a chance. I also learned recently that 1,000 people a day are moving into the surrounding shantytowns. But things seem a *little* better than last year — the peso is up slightly, due to higher oil prices, which my buddy Erik at Moto Altavista [the BMW dealer] told me accounts for 60 per cent of Mexico's exports.)

After sitting there for a couple of hours watching the candles burn and sifting through some memories of Selena, letting the tears fall as they would, I went out and wandered around the streets of Mexico City in a jetlagged (and grief-drained) daze for the rest of that day, then had a good dinner and went to sleep.

Next day, I made another visit to the Museo Antropológica to have a look at the exhibit on Palenque, then went down to San Angel to have a look at my bike, the poor old Viajero Fantasma. And don't she look sweet now!

All cleaned up, and fixed up with a new front fender, some other new "nose bits," the scratched-up windscreen polished like new, and they even repainted the tank. On the negative side, they lost my little spare gas can (every time I've tried to buy one here, they've offered me a *milk jug!*), one passenger peg has disappeared, they forgot to install the tank-bag mount (noticed too late — they'll mail it to me), and the "rider information display" doesn't work, so no temperature gauge, fuel gauge, or clock. Oh well. (Not that *we* care.)

Some more Mexico City facts for you: the population is thought to be 18 million now, and I saw an article in the *Los Angeles Times* about the dog-shit problem in the streets — apparently it dries up, floats into the air, and lands on the street food. (I can tell you what *I* wasn't going to be eating in Mexico City.)

Once again I noticed lots of heavily armed soldiers all over the city, especially outside the banks — I saw an armored car parked outside one bank, surrounded by about *10* soldiers with big guns.

For obvious reasons, I planned my departure from Mexico City for Saturday morning. After four months off the bike, let's start off with *that* kind of traffic. You know about that ('course it wasn't *dark* too!), and it sure felt weird for an hour or two. That first day I headed north, around the old Periférico, then a long stretch of "cuota" [toll highway] to San Luis Potosí, and over to Zacatecas.

Much easier to find the Quinta Real *this* time! (Why, they even had some *signs* around town to help.) That place was great once again, at the end of a 640-kilometre [400-mile] first day, and they even had that same waiter in the restaurant — the guy with the amazing decorative orthodontics who chased us to our rooms to sign the bill. He looked older though. Not like *us.*

Next day I finally got on some proper roads, empty two-lane through dry yellow country with scrub mesquite, prickly pear, creosote, and some tall yucca trees, similar to Joshuas, stretching back to the haze of distant hills. I made a brief photo-stop at Canutillo, the hacienda the government bought for Pancho Villa (to keep him quiet, I'm sure), then 80 kilometres [50 miles] north to Parral, where he got his "just deserts." A group of townsmen, fed up with the dictatorial ways of the "generalissimo," shot him and his buddies in their car. Now they have a huge equestrian statue of him there (though not as cool as the one on La Bufa in Zacatecas, which I could see silhouetted from my room at the Quinta Real), and apparently the Dodge touring car he was driving at the time is on display in Chihuahua. Bullet holes and all.

And speaking of guns and bandidos, I had to go through a few army and police roadblocks today, but only one T-shirt-wearing cop felt he had to poke through my stuff. Man, I hate that. That one spoke English, at least, though that doesn't really help — makes him more insistent in his questions, and me "mouthier" in my answers. Really ought to watch it.

Just last night I finished reading *Treasure of the Sierra Madre*, which ought to remind me of what Mexico can be like! Then I started *In Cold Blood* (another cheery story) which mentions *Treasure* early on, as one of the bad guys' favorite books.

Anyway, that was another pretty long day — almost 700 kilometres [438 miles] — but by then I was back in the old scooterin' groove, and it's a good thing, because I was ready for *today*. I hadn't been thinking of coming this way, but my buddy Erik told me the road through Copper Canyon was "the best motorcycle road in all Mexico."

In mock disbelief, I asked, "Better than *El Espinazo del Diablo?*"

He laughed at that, and said, "Even better."

He wasn't lying.

Everything good about that ride we did back in '95 — the high Sierra, fragrant pine woods, incredible views, stunning rock formations in red and gray, twists and turns and terrifying dropoffs — but almost no traffic, and perfect pavement all the way. The bluest sky, the freshest air, the sweetest smell, the bestest riding. I thought of you *so* much. (Don't think you'd have been able to keep up, though; I was using a lot of my Freddie Spencer moves. And *all* of my tires!)

Then there was a side trip, about 60 kilometres [38 miles] of dirt leading to a Tarahumara [Indian] village at the bottom of the canyon. Well, yeah: we're *there*, right? It combined the scariest elements of the road to Mike's Sky Rancho (narrow track of rock, stones, dried mud, and loose gravel and dirt) and the road to Telegraph Creek (lonely, winding, tight switchbacks, and appalling dropoffs right beside you; don't look down!), and it got hotter all the time. About 30 kilometres [19 miles] in I stopped at a sign in the middle of the road, "Camino Cerrado Por Obras." Now, I figured if a *Mexican* road was closed, it must be *really* bad, and being sweltering, dusty, and scared enough already, I decided on "the better part of valor," and turned around. Later I met some guys on a dual-sport tour (company called "Rosen-Rides," out of Texas), who said they'd gone through and it had been "no worse," but . . . well, I'll save the rest of it to share with *you*.

You'd like this town, too. Three thousand people, many Tarahumara *indígenas* (handsome people, with dark coppery skin, resembling the old pictures you see of Apaches), at 7,670 feet, with the smell of the sawmill, wood fires, and lots of little restaurants. A few decent motel-type places, too, as it's a main stop on the Copper Canyon railway, and the main entrance to the park. Lots more to do and see around here. So hurry up!

A funny moment at Moto Altavista: while they prepared my bill, I was standing outside having a smoke, and when they said it was ready, I asked if it was alright to smoke inside.

Erik laughed and said, "This is Mexico — you can smoke in a *hospital* here!"

Right on.

I had a bad moment over dinner last night, when they were showing the movie *Grease* on the TV in the dining room. That had been one of Selena's favorite movies, and it soon had me in tears. Somebody seemed to read my mind and came and changed it.

Then this morning they were showing the funerals of those teens killed in Colorado, which made me sad and teary all over again. Ach.

Holiday Inn,
Deming, NM

Yup — right on the Interstate, and from my window I can see semis, and even occasional trains rolling by. God bless America! (I know *I* do, though *you* may not.)

I just read that they used to round up outlaws in Arizona and give them a ticket to Deming — must have been a fun place.

Another great ride today, starting off this morning in the High Sierra pinewoods (with turtleneck, heated vest and grips on), then winding down through junipers and dramatic rock formations to the wide, lovely creosote desert, with distant mountains, occasional ranches, and a few areas of irrigated farmland (now when I see that, I can't help wondering, "where is that water coming from, and who is it hurting?"). Amazing dust devils too, towering hundreds of feet high, sometimes four or five at a time. Then some long, straight stretches, to remind us why we love desert riding. (Yep, even some singin'.)

I passed a crow attacking a roadrunner, trying to steal its snake, and shortly after that I rode straight into a dense cloud of killer bees (I was told later), which hit me like a spatter of gravel and completely covered my helmet and the front of the motorcycle. I had to pull over and clean off my face shield to see the road. Yikes!

The Columbus, New Mexico, border crossing was a breeze, I'm glad to report (you never know, eh?), with only a brief wait to hand in my "Temporary Vehicle Import Permit" — the one I picked up way back when in Mexicali. Then I had to stop at the museum in Columbus (continuing the Pancho Villa theme, it's the only place in the U.S. ever to be invaded by foreign "troops," though apparently *El Generalissimo* himself didn't attend, just incited his followers with, "Let's go kill some gringos!"). Then up here, for another 700 kilometre [438 mile] day (seems to be the magic number lately). I poured myself a big ol' glass of duty-free Glenmorangie (bought on the way down), and pulled out the Western U.S. map.

The question now, of course, is "now what?" Well, I called up the Rich family in Palm Desert, and arranged to get together with them, then called the good old Ingleside Inn (I had to use your name to get a room!). So I'll stay in Palm Springs a couple of days, then maybe mosey into Hollywood and hang with Andrew and the rest of the expat gang there. Now that I can see ahead a little clearer, I could probably wind my way northward through the mountains and the Great Basin and make it up to visit the Lindley-Peart family in San Vancisco. That's a sort-of plan, which has evolved over the past hour or two.

Otherwise, yeah, this was definitely the right thing for me to do now, and I'm glad I gave myself the necessary kick in the ass to get us back out and on the road again. I know *you* are too.

Once I get settled somewhere long enough (probably L.A.), I'll give you a call and hope to speak to you. I did call from Mexico City on Thursday morning, hoping to hear from you that night or on Friday, but never did. I hope the court thing went okay. There's a lot of stuff going on out here that needs *you* in it. Lots of chicks too, ditto.

Not that *we* care.

> Big 10-4 from the Superslab westbound,
> good buddy, and the hammer is down
> *Ghost Rider Redux*

> *Just an escape artist*
> *Racing against the night*
> *A wandering hermit*
> *Racing toward the light*

GHOST RIDER, 2001

Chapter 12

SPRİNG FEVER

We can wear the rose of romance
An air of joie de vivre
Too tender hearts upon our sleeves
Or skin as thick as thieves

FORCE 10, 1987

"Springtime in the desert," I thought, admiring the subtle transformations in the desert dreamscape as I left Deming and rode west on Interstate 10 across southern New Mexico and into Arizona. In such an exacting land, all life is normally conservative and even puritanical in its guarded displays, harboring every drop of moisture in its cells, while minimizing the surface it exposes to the arid heat. In the Sonora Desert, a brief rainy season passes through in the spring, and it only takes a couple of rainfalls to bring out the brief and urgent, yet still restrained, decorations of reproduction and germination.

The wispy palo verde trees carried an array of tiny yellow blossoms; the spindly arms of the ocotillo cactus were studded with vibrant red; a host of small plants and bushes displayed their subtle jewellery, and the mesquite, cholla, and giant saguaro cactus wore their full-dress greens. The wind blew fierce and steady from the west, raising dust clouds along the roadside, and it was a "quartering" wind against me and the motorcycle. Bad enough riding against a headwind that buffeted my helmet around and drove stubbornly back against the bike and my body, but trying to steer the bike into a wall of wind that was slightly off-center like that was even worse, combining the wind of my passage at 80 mph against the 40-mph wind vectoring in at me.

Stopping in Tucson for a maintenance check at the excellent BMW shop, I carried on westward on I-8, still fighting that vicious, punishing wind. By 4:00 I was ready to seek shelter for the night, and took the loop off the Interstate leading to the town of Gila Bend, Arizona — or what's left of it.

Named for the Gila River (or what's left of it), which meandered south from Phoenix, then turned west toward the mighty Colorado — or what's left of *it* — only the town's status as seat of Maricopa County seemed to hold off true "ghost town" designation, as waves of dust blew along the short main street, and freight trains rumbled by every few hours. Neither the wind nor the trains stopped at Gila Bend. A new police station and courthouse were the only prosperous-looking buildings, though the people of the town did seem to be resisting its decline. A few areas of the roadside had been landscaped in the natural style of "xeriscaping," using the native plants in a decorative arrangement, but they had soon become covered with dust and litter. A recent attempt at a strip mall seemed to have failed, but the laundromat was apparently thriving, and the half-moribund main street offered a supermarket, video store, and a few motels and gas stations interspersed with a decrepit auto repair shop, a woodworking place (somewhat ironic, with no trees of any size for hundreds of miles), and an abandoned *Llantera,* or tire repair shop, a taste of Old Mexico.

Tall palms whipped in the wind above the local Best Western, called the "Space Age Lodge," which was set apart from the usual run of motels by its theme: the lobby featured a mural of outer space, and the guest rooms were decorated with framed photographs of the Space Shuttle. The restaurant was called "Outer Limits," but had been destroyed in a fire recently and was under reconstruction. This was one of the times I wished I were a more *sociable* reporter; I would have liked to interview the person whose vision this was, but I was content just to experience it — and send Brutus and my grandfather a postcard from there.

The gravel bed of the Gila River was dry, even after the recent rains, for its flow was channeled into a concrete canal, which was full. The girl behind the front desk at the Space Age Lodge told me the water was "foul" because of Phoenix, and you weren't even allowed to fish in it. And far from acting as the "flood control" the builders of such projects always tout to justify their short-term profiteering, one year that canal had overflowed and washed the few irrigated fields completely away.

A more dramatic example of such high-handed fumbling dominated my next day's ride, as I rode around the shore of the so-called Salton Sea. This depression in the earth's surface had formerly been called the Salton Sink, until the Colorado overflowed its artificial banks in 1905 and flooded the whole area. Too salty for drinking or irrigation, the new inland sea soon became a "sink" of another kind, contaminated with agricultural runoff from the irrigated Imperial Valley to the south and the date palms, orchards, and vegetable farms of the Coachella Valley to the north, until it became known as the "Salton Sewer."

29 Apr Gila Bend — Palm Springs CA
106,786 (486 kms) [303 miles]

Awake at 4:00 a.m. (bad), cool and less windy (good), free continental breakfast (bad), nice ride across I-8 to Imperial Valley, then up along Salton Sea (smelly).

On a cool, overcast morning I took a detour to explore the ragged remains of Salton City, once planned to be among several resort and retirement communities on the shore of the Sea, which would have offered a desert climate and superb scenery of the surrounding mountains — had they not been sited on a cesspool. Then west into the Borrego Mountains, north on the high plateau connecting to the San Jacinto Mountains, and back down again to the Coachella Valley and the resort and retirement community of Palm Springs. This true oasis, in one of the hottest regions of the desert, was facing its own decline into urban pollution. It was in danger of becoming a miniature Phoenix (alas!), with its own spreading suburbs of Cathedral City, Palm Desert, Rancho Mirage, La Quinta, Indian Wells, and all the way to Indio.

After riding down the steep highway into the "greater Palm Springs area," I stopped and phoned Cathy Rich for directions to their home in Rancho Mirage. Greeted by an artificial waterfall at the entrance, I was cleared into the gated community by a security guard, then rode through the manicured streets between high walls and the low, tile-roofed condominiums built around the shores of two artificial lakes. So much *water,* the symbol of wealth in the desert, but no doubt it was psychologically soothing in the blistering summer, when the thermometer might hit 120° Fahrenheit for days on end. I remembered talking to Cathy on the phone once on such a day, when she had said, "I am living . . . in hell."

Nowhere is perfect, of course, and the Palm Springs area was certainly beautiful in its way, an expanse of green palm trees and golf courses set against the steep rise of the San Jacinto Mountains to the west and facing across the valley to the Indio Hills and the Little San Bernardino Mountains, brown and gold under the sun that always seemed to be shining there. Or nearly always — the Ghost Rider managed to bring rain to this desert too, and over the three days I spent there, light showers began to fall from an uncharacteristically gray sky. Rain in the desert had an effect different from the unwelcome gloom it often brought to other climes, for the attenuated light dimmed the usual unrelenting glare of the sun and brought a lighter kind of melancholy, illuminated by the knowledge that this rain was rare and life-giving.

Once again, it was like exhaling a long-held breath to park my bike for a few days, this time at the Ingleside Inn, where Brutus and I had stayed during rehearsals after the mid-tour break on the *Test For Echo* tour, in the spring of 1997. The cozy little rooms and cabañas set in lush gardens on a back street of Palm Springs were an oasis of another kind for my little baby soul, as rabbits hopped about the lawns, mockingbirds and doves called, and hummingbirds darted among the flowers. The steep mountainside rose almost at the back gate, where I saw a roadrunner and a family of quail among the cactus of an "xeriscaped" garden, and that night, I heard coyotes yipping at the full moon.

And once again during my visits to the Rich family I sank into the peaceful ease of being in someone's *home*. Cathy and Steve and I shared the dumb jokes that had sustained us during the frantic and exciting weeks of recording the tribute album in Manhattan, and I bonded with Nick, now 15, in the same way I had when we had first met, when he was nine and we were both performing at a Buddy Rich Memorial Scholarship concert in New York. Two hours before show time, I had been tapping nervously on the practice pad on my lap, and Nick had appeared at my dressing room door, wide-eyed and frantic, and said, "I am *so* nervous — can I hang around with you?" I had said, "I'm nervous too, come on in," and we kept each other company until showtime. A few weeks later, Cathy told me that when she got home one day and told Nick that she'd had a letter from me, he looked up from the ditch where he was catching frogs and said, "I love Neil — can he come and live with us?" Aw, shucks.

I had felt the same way about him, and now I found he was helping to fill a void in my life, a smart, sassy kid to roughhouse with and tease the way I used to do with Selena. There was still an immature teenager in me, I discovered, and being around a great kid like Nick was both a torment and a comfort. Together we visited the outdoor zoo and gardens of The Living Desert, where the day's light rain brought out the elusive animals like cheetah and mountain lion from their shady retreats, and we hiked a little on the mountain trails, talking and joking comfortably together. It was good for my soul.

After three days, I went back to Los Angeles for what I hoped might be another entertaining visit. Once again, Andrew was determined to get me "out of myself," and took me on a hike in Topanga State Park, above the wide blue Pacific at the end of Sunset Boulevard, accompanied by his Jack Russell terrier, Bob. On the way back, Andrew grabbed my arm and pointed to a rattlesnake across the trail just ahead of us, and as we froze we saw that Bob was somehow on the other side of it. Afraid Bob might be tempted to "play" with the snake, I told Andrew to concentrate on keeping him away while I stamped on the ground and threw stones until it finally slithered off into the chaparral.

Andrew also kept my social calendar filled with nights out with the Canadian ex-patriate gang, Matt Stone (an "honorary Canadian," we decided, as he was from Colorado), and Andrew's room-mate, Wil, an intelligent, articulate young urbanite from San Francisco. We all had some long dinners and kitchen-table forums back at Dave Foley's house (though Dave himself was out of town at the time, several of the other guys were staying at his "Canuck drop-in center"). And then there was Gabrielle, the girl Dave had been dating during my last visit. Andrew told me they weren't dating anymore, and her attitude toward me seemed very warm.

My Air of Tragedy was striking again, apparently, and one night when Andrew and I were about to leave a party at Dave's house a little after midnight (Andrew had an early photo shoot), Gabrielle stood in front of me and said, "*You* don't have to go." She looked straight into my eyes with a telepathic ray, it seemed, and I was totally galvanized for a few seconds. Shaken (and stirred), I mumbled something about "saving Andrew from himself," and left with him (saving myself from *myself,* more like).

The next afternoon, I was out walking around Hollywood on some errands, to the post office, the bank, and the excellent bookstore on Sunset Boulevard, Book Soup. On the way back I thought about Gabrielle's invitation to stop by the restaurant where she worked (while waiting for acting calls, like many young people in Hollywood). Working as a hostess in the main restaurant, she was too busy to talk much, but gave me a big smile and a hug as I took a seat at the bar. I ordered a bowl of pea soup, a Coke, and an espresso (obviously in need of caffeine, after all those long nights), looked over my purchases (Nelson Algren, Joseph Conrad, T.C. Boyle, Saul Bellow, Graham Greene, and *Great Plains* by Ian Frazier) and caught up on my journal writing. "Could be fun here, if it wouldn't *kill* me . . ."

Truman Capote once wrote that he believed that anybody who loved somebody else and pursued them ardently enough would eventually *get* them, for no one can resist being *loved* that much. I think there's truth in that, and to a lesser degree, I was finding it hard to resist someone (well, an attractive woman) who was apparently interested in me. Or maybe my little baby soul had decided it was time to *respond* to the idea. In my journal I tried to be the voice of reason, "Slight attack of 'girl fever.' Keep telling myself no, no, no. Hope I listen! Nothing but trouble there."

But it was no good.

That night, a bunch of us met at Club Largo for an excellent performance by Aimee Mann (who had sung on the Rush song, "Time Stand Still," back in 1987) and her husband, Michael Penn. Afterwards we went from bar to bar, led by the irrepressible Gabrielle. On the way home in a cab, there were four of us crammed into the back seat, so that I was helplessly pressed against — her. A fumbling goodnight kiss, half friendly-on-the-cheek, half lipsward, and she murmurs, "Don't leave town without talking to me," carrying a freight of meanings to my tormented brain.

I said I wouldn't, but I did. Having not only told everyone, but pretty much decided to stay another day, the next morning, with a crushing hangover, found me throwing my bags together, loading the bike, and getting the hell out of Dodge.

Unable to deal with that confusing upwelling of feelings I was not ready to face, or even *acknowledge*, feelings I had thought were dead (maybe forever), I decided to get away from there for awhile, try to think this through "like a *sensible* person."

So, I rode across the Hollywood Hills to the San Fernando Valley and stopped in Encino to visit Freddie Gruber — a man who definitely deserves some introduction. Freddie was a native New Yorker who as a young man had been a drum prodigy in the jazz world of the late '40s, but fled that self-destructive scene and worked his way west through Chicago, Las Vegas, eventually settling in Los Angeles to play the after-hours clubs, and develop a whole new career as a master teacher. He had been Buddy Rich's best friend until Buddy's death in 1987 (so often I would hear Freddie say, "I still miss him, man"), and remained close with many of the prominent musicians of his day, as well as many of his students, who had become the prominent musicians of *this* day. Their names may not be well known to the average listener, but their playing would be heard on the radio every day.

A lifelong bachelor, at 70, Freddie was full of energy and enthusiasm, and was a certifiable one-of-a-kind (Buddy had once called him that, Freddie told me, then a year later had said, "I've changed my mind — you're *none* of a kind!"). To be around Freddie was to hear a thousand stories about Buddy, and about his own eventful, even outrageous, life. Freddie's stories would meander from the streets of Harlem or Greenwich Village in the '40s and '50s, or the Hollywood Hills in the '60s and '70s, and inevitably end up with a capper like, "and that young man on the Harlem rooftop who called himself Detroit Red later became known as . . . Malcolm X," or "That young actor in New York who stole my girlfriend was . . . Marlon Brando," or, "the man with the English accent by the pool next to Jack Nicholson's house on Mulholland Drive was . . . Stanley Kubrick."

I had first met Freddie during the *Burning For Buddy* sessions in 1994, when I listened to Steve Smith's playing — always a great drummer, he had suddenly become a *monster*, so musical and with such beautiful technique — and I asked him, "What happened to you?" He had smiled and said, "Freddie."

So I arranged to get together with Freddie myself later that year, in New York City, and over that week (and the next year or so of daily practice) he guided me through a complete reinvention of my approach to the drums (no small undertaking after 30 years of playing, but a challenge that proved rewarding and productive). Thus Freddie had become one of the key people in my life — those who appear exactly when you need them, and only when you are ready for them. I call it the "principle of serendipitous confluence." Or more simply, finding the right person at the right time.

[Letter to Brutus]

May 6, '99
Encino, CA

Buenas días, compañero —

Yep, here I am, hangin' at Freddie's "pad," man. How can I begin to put you in the picture? Well, it's a quiet suburb in the San Fernando Valley, tidy streets with manicured postage-stamp lawns, cypresses, pines, lemons, and orange trees symmetrically placed, and the small lots entirely filled with narrow bungalows, and back yards usurped by modest swimming pools. One of those narrow bungalows is Freddie's, and the driveway features a faded brown Rambler two-door from about 1960 (his late mother's) and a '71 Firebird, also faded brown, and also a neglected non-runner. Behind them is an early Infiniti, a black convertible-conversion job, and on the street out front is a mid-'70s Dodge four-door, the "daily driver."

Inside is where the description becomes difficult. Small rooms filled with bits and pieces of flea-market furniture, boxes stacked against walls, table covered with neatly stacked papers and photos, an ancient stereo, a built-in bar with white naugahyde padding, behind it a four-foot stack of bags and boxes full of stuff, closets and racks of hanging clothes that probably go back 50 years, those crammed into a room with a battered drumset, muffled with pads and towels, and the little kitchen, wallpapered long ago in formerly bright yellow flowers, every surface covered with dishes, pots and pans, unused appliances, bits of paper, and a miniature TV. Everywhere in the house, thousands of magazines about drums and jazz, and nothing else. (No current events, no gossip, no American "lifestyles.")

And you know, I *like* it here. After escaping the insidious temptations of La-la (more about that in a minute), I rode up through Laurel Canyon to Mulholland Drive (given new meaning these days, not only knowing who he was, but what a gigantic figure he was in local history), with hazy L.A. on one side and the hazy valley on the other, and some truly great riding through those treacherous and famously deadly curves. I stopped here yesterday afternoon, just to see Freddie and maybe have a coffee, let him talk for awhile, then continue on my way.

But now I'm settled into the sweltering back bedroom with the roll-away cot, Mickey Mouse comforter, boxes, magazines about drums and jazz, a "trilight" pole-lamp in the corner, a broken aluminum lawn chair, a TV table (no TV), a bedside lamp that doesn't work, and a bottle of The Macallan — and I don't want to *leave!* It's a hideaway, a sanctuary, a place where a guy can just *hang.* Though it's obvious that Freddie totally puts me to shame at being "bachelor with a vengeance" (an inspiration!), the whole thing simply *works,* perhaps like Le Corbusier's description of a house: "a machine for living." Like the old Rambler or the naugh-ahyde bar, it might not be exactly fully *functional,* but really, what's that got to do with it?

In context of Freddie, it's simply *right.* The machine works. You don't use the dishes in the cupboard, for they've been stacked there since he moved in — 14 years ago. So you use the ones in the drying rack. The freezer is packed with white plastic bags of something-or-other, but no ice. The fridge has a few containers of prepared deli food, stuff that Freddie can heat up in the middle of the night when he gets hungry. If the gold velvet couch is covered with bags of laundry and magazines, Freddie moves them aside, covers them neatly with a striped towel (!), and you stretch out. Apparently the blinds in my little room haven't been opened in 14 years — never mind the window — but hey, they open! The old Dodge runs. The pool is clean. Lemons grow in the yard. The sun shines. I'm not leaving.

See, I had a very *confusing* time back there, "over the hill." And yes, as you might expect, it's about a *woman*. Oh man. You remember I told you about meeting that young Canadian girl, Gabrielle, the last time I was here? At the time I didn't even *think* about thinking about her (for about a million good reasons), not even for a second, but later Andrew told me that she was always talking about *me*, and said I was a "hottie" (nobody ever called me *that* before!). I blushed and was pleased about that, especially given my present state of existential insecurity, but I didn't take the idea at all seriously. Especially given my present state of existential insecurity.

This time, however, she got to me. You know — she shot me with that *look* that wimmen have. *[Recap of the "Don't leave town without talking to me" night.]*

So, as we began, I'm hiding out at Freddie's pad, my retreat, my hideaway, my sanctuary, where hopefully I can talk some sense into myself, and stop thinking about that girl.

Say it again, "No, no, no."

You know me well enough to understand there's no being "casual" about a thing like this, and I sure don't want to mess with *her* life — especially given my present state of etc.

I mean, really.

But of course, one is helpless in the grip of such thoughts and feelings, and I can only try to summon the strength to keep *running*. Get back on the road and ride. I'm far from ready to deal with the ramifications of what all this means — even presuming the notion should even be entertained for, like, two minutes. How stupid can a guy be? Well, in the words of the Brain, "Time will tell, Pinky, time will tell."

I'm sure you get the picture. One confused and scared little soul sitting here on Freddie's gold velvet couch. Drinking. Freddie's out at the dentist and nutritionist, or I'd never have got a word in edgewise (even on paper), but even when he's here, part of Freddie's uniqueness is that he's so damn oblivious to the rest of the world. Right now, this *works* for me.

He has this radio station playing all the time (from the bathroom, at the moment) with a format of "America's greatest music," pretty much regardless of era or style, and they do play a lot of great songs. Like, "Go Away Little Girl." "Crazy." "Unchained Melody." "I Got it Bad, and That Ain't Good." "I've Got a Crush on You." "I've Got You Under my Skin."

And one that got me last night, dedicated to you and me: "Our Day Will Come."

Now they're playing "The Way We Were." Oh man. Weigh that one up, for you or for me, and fall to little tiny pieces.

May 8, '99
Bishop, CA

I stole away from Freddie's place about 10:30 this morning, leaving him a note, then headed up the "eastern California" route — 395 through Mojave, Big Pine, Lone Pine, and past Owens "Lake" to Bishop, the center of the whole Owens Valley ripoff. The same road goes all the way up through Reno, then back into northern California, Oregon, and right into Washington. The other day I noticed the Grand Coulee Dam (the biggest?) on the map, so I might pass by there on the way (to *where* I'm not sure — maybe Vancouver again).

Right now, the main thing is: Get the hell out of California! Especially given my present state of existential insecurity.

> Bye Bye, love —
> Or at least infatuation . . .
> *A rattled Ghost Rider*

My little baby soul had been thrown into total disarray by these totally unexpected — and just as totally *unwanted* — feelings, and as I rode northward, I went over and over it in my mind. In a way it seemed simple enough; if this girl was interested in me, and I was interested in her, I should just ask her out on a date and see how it went. But it was not in my nature ever to be so casual, about *anything,* and there were so many complications my wretched brain had to sift through, from trying to understand the real nature of my feelings (never easy), to the heavy-duty question I couldn't help asking myself: What would Jackie and Selena think about this?

My journal entry that night captures my state of mind pretty well:

> *Still tormented and confused, but moving in the right direction —* away.
> *Can't believe the state of me, in all ways. Trying hard to get a grip, but part of me says "surrender" — turn around and go back.*
> *How did I let this* happen?
> *After all my big talk about bachelorhood etc.*
> *What a fool.*

So for the time being I just kept riding, hoping time and distance would help me regain whatever "balance" I had attained before that fateful second stay in Los Angeles. I was learning a lesson about how much I could "control" my feelings, and along the way I adopted a new motto: "You can't tell yourself how to feel."

With the kind of serendipity novels sometimes provide, or reveal, it happened that at the time I was reading Joseph Conrad's *Victory* (which I had been inspired to pick up because of a fan letter Jack London had written to Conrad praising it), and I was struck by the parallels with my recent experiences and their effects with those of the main character, Heyst. While I was reading, a couple of times I made myself stop and copy out a passage into my journal, so wonderfully did they reflect my own state.

> *Where could he have gone to, after all these years? Not a single soul belonging to him lived anywhere on earth. Of this fact — not such a remote one, after all — he had only lately become aware; for it is failure that makes a man enter into himself and reckon up his resources. And though he had made up his mind to retire from the world in hermit fashion, yet he was irrationally moved by this sense of loneliness which had come to him in the hour of renunciation. It hurt him. Nothing is more painful than the shock of sharp contradictions that lacerate our intelligence and our feelings.*

> *"I'll drift," Heyst had said to himself deliberately.*
>
> *He did not mean intellectually or sentimentally or morally. He meant to drift altogether and literally, body and soul, like a detached leaf drifting in the wind-currents under the immovable trees of a forest glade; to drift without ever catching onto anything.*
>
> *"This shall be my defence against life," he had said to himself with a sort of inward consciousness that for the son of his father there was no other worthy alternative.*
>
> *He became a waif and a stray, austerely, from conviction, as others do through drink, from vice, from some weakness of character — with deliberation, as others do in despair. This, stripped of its facts, had been Heyst's life up to that disturbing night. Next day, when he saw the girl called Alma, she managed to give him a glance of frank tenderness, quick as lightning, and leaving a profound impression, a secret touch on the heart.*

[Letter to Brutus]

May 11, '99
Salish Lodge
Snoqualmie Falls, WA

Hey-Zeus,

This is definitely a Scooter Trash kind of place. Overlooking the actual falls from the opening of "Twin Peaks" (a lot of the locations were shot in this area, according to Deb's TV America book, which we'll have to get. For example, did you know that "Grizzly Adams" was shot in Kanab, Utah?). It's a four-diamond hotel, with a four-diamond restaurant — which is where we two are now, just finishing an exquisite salmon chowder with a delicate Sonoma wine (we're snobs about that now, after our visit to St. Helena last fall, where we found the relatively quiet Sonoma Valley — and Jack London State Park — much more simpático than the parade through Napa), and awaiting the main course of sturgeon (had to try it; how often do you see *that* on a menu?), though you might opt for the venison, or the rack of lamb.

So, since my last letter, mailed from Alturas, California, another superlative day on 395, which we hereby christen one of the great American roads. This morning I rode through the treeless grasslands and center-pivot-irrigated farms of eastern Washington, thoroughly enjoying the underrated scenery and empty, winding roads of the Columbia basin, and stopped at the Grand Coulee Dam (it was large).

But first let me tell you about yesterday's ride: 834 kilometres [521 miles] from Alturas to Connell, Washington, a tiny farm town, where I got tired enough to stop. Looking over my journal notes, they might give a good sketch of those two days. So here goes:

May 9 Bishop — Alturas
108,208 (620 kms) [388 miles]

Here at the "Pizza and Pasta Place," for the lasagna special. Nice enough day, bright and sunny, though cold — always around 5,000 feet, with snow-capped mountains in view most of the time. Sagebrush and junipers, rather than forested mountains I expected from map — or half-expected, more like.

Restaurant full of older couples for Mothers Day, which is both cute and cruel. One presumes that Alturas hasn't much more to offer than this place. Note Super 8 guy described it as an "Eye-talian" restaurant.

Called Mom this morning (two years ago, Brutus and I called our Moms from Coalinga, not so far away), but got no answer. Caught her later, and talked to Deb too.

Playing in Reno: James Brown, Lou Rawls, Engelbert, Wayne Newton.

Small town trying to stay alive — county seat of Modoc County, with courthouse, few motels and restaurants, one old hotel (are any of those places habitable?), sporadic cinema, video rental store, grocery store, bottle shop, couple of "antique" stores. Nice little place, really, with park, museum (closed unfortunately) and decent-looking streets, murals on many old walls — cross-country skier, cyclist, fly fisherman, old cars on GM dealer wall. Altogether, probably in better shape than 10 years ago.

Reading Great Plains *by Ian Frazier — obviously a kindred spirit.*

May 10 Alturas — Connell, WA
109,042 (834 kms) [521 miles]

Onward up 395, truly a great American road. Cold this morning: ice under irrigation wheels. Saw temp. 44°F at noon. Farmland, range-land, sage and juniper, alkali lakes, long stretch alongside Goose Lake with "rimrock" formations, Hogback Summit at 5,039 feet, then pure sage and rocky outcrops to Wagontire, Oregon. Up into pinewoods around John Day (got in trouble for passing in "pilot line"), then out to rounded grasslands after Battle Mountain. Suddenly open far and wide. Across the Columbia twice, through franchise nightmare of "Tri-cities," Pasco, Kennewick, and Richland [at confluence of Columbia and Snake], and on into irrigated farmland.

Now dinner at Michael Jay's family restaurant. Staying next door at M & M Motel, $30. Lots of truckers and construction pickups. Good long ride for thinking. Only busy around Columbia, otherwise smooth cruising.

And we're in the bar now, enjoying a Martell Cordon Bleu with espresso. Quite a step up from the past few days of Super 8, M & M motels, and "family restaurants."

And well-deserved, after the day that today turned into. The only two times on this whole long journey (taking it all together, from the beginning in Quebec last August) when I've had serious stomach problems were after a dinner at the "Home" restaurant in Hope, B.C., and after breakfast at "Michael Jay's Family Restaurant" this morning in Connell, Washington. And that includes criss-crossing Mexico and Belize. Today, caught out in the middle of wide-open sagebrush and low, irrigated fields, without a stick of cover, found me crouched behind a couple of hay bales at the roadside, groaning and purging . . .

Then there was the weather. Here's the journal entry, with a couple of early scribbles I didn't want to forget:

May 11 Connell — Snoqualmie Falls
109,588 (546) [341 miles]

Lind, WA — Combine [harvester] demolition derby!
Center-pivot irrigation everywhere.

Bird: orange head, black and white wings [Yellow-headed blackbird]

[Later] Well, here at Salish Lodge. Seems to me only the waterfall was in "Twin Peaks," but it is cool. Made the run to Grand Coulee Dam, great ride on excellent, empty roads, and even better after: river bluffs, lakes, winding road. Great part of Northwest around there, for scenery and weather.

ALSO: actually called Gabrielle! The words came into my head this morning: "The answer is yes." Felt like a goofy teenager about it, but got her number from Andrew and made myself call her. Made a date to go back there after Vancouver. Now I'll be increasingly terrified for the next week. Oh well. It's certainly sparked up my life already, just thinking about her. And now, making a move. Well done.

I think . . .

Great to have called her from Grand Coulee Dam too. A place to remember.

I hope . . .

Never mind these doubts and fears. Trust that voice inside.

Unfortunately, the day went downhill from there. Bad stomach, bad weather. I-90 increasingly cold and rainy, trucks roaring by, blinding and treacherous. Fear of ice.

Once again, cheated death and made it.

Talked to Deb, but just said I was heading back south, and might see my "new friends" in L.A. We'll see how things go before I tell her — hope she understands. She's the only one who might take it weird, and I'd hate that.

We are links for each other.

May 14
Vancouver

Hey Razor Willie!

Here I am, back at you — from my rather *cramped* guest quarters, at Danny and Janette's house. Only one bathroom too. I keep telling them we need a bigger place here, especially as they, the landlords, keep collecting more dogs and babies and stuff. But they're too busy.

However, I've been making the best of it, as one does. Down on the floor playing cars with my pal Max, walking Tara and "Barfy" through the woods with Janette (seriously pregnant, in her petite way, but no less active in work or fast walking), and hiking with Danny up the Capilano River to the Cleveland Dam (named after Vancouver's first water commissioner; wonder what kind of a character *he* was?). Later today, Danny's proposed either a bike ride or a swim in a local pool, and tomorrow he's booked rowing boats for us to take out in the Burrard Inlet, like we did during my visit last September. It was very cool to be out there among the freighters, huge steel marker buoys, sea birds, seals bobbing to the surface, and all around us the splendid view of city, Stanley Park, Lion's Gate Bridge, and the mountains above, green with snowy tops. They keep me busy here.

This morning I left a message with your "service," so I'm hoping to hear from you by tomorrow. Your most excellent letter to "Pancho" was here when I arrived, and I thank you for some of the nice things you had to say. It matters, brother o' mine.

For now, I'll close this off, and we'll no doubt talk about the rest of recent events "on the wire."

Carry on, major
El Romancero

Other than Brutus, the only person I told about my plans was my Mom. She knew better than anyone what I had been through for nearly two years by that time, and she and Jackie had also been fairly close, so I knew her response would be a fair one. I needed someone to tell me that what I was doing was okay, and when I called my Mom and said I was headed for Vancouver, then back to Los Angeles because I had "a date with a girl," she was *ecstatic* for me — so excited that I was taking this big step back into life. That made me feel a little better about my rash decision.

When I arrived in Vancouver and told the whole story to Danny and Janette, their feelings must have been mixed, partly concerned and partly amused at my "infatuation," but they were supportive all the same. While my motorcycle was in the local BMW shop for servicing, Danny took me shopping for some nicer "dress-up" clothes, and three days later I picked up the bike and headed south again — this time by the "express route," the Interstate, through the rain and wind and cold of Washington and Oregon.

The first night, in Salem, Oregon, I tried to put all my feelings in a letter to Deb, telling her what I was doing — what I felt I *had* to do — then faxed it to her, asking her to call me in Los Angeles and, "laugh at me — so I'll know everything is okay between us."

For myself, even though I had made the big decision to go back there and see Gabrielle, I was far from comfortable with the idea. In my imaginary presentation of the case to my ever-present "ghost jury," Jackie and Selena, I eventually decided that if I told Selena I had a date with a glamorous beauty queen, she would probably say, "All right Dad!" Jackie, on the other hand, would hardly be *excited,* but I could picture her rolling her eyes to Selena and saying in her dry way, "Well, I guess we have to let your *father* have his *fun . . .*"

The second day carried me 994 kilometres [621 miles], from Salem, Oregon, to Stockton, California, riding through the magnificent scenery around the Oregon/California border, past the gleaming white peak of Mount Shasta and the blue expanse of Lake Shasta. That day I passed from cold rain to hot sun, from Douglas firs to California live oaks to palm trees.

That evening, as I walked back to the inevitable Best Western from a

Carrow's restaurant, I passed under the Interstate and noticed the on-ramp I would be taking the following morning. Looking at the "I-5 South" sign, I felt a strange sense of *disbelief,* and realized that it was a reflection of my inner distrust of anything in life. I had no faith in the future, even as far as getting on the highway again the next morning.

But of course I did, facing another cold morning, clear and bright, through the irrigated farms and ranches of the Central Valley, and what I called "those tawny, wrinkled, 'Shar-pei' hills." The Tejon Pass, at 4,000 feet, was cold and hazy, and it stayed like that all the way into Hollywood, and back to the Sunset Marquis.

The previous night I had called my brother-in-law, Steven, and told him "the news." He was cautiously supportive, but typically, he had his concerns about me. "I'm only worried about you getting hurt."

I wrote in my journal, "Me too, but . . . you can't tell yourself how to feel."

Unfortunately, Deb couldn't hold back her feelings either. As I had asked her to do, she called me at the hotel, and I knew right away she wasn't going to be "laughing" at me. She was obviously in tears, her voice breaking as she said, "I've got some problems with this." Oh dear.

She was very upset, and sobbed, "I didn't think you had any interest in *dating* right now." I began to feel pangs of guilt, and an ache of doubt as I told her that I hadn't thought so either, but it had just happened — I was sorry she was so upset about it. I told her I would call her later in the week, hoping that she would get a little "used to" the idea. Or maybe this "experiment" would just fizzle out on its own, and become a non-issue.

In any case, my own chaotic emotions were stirred up even more by this conversation, and later that day I stood in the shower and was suddenly overcome by a helpless attack of weeping, sobbing my own heart out — about everything.

But in my characteristic, obsessive way I threw myself into this fresh adventure, throwing caution to the proverbial winds and romancing that girl, in a nervously determined (not to say desperate) sort of way. Renting a sleek Porsche Boxster, I first escorted Gabrielle on a double-date with Andrew and his friend, Rich, and later back to my hotel for drinks, where we stayed up all night talking about our lives and past heartaches.

As a man who hadn't done anything that could be called "dating" in more than 20 years, I was surprised how well I slipped into this new role, but once again, I seemed to have evolved a new "adaptive persona" for this mission, a new mask (without armor, alas) called "Ellwood, the Hollywood party boy." During those heady days Andrew and I had even begun to talk about renting a *house* together in the Hollywood Hills, so that I could spend more time there, and it's certain "the fool I used to be" would simply have *laughed* at that idea.

But somehow it didn't seem so crazy now — to Ellwood, at least, as he dressed himself up and squired Gabrielle to the new Getty museum, to dinner at the Bel Air Hotel, on a couple of shopping expeditions, and to dinner at a restaurant on the ocean in Malibu with a full moon rising through the palms, then driving back to Hollywood with the top down in the cool, fragrant night. I drove her and Andrew in his SUV to Death Valley, so he could scout some photo locations, and showed them around some of my favorite places there.

One afternoon, Gabrielle and I strolled beneath the California fan palms that line the beachfront in Venice, taking in the surreal stage set (or movie set, really) of souvenir shops, sidewalk vendors, fortune tellers, street musicians, and the passing parade of strange-looking individuals. There were several tarot-card readers, and I was a little curious about that. Though I've always been a card-carrying rational-scientific-skeptic, I try to remain open to all possibilities (the difference between a cynic and a skeptic, I like to think, is one is dismissive, the other only *doubtful*), so I thought it would be entertaining to have my first tarot reading. The graphics of the tarot cards had always seemed romantic and mystical to me, and the few names I knew were also intriguing: The Tower, The Hanged Man, The Lovers, The Fool.

From among the sidewalk readers I chose the one who *wasn't* dressed in gypsy garb, a spare, fit-looking man of about 60 years with a weathered face. As I sat at the folding card table beside him, his expression was calm and intent. (Later I learned he was a Vietnam veteran, and a practical, down-to-earth sort of man.) His well-worn deck of cards was spread before us, face down and cut into separate stacks that were bound with elastic bands. Without asking any questions or trying to gather any "clues," he fanned one of the stacks toward me and told me to choose five. I plucked them out in a way I felt was random, and he placed them on the table, face up.

Death, Wisdom, The Tower, Wheel of Fortune, High Priestess.

After a few seconds of silence, he shook his head and said, "This is most unusual." Then he gave me his interpretation, which so galvanized me that I was compelled to ask him to write it down for me.

"After great tragedy and tribulation you are trying to rebuild yourself and your life. Pain from separation is causing you unhappiness, and you're dwelling on past conflicts, travelling with regrets. You work in the performing arts of some kind — actor? musician? — and your job offers you abundance, but this has deteriorated as you've been moving in a different direction. Now you are travelling far from home, trying to begin a new cycle, but you're not ready. You need more insight."

Then he had me choose five cards from the next stack, and carried on. "After a time of difficulty, of unhappiness and financial problems, you will find a new beginning with a relationship, and a time of superabundance. This person will not only provide you with affection, but will help you straighten out your money problems as well. She will be a true *partner* to you."

My jaw dropped, and it's *still* dropping. That little oration was so true in every respect, then and now, that, as I said at the time, "It rocked my world." It was so far beyond the possibility of guesswork or generality, and subsequent events and future readings only reinforced that experience, gave me the "empirical evidence" of repeatability.

For days after that reading I walked around shaking my head. One part of my brain was seeking in vain for a rational explanation, while another part was trying hard to find a way to incorporate this understanding into my world-view. How does a rational-scientific-skeptic find a place in his orderly philosophy for that? (Though I could say the same thing about death.)

As for the progress of Ellwood's efforts at romancing, everything *seemed* to be going very well, but Gabrielle held her feelings close. I couldn't tell if we were just having some fun together, or *starting* something. Ellwood was happy just to be playing the "romantic superhero," but the rest of "us" had more serious concerns.

I tried to clarify my feelings in my journal.

> *With Gabrielle, it's all getting complicated, both feelings and realities. This fool is definitely falling hard, but can't tell if it's reciprocal. My need is rather pathetically desperate, but again, you can't tell yourself how to feel. She's got "powers," no question. I'm so stirred up inside, agitated, and alternately miserable and ecstatic. I don't think I'm strong enough to be facing this right now, but again — it wasn't a choice.*
>
> > *In the heartbreaking words of Grace Bailey from "Wind at My Back," "Don't let me lose again."*
> >
> > *These are dangerous times, and I fear the future — for the first time in 11 months and 5 days [since Jackie's death]. I'm afraid if this doesn't go well it could really mess me up bad again. Still, I wouldn't do it any differently. That would have been a bigger mistake.*
> >
> > *But . . . Don't let me lose again.*

> *Look in*
> *Look the storm in the eye*
> *Look out*
> *To the sea and the sky*
> *Look around*
> *At the sight and sound*
> *Look in look out look around*
>
> FORCE 10, 1987

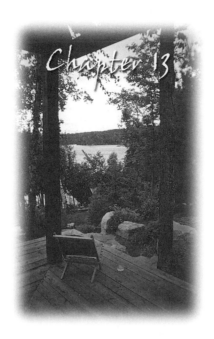

SUMMERLUDE

Got to keep on moving
At the speed of love
Nothing changes faster
Than the speed of love

THE SPEED OF LOVE, 1993

After five days and nights of "extreme romancing," several indicators seemed to tell me it was time to get riding again. Gabrielle had to return to working her usual long hours at the restaurant, when she wouldn't have much time for me, and also, the arrival of June was calling me back to the house on the lake. It would be summer there now, green and gentle after the harsh white winter, and I was yearning to be there. Gabrielle and I agreed to meet up again soon, maybe in Canada, or maybe in San Francisco, just a short flight from Los Angeles, and we had a sweet parting at the Sunset Marquis.

It was time for me to regroup, to try to sort out the chaos of my feelings, and I knew a long cross-country ride would be just the forum for that. So, instead of my usual meandering routes, I got on the Interstate in Los Angeles and just started *riding,* my feverish thoughts ticking off the miles across California, Nevada, Utah, Colorado, Nebraska, Iowa, Wisconsin, the upper peninsula of Michigan, Ontario, and — in only five days — back to the house by the lake.

I was so excited to be there again that I was dashing around the house, the woods, and down to the lake, trying to look at everything at once. Keith had taken his usual perfect care of the place, and the gardens were a vision of carefully tended splendor. Altogether, it was quite a different scene than the one I had left back in mid-April, a reflection of the seasonal changes as well as the changes my little baby soul had been through in the intervening time.

We also seemed to have a new member in that splintered, multi-faceted soul of mine, a persona (perhaps not "adaptive" this time, but rather "developmental") I could best describe as a 14-year-old girl, given my sudden taste for "teen-pop music," especially the lovey-dovey songs, and my tendency to burst into tears over even the *happy* parts of my Sunday night TV show, "Wind at My Back" (on CBC, of course, a family drama set in the '30s, kind of "The Waltons" of Ontario). Thinking that perhaps my little baby soul had grown into an adolescent girl, I called her "Gaia," after a primitive goddess.

As I settled into summer, I was hoping to build myself an active routine once again, writing my therapeutic letters and getting outdoors for thera-peutic exercise, alternating weeks alone with therapeutic visits from friends and family. (Yes, life was all about therapy.) I even dared to harbor a secret hope I might get started on some *serious* writing work, whether it meant getting back to my half-finished book about the Rush tour, or working on the Ghost Rider's story — but I would just have to see about that.

A passage from George Eliot's *The Mill on the Floss* expressed the post-traumatic state I was embarking upon, and gave me a clue that I was still in for some tough times:

There is something sustaining in the very agitation that accompanies the first shocks of trouble, just as an acute pain is often a stimulus, and produces an excitement which is transient strength. It is in the slow, changed life that follows — in the time when sorrow has become stale, and has no longer an emotive intensity that counteracts its pain — in the time when day follows day in dull unexpectant sameness, and trial is a dreary routine; — it is then that despair threatens; it is then that the peremptory hunger of the soul is felt, and eye and ear are strained after some unlearned secret of our existence, which shall give to endurance the nature of satisfaction.

In my early days of settling into the house on the lake, I wrote to my friend Mendelson Joe, to tell him all about everything.

June 9, '99
Lac St. Brutus, Que.

Good day Joe,

This is one of those times when I can't believe it's been so long since the last time I wrote to you — late February, according to my files. However, these days I'm often *glad* to notice a few months have slipped by on me. It means that I've been filling my days well enough to allow Time, the presumed healer, to get on with its job.

I've just returned from picking up my bike in Mexico City and riding it home through northern Mexico and the western U.S., via the six-week, 14,000-kilometre [8,750-mile] route. Most of that time was spent meandering around the West Coast, visiting some Canadian ex-pat friends in Los Shmengeles, and my brother and his family in San Francouver (the B.C. one). Last week, I decided it was time to get home, and took the "express route" back from L.A.

You know I prefer the back roads, the empty two-lane blacktop thrill-rides of the West, but there is still something special about a long, relentless journey, even on the "Superslab." Brutus and I did a couple of cross-country marathons during the Rush tour (Virginia to Frisco in four days, Toronto to L.A. in five) and we got to like the way you just keep humming along, stopping only for gas and "biological breaks," with a mental jukebox dredging up every song you ever knew and playing it back to you. Sure you get stiff and sore, and maybe cold and wet, but that's the price of admission.

This time I made a truly epic crossing ("Five Thousand Ks in Five Days" is the pithy headline) because I just wanted to be *here,* and because the idea of a long ride in that "Interstate-of-mind" appealed to me.

Across the Mojave (101°F on the World's Tallest Thermometer in Baker, California), into the high desert of the Great Basin, Nevada and Utah, and one of the best Interstate routes in all America — I-70 winding through Utah's monumental rock formations and wide blue sky, then up and over the Colorado Rockies.

The weather got kind of "bitchy" around eastern Colorado (though never "beastly," as it had been in the Pacific Northwest; these are a couple of my new meteorological classifications for motorcycling weather), with clouds and wind and occasional rain, but it was never too serious. I avoided the Shmegmopolitan rat-warrens east of the Mississippi by riding up through Nebraska, Iowa, Wisconsin, the upper peninsula of Michigan, and crossing Our Nation's Border at Sault Ste. Marie, right past that old arena where, I recall, we did a show together in the long-ago time. [In the mid-'70s Joe opened for Rush on a few shows in northern Ontario, the audiences typically bemused by his quirky singing, guitar playing, and amplified boot-stomping.]

Then across (ridiculously over-policed) Ontario, through

Sudbury, North Bay, and Our Nation's Capital, and back to my garage. The GS had covered 60,105 kilometres [37,566 miles] since leaving here last August, and its odometer now shows 117,312 [73,320 miles]. And it's still running like a champ.

Despite covering such a distance in that short a time, it was actually a very *safe* crossing (as much as there is such a thing, of course). Relative to suburban streets and meandering highways with sudden tractors and cows, cruising on the Interstate is what the Brits call a "dawdle." Especially out West, where the traffic is so much lighter and you can often see around you for *days*. Even travelling through the American Memorial Day weekend, that was a pretty smooth route, and I made much better time than I'd expected. I'd allowed six or seven days for the crossing, but once I got into that Interstate-of-mind, I just kept *cruising*.

Simply making "Big Speed" is not the way, of course. For one thing, you only invite the attentions of the Law, and who needs the hassle? Not me. The Western states all have limits of 70 or 75 mph anyway, so you can cruise safely in the low 80s, and that's plenty fast enough to make time. Then I just try to keep the "two-second cushion" between me and surrounding traffic, keep out of their blind spots (while remembering that no matter what, I remain totally *invisible* to them), and ride on — one fuel stop or rest area/pee stop at a time. So pass the miles, and the days.

For many excellent reasons, I don't like riding at night (well, I *like* it, but I don't think it's a good thing). One big reason is that there's certainly no point in riding through scenery you can't see, but there are also all the *other* things you can't see, like broken mufflers or strips of truck recap in your lane. And obviously I don't want to get too tired and possibly make a dumb mistake, so I was off the road by 5:00 every day, and away again early, early in the morning. The last day, as I got close to home, I went longer — 1,300 kilometres [813 miles] in 14 hours, but even then I arrived before dark.

And I can see now it was the right thing to do, back then: taking off during the change of season. I was "sinking" a little, day by day, and needed to make a change. Take my little baby soul for a ride.

Plus, that Last Big Ride from L.A. homeward was special in another way, because now there's gold at either end of that rainbow — my beautiful house at this end, and a beautiful girl at the other!

[Recap of the Big Romance.]

You can probably imagine what a huge transformation this has made in my life. Your most recent letter advised me to travel in this direction, so to speak, though I must say I had been giving it precious little thought myself. I just wanted to carry on in relative solitude, to be a hermit in the winter and summer, and a gypsy in the spring and fall. That was my little plan for life, and I certainly had no intention of becoming attached to anyone. To the contrary, I wanted to shut myself off from all that — "I touch no one and no one touches me."

But as I have been saying often lately, "You can't tell yourself how to feel."

Certain electromagnetic and biochemical signals were exchanged — to take the unromantic view — and everything was suddenly different. It's a hell of a thing. Another one of my current mottoes: "What a difference a dame makes."

All I know is that I saved a bundle on tire wear, because all the way from California to Quebec, my wheels never touched the ground.

And that's my little story for today, Joe. Definitely a lot brighter than most of my stories lately, and it just goes to show . . . well, something. There is always a dark side, of course, and now I sometimes find myself tormented by doubts and insecurities and fears and guilts of an entirely different order, but again — you can't tell yourself how to feel.

Another motto, from the French, that applies well to my current attitude about life-in-general: *Ça vaut la peine.* "It's worth the trouble."

That also goes to show . . . something.

Otherwise, I'm trying to get myself oriented for summer activities — already out rowing every day, and wanting to get into cycling — and also into doing something, I don't know, maybe productive?

Nothing like Romance to get a guy fired up about "doing something" (probably just a variation of "showing off"), but we'll see what, if anything, comes of that notion. For now, I'm just glad to have all those new sparks lighting up my little baby soul.

> Ain't love grand?
> Sometimes it is . . .
> NEP

[Letter to Brutus]
le petit oiseau d'été

June 11, '99
Lac St. Brutus, Que.

Hey Schnitzelgrüßen!

Good morning to you from a golden day of early summer, bright yellow sunshine, immaculate blue sky, ripples sparkling on the lake, curves of green all around, and even at 9:30 a.m. it's around 75 of your quaint American degrees.

Winds light from the southeast, barometer steady, humidity 80 per cent, and it looks as though we're under the influence of a fairly stationary high-pressure zone. After a somewhat gloomy week, both exterior and interior (that would be me), the change is welcome.

Easing into the summer groove-thang, this morning I was up

before the sun cleared the trees, pressing the juice and making coffee, then standing at the kitchen window to watch the birds at my feeding station while I wash a few dishes. A little Sinatra playing quietly, so as not to disturb the guests (Steven and Shelly in the house; Deb and Rudy over in the guest house), while I do the morning clean-up chores.

Imposing Bachelor's Rules on the household, where the kitchen must be cleaned up the following morning and *not* right after dinner, has had the unintended effect that the earliest riser faces the task. That would be me. However, I'm sure you can imagine that it's not so unpleasant *dans une scène si belle comme ça ici.*

Yesterday morning I had a wonderful little set-piece: a bright yellow goldfinch perched opposite a bright red house finch, while a ruby-throated hummingbird sipped at the nectar right outside the window. Even in summer, Chef Ellwood's Birdbrain Café is very popular in the neighborhood, and I get to see a lot of birds that would otherwise pass unnoticed.

Slowly I'm getting adjusted to this latest change of seasons, trying to find the patterns of activity and a "mind-set," I guess you'd call it, that will get me through the days and nights. This first week back I've been feeling kind of out of sync with everything, including the environment. It seems I'm still fairly confused and disoriented, from the inside out, and I've had trouble getting centered, or even motivated toward the ever-necessary activities. Basically, I'm just stirred up inside. Agitated, like.

I've gone out for a row most days, but often I fail to "surrender to it" or something, and don't get the lovely trance-state that makes all those kinds of motion so valuable to this little baby soul o' mine. It seemed like I was hauling at those oars and driving down through my feet with a feeling more like agitation, frustration, and even anger — beat up that water!

It's hardly surprising that I'm finding it a little difficult to get settled down. I've got that old "caught in a whirlwind" feeling again, with so many emotions whipping through me, some of them *big* ones, that my poor brain can't even keep up, let alone make sense of it all. Still, that inadequate little organ keeps trying, cranking away like the primitive computer it is, continually attempting to solve impossible questions and make impossible decisions. That would be me.

The time of year is rough too, as June is another of the "cursed" months in my year these days. It occurs to me now that the whole *season* is cursed ("Cruel Summer"), as July and August will each bring their "days of doom and gloom" too. Man.

The birthdays aren't so bad, because at least you can still *celebrate* them. It's the others, what I have come to call the "D-Days," that are really tough.

I had been hoping that this next one [June 20th, the anniversary of Jackie's passing] could be "marked" by the completion of the memorial at Mount Pleasant, but that project has suffered setback after setback (nobody's fault, really, except perhaps mine for not bugging them enough), and it's not going to be finished on time. So that's depressing.

Wednesday I'm driving into Toronto (reluctantly) to take care of some medical, dental, business, and social obligations, and I had planned to spend Sunday, the dreaded 20th, at the memorial, and fly out that night to San Francisco. (A certain ugly irony there, I know, but it just worked out that way.) So now I don't know what I'll do that day, but it won't be nice.

Yesterday Deb and I were going through some of Selena's things, and putting up her collections of key rings and shot glasses (how many of those you and I picked up on our travels!) in the Selena Memorial Library. At first it was okay, and we were laughing at different things and talking about Selena, but then, as Deb opened more boxes and I saw more and more different "souvenirs" of her — stuffed animals and little things from her room — it started to get really bad. I went downstairs and sat at the kitchen counter weeping uncontrollably, and it went on for a long time.

I poured myself a large Macallan or two, and played all my saddest songs really loud (to try to kind of "wallow" in it) but I simply couldn't stop crying and sobbing for about two hours. Eventually I went and lay down and passed out for awhile, then woke up exhausted, but calmer. That happened before too, a couple of weeks ago in L.A., when I was alone one afternoon and it just swept over me, like a wave of abject sorrow. Well, no surprise if I should be afflicted like that from time to time, I don't imagine.

Sunday, June 13

The very next day after the very next day . . .

All my guests are gone now, it's a hot afternoon, and I'm presently wallowing in peace and nakedness. ("Don't you look at me!")

Since yesterday morning, I'm pleased to report that the world is moderately transformed around here, and by one simple plunge: I went swimming. Now the lake is part of my world too, in a more tangible way — a more *sensual* way — and what a difference it makes. I think it's fairly early in the season to be swimming, though I've seldom been here this time of year. Apparently it was pretty hot for a couple of weeks while I was gone, so maybe there's global warming in my lake. In any case, I like it.

It took a couple of "hangs off the ladder" to get up my nerve, but once I got in, it was fine. I swam way down the shore to what I still consider to be your little dock and back, for a preliminary "sea-test," after a year of (I realize now) almost no swimming, save for a couple of brief dips down there in Loreto, in the Sea of Cortez. But right away, getting into that long-distance, three-strokes-per-breath rhythm was really good for soothing my brain.

Better than rowing, somehow; more like the trance that comes from cross-country skiing. Don't know why, but so it seems to be. Research into trance-states will continue.

Last night I was telling Steven and Shelly how you had been "The Discoverer of This Land," and as such you'll remember how good this water tastes on your lips, and how good it feels on your skin. As I stroked along, steering by the shoreline, I couldn't help thinking of another summer "Once Upon a Time" (one of my current fave sad Sinatra songs), and I remembered all those swims along that shore to the rock in front of your dock, calling out "Kee-ah-kee!," and consulting on crossword clues and such before the swim back.

But enough about that. I've had enough abject sorrow for one weekend, thank you.

Today, on another immaculate morning, I went out early for a long row around the whole six-island loop, a route I call "all around the circle." After Steven and Shelly drove off to the airport, and Deb (things are better between her and me, but not quite the same) and little Rudy for home, I dozed in my chair for a while in unalloyed silence, then went down to the dock, dumped my clothes, and swam the other way up the shore past Louie's and Chalmers's, all the way to Duddy's rock. Then back in a perfect, unconscious trance.

Since I started this letter, the combination of a little sun, a little water, and a little exercise has accomplished wonders. (A little peace and quiet doesn't hurt either.) I feel better. Why, I bet I *look* better too. If that's at all possible, for a Hollywood babe-magnet like me.

Or at least, like Ellwood is. See, in my ever-splintering personality (way past schizophrenia now, through triphenia, and quadrophenia, and well into polyphenia), there are now a few different guys who are sort of . . . collaborating . . . on being the boss of my life. As the most righteous dude of us all, Ellwood has arisen to be the Hollywood facet of our personalities, the Romantic Superhero.

He's not like that old guy we used to be, that drummer-goof, the one with the weird name nobody could pronounce. For sure, Ellwood is not like whatever shreds of that old guy might remain in us now. And Ellwood is not at all the same as John Ellwood Taylor ("all blues, all the time"), or Chef Ellwood, nor even like the fabled Ghost Rider. And he's certainly nothing like little Gaia, the adolescent girl who's all weepy and sentimental over pop songs.

Although, it has to be said, when Ellwood attains his most exalted state, it's not too hyperbolic to say that Ellwood Embodies All.

In a Walt Whitman sort of way, "I am large, I contain multitudes" and all that.

In a more practical vein, I just hope my Sybilline filofax can accommodate the increasing activities of my "cast of thousands." It was fine when we were just pieces of that other guy, along with John Ellwood Taylor, Chef Ellwood, and the Ghost Rider. But even adding the romantic superhero, Ellwood, to the plot has been a bit of a strain.

I mean, *really*, dear boy! First we had to interrupt the Ghost Rider's travels while Ellwood made us all ride back down to Los Angeles, just so he could tart himself up like some popinjay and pitch his agéd woo at some fair young damsel. And now, the road-weary Ghost Rider is barely back in the garage and trying to relax his way into summer (hangin' with John Ellwood in the hammock), when our Romantic Superhero decides he wants to turn around and fly us all out to San Francisco to dress up and play El Romancero again.

You see the problem.

Well, if there's one thing I've learned in this topsy-turvy world of ours, it's that it's pointless to try to steer this crazy roller-coaster ride called Life, so you might as well just hold on.

So saith the prophet, the Reverend L. Wood Hubbard.

And speaking of inspirational writings, I'll enclose a couple of prophetic quotations from Joseph Conrad's *Victory,* which I happened to be reading throughout my *crise de coeur* a few weeks back, through Alturas, Grand Coulee Dam, Snoqualmie Falls, Vancouver, and back down to L.A. I think you'll see the relevance. It was another one of those West Coast synchronistic experiences. Man.

I hope you're doing okay there. Be a darling boy and give us a call soon, will you? (We'd *all* love to hear from you!) When we get back from the coast — say the 25th or 26th. There's a good chap.

And say, when Reverend L. Wood finishes his book of stern-but-sensitive inspirational thoughts, we'll send you a copy. You and your mates could be his first "flock."

Now, let us pray for redemption, brother.

Blah, blah, blah . . .
From "all of us"
To all of you . . .

So . . . the romantic superhero among us, Ellwood, hitched a ride to Toronto again, took care of some business, had dinner with Alex and his wife Charlene, and with Geddy and his wife Nancy (no doubt thrilling them all with tales of his romantic exploits), visited the cemetery plot for a tearful few hours, then flew off to San Francisco to meet Gabrielle.

Once again Ellwood did his utmost to impress, booking a luxurious hotel suite on Nob Hill overlooking the beautiful city and out to San Francisco Bay, taking her on driving tours around the town, a boat trip to Alcatraz, a performance of the musical *Rent,* and a night of Stravinsky at the symphony, but it didn't seem to be working. Perhaps he was coming on too strong, an inevitable conflict between his serious intentions and a young woman who now seemed to personify the song, "Girls Just Wanna Have Fun." Or maybe it was his constant sighing and occasional tears. (Or was it time to consider the *reverse* of our "principle of serendipitous

confluence" — maybe she was just the wrong person at the wrong time.)
In any case, she had turned unaccountably "cool" toward him, and after
four days he flew back to Montreal, crestfallen and confused.

Now what do we do? If life were a Sinatra song, when you have
"woman trouble" you simply get good and *drunk*. So I used that "temporary escape hatch" one more time, and went on a binge for a couple of
days. (In Selena's teenage years, I once tried to instruct her about such
things with this motto, "Everything in moderation, with occasional
excess." She replied, "Alright Dad — I can live with that," and I said,
"Daughter, I have!")

I emerged with a crippling hangover, and as sometimes seems to
happen, a fresh outlook of *clarity*.

It was obviously time for radical action, desperate measures, and I had
one last refuge to explore — drumming. In the past, I had always found
playing the drums perhaps the ultimate escape, an engrossing, inspiring
trance-state that always made me forget everything else in the world, and
I decided it was time to try that.

Not wanting to put any pressure on myself, or give any false hopes to
my professional "associates," I secretly booked a room at a studio nearby
(where I had so often worked with Rush over the years, going back to 1979,
my first introduction to the area that would be so important to my life),
making the arrangements through Sheila at the office (who could always
be trusted with a secret), and Nathalie, the studio manager, who listed me
in her records as "The John Taylor Project."

Keith was away visiting his family in Toronto, so my friend Trevor
helped me transport my yellow Gretsch drums, which had been stacked in
the furnace room beside the neglected little practice kit, over to the studio.
I started going there every day for a couple of hours, just playing aimlessly
through various patterns and seeing where they took me. I hadn't played
at all for almost exactly two years, since the last show of the *Test For Echo*
tour, but after playing the instrument for more than 30 years, the physical
technique came back readily.

What surprised me was what happened *musically*. I soon realized that out of the random patterns and tempos I was playing, a larger "theme" was appearing — I was "telling my story." Not in musical or lyrical terms, but just thinking while I played a certain passage, "this is *that* part."

I once defined the basic nature of art as "the telling of stories," and never had I felt that to be more true. I played the anger, the frustration, the sorrow, and even the travelling parts of my story, the rhythms of the highway, the majesty of the scenery, the dynamic rising and falling of my moods, and the narrative suite that emerged was as cleansing and energizing as the sweat and exertion of telling it.

I also continued telling my story in the more usual, verbal form, in the inevitable letters to Brutus.

le corbeau dans la pluie
(or "Ravin' in the Rain")

July 6, '99
Lac St. Brutus, Que.

Hey Schmützfink!

A dark and gloomy morning today, with a couple of heavy showers. And wouldn't you know it? That's just how I feel — dark, and gloomy, and heavy.

So I'll take it out on you! (What are pals for?)

There's a gray fog sprawled across the lake, and a gray fog sprawled across my little baby soul. Today's ritual wolf-howls spiral off in a descending lament. These are confusing times, oh my brother, and yea, my brain is sorely vexed. The Mysteries of Life, the Mysteries of Woman, and especially, the Mysteries of Grief. Lately I realize that I'm still far from over all that. Not that I should be, but sometimes I fool myself for awhile.

Back in England, when I was reading all those "grief books," I found some of the information in them unacceptable and unbelievable at the time, because I wasn't *there* yet. Then later I would go through that phase, and find that the cumulative human experience represented by these books was, not surprisingly, pretty true. One such unacceptable piece of information was the notion that "the second year is worse," which, all through the first year, I couldn't imagine could *possibly* be true. Now I'm beginning to get it.

It's hard to describe, and maybe too early, for I've only started to think about that idea this week (as the second second-year begins, if you know what I mean), but it seems as though at this point the abject sorrow starts to modify into a less-dynamic, less emotional state, into a feeling of emptiness, a day-to-day malaise of directionless stasis. I'm finding this is somehow more difficult to face. Or to figure out what to do about.

It's as difficult as ever to get motivated to do anything, to care about anything, to go on facing up to the everyday frustrations and worries — and it's harder not to *drink*. Lately it's almost a fight to hold out until cocktail time, and also to keep to the "basic dietary minimum" of a couple of whiskies and a glass of wine at dinner.

Because I'm not too fired-up about life right now, it seems like I'd sooner be numb. If I'm not *into* it, I want to get *out* of it.

And fair enough, for awhile, if it helps me get through a particularly difficult time, as it did in the early part of last year, and then stops. But I do not want to find myself degenerating into the so-called life of a pathetic and decaying boozer. Insofar as one can "choose" what kind of a life to have (and we don't rate that element of "free will" too highly, do we?), there are certain futures I do not wish to contemplate. One of those is certainly the thought of being any version of an alcoholic. Especially, horror of horrors, a *recovering* one.

So I'm keeping a stern and watchful eye on the situation, and

I really don't think I'll let it get out of hand. Still, I hate even having to worry about that, you know? (No, actually; you don't! You *wish* you could worry about being a boozer!)

Anyway, let's talk about the weather, shall we?

Night before last I was awakened at 2:00 a.m. by thunder, wind, and rain, and then stayed up to watch a most amazing electrical storm. The lightning flashes came so rapidly and constantly it lighted my way all around the house as I ran up and down stairs closing windows. Then I just lay on the bed and watched the show over the lake, a steady artillery barrage of retina-searing bolts and rapid, distant flashes and even small, spidery "bursts" in the sky, sometimes several exploding simultaneously — reminding me of looking down from the plane over Montreal last week and seeing the St. Jean-Baptiste Day fireworks above La Ronde.

Imagery-wise, I was thinking of World War One artillery, battles at sea, flashbulbs popping at a Beatles concert, fireworks, that sort of thing, but Nathalie at the studio nailed it best (insert French-Canadian accent), "It was like a . . . *disco!*"

According to last night's CBC News, the storm caused a lot of wind and lightning damage in the area, and parts of the Laurentians are still without power, though mine only flickered a couple of times. I did see a lot of trees and branches down yesterday morning, as I rode the scenic route down to Laval and back.

In regard to other types of "weather," I mentioned to you that things seemed kind of "cool" in San Francisco, and I came home a little . . . disappointed. Okay, a lot. I have still been calling her every few days, but I sense a certain *restraint*. You never know what's up with wimmen, eh?

Also in the weather today, there are my concerns about future "security." According to the cheques Sheila just sent me to sign, with a note saying, "I may need them now that you are a jet-setter," I'm presently living at about six times my income. (Or Ellwood is, anyway, and I can't control that guy!) It seems that dealing with all this bad luck and tragedy has not only been unpleasant but also *expensive* (after those long stays in London and Barbados, plus abandoning my investments to an increasingly "creative" broker), and the old "nest-egg" has taken a heavy beating in the past few years. Ach. I didn't expect to have to worry about *that* yet. You understand, I've still got a few *huitlacoches* in my tank-bag, and there's always the principal to spend (and the principle "to spend"). So as long as I don't live too long, I should be okay . . .

Or — I go back to work. However, it's clear to me this notion still scares my little baby soul witless. True, my drumming explorations over at Le Studio are going well, and have confirmed that not only am I still capable of playing technically, but that I can still *communicate* through the instrument.

This "narrative" approach has taken me some interesting places musically too, and just doing that everyday — having somewhere to go and something to do — has been good for me right now. An outing and a good sweat alone are "worth the trouble," even if just for now, but I still don't feel ready to dive into a big "project" with the other guys. I guess the difference is that I may be ready to *play,* but I'm not ready to *work.* So I'll let it rest again for awhile.

I had always thought that if any of my former enthusiasms were going to return, then prose-writing would naturally be the first — a solitary and peaceful activity that I could ease myself into gently. And I certainly have some stories to tell. However, I still feel very far away from having the strength and discipline for a big writing project, though at least I know I can play the drums if I want to. Or need to.

"To pick up a little gas money along the way," to quote Ray. You'll remember that he was talking about *touring,* but forget about that. I sure couldn't conceive of thrusting myself into *that* circus right now. I wouldn't have the strength or the tolerance. (Or the navigator.)

But, for now, I'm still working at the drum-thing in secrecy, unsure of what I really want to do with it. If anything. And if anything, *when?*

It's another big consideration for me to contemplate making such a huge commitment of time right now — to agree to go somewhere and work all the way through this fall, or this winter, or next spring. What would the Ghost Rider say about that? Or John Ellwood?

Those two are already feeling a bit restless, and lobbying for a journey; reminding us only yesterday, as we rode the GS through the farming country outside Lachute, how nice it was to be riding, and how much nicer it would be if we were packed up and blasting the whole day through down the road to Havre St. Pierre, or Twin Falls, Idaho, or Moab, Utah. Those guys also assure the rest of us that travelling would be much better for our mental-state(s) right now, and help control the drinking and smoking too.

So what am I supposed to tell *those* guys? And you can imagine what Ellwood's response would be to the idea of hiding away in some Toronto studio for four or five months. Not his style at all. And Gaia's a 14-year-old girl — what's *she* care?

So we're in a quandary, a couple of conundrums, a few enigmas (with friends like you who needs enigmas?), an ambiguity, several dilemmas, and a very large confusion.

Ain't life grand?

Not tonight, darling — I've got a heartache.

After the unbelievably accurate tarot reading I had in Venice Beach last May, I have learned to do simple readings for myself (through one of those "Idiot's Guide" books). Last night I did a "three-card spread," and laid out The Fool, the Six of Cups reversed, and the Nine of Wands reversed. Briefly, here is my interpretation of the first two cards:

"You are trying to set out on a new adventure, to explore new paths and commit yourself to the future in a brave and carefree manner, but you're not ready. Your emotions are still caught up in the past, with feelings of nostalgia, and you have to cut yourself free of that before you can move on."

And here's the last card, right from the book:

The Nine of Wands reversed still has the desire to protect and be of help to others, but this man can barely take care of himself. Most of the time, the reversed Nine of Wands indicates the lack of stamina and physical strength to see things through. You've been beaten down either mentally or physically, and your health isn't good enough to follow through on the difficult tasks ahead.

You need to rest and recuperate, rather than go out and fight the battles again. You're not prepared, and need to check on things before you make your next move. You could be vulnerable, too weak to fight, or just plain exhausted. Sometimes this card comes up when you feel let down by others or are worried about something. The Nine of Wands reversed suggests it's best to regroup and calm yourself before taking another step.

I'll let that reading speak for itself, regarding not only my romantic misadventures, but also my experiments with drumming. Like, take it slo-o-o-o-ow, baby. Yeah, sure.

Anyway, that's about enough out of my fingers for one day, and I do hope this hasn't been too "dark" of a letter. Don't you go worryin' about me, now. I've got enough to do, what with worryin' about you *and* worryin' about me, and I don't need to be worryin' about you worryin' about me too. Ya got that?

I hope so.

Better days ahead, right?

Right . . .

le petit nuage noir

July 22, '99
Lac St. Brutus, Que.

Hey Booger-Breath,

Trying a new approach here: sitting at the kitchen counter with my Powerbook on this perfect summer morning. I felt like "venting" at you a little bit, but this morning is too glorious a specimen to consider shutting myself away up in the office, so I thought I'd try this. A nicer scene. The hummingbirds make repeated visits to the window feeder, a few bright goldfinches flit around Chef Ellwood's Birdbrain Café, the sprinklers are spitting, the insects buzzing, and the dishwasher churns quietly.

Like you, I'm sure, I've been up since 6:30. After squeezing the juice, I pulled open the garbage thingy under the counter and looked down into a pair of dark beady eyes: a lively, if rather bedraggled, little mouse. I couldn't think what else to do with it, so I carried the bin outside and turned it on its side, and let the little bugger scamper away.

Checking the composter beside the garage, I was satisfied to see the raccoons hadn't been able to get past the cinder block I'd put on top of it yesterday — after the pesky varmints had managed to shift the two big rocks we had there, each the size of a loaf of bread. I also noted with satisfaction that those masked bandits had once again been knocking away at Chef Ellwood's Birdbrain Café, but without success. (They seem to be *mad* for sunflower seeds, and had easily overcome my previous squirrel-proof defences by climbing up and knocking against the sunflower-seed feeder until all the seeds spilled out, but I think we've beaten them now.)

Then I wandered down to the dock and went for a row, out

across the still lake. On the shores of Sammy Cay, I finally managed to spot the loon's nest which [neighbor] Charles had been telling me about the other night. He has been keeping an eye on the loons all summer, and he told me where to look for the nest with two eggs in it, but warned me not to go too near it if there were crows around, for I might scare the parent off the nest (they take turns) and give those nasty scavengers a chance to attack the eggs.

Probably true, and yesterday I rowed by to have a look, but stayed away when I saw a pair of crows lurking about up in the pines like Heckle and Jekyll. This morning I brought along my binoculars and drifted quietly along the shore of L'Île Selena, scanning across among the rocks and trees at the waterline of Sammy Cay. It took some looking, but finally I spotted the black-and-white checks of the nesting bird (they look so big out of the water), and then picked out its baleful red eye — so demonic and primeval looking.

After a fine breakfast of scrambled eggs and toast (with a new supply of partridgeberry and apple jam that Deb brought me from the Newf store in Brampton), I found myself at "loose ends" again (like, "okay — now what?"), and decided to try this new activity, letter-writing-in-a-different-scene. It makes a change, and maybe I'll feel better. In L.A. speak, my recent mood might be expressed thus, "I'm *so-o-o* not happy."

This week has been a little better than last week (considered in "degrees of misery"), but lately I'm finding that getting through the days in a halfway healthy fashion just takes so much fucking *effort*. Trying to pull myself together, I've been out rowing every day, and the past two days I've kicked my ass out the door for a mountain-bike ride around the loop of Lac St. Ellwood, which makes a good, hilly, 10K training ride — though training for *what* I don't know. Maybe if I decide to take it further. (Or *force* myself to.)

It's all about *will*, isn't it?

This must be true for you as well, to some degree. You certainly couldn't "weather" your present circumstances without a fairly constant exercise of the will to do so. And you know, it does become wearying.

But again, the "choices" are limited, so all we can do is try to get through the days and nights. Tiring myself out with some exercise like that during the day also seems to allow me to relax in the hammock and read for awhile in the afternoon, with a clear conscience and tired body, and even doze off — sometimes until well after cocktail time. So I'm keeping things under control, anyway. But again, it just takes so much effort.

[Later]

It's a spooky sort of night. The moon's a little past half-full, standing high and bright among the passing clouds (that ever-popular "ghostly galleon" effect), while distant lightning flashes behind heavy clouds to the north and east.

July 23, '99

Morning again. Hotter today, as I noticed when I rode the GS into St. Sauveur, then made a stop at Vaillancourt's to fill the hard cases with oranges and coffee and bread. I wore my regular leathers, but could have used the Vansons; probably wear them on my trip to Toronto, as the forecast seems to be on the rise.

Talking to "that woman" last night I learned that she will be in Ontario for most of August, as she has the lead role in an indy film being shot there. Hopefully we'll have an opportunity to get together then and . . . see how it goes. She seems to be up for it. As far as a mere man can tell, anyway.

Last week, I was writing to Dan Hudson [my artist friend, visited in Alberta early in the journey], who had recently split with his long-time partner, Laurie, and offered this observation: "'Man Bewildered by Woman' is hardly headline news."

Otherwise, life around here is dull, and often rather annoying. I'm in a foul temper much of the time, sometimes hating the slow passage of time, and equally resenting the sense of life moving on without me — though of course there's nothing I need more than for time to pass (you know about those things too, no?). But it's the old cycle: when you're down, other small nuisances just bring you lower. Seeing things around here that I could do, or should do, and not doing them, twitching around restlessly between forced "scheduled activities," cursing and growling to myself a lot. Not much company for my guests either. They'll understand, of course, and can entertain themselves, but I wish I could shake myself out of it. I'm tired of being *so-o-o-o* not happy.

I've been making some tentative travel plans toward the end of next month (or at least imagining some tentative travel plans that I might make). I could take the *Nordik Express* [boat] down to Labrador, like we did, then circle around Newf for as long as seems good, then cross to Nova Scotia and hang with Lesley Choyce and the Williamses for awhile. Then there's that ferry across to Maine, which would set me up for a stay in NYC, and that might be nice for a week or so in September. However, it would be hard to pass on a ride around the Gaspé instead, then maybe cut down through the Adirondacks to NYC. Then, I suppose, "Go west, old man." I dunno.

July 24, '99

A rainy Saturday morning, and I feel unaccountably better. Despite the effort it cost me to get through this week, it is done, and I managed to accomplish my goals — getting out for two "activities" every day (back to the long-swim-up-the-shoreline the last couple of days, plus either a bike ride or a row), and I managed not to drink and smoke too much. That will do for one week's ambitions, humble though they be.

Next week combines the Toronto taking-care-of-business trip at the beginning of the week with the Reunion of the Front Lounge Club [Alex, Liam, and Andrew, named for the "smoking section" on the tour bus] at the end, and there's not likely to be much "clean living" then. However, there will certainly be some laughter, and that couldn't hurt. (According to *Reader's Digest*, it's the best medicine, eh?)

Then I've got a few days "turnaround" before Brad and Rita arrive for the second week of August. I haven't booked any other guests after that, and don't think I will. Having guests is a mixed experience. Diverting, but demanding. Companionable, but messy. Less solitary, but . . . well, less solitary.

If "that woman" is going to be in Canada in August, I guess I want to be available, and considering that last year I set out travelling on August 20th, that's probably a good target date for this year too.

It just occurred to me that the only two notions which get me even a little bit excited right now are wooing and scootering. But still, that's two things!

And once again, this letter has taken us all over the emotional map. Since we're on a relative "high note" on this rainy Saturday morning, it might be a good time to wrap this up. That way I can get it mailed before I ride off to the big city, and before all the other madness begins.

Meanwhile, let us reflect on the following Maasai proverb:

Meetai dikir nemesheyui.

There is no hill that never ends.

Or perhaps this one, from the Swahili, might be more profitably contemplated:

Ukenda chooni na giza basi shetani atakupiga kofi.

If you go to the lavatory in the dark, the devil will give you a box on the ears.

Just think about that, boyo . . .
NEP

[Letter to my colleague, Geddy, on his birthday, which was also the anniversary of my joining Rush, in 1974. In years past we in the band had always tried to work "schoolteacher's years," recording and touring through the autumn, winter, and spring, then being home all summer.

While always remaining the best of friends "at work," we tended not to see each other too much in the off-time, so that my annual midsummer birthday message to Geddy was often a personal update and "catchup letter" as well. So it was that year . . .]

July 29, '99
Lac St. Brutus, Que.

Can it really be?

Apparently so.

Yes, according to my calendar, it's time once again for the Annual All Singing, All Dancing, Birthday Greeting and Summer Update, coming to you live from the balmy shores of Lac St. Brutus.

I just got back here myself late last night, after a quick one-day stay in Toronto to see to some medical matters, and two all-day Brutus-style backroads motorcycle tours there and back.

Yesterday morning I was setting off early from the Four Seasons to my folks' place in Severn Bridge for breakfast, but when I brought my bike up from the parking lot, I found the rear tire was flat. Nothing else to do — I got out my repair kit, located a big nail sticking out of the tire, removed it, and plugged the hole, as I've had to do several times before, in various exotic locations.

And here's where a real hotel shows its mettle: instead of "boging out" about having me there lowering the tone of their front entrance — leather-clad Scooter Trash sitting on the ground behind his dirty old motorcycle with tools spread around — the bellman ran off to get the hotel's electric compressor to help me fill the tire, and the doorman brought me a bottle of Evian and a towel — because of course it was sweltering hot in the city yesterday, even at 7:00 a.m.

So that was pretty nice, for a bummer situation.

Plugged and refilled, I set out northward, but when I arrived at my folks' place, I found the tire was still going flat. Not knowing what else to do, I put in a larger plug, and set out for Huntsville. I had planned on taking the Algonquin Park route across Ontario and home, as every time I've had to ride to Toronto this summer I've taken a different route, and that was the one remaining. Plus it was a beautiful day for it.

When I got to Huntsville the tire was still going flat pretty rapidly, so before I headed off into the hinterland of Ontario (next stop, um, Barry's Bay), I stopped at Thompson Tire on Highway 11, which had been recommended to me at the last gas station. Right away I could see they dealt more in truck and tractor tires, and when I asked the guy ("Bob," of course), he told me he didn't know anything about motorcycle tires. But instead of sending me on my way, he agreed that if I would take the wheel off, he would have a go at it. But he soon determined that the nail had dug right through the sidewall of the tire as well, and it was unrepairable.

For a few hours already I had been a little tense, riding around with a tire I knew was losing air, but now I got *really* concerned, for I was pretty sure my tire was an unusual size. Sure enough, as Bob called around to all the cycle shops and suppliers, as far away as Barrie, he came up empty.

Meanwhile, I was trying to decide whether I should truck the bike to Toronto, or have them send a new tire up by bus, and trying to contemplate the reality of being stuck there for another day, and probably staying the night at my parents' place. I've been pretty restless lately, and didn't think I was up for that.

Then the receptionist suggested a place her bike-riding brother bought used parts and such. Incredibly, the proprietor ("Johnne Smith"), came through — apparently he'd once ordered a tire and misplaced a digit, and had ended up with this "oddball" — the size I needed. Bob told me to take his car and go have a look at it, and if it suited me, he'd install it for me.

As he handed me the keys, he pointed out the window to a dusty black Bonneville, and said, "Just be warned that it's a mess inside, 'cause I don't clean it — and don't roll down the driver's-side window or it will fall off the track."

So off I went. It seemed like Johnne Smith was as glad to get rid of that tire as I was to have it — it was a cheap Pacific Rim brand, but it would certainly get me home again. And it did. Although it was after 4:00 before I had everything back together, and I had a long journey ahead of me yet, it was still a beautiful day, and a beautiful ride, with lakes and cottages and pines and hills and farms.

Through the Ottawa Valley I enjoyed the world's longest sunset, sinking so slowly down a clear sky and silhouetting the moving shadow of me and my bike on the roadside embankment. Twilight didn't dwindle into darkness until I was over the river into Quebec, and back on familiar roads, so I didn't have to ride in the dark for more than a half hour.

When the bike was parked in my garage, I was enjoying my well-earned glass of Macallan at the kitchen counter, and started to smile about it, thinking, "You know, that was a real adventure today."

And so it had been — both the good and the bad. For of course it could have been much worse, in many ways, and those ways had been avoided in large part by the "kindness of strangers." At the end of the day I was left feeling a little better about the world, and about life — for I also had to smile at a thought that sometimes crosses my mind at the end of a long, perilous day. "I have cheated death again."

(Though always knowing that I'll never even *that* score . . .)

Today I drove my Audi to the post office and for groceries at Vaillancourt's, and that was adventure enough.

In general, lately I've been pretty up-and-down. The "yo-yo" comparison occurred to me yesterday, for while I'm going up and down, I'm not really going anywhere. And sometimes I do feel like I'm holding on by my fingertips, to something. Life, I suppose.

Back in London, when I was reading all those grief books, I was struck by one quote: "the second year is worse." Ach. At the time that seemed impossible to imagine, and I simply rejected it. But now here I am, in the middle of two second years, as it were (sentences served concurrently . . .), and it is tough. It seems like the abject sorrow and emotional outpouring starts to dissipate a little, but it leaves behind such an emptiness.

Here's what I wrote to [a former employee who had long battled heroin addiction, and after six "clean" years, had suffered a relapse during the *Test For Echo* tour] last week, when I was trying to tell him that he needn't feel guilt and shame about what he went through on the last tour, writing that my responses to his plight had been, first, "poor fuckin' guy," and second, "that could be me."

If the first is the year of sorrow, then the second is the year of emptiness. Somehow it's even harder to deal with, to work around, and to kick your ass out of, and no doubt I'm already pretty worn out from trying to keep myself 'together' this long. As you know too well, any kind of day-to-day existence that demands too much will — either to do something or not to do something — can wear you down, and 'get' you when you're weak.

Though I'm certainly still fighting. A month or so ago, I came back from San Francisco confused and bewildered by the Great Mystery of Woman, but I responded to that bewilderment in a healthy fashion, by going and beating up my drums.

[Recap of drumming experience.]

Along the way other questions were answered too. I realized that while I might be ready to *play* again, I was not ready to *work* again. Not yet, anyway. So I put the drums away for awhile, but knowing that the power was still there, and that I could do it if I chose.

That was good to know, but somehow it was clear to me that I was not ready for commitment, for collaboration, for taking on a serious "project." This is the same boundary I've reached with prose-writing — nearly every day I sit down and write to somebody, often my erstwhile riding partner at his House of Incarceration, or to someone I've fallen out of touch with but feel I still want in my life. I've written hundreds of pages like that over the past months, and they often function like a diary and confessional for me. (Last week I had a phone message from Mark Riebling, commenting that the letter he'd just received was "awfully close to literature, my friend.") Yet the same limits apply — I'm ready to "play" with words, but not to "work" with them.

Fair enough, of course. Progress is being made, but it ain't going to be fast, and it ain't going to be easy. Time, time, time . . .

On this occasion, which also marks our 25ᵗʰ anniversary, I just wanted to let you know "where I'm at" in those departments.

The rest of this summer is still a bit vague for me. For awhile now I've been itchy to go "Ghost Riding" again, for that has definitely proven to be the best therapy, but I'm trying to hold off leaving until later in August, like I did last year. Avoid the crowds, and the heat, of summer. I'm thinking of going eastward at first, to virtually repeat my first-ever motorcycle tour, with Brutus, which took us to the "end of the road" on the north shore of the St. Lawrence, by boat to Labrador, then around Newfoundland

and Nova Scotia. I've got a couple of friends in the Halifax area, so I'd probably hang around there for a few days or a week.

There's a ferry from Nova Scotia to Maine that would make a nice boat trip, and set me up to spend some time in NYC, which would be pleasant in September.

Then, I suppose, I'd carry on west, and see any parts of Canada and the U.S. I missed last time, and revisit a few fave spots — the national parks, the great small towns like Moab, Utah, St. Helena, California, and maybe back to Baja and the rest of Mexico. We'll see.

And that's basically my story. (Art may be "the telling of stories," but of course that doesn't mean that the telling of stories is necessarily *art!*) I'm hanging in there, despite all, and my basic philosophy of life these days resides in a phrase I learned from our old Berlitz School buddy [Geddy, Alex, and I had taken French lessons before our shows during a couple of tours, from teachers sent out in the various cities by Berlitz], Jean Gallia, "*Ça vaut la peine*" — "It's worth the trouble."

Interesting that *peine* also translates as "sorrow," and some days I can almost get my mind around the notion that it was worth the sorrow of losing Selena and Jackie for the joy of having known them.

Almost . . .

My other favorite motto lately comes from the Swahili:

"Hyena says, 'I am not lucky, but I am always on the move.'"

Hyena, *c'est moi*.

I hope things are good with you and yours, and that you'll have a fine day today. (And other days too.) Drop me a line if you feel like it, and chances are I'll have to make another trip to Tarawnna one of these days, and we'll get together then.

My best to you, my friend, and I look forward to seeing you/ talking to you soon.

P.

[Letter to brother-in-law Steven]

Aug. 5–6, '99
Lac St. Brutus, Que.

Hey there, brother,

Long time no hear, eh?

No, I mean you, not me. Well, okay, it's been awhile since you've heard from me too, but that's not what I'm talking about right now. I'm talking about *you,* boy!

Okay, that's enough about you. What about me?

Well, starting with the weather (logically enough), it's a spectacular sort of evening here, with great reefs of gray cloud off to the east, bright blue sky above, and a purple sunset to the west. Three loons are silhouetted on the lake, which reflects pastel light from the luminous sky. Madonna's *Ray of Light* plays from the library, and I sit up here tapping out a message to you.

I know that you've been exposing yourself to the toxic atmosphere of the Niagara Peninsula of late, and I'm sure that's part of the reason for your recent silence. I can only plead the same kind of "distractions." For instance, last weekend I hosted a reunion of the "Front Lounge Club," starring Alex, Liam, and Andrew (veteran of two tours as "personal assistant," as well as being our long-time photographer). As you might imagine, we ate a lot of great food, laughed a lot, and overindulged ourselves in most other ways as well.

I just walked out on the balcony for another look, and now the eastern sky is all pink and gray, the calm water is a steely mauve, and a low mist is creeping out across the lake from down by the "Porcupine Highway" [a snowshoe trail Steven and I had pioneered, following the unmistakable depression in the snow left by a porcupine]. Not bad.

Anyway, now I've got a few days on my own before Brad and Rita arrive, on Sunday. They're staying until Friday, and are my last "guaranteed reservations" for the summer. "Closed for the Season," or something like that. No firm plans after, but various . . . possibilities.

After my musical experiments last month, it is clear to me that I'm not strong enough (yet?) to think of taking on a project with the other guys, nor am I ready to commit to the chunk of time such an enterprise would demand of me. Internally, we all agree on that: John Ellwood wants to remain a melancholy loner; the Ghost Rider still hears the call of faraway roads; and as for Ellwood . . . well, Ellwood wants to get a house in the Hollywood Hills and be an international playboy. At least until he blows all our money . . . The Ghost Rider is definitely agitating for another journey, the sooner the better, and good old J.E.T. will also be glad to get back to being the solitary, melancholy stranger drifting from town to town. (Gaia doesn't mind; she can pout and sing along with "boy bands" anywhere.)

Just today I faxed Terry Williams in Halifax to let him know I was thinking of heading that way "sometime in late August or early September." Talking to him later on the phone, he didn't seem to think that was *specific* enough, but he doesn't understand the way we work these days.

If I go around Newfoundland before I hit Nova Scotia, there's a ferry from there to Maine, which would set me up for an easy run down to New York City, where I'd also like to spend a week in September — get me a culture injection. I've also recently sent messages to friends in that area, who also urged me to let them know exactly *when*. Geez, I don't know . . . *sometime!*

One way or another, I'd be heading west again while the weather's still good, and probably more-or-less follow my pattern of last fall, drifting south and maybe catching some parts of the American West I missed last time.

Otherwise, lately I feel kind of like a yo-yo: bouncing up and down a little bit, but not really going anywhere. And hanging on by my fingertips . . .

Strange to think that as I look back on last winter, it seems like that was a season of relative peace and balance! It didn't feel like that *then*, of course, but so it appears now. It's been a hard summer — trying to function in the middle of a big empty *ache* — and it ain't over yet. But in more than one sense, we're "over the hump," and although this summer wasn't what I hoped it might be (I had some fantasy in one of my brains I'd be getting into a fabulous routine of exercise and creative work), at least I can see the end is in sight. The end, I suppose, being "the road."

Well, that's still what works the best, so I'll go with it. I'm glad to have that alternative, at least, for these days nothing else is appealing enough, or compelling enough, to keep me going. I just scrape through the days, it seems, writing a few letters, doing a few chores and errands, making myself a decent dinner, and not drinking too much. (Except during Front Lounge Club Reunions.)

At the same time, I score some "little victories." Today I mailed off a nice letter to my niece, Hannah, in response to one from her, and sent a copy of my instructional video to my 16-year-old pal, Nick, out in Palm Springs, an aspiring drummer and Buddy Rich's grandson. In these small ways I allow myself to feel I've made some mark on the day, and on the world.

Little baby challenges I set for myself: maybe drive into town, get some fresh flowers, fill the bird feeders, go for a row or a bike ride, clean up the kitchen, do some laundry, whatever; it is thus that I score some small, attainable victories.

A life measured out in tiny challenges and little victories. I guess that's not so bad, and probably a lot of good people get through their days like that. And perhaps they also wish those little victories could be a little more demanding, or even rewarding, but one does the best with what one has, no?

I do kind of wish I had the "whatever" (the interest, the drive, the ambition) to think about a more *adventurous* journey, like to southern Africa, Europe, or Australia, but it would take so much planning, and I'd be more-or-less locked into an itinerary in places like that, or at least having to plan pretty far ahead all the time. I wouldn't be able to simply ramble around from Best Western to Super 8 to Pelican Reef Beach Club [charmingly funky place we stayed in Belize]. For now, I think I'm more comfortable with that kind of mindless freedom.

Ah yes, mindless freedom. I guess that's my preferred state of mind these days, whether I'm "hermiting" here or "gypsying" across America. Perhaps that is "sufficient unto the day," but still, what I wouldn't give for some enthusiasm, some drive. But along with several other precious commodities, you can't buy that stuff.

Anyway, those are my cheery thoughts for today. Or rather, last night and this morning, for it's "tomorrow" now, another cool and cloudy one, with the lake so calm the loons leave silver ripples against the reflected forest.

Let me know how things are with youse, willya?

NEP

[Letter to Brutus]
le plus grand yo-yo du monde

Aug. 14, '99
Lac St. Brutus, Que.

Hey Fleischkopf,

Hard to believe three weeks have slipped by since my last crabby letter to you, but at least we had a good talk on the phone last week. And now that we've got all that laughter and good cheer out of the way again, why of course it's time for another crabby letter. Aren't you glad?

I know I am . . .

Lately we've had mostly cool and cloudy days at Camp Ellwood, and quite a lot of rain through the day yesterday, but I can't say I've noticed even the weather very much. Too hung up on the "interior weather," I suppose. Once again, I've just been getting through the days and nights, still feeling that yo-yo effect: up and down a little, going nowhere, hanging on by a fingertip. And saying a lot of bad words.

Yep, it's been another rough week at Camp Ellwood.

Especially, of course, that darkest of days, the 10th [second anniversary of Selena's passing]. I didn't know what to expect that day, but I knew it wouldn't be nice. I thought I was preparing for the worst by starting the morning with a Bloody Mary and a valium, and continuing on from there, but just like at the beginning of it all, two years ago, nothing really helped.

(Later that day, Brad would remark, "You know, sometimes booze and drugs just aren't enough." I had to protest, "Hey man, they're doing their best!")

Anyway, I'm sure glad Brad and Rita were here with me, for of course nobody could be stronger or more understanding.

A couple of weeks ago, Deb and I took Selena's bedframe (the gold-painted wrought-iron canopy job from Toronto) and set it up in the woods between here and Louie's place, above Deliverance Point. The whole elegant structure fit perfectly over Deb's tiled picnic table, which was already there, and altogether it looked very cool among the trees.

I hadn't been back there until this week, when I showed the spot to Brad and Rita, and when I saw how really perfect that whole scene was, I realized it might make a better setting for a little "memorial service" than the island.

Later that afternoon, I called Keith to leave his work in the garden to join us, and we took a bottle of champagne (with proper glasses), some smoked salmon, paté, and crackers, a vase of flowers Rita gathered from the garden, lit the three-wick candle, and sat there for awhile in that elegant little arbor among the trees, with glimpses of the lake between. A toast to the princess.

After a while, I walked down the path to the lake, and when I came back up over the rocky rise, I had to pause and take in the surreal tableau before me, the Fellini set of this gold canopy-bed framing the table, the glasses and food, the candle and flowers, and Brad, Rita, and Keith — all in the middle of the woods.

Later, back at the house, I was sitting at the kitchen counter (with a Macallan in front of me "doing its best") while Brad and Rita worked on dinner. Though I'm usually fairly useful in the kitchen these days, I had already announced, "I'm not doing nothing," and of course they understood. So there I was, just sitting there, drinking, with some CD playing, when suddenly I just started flooding. The memories flowed, the tears flowed, and it went on and on.

Everything made me cry — everything I looked at, heard, or thought. Every song I played, happy or sad, every pretty little bird at the feeder, the trees, the flowers, the lake, every memory. Everything was dark, because Selena was not there. As usual, in the middle of this torrent of emotions, I was trying to figure it out, and eventually got down to the one feeling that lay at the root of all these sorrows and memories, and once again, that little voice spoke in a clear sentence: I miss her so much.

Other people sometimes put that in words to me, telling me they miss Jackie or Selena, but I can't say it registers much (like, "*You* miss them?"). Even Deb and I never say such things out loud; because it seems so obvious, I guess. But of course, that just means it's obviously and totally *true*.

And equally, it's true all the time, and not just when I stop to cry about it. I guess after a while you learn to pretend to put it out of your mind. For a while. But the thought that it's been two whole years since that terrible time, and the thought of all the terrible times since, sure doesn't feel like any kind of an accomplishment. In fact, it kind of makes me sad . . .

However, I've got at least one good day to tell you about:

Thursday, day before yesterday, I finally put together a "work gang" and spent the whole day cutting firewood. That, at least, was good for my soul — in many ways. Last winter I spent so much time here (four months instead of the usual three or four weeks) that I burned pretty well every stick of wood around the place (and was starting to cast a covetous eye at the siding on the carport).

Last month I tried to get a work team organized, but both Ron and Pierre [local woodsmen] have been busy this season. So now I found myself with the summer wearing on, me still without a woodpile to call my own, and I couldn't bear it. I was feeling so inadequate as a northwoodsman, unprepared for winter like that. (In L.A. speak, "I'm like *so-o-o* not ready.") So, last week I simply announced to Keith that I couldn't stand it any longer, and this Thursday was going to be the day, even if we had to do it ourselves.

His mental picture of me chainsawing solo and dropping trees on his head must have inspired him to get more persuasive, for we ended up with Pierre leading the chainsaw brigade (me), and Keith and Brad doing the clearing and schlepping. We only went after dead trees that were close to the road (but not too close to the power lines), and felled and sectioned them on site, while Keith and Brad ferried them back in the pickup and dumped them by the carport to be split sometime later, even in the fall when I'm gone. (You'll understand, I had to be there for the cutting, as a matter of pride, but not the splitting. After all, the successful hunter need not skin the beast.)

By the end of the day, Pierre estimated we had about 15 cords of wood piled up beside the carport, much of it good maple, so I should be set for this winter, anyway. Since it was all dead stuff, I don't have to worry about seasoning either; it's ready to burn.

But man, I'll tell you, that lumberjackin' is hard work. Brad looked at me at the end of the day (as he drained another Budweiser) and said in his best Cockney, "You look all in, mate."

Yeah, man. We both felt pretty beat, though we agreed we didn't feel any specific aches, just an overall feeling of fatigue all over, from fingertips to toenails. After dinner, I fell dead asleep on the couch, and yesterday, after Brad and Rita left, I spent most of the day back in bed. Worn right out.

But the important thing is, a basic need of my soul has been satisfied: wood has been collected for the coming winter, and the weight of its lack troubles my conscience no more.

I can shout to the world from the highest peak, "I am *not* a total loser — I have *firewood!*"

Now if I could just put together one more day like that, and get a crew out in the woods to do some trail-clearing, I would have done at least *some* of the stuff I hoped to get done this summer. I was writing to Steven the other day about the way I imagined it last spring when I was thinking ahead to this summer, daring to imagine all the good things I was going to do: the exercise I was going to get, the creative work I was going to start on, and how great I was going to feel.

Well . . . I have firewood!

And besides, there are other troubles in the forest: why, not since the Great Squirrel Skirmish of April has there been such a flurry of clandestine activity around here. A new Cold War has begun, and once again I exist in a state of siege, fighting vainly to repel the nightly attacks and depredations on Chef Ellwood's Birdbrain Café. I refer, of course, to my latest quixotic campaign of counter-insurgency, this time against those who attack by night. The Masked Bandits.

At first it was just the Mom, but now the three little ones are big enough to get up that feeder too, and man, do they love sunflower seeds. And I'll tell you what: those fat buggers are a lot harder to outsmart than the squirrels. (I've settled into peaceful coexistence with those former foes, content to allow them to pick at the scattered "leavings" on the ground.)

But the raccoons — unbelievable! I've tried greasing the pole, gluing thumbtacks onto the anti-squirrel plate, then carpet tacks, then pouring Tabasco sauce over it (somebody's suggestion, don't remember who), using two anti-squirrel plates at various distances apart on the pole, and even hissing at the thieving bastards out my bedroom window when I hear them rattling around on the feeder at three in the morning. Nothing has kept them off!

Now . . . Brad just left me a cute little Remington .22 rifle that's been kicking around his basement, just for shooting at cans and stuff, but it can't help but give a fellow ideas. (Not *those* kind of ideas, you silly man — like Brad, you know me better than that — but thoughts about raccoon-snuffing.) You can bet that's Keith's preferred solution; he *hates* those guys, and the groundhog that eats the flowers and tears up the lawn. But, regardless of morality and my delicate sensibility, I don't think I'd be satisfied beating them that way.

I am determined to be smarter than a rodent. (After all, I have firewood!)

During last night's surveillance I hatched a new plan: why not wrap the pole in strands of barbed wire? I think it would work, and it's starting to seem like the best idea yet — though who'd have thought they'd get past axle grease, or thumbtacks?

Bastards.

If the barbed wire doesn't work, it's gonna be Mace land-mines . . .

Anyway, in sum, I guess what I'm going through right now is a repeat of last April. I know that it's getting to be time to hit the road again, because I feel so low and only that seems to work. But *because* I feel so low, I can't get motivated to start making any arrangements. (Maybe I'll find something to inspire me, like happened last time with the flag babes on the road by Lac Cochon.)

Why, even now I should be getting myself organized to ride to Toronto, for I've got an appointment with Dr. Earl on Monday, along with the usual list of other city things to take care of, people to see, etc. But up to this moment, I just haven't felt like it, and haven't even booked a hotel room. Like, fuck it. Earl's just going to suggest another test, probably a gastroscopy (oh yay), and that will take at least a month to set up, and by then I'll be away anyway, and . . . well, it just doesn't seem worth it right now. I could just call up and cancel it, and then I wouldn't have to go anywhere tomorrow, because I don't think I really want to.

Unless . . . I were to receive a call from a certain young lady . . .

I had a phone message from her earlier in the week, saying that she was in Ontario, but didn't have a phone or a number to leave, and would call again in a couple of days. She hasn't yet, but, truth to tell, that whole situation weighs on me less all the time. I may be stubborn by nature, but I don't really try to resist the inevitable; or the *un*inevitable either. It ain't over for me, but I can say that unless the "input" changes from her end pretty soon, I will continue to gradually . . . cool . . .

Sayin'?

Sure you do.

And you know what else? This letter didn't turn out as grim as I feared it might. Starting a letter to you is always a mystery, because I have no idea what's going to come out. Equally, however, starting a letter to you is always *comfortable*, because I know it doesn't really *matter* what comes out; you'll accept it, even welcome it, whatever I've got to say.

Same with me for you, dude. Like I've said before, in our respective positions I don't think we can really bring each other down any lower, so we can let our feelings spill out willy-nilly, knowing they will be received in the spirit with which they are offered:

Crabby!

> Yours in bitchiness,
> The soon-to-be departed —
> *Ghost Rider*

> *Summer's going fast*
> *Nights growing colder*
> *Children growing up*
> *Old friends growing older*
> *Experience slips away . . .*
>
> TIME STAND STILL, 1987

Chapter 14

EASTERING

You move me
You move me
Your buildings and your eyes
Autumn woods and winter skies
You move me
You move me
Open sea and city lights
Busy streets and dizzy heights
You call me
You call me

<small>THE ANALOG KID, 1982</small>

On August 29th, the Ghost Rider hit the road again, riding east this time, on a cool, sunny, and windy morning. It had taken me this long to get motivated to travel again, caught in the same trap as the previous spring — feeling so low that I knew it was time to get moving, but unable to stir myself up enough to *go*.

After riding along some pleasant back roads through the farming country of central Quebec, I joined the main highway, the Autoroute, for a short distance through Quebec City. I noticed signs had been posted by the provincial government calling it the *Capitale Nationale.* Obviously a deliberately provocative move by the nominally separatist powers, whose sole accomplishment — like many political movements — seemed to be *annoying* people.

Because the GS was awaiting a few parts for some last-minute service work, I took a different motorcycle on this journey, a sleeker, more powerful BMW called the K 1200RS (the fourth and newest in my stable of red machines). Because of its limited luggage-space, I left off the camping gear, but otherwise I was fully equipped, down to the small container of spare gas — even more advisable on this machine, with both a smaller fuel capacity and a "thirstier" four-cylinder engine.

My plans remained as loose as ever, just a vague desire to revisit Newfoundland, and I had advised some friends in Halifax, Nova Scotia, that I would be coming to visit them . . . sometime soon.

One week later, after writing a letter to Brutus in my head for six days, I finally put it down on paper. The name "Snorri" refers to the first European born in North America, a Viking girl born in what would become L'Anse Aux Meadows, Newfoundland. Brutus and I had learned about all that on our first motorcycle tour together, back in September, 1995.

During that tour we had also been joined by Jackie and Georgia, flying into Halifax and renting a car to follow us around the scenic splendor of the Cabot Trail in Nova Scotia for a few days. So I was also running across some of *those* ghostly memories.

Sept. 4, '99
Northern Lights Inn
L'Anse au Clair, Labrador

Hey Snorri!

It goes without saying that I wish you were here, but I'll say it
anyway — I *miss* you man! And I have no doubt that you wish you
were here too. Or "anywhere but there," eh?

For the past six days I've been dictating letters to you in my
head, so I thought it was about time I put some of those thoughts
on *paper*. There's already so much to tell you that I hardly know
where to begin, so I guess I'll just start at the beginning. That
would be last Sunday, August 29th, when I hit the road at about
7:00 a.m., riding down to Lachute, then east on 158 to
Berthierville, through Quebec City on the Autoroute to the
Saguenay River, across on a packed ferry to Tadoussac, along the
back road through Baie St. Paul (also busy, and with a big bicycle
race going on), then east, checking the ferry times as I went [to get
across to the south shore of the St. Lawrence River].

The Grand-Escoumins to Trois-Pistoles boat was hours away,
but the one from Forestville to Rimouski was only a couple of
hours later, so I decided to wait, rather than race to make the one
from Baie-Comeau to Matane, which went at 5:30 or so. Good
call, because this one, advertised as "the fastest ferry in Quebec"
(compared to the Quyon to Fitzroy Harbour one, maybe?), it
smoked, making that crossing in 55 minutes, with two rooster-tails
of spray shooting out behind. By then it was 5:00, so I stopped in
Rimouski at the Hôtel des Gouverneurs, right on the river —
which already smelled like the sea.

Next day I continued around the Gaspé, the morning cool and
cloudy, then gradually clearing, but never *warm*. The northern
side was as scenic as I remembered from our previous tour, but

much more *populous,* and it seemed like I was constantly slowing for towns and villages, and having to pass cars, trucks, and convoys of RVs. A 700-kilometre [438-mile] day brought me around to Campbellton, New Brunswick, with pauses to admire the lighthouse near Forillon (Canada's tallest, apparently), and of course, the big-rock-with-a-hole-in-it, at Percé. Though tempted to stop there, I carried on, for I'd booked the ferry from North Sydney to Port-aux-Basques on the 2nd, and somehow had it in mind that August had only 30 days.

For once, that typical Scooter Trash miscalculation was advantageous, for when I turned on the Weather Channel the following morning and saw that it was the 31st, I knew right away what I had to do: cross that new Confederation Bridge to P.E.I. [Prince Edward Island]. In the words of that book you gave me years ago (about Labrador, as it happens), "And So I Did."

(By the by, can you believe it? The Howard Johnson's in Campbellton was *full:* the only time that's happened to me in six months and 60,000 kilometres [37,500 miles] of travelling — with the sole exception of the Sunset Marquis in Los Angeles that one time, but it had been "Book Week" or something. Fortunately Campbellton had a new Comfort Inn, which was probably better anyway, perhaps even including the mediocre Chinese restaurant next door.)

(And what about the *music* they were playing in that restaurant? "Knock on Wood," "The Letter," "Time Won't Let Me," "Midnight Confessions," "Kicks," "Spooky," "Kind of a Drag," "Windy," "This Diamond Ring" — play some of *those* in your helmet for awhile.)

Sublime weather down through New Brunswick, sunny, clear, and cool, and the bridge . . . was long: 12.9 kilometres [8 miles], to be exact, and from there I did a loop of eastern P.E.I., past all them farms and B&Bs (often both at once). My journal sums up a confirmation of our previous impression: "Pretty, but uninspiring, I'd say," though I did stay at a nice place, a golf-resort kind of riverfront hotel with pleasant little cabins and a good restaurant, at Brudenell.

There I finally finished Saul Bellow's *Herzog*, which I'd been chipping away at for months, between other things, and decided it was "definitely a great book — so different from *Henderson the Rain King*. Deeper and wider." I've been reading a lot this trip already, including Jack London's first book of Yukon stories, *Son of the Wolf*, a comical 19th century romp called *Three Men in a Boat*, by Jerome K. Jerome, which I heard of on my Sunday night CBC show, "Wind at My Back" (its sentimental innocence appeals to my 14-year-old feminine side!), the books by Max Braithwaite which apparently inspired it, and *Night of the Caribou*, which I picked up on the Newfoundland ferry of the same name, about the 1942 torpedoing of that earlier "Caribou" by a German U-boat. Now I only have one book left, Wallace Stegner's *Wolf Willow*, after which I may have to actually read *Moby-Dick*, which I've been carrying for six months "in reserve" — like in case I got trapped somewhere because of a breakdown or something.

It occurred to me today that last year at this time I was in *Alaska*, about as far away as you could be on the roads of North America. And the year before that, I was in *England*. Ach.

Next morning
L'Anse au Clair

Well, after seven days of near-miraculous good weather, it rained during the night, and is cloudy and gray today. Now I'm just waiting for ferry-time, thinking of heading down to Rocky Harbour, and maybe do a hike in Gros Morne [National Park] tomorrow.

So . . . from Brudenell it was across on the ferry to Pictou, then down to Cape Breton and around the Cabot Trail, like the four of us did back in '95. Again, the weather was stunning, and again there were too many other people out in it.

That really is a spectacular *ride*, however, though the tight stuff showed up some flaws in my relationship with the K-12. It's certainly not the *power* (I love to turn that "loud grip" alright), and despite its weight and length, it certainly handles willingly, even scraping the pegs a few times, but when you're leaned way over, carrying high RPMs in lower gears, it's *very* hard to get smooth throttle control. It will tend to sag, or surge, or flatten out, and doesn't seem to offer the seamless balance of speed and lean angle I can achieve with the GS.

Journal entry:

Had thought of stopping at Keltic Lodge, but ... didn't need memories. And, did *need synthetic oil, and* real *whisky, and probably won't find either for awhile. Had also thought of changing plans and heading for Halifax for tires, but they don't look any worse today, so hopefully they'll get me around and back.*

Amazing how much I've remembered *of those rides — even opposite way around Gaspé, and places we stopped etc. Especially poignant today, around Cabot Trail. Often best not to think about it — which may be a deeper insight than it first appears.*

So, I got into Sydney in time to buy oil and whisky, stayed at the nice Delta Hotel there, then caught the "Caribou" the next morning — another sparkling one, and warmer every day. When I came off the ferry it was about 6:00 p.m., and I'd thought about staying in Port-aux-Basques, though I noticed that "one of us" (probably the Ghost Rider himself) decided to put in earplugs.

And sure enough, it felt too good to be riding, and once clear of the ferry traffic, it was a lovely, *fast* ride. Touched 220 once [137 mph], and 200 several times; looks like 250 should be an easy reach, given the right piece of road. Gorgeous weather, rolling spruce country, sweeping turns — what this bike was made for, I guess. Fast touring . . .

Until the next morning, riding out of Stephenville on the TCH [Trans-Canada Highway], when a Mountie appeared in my mirrors, lights and siren going. Fuck — 136 in a 100 [85 in a 60], he clocked me at — and ticketed me for it. Bastard! Now my nice clean record is besmirched by what will probably be a whack of points, and I'll have to worry about it whenever I travel in Canada. For *two years!* Die, die, die!

But on we went (cautiously now, alas) up the Great Northern Peninsula on the Viking Trail. Passing the home village of "that woman," I rode around the few streets and paused on the wharf to toast her with a smoke — wherever she is, whatever her thoughts and feelings are. (Perhaps her "job" with me is done? If so, amen.)

Back at you tomorrow, I'm sure . . .

Later I looked back on that scene. I had stood on the wharf in the small fishing village that clung like a barnacle to that harsh, barren coast, looking around at the huddle of plain little houses, the scattering of equipment shacks along the shore, and the work-scarred fishing boats in the harbor. My mind's eye could conjure the little girl who had grown up in that setting, and compare her with the ambitious, "hardening" young woman I had met in Hollywood.

It was a long way from that fishing village to Sunset Boulevard, by any measure, but, for better or worse, she had made that journey. When referring to my own character, it pleased me to say, "I am what my life has made me," and so it was with her. For one so young, she had lived much.

I smoked a cigarette among the lobster traps and concrete blocks of the breakwater, and all unknowing, began to get a grip on reality. She wasn't "from there" anymore; she wasn't who I had thought she might be, and I was free of my foolish illusions. From that moment on, I came to realize, I was completely over her.

Sept. 5, '99
Ocean View Motel
Rocky Harbour

Back again, Spaceman Spiff —

(As I was calling you on that long-ago trip here, on account of the *very* cool sunglasses you were wearing. And leaving everywhere.) Riding out of St. Anthony yesterday, I smiled to think of us using those hare-brained "communicators" on that trip, remembering our morning ride out to Goose Cove, and you announcing, "I'm down."

My ride across from St. Barbe to St. Anthony this time was not unlike that day: blowing like the *devil,* and cold too. Checking the Weather Channel when I got in, I learned that it was 8°C [47°F], blowing 40–50 kph [25–31 mph], and giving a windchill of -1°C [31°F]. And that's if you're standing *still.*

I stayed at the same Vinland Motel (the years haven't been kind to it, though it's undergoing some kind of renovations), and the next night I had wanted to stay right in Red Bay, on the Labrador side, but all four cabins were full. I even considered stooping to one of the two B&Bs, but no; after a walk around the brand-new Visitors Centre, I followed that excellent road back to L'Anse au Clair. (I think we were probably too *freezing* that morning to appreciate what a great road that was.)

I noticed how so many of the houses on both sides of the strait seemed *new:* bright siding on variations of pre-fab designs, and many with attempts at decoration — garden gnomes, old bicycles with handlebar baskets filled with flowers (ditto one-lunger stationary engines, coaster wagons, sleds, wheelbarrows), flags, two little plaster boys, black and white, on a bench.

There were also several closed schools, one being converted to a Seniors' Home: ironic and telltale. [Because so many of the young people of Newfoundland left in search of jobs and raised their families elsewhere, so that only the old folks were left at home.]

Tomorrow I'm going to try the hike up Gros Morne, then maybe head for Fogo Island, then into St. John's for a couple of days. I'll see if I can get a cabin on the Argentia ferry, and if not, probably ride back across to Port-aux-Basques.

Then Halifax — and . . . ? I don't know, we'll work it out.

I want to get this mailed tomorrow, and I'll probably talk to you in St. John's, before you even get this, so I'll close for now.

Down and out from Down East, your —

Skipper

Sept. 7, '99
Fogo Island Motel

Yr Brewis,

[All salutations in this letter refer to obscure Newfoundland foods.]

Sure, I know I just mailed a letter to you last night, from Rocky Harbour, but jeez: who else am I going to write to from *this* place? After all, wasn't it our plan to ride from Rocky Harbour to Fogo five years ago? At least, until we realized that you'd gone and buggered everything up. (Again.) (And again.)

I had a great ride down from Rocky Harbour along the Viking Trail, and I got to thinking about Wallace Stegner, the way he described the torments of his boyhood, then grew up to be a great writer (*Wolf Willow* was *such* a good book), and yet . . . now he's dead. And you know, that reality colors all my thoughts about anybody doing "good work" and achieving "immortality." Like, what good is it? You're *dead.*

Cynical, I suppose — like Paul Theroux's definition of a cynic being a disappointed idealist. That's me, all right.

And all the time I'm thinking about all that heavy stuff, "Invisible Man" [by 98°, Gaia's favorite "boy band"] is playing in my head, in the "background" (amazing how many levels one little brain can work on sometimes), and I'm riding that great road, lost in it all.

That's the reason for Ghost Ridin'.

So, when I finds myself at Notre Dame Junction, and it's only 12:00, what else can I do but go for them *all:* "all around the circle," right? [From a Newfoundland folk song, "I'se The B'y," with the line, *"Fogo, Twillingate, Moretons Harbour, all around the circle."*] So off I go, "down north" to Twillingate, take a photo of the bike in front of the Masonic Hall (built in 1906), then whip 'round to Moretons Harbour, take a picture in front of the museum, then race over to Farewell and catch the Fogo Island ferry. ("Farewell to Fogo," cool.)

Course, don't it start to rain like blazes about then, as we stop briefly at the lonely looking Change Islands, then wallow over to Fogo. Before leaving this morning I'd checked out the Newfoundland travel guide for accommodations, settling on either the Quiet Cannon Hotel, or this eponymous establishment. Well . . .

The Quiet Cannon squatted in the rain just past the ferry dock, like an overgrown Legion Hall, with restaurant and "lounge," so I rode on up toward Fogo town, picturing this quaint New-England-style village along the harbor, with a cute little motel, and (ha!) maybe even a bookstore to browse in.

In turn, the Fogo Island Motel squatted in the rain in the

middle of nowhere (at the junction with the road to Joe Batt's Arm) and looked . . . equally uninviting. In the pouring rain, freezing cold, and with my reserve light coming on, I rode on to Fogo town.

On another day, the town is probably fairly picturesque, with a few old Victorian houses and three churches huddled around a circular cove, where the surprisingly well-wooded island of white spruce, balsam fir, and tamarack gives way to barren headlands blasted by wind and salt spray. And did I mention it was raining? Hard.

So, I circled the town, took a photo in front of the post office to complete the "all around the circle" set, then swallowed my illusions and headed back to the Joe Batt's Arm crossroads, and this place.

Turns out, of course, it's clean, friendly, and cheap (or at least reasonable, at $55), and I had a decent dinner of "homemade" turkey-vegetable soup (well, I'm sure they opened the *can* at home!) and catfish with "mash" potatoes and a glass of drinkable white wine.

Speaking of meals, I forgot to tell you I went back to the Lightkeeper's Café in St. Anthony, and it was still really good. Far out on the white-capped sea a couple of icebergs drifted by as I feasted on chowder and the special of steamed snow crab. That last time there with you was my first taste of bakeapple parfait; this time I had partridgeberry; and the next night, in L'Anse au Clair, partridgeberries and ice cream, and the last two nights, in Rocky Harbour, partridgeberry pie. I loves them some lot.

I also meant to tell you about the "fisherman's plate" in L'Anse au Clair, with shrimp, salmon, halibut, smoked capelin, scallops, and cod tongues (kind of "mooshy").

But the biggest flashback I had was at the Gros Morne Visitors Centre, of all places. I don't know if you'll remember, but I'll never forget walking back out to the bikes that day and telling you how *good* I felt, how happy, how full of life, how simply, existentially, complete. Ah, will we ever feel that good again?

Probably not for a good long while.

Anyway, yesterday I did the hike to the summit of Gros Morne. At least, I took a picture of the sign up there. It was raining all the way, and so foggy I could only see about 50 feet around, but it was still a good hike, and since I was not "distracted" by the fabulous scenery, I did the 16-kilometre climb in four-and-a-half hours, rather than the seven to eight hours the guidebook suggested it would take.

Then I went back to the Visitors Centre, watched a slide show of all the stuff I *would* have seen, and took my wet and muddy clothes to the laundromat in Rocky Harbour. Then a "battered cod" dinner at the Fisherman's Landing.

Now, here in Fogo, it's getting dark, and still raining hard, though the air does *smell* great. Why is it that the Atlantic coast always seems to smell more "oceanic," more pungent, fragrant, saline, and "estuarine" than the Pacific? Is it the tides? The sea-life?

Anyway, the ferry is at 7:00 tomorrow morning, so I'll be rising at 5:30 and heading for St. John's. I've got a couple of different scenic routes to choose from, depending on the weather. And then I guess I'll be *talking* to you.

Later, tickleace . . .

Sept. 8, '99
Hotel Newfoundland,
St. John's

Hey Scrunchions!

The rain poured down most of the night, then let up before the cloudy dawn, when I was loading up and riding down to the ferry. I took the long way around, through Musgrave Harbour and Wesleyville, and it was a very nice ride, much of it along the sea, with the sun peeking out occasionally through *three* layers of cloud, each at a different altitude.

Not finding anywhere suitable for breakfast until I got on the Trans-Canada Highway at Gambo, I had to survive on the coffee and muffin I had on the ferry. The rest of the ride in was quite pretty, though the weather was a bit . . . fickle. Cold, then warm, then drizzly, then clearing, then, just as I struggled out of my rain gear, of course it came *flooding* down, and I had to do the classic under-the-overpass change again.

I was into St. John's by about 1:00, so I rode out to Cape Spear [the easternmost point in North America]. Man, I can't believe I did that so blithely on a bicycle all those years ago; it's quite a climb.

I just got off the phone with Andrew in Los Angeles, who tells me "that woman" has been trying to get hold of *me* lately, and is back in L.A., and wanted him to give me her new number. Well, we'll see about that. He's also sending me a Polaroid of the photo assistant he's been telling me about, who's young and pretty and smart, and "*so* wants to meet you." Yep, it's a nonstop babefest for old Ellwood . . .

[Later] Now I'm in the Cabot Club restaurant, here in the Hotel, with a view of the harbor and the Narrows, the shores lighting up as it gets dark, reflecting on the still water. And, oh dude — it just wouldn't be fair to tell you about the meal I've just had. I'll only say that, after everywhere I've been so far, and all I've been through to get here, "Ça vaut la peine."

Sayin'?

Tomorrow I've got a lot of "service and resupply" sort of stuff to do, like post office, bookstore (get some *new* books to read, though I just picked up a new collection by Ray Guy), book a ferry to Nova Scotia (no cabins available on the last Argentia one, going Saturday, so it looks like back across the island to Port-aux-Basques), find out how much my freakin' speeding ticket is and pay it, a few drugstore-type things, and all like that.

Just now I took a quick walk around town, down Duckworth and back up Water Street. It's so *warm* out, with just a scattered raindrop here and there, and even on this Wednesday night, there's *life* on these streets. Nice to see — if not to be *part* of. (A fine grammatical point there, with that "dangling participle." Usually one can write around them, if one chooses to be pedantic, but that one's a puzzler. Like the example I heard in an English play, where a mother complains about her son's American girl-friend dangling her participles, and the son replies, "Yes, I know, Mother, and that is something up with which you will not put!")

I had to grin when I turned down the steps at the courthouse, remembering your tale of "attempted suicide," and your poor, unfor-tunate cell-mate — who you were going to take with you when you busted out of there [one of Brutus's hilarious tales of his misspent youth, when he — well, I'd better let *him* tell that one someday].

Dude, you are still my Number One favorite person, even when you're not here. You are still so *here,* sayin'?

I'm going to close this one off, so I can mail it tomorrow. Terry Williams tells me there's a letter from you waiting at his house, so I'll start a new one there. Or before, even.

You gettin' sick of me yet, my little cloudberry?

Your faithful,
Langue de Morue

I spent a day in St. John's taking care of some errands, like the post office, booking my ferry from Newfoundland to Nova Scotia, shopping in the used bookstore, visiting the museum, and calling about my speeding ticket (relieved to learn that, as a "foreigner," I only had to pay a flat $75, and no demerit points).

Now that I could predict my arrival in Halifax with some confidence, I called Terry Williams to let him know. Since I was calling his cell phone, when a voice answered I said (in my best "radio voice"), "St. John's is *rocking!*"

An unfamiliar voice said, "I'm sure it is . . . I'll get my Dad for you."

It was Terry's 18-year-old son, Aaron, and I had to laugh at his quickness. Smart-aleck kid.

My friend Andrew was still trying to look out for me (even all the way from Los Angeles), and he made me call the wife of a friend he had worked with there, Alan Doyle, from the band Great Big Sea. Alan's wife Joanne, brother Bernie, and his wife Lisa joined me for dinner at an Italian restaurant, La Dolce Vita, and they can best be described, like most Newfoundlanders, as "lovely people."

Then the long ride back across Newfoundland, sticking to the Trans-Canada Highway this time, and on the long, open stretches I was tempted into letting out the K-12 a little once again — until I got another ticket, on the same stretch of road as the one I'd just paid. However, this time I knew the modest penalty, and didn't care so much.

After an uneventful (but always enjoyable) ferry ride to Sydney, Nova Scotia, I rode on to Halifax and parked my motorcycle in Terry's MG-filled garage. I had known Terry since my early 20s in St. Catharines, when we had both driven MGBs, and he had been a DJ at the local radio station. Though no longer "behind the mic," Terry was still in the radio business, and he and his family had followed it from St. Catharines, to Hamilton, to Kingston, to Halifax, to Sudbury, to Winnipeg, to Toronto, then back to Halifax again. Fortunately, they liked it there.

I had known Terry's wife, Christine, for nearly as long; she was a pert, spirited woman and shared Terry's ebullient high spirits and great sense of humor. Aaron was quietly intelligent and polite (especially for an 18-year-old), and his older brother, Zak, was another treasure in the family. Born with Downs Syndrome, he had the characteristic sweetness and affectionate nature, and since he and I were the earliest risers in the household, we often shared the breakfast table with boxes of cereal and a comfortable, friendly silence. After a few mornings like that, one day he said, "Neil, I'm going to miss you all day at school today." That made my heart smile.

On September 12th, I snuck through my 47th birthday without telling the Williamses about it until the next day, countering their dismay by explaining that I hadn't wanted them to make a fuss, and that I had celebrated in my own way (by buying two boxes of my favorite candies, Bridge Mixture, and eating them while I drank a glass of whisky and read my book — that's *my* kind of party). That wouldn't do for them, though, and the next night they had a cake and sang to me.

Another present arrived for me that day — a FedEx envelope from Andrew with two Polaroids of a photo assistant he had been working with, Carrie. Just before I left home he had told me about her, and wanted me to come right out there to Los Angeles and meet her. But, having just got over one upsetting romantic experience, I wasn't much interested in exploring another, so I just told him I would wait until I got there, then "we'll see." (She did look pretty in those Polaroids, though, long dark hair, slender figure, sexy smile.)

The K-12 went into the local dealer for new tires and a 10,000 kilometre checkup, and Terry drove me around on some errands of service and resupply — including a new pair of Rockports, my combination hiking-and-dinner shoes, as the old ones were starting to get rather disreputable for the latter purpose. (I once read that waiters judge you by your shoes.) I also booked a ferry from Yarmouth, Nova Scotia, to Portland, Maine. I had decided to carry on to New York City, then ride back home to change motorcycles before I headed west again. The road was still the best place for a Ghost Rider to be.

After a pleasant few days with the Williamses, I said goodbye and rode the cleaned-and-serviced K-12 into downtown Halifax to meet with Lesley Choyce at the university where he taught (prolific author, poet, teacher, publisher, TV interviewer — he was a hard-working writer-man). Later that afternoon I rode out to his home at Lawrencetown Beach (where he surfed almost every day — he was also Canada's surfing champion at one time) to meet his wife Terri, and look around their 200-year-old farmhouse, on which Lesley had also built some impressive additions. A renaissance surf poet, he was.

Their guest house was a small house trailer in the back yard, and after a fine dinner and some good music and conversation with Lesley (he made an interesting comment about my "special relationship" with books, "You take them into your *life*"), I enjoyed spending a night as "trailer trash," with heavy rain pounding on the metal roof.

In the morning, I set off on the short journey to the ferry terminal at Yarmouth, then started a letter to Brutus.

Sept. 17, '99
Yarmouth, N.S.

Hey there, Grossglöckner —

"Mi casa es en su boca." Get it? My house is in your mouth. *Yarmouth*, now ya get it? Geez.

Yep, ol' Floyd [the hurricane] has decided I should hang in this town for awhile, cancelling my ferry due to high winds and waves (buncha wimps, if you ask me!), so I've been out scouting apartments, checking job availabilities, and pricing used pickups.

It's a nice little town too, even measured by the exacting John Ellwood standards (he's the one of us who looks after that sort of thing, of course; the Ghost Rider just rides, Chef Ellwood just cooks, Ellwood just parties, and the 14-year-old Gaia just moons over teen music and Love). We've got the requisite decent motel (Best Western "Mermaid"), restaurant (Captain Kelly's), museum (mostly nautical stuff, as you might expect, though Gaia was moved to tears by a photograph of a dog sitting in front of a burned-down house where it had tried unsuccessfully to drag its unconscious master from his bed, and, eight hours later, still sat in front of the ruins of its life — we know how that dog *felt*, sayin'?), liquor store, and post office (neither of which we needed today, but they've got to *be* there, eh?).

No doubt you'll notice our new writing paper: rather thin, and a little small, but since 1988 I've been using the same Hilroy typing tablet as a travelling letter-writing kit, and you can't buy a thing like that anymore, for obvious reasons of technological change. The key element is the front and back cover, to protect it in your bicycle or motorcycle panniers. I've kept it going the last few years by taping refills into it, but you can imagine it was getting a little travel-worn, and since it (and you) are often my dinner guests at the nicer sort of restaurants, well . . . it was getting to be a tad declassé.

The K-12 was also pampered with new tires, a 10,000-km service, and a new front rim (victim of a pothole in St. Anthony, near the Lightkeeper's Café, though I only hit it at about 50 kph [31 mph]), which cost *$800.* I am growing ever more close to this bike — *into* it — and find myself wanting to ride *it* cross-country when I head west. But no, the GS is still the "one," of course, and I miss the luggage capacity, the fuel capacity, the all-day comfort, and being able to carry my basic camping gear. Red Bay was a prime example of that kind of situation, but even here, the first place I called was booked up, and if the desk manager and I hadn't decided to book me in for two nights *last* night (just in case), I might have been in trouble tonight, with dislocated people here from *four* ferries (today's and tomorrow's to Portland and Bar Harbor). However, after 12,000 kilometres [7,500 miles], it seems as though the K-12 and I finally understand each other. Even the delicate throttle response seems to be coming together, though I need another stretch of tight stuff, like the Cabot Trail, to be sure (maybe on the ride from New York City back to Quebec). No doubt my threat to trade it in on a new R-1150GS has been a factor!

So far, Floyd has proved less dramatic than expected (or *hoped* by me; I figured if my ferry was cancelled, I could at least get some *adventure* out of it, and was ready for the worst: Maglite and smokes on the bedside table). We only saw a little rain and moderate winds here, and according to the Weather Network, the media in New York are calling the hurricane "Fizzling Floyd."

I spent much of the day reading Tim O'Brien's *Tomcat in Love*, and it is *great*. So different from his others, funny and ironic, like some of Nabokov's, using the "unreliable narrator" device.

This morning I finished a book of stories by David Guterson (author of *Snow Falling on Cedars*) which was also good, and along with my dented rim, which I left with Terry to send home for me (an $800 wall-hanging?), I left two collections of stories by Patrick O'Flaherty, one by Ray Guy, and *Wolf Willow*. Now I'm carrying another one of Stegner's, *The Spectator Bird*, and Saul Bellow's *The Adventures of Augie March*. So I've still got some reading to do.

Anyway, I'd better wrap this up and get it mailed —

Ghost Rider

That ferry crossing became something of a drama, not to say nightmare, though it was not really any kind of *adventure* — just a nuisance. The ferry was about eight hours late arriving the following day, and was already filled with passengers who had been on a weekend gambling jaunt. Already a day behind schedule, they were told they could stay aboard for the return sailing — along with all of *us*, who had booked those same cabins.

At a crowded, unhappy meeting in the ship's bar, people were assigned the few remaining cabins in order of priority, from handicapped, to families, to couples, while those travelling alone were shoved together into small four-berth cabins far below deck. I shared with a drunken partyboy, Al, and a bus driver, Joe, but when I came back later that night (after waiting hours in line for dinner, and wandering on deck for awhile), Al was sleeping in the upper bunk and Joe was gone. When I saw Joe in the morning he told me Al had staggered in, thrown up, passed out and started snoring, so he had gone to sleep in his bus.

While waiting to disembark, I talked with a motorcyclist from New Hampshire, and when I told him I was headed for New York "to get some culture," he sniffed and said, "I don't know how much *culture* you'll find in *New York City!*"

I got exactly the same response, word for word, from the female officer at the Customs and Immigration post in Portland. Then she asked me, "Have you ever been arrested?"

"No."

"Have you ever been fingerprinted for any reason?"

"No."

"Have you ever been in the armed forces?"

"Um, no."

Then she asked the strangest one of all, "Do you have a return ticket?"

I just pointed to the motorcycle, and she frowned and waved me away.

Then off through Maine, New Hampshire, Vermont, Massachusetts, New York, and a corner of New Jersey (six states in an afternoon — only in the East), and I was in the mean streets of New York City.

A hotel on Central Park South, with a view over the park and the "canyon walls" of Manhattan, a rowboat on the lake on a glorious September morning, a rainy day walking those buzzing Manhattan streets in a forest of umbrellas, visits to the Museum of Modern Art and The Metropolitan (triggering some long-dormant "religious" responses to great art), a night out with the two friends who produced and directed my drum video, Rob and Paul (which included attending a Paul McCartney record-release party, a most strange episode), and a couple of long, talk-filled nights with my writer friend, Mark Riebling — which included forcing him to yield to the preferences of his girlfriend Mindy and me and attend the musical comedy *Chicago*. Mark's Teutonic soul being somewhat lacking in what you might call "frivolity," during the performance of this "all-singing, all-dancing" bit of fluff, I found myself smiling just to think of him sitting there. It was an entertaining bit of fluff, however, and Mark seemed to suffer it gracefully, if not gladly.

I had one awkward moment at the Paul McCartney party, the kind I always dreaded, when somebody recognized me and wanted an autograph. He was polite and well-spoken, perhaps a journalist (he said, "I didn't expect to see *you* here," which I could understand), but when it happened again a few minutes later, I began to feel nervous and uncomfortable, and got out of there as soon as I could.

Throughout my Ghost Rider travels I had only been recognized a few times, to my relief, but of course I was often "on guard," especially when I saw someone looking at me a certain way. The "John E. Taylor" credit cards had forestalled any "name recognition," which is actually more frequent for me — perhaps a result of being hidden at the back of the stage (or video) as "the drummer."

On my first night in New York City, Mark Riebling and I had gone to the restaurant in Grand Central Station and sat at the big square bar facing the vast concourse and the star-speckled ceiling. I saw a patron on the other side talking to the bartender, who came over and asked, "Is one of you guys a drummer?" I felt justified in denying it, and later smiled to myself when I saw him studying my credit card carefully, then shaking his head at the other guy.

Despite 20 years or so of modest celebrity, I had never grown comfortable with such encounters, but now, after the terrible events in my private life, it seemed exactly *twice* as bad. Whoever I was, I was definitely not the person *those* people thought they knew.

I commented in my journal, "Upsetting more than ever these days — I'm not 'that guy.'"

Cast in this unlikely role,
Ill-equipped to act
With insufficient tact
One must put up barriers
To keep oneself intact
LIMELIGHT, 1980

Chapter 15

RIDING THE
JETSTREAM

Rising, falling at Force Ten
We twist the world and ride the wind

FORCE 10, 1987

In the pre-dawn darkness, just after 6:00, I loaded up the K-12 and rode through Central Park and over to the Henry Hudson Parkway, then up to the George Washington Bridge. On the way across, I stole brief glances back at the twilight mist over Manhattan, always an impressive sight. Riding along the Palisades Parkway, I looked across the river between dark green walls of groomed hemlocks, pines, and hardwoods, as the red sun edged above the smoky tenements and warehouses.

Once the New York State Thruway had carried me out of the urban sprawl, I made an exit to the two-lane highway across the Catskills, then turned north on Highway 30, which winds all the way through the Adirondacks to the Quebec border. A bright sunny day, pleasantly cool, with little traffic on a near-perfect road of sweeping curves through the mountains, forests, and lakes. My soulscape again.

As soon as I crossed the border into Canada, however, the rains came, in proportions both "Floydian" and biblical. Caught by this unrelenting downpour on the little ferry from Hudson to Oka (my 10th ferry of that eastern circuit), I had to stand with my back to the onslaught, helmeted and half-rainsuited, pelted and dripping, looking at all the people warm and dry in their cars, until the other side where I could put on the rest of my raingear.

I arrived at the house on the lake wet through, deeply exhausted, and numb with cold. Still, only the last couple of hours of the journey had been miserable; the first eight hours were pretty much perfect.

(A metaphor for life. Mine, anyway.)

I awoke to another pre-dawn mist, this time steaming up from the lake, and another bright sunrise, this one yellow and gleaming through the trees, wearing their early autumn wardrobe of glory. When I stepped outside into the sudden chill and breathed that air, I was freshly amazed at how delicious it tasted.

I couldn't help thinking, "Why do I go anywhere else?"

But I knew why, and I was only pausing there at all to change mounts, like a Pony Express rider. I still needed to be moving, and I still needed to be *away* from that house for awhile. Three days later, I loaded up the GS and hit the road again, not knowing how long or how far I was going. My only plan was to head west toward Vancouver and visit Danny, Janette, and Max again — and my new nephew, Nick, who had been born in June. The rest I would decide along the way. "Something will come up."

As usual, I took up the story with my friend Brutus . . .

Oct. 1, '99
Sauk Centre, MN

A-2 Bruté —

Yeah, that's one possibility we haven't discussed for your future: what about professional wrestling? You'd probably have to "bulk up" a little (like Cartman's "Weight Gain 2000"), but with a good manager (like me) and a good hype (how about "From Hard Time to the Big Time"), you could make a go of it, dude. And no telling where it might take you: consider Jesse Ventura, the governor of this very state, whose opinions are now quoted by the likes of Mark Riebling, for pity's sake.

Man, you have to admit, your future's so bright, we don't have to wear shades. Just rainsuits . . .

And I've been wearing mine for the past four days, with no relief in sight. I'm riding "mad from hell" southward now, trying to escape a vicious cold front across the Prairies and the Dakotas, and I may end up in Oklahoma before I'm warm again. I started out on that nice route we discussed, on the Quebec side of the Ottawa River, to where 148 ended at the Île des Allumettes (Matches Island?), then across to Ontario, and into the pouring rain. I gave up in North Bay, staying in a nice place on the lakeshore, and enjoying a good meal at Churchill's (prime rib was their specialty, and even a rabbit-food lover like you would have liked it).

There were righteous thunderstorms that night, and again the following morning, but as I was riding out of North Bay a marbled gray sky and a brief ray of sun emboldened me to stick with the "scenic route," and I headed north to Temagami. Wrong.

Rain and trucks and construction and mud and cold. I huddled under the dripping eaves of a driving-range shack for a smoke, thinking, "Why am I not at home, warm and dry, writing a great book or something?" And you know, I could just *imagine* it, and it made a lovely picture. But the answer remained the usual one, "Shut up and get back on the road."

So I did. Through the mine-towers of Timmins, the "Shania Twain Way" (oh god!), Pegi's [long-time employee of Ray's and the band who had also been a great support, especially for Jackie, in the House of Mourning] home town of South Porcupine, long-ago memories of high school gigs up there, then into the lonely, rain-washed, green-and-yellow woods, through Chapleau, and all the way to good old Wawa. A journal entry that night:

Weather shows single digits all across the Prairies, and I feel . . . lost. Teary and uncertain. Don't know where to go, or what to do. Once again, reading soothes me, takes me away to Augie's problems [The Adventures of Augie March, *by Saul Bellow]. But I'm still lost.*

However, next day, back at it again, around Lake Superior through rain and trucks and construction and mud and cold. Glimpses of glorious scenery between showers, and even a few blinding rays of sun through Thunder Bay, then the clouds darkened again, and the heavy rains came down.

For reasons fanciful (and ultimately erroneous) I had my heart set on Fort Frances, or even Rainy River, but by Atikokan, that heart was weary, sodden, and chilled, and I settled for the White Otter Inn, with gangs of utility and construction crews. The Weather Network showed my foolish heart the error of its westward ways, and this morning, when it was 3°C [37°F], and raining again, we finally got the message. Despite a potentially beautiful and almost pleasant ride along that deserted two-lane to Rainy Lake (aptly named today), when we got to the hellish pulp-mill steam and smoke and stench of Fort Frances, we crossed to the ditto of International Falls (which, on the Stuart Hall weather reports from Burlington, Vermont, was alternately the coldest spot in the U.S., sharing that distinction with Caribou, Maine, which was definitely warmer today!), and headed straight *south*, on Highway 71.

Ever colder, I noted 41°F at 2:00 p.m. on a bank sign in Wadena, Minnesota. Bright spots from the journal of Mr. Ever-the-Optimist: "Red pinewoods on the edge of prairie farmland, lakes and rivers, a pair of bald eagles, traffic going the other direction (weekend hunters), rain tapering off, and — no bugs!" [Meaning splattered on my faceshield.] I made myself laugh at that hopelessly optimistic observation.

(By the way, I saw an item on the Weather Channel which confirmed that the fall colors are triggered by the angle of the sun, as I had thought, and not by cold or frost. Apparently some response to the sun's angle stops photosynthesis and cuts off the chlorophyll. The key *fact* is that the local weather only affects the *duration* of the colors — whether or not the wind and rain knock the leaves off.)

So many connections to our experiences at this time of year, near the beginning of the Rush tour in '96: Michigan, Wisconsin, and, yes, Minnesota (today I saw a bumper sticker: "Our Governor Can Beat up Your Governor"); the ride to Minneapolis, and from there down to the "Quint Cities," and even the ride cross-country, with our feet pigeon-toed under the bikes to catch the exhaust heat.

I was even doing that today, while wearing full-out cold weather rainsuit, balaclava, sock liners, and all heating systems on full. And as on those other occasions, it was far from enough, with a cruising speed windchill of, say, -90. (I don't even have to say "Sayin'?" You know what I'm talking about here.)

Late in the afternoon I saw this place on the mileage signs, and it rang a bell. You ever read any Sinclair Lewis? His *Main Street*, published in 1920, was set here, in the town where he'd grown up (called Gopher Prairie in the novel), and caused a big to-do at the time, especially among the townsfolk he'd lampooned so mercilessly.

So as I rode in, I wondered if even today they would acknowledge their ungrateful native son. Well, my first clue was when Highway 71 became "The Original Main Street," then led to Sinclair Lewis Park, and the main intersection in town with Sinclair Lewis Avenue, leading to the Sinclair Lewis Boyhood Home, then farther along to the Sinclair Lewis Museum and Interpretive Center (where the nice old lady promised to send me a Sinclair Lewis sticker, as soon as she got some more), beside the Gopher Prairie Motel. So yeah, they sort of acknowledge him: he's America's first Nobel-Prize-winning writer, after all.

Here at the "AmericInn," surrounded by the usual Interstate exit (I-94) detritus of truck stops, McDonald's, Hardees, Super 8, and supermarkets, I wonder what old "Red" Lewis would say about the modern version of Main Street. Probably not much, because he's dead . . .

Oct 2, '99
Maryville, MO

Ha ha, what a card! And I had lots to laugh about today, boyo, starting with scraping the ice off my saddle this morning, at 30°F, then riding through the snowy fields of southern Minnesota and northern Iowa. At least the road was dry, the sky was clear and blue, and there were no bugs!

Though I have to say it was actually a pretty nice ride, as Highway 71 continued to carry me southward through brown cornfields alternating with stubbled wheat and soybeans, gentle hills and occasional neat towns with Sci-Fi grain towers, monumental courthouses, and vast implement dealers. The Saturday traffic was light and unhurried, and town names like Sacred Heart, Minnesota, and Spirit Lake, Iowa, kept me entertained.

Judging by the Weather Channel, a move westward seems prudent now, and I'm thinking of picking up Highway 36 across northern Kansas, hoping to hit Colorado on Monday, and maybe a BMW dealer for an oil change, say in Fort Collins. (Now I'm navigating by the jetstream *and* the dealer directory!)

Rain coming in around here tomorrow, and colder air, so no sense sticking with 71; it's done its job. During dinner tonight at the excellent (not) Country Kitchen (next door to the equally *not* Super 8), I finished the epic *The Adventures of Augie March,* and it is definitely going on my book list for you, with *Wolf Willow* and *Tomcat in Love.* If there's anything else I've mentioned you'd particularly like, let me know c/o Danny and Janette, for (despite appearances) I am still Vancouver-bound, and will be trying to organize some reading for you.

Otherwise, I'm going to close this one off for now, and aim to get it mailed before the first of the week. (And I still hate this cheesy, thin writing paper, but even in New York City, at the main Staples store, I couldn't find one of those old-fashioned typing tablets. What a world we live in, huh?)

That's all from Maryville, MO, and I'll talk at you again soon.

El queso pocito

Oct 4, '99
Santa Rosa, NM

El Cuervo!

(Which I just passed a couple of hours ago.) Yes, this is how far south I had to go to get *warm!* When I mailed your letter this morning, from Garden City, Kansas, it was 30°F. Do you believe this mu-fu'n weather?

True to my pledge, though, I just kept riding south until the temperature reached at least 60°F, and this is how far I had to go. And yes, I am still on my way to Vancouver; although I just talked to Andrew, and he says "everyone" wants me to come to L.A. (I still haven't called that woman, for I'm into this good self-contained travellin' groove, and I just don't *need* all that right now, sayin'? Ghost Rider redux. Far as I'm concerned, I'm *over* her. However, now Andrew keeps talking about this other girl he's been working with, Carrie, who "can't wait to meet me." He sent me some Polaroids of her in Halifax, and she looks real pretty, but — I just don't need all that right now.)

So I guess I left you hanging back in Maryville, Missouri. Next morning was cold and rainy (surprise!) as I made my way around old St. Joe, then west on the Pony Express Highway, 36, which was actually a very nice ride, especially as the rain tapered off after a couple of hours. The Great Plains began abruptly, and unmistakably, around Norton, as I turned southwest on 383, running between open views over brown fields, the railroad tracks over quarried-stone culverts marked "1897," and turkey vultures lifting off the roadkill. The sun finally appeared, though the bank-signs in the towns never showed above 50°F, and around there, on Highway 83, I must have joined the historic Scooter Trash Route: the one we took from Ogallala down through Dodge City, and Pratt, to end up in Fairview, Oklahoma.

And, in the here-and-now of Santa Rosa, I'm just back from the "Route 66 Restaurant" (looks like it could be an original), where I had the #1, Full Mexican Meal, with enchilada, taco, tamale, and beans and rice. (You wouldn't have liked it, though, 'cause of course it had *meat* in it.)

Now I'm back in my spacious "pod" (sorry) at the Ramada Limited, which is actually pretty nice. After several nights of Super 8 and Best Western, the Wheat Lands in Garden City, Kansas (whose envelope you should have received), was an unexpected treat. As I was checking in, I noticed a large black-and-white photo of Truman Capote, looking very cool in a tall billed cap and turtleneck with double-breasted pea jacket, and standing in front of a '50s-style sign for the Wheat Lands Motel. He'd stayed there during the making of the movie of *In Cold Blood* (which I just read during my travels last fall — yet another "Ghost Writer" connection). The manager told me his father or grandfather had taken the photo, and that old Tru used to come back there a lot in those days, for he'd become "friends" with a local high school teacher. Whoa, eh?

Last night, I took a walk by the Finney County Courthouse, where Dick and Perry had been held, and this morning rode out toward Holcomb, looking for the Clutter house. You'll understand that I was kind of shy about asking anyone where the house was, but I found one that fit Capote's description, and whether it was or not, I rode away from there well "creeped out."

The house is also mentioned in that book, *Great Plains*, I was telling you about, and which I've been reminded of the past couple of days. I've added it to your book list, along with Lesley Choyce's *World Enough.*

From there, I rode south on 83 again through Liberal, Kansas, then Highway 54 took me southwest through the Oklahoma panhandle, a corner of Texas, and into the sage and juniper high desert of New Mexico. As so often happens, it seemed to change right at the border from flatter, open range land, vast areas of our old favorite, center-pivot irrigation, on soybeans and winter wheat, and towns grouped around those immense, metallic, fearsome-looking grain towers. Plenty of stenching feedlots too, reeking so that I almost *gagged,* and stretching for acres sometimes, countless rounded cattle-backs like hills of strangely colored boulders. All those cows getting fat for you to eat . . .

Our BMW buddies in Albuquerque were closed, so I figured instead of racing in there, I might as well make an easy day of it — only 657 kilometres [411 miles], versus 855 [534] yesterday) —

and I stood in the parking lot here, feeling overdressed but relaxed, thinking *"I'm warm!"*

At last — 2,913 kilometres [1,821 miles] from Atikokan — I'm warm.

Oct. 5, '99
Cortez, co

And today, hooray, I'm even warmer. A strange sort of day it was, though. In the words of the Talking Heads song, "Some good points; some bad points — ah, but it all works out." (So he says.)

Awake at about 4:30, after those two sudden time-zone changes, I went back over to the "Route 66" place for breakfast just after 6:00, with the air pleasantly cool, stars and planets and a bright quarter moon with earthshine on the rest, then hopped on I-40 a little after 7:00, sun rising in my mirrors, shades of former crossings as I cruised past the big semis from Jim Palmer, Covenant ("It is not a Choice, It is a Child") [anti-choice slogan on each of their trailers], England, Dick Simon (with the skunk), and the rest. Needing gas, I couldn't resist Clines Corners, where I also scored some great vintage stickers of some of the western states.

While waiting for an oil change and a new front tire — 17,000 kilometres [10,625 miles] on it, and still okay, but I thought I might as well get it now) — I noticed a place on the map of Albuquerque labelled "Ernie Pyle Memorial Branch Library," so I got a cab and went to check it out. Years ago, someone sent me a collection of Ernie Pyle's newspaper columns called *Ernie's America,* and I'd become interested in his life and work. Another one of those interesting guys, a "roving reporter" during the '30s, driving around with his wife, Jerry (to whom he always referred as "that girl who rides with me"), and talking to people and telling their stories in a folksy, understated way. Later, he was a tremendously popular correspondent in World War Two, until he was killed by a sniper near Okinawa, in April of 1945, just a few months before the war ended. Unfortunately, Ernie and Jerry were not very happy people — they were both alcoholics; she was mentally unstable, and he was impotent. (Obviously, all of those conditions may have been linked!)

Anyway, it turned out that this had been their house, and although it now functions as a library, with books in every room (and closet), it is otherwise as it was, with some interesting mementos of Ernie's life and career, and some wonderful black-and-white photos of their life in that house. So that made a worthwhile diversion.

Then back on the road. But — why didn't you *tell* me that Highway 44, despite its scenic "dots" [many maps use dotted lines to signify a scenic route], was actually a straight, busy highway, with lots of trucks, and fairly ordinary scenery of sage and juniper with a few rocky outcrops? Or that Farmington was a busy, dusty oppression of four-lane traffic, franchises, and unaesthetic Southwest glut? (Don't know what's going on there; gamblers, retirees, or what; but it's definitely the bad side of the Four Corners.) And why didn't you tell me that there was absolutely *nowhere* to stay in Shiprock? Because it's in the Rez [Navajo reservation], I guess.

However, it was 90°F there, and about 80° here in Cortez, and it was awfully nice to be riding all afternoon in leathers and T-shirt. And there were lots of places to stay here (Best Western was my choice tonight) and a good restaurant, the "Main Street Brewery." So you're lucky. (Oh yeah.)

There's a good motto on the wall here (part of an extraordinary "mural"): "Never approach a bull from the front, a horse from the rear, or a fool from any direction."

I'm reading Stephen Jay Gould's *Wonderful Life* right now, about the difference between the "survival of the fittest" and the "survival of the luckiest," but I'm finding it hard to get engaged with this book. Like, who cares about the contingency of primitive life? What about the ditto of *modern* life? Yeah . . .

Say, on that subject, it occurred to me today that if you are to be banned from riding the roads of America hereafter, at least you know you have ridden the best already. If it's any consolation . . .

I'm sure it is.

Oh yeah — happy anniversary, tomorrow, I think.

One whole year of injustice.

Oct 6, '99

Moab, UT

Now, this is better. Not just *being* here, but *getting* here too. Tell all your clients that Colorado 141 is a "must;" the best ride of this fall Ghost Riding season, and certainly one of the all-time Scooter Trash best as well. Need I say more? Of course!

After all, I am *your* Ghost Rider; it's my *job,* right?

Well, you start off out of Cortez climbing through tall yellow-and-green forest to Lizard Head Pass, at 10,222 feet, where it was cold, but not *too,* then down to Telluride. I believe you've been there in ski season, no? Well, it looks pretty good in autumn too, and would be worth staying there for a day or two, I reckon, for bikin' or hikin'.

Now, yesterday I found myself wondering if I wasn't getting just a little *jaded* about the fabled Southwest scenery, noting in my journal about yesterday's route, "scenic, but perhaps too familiar," but then I absolved myself, "But no. As always, it's the *road.*"

And sure enough, just a day later, I was ga-ga; and it was the *road.* In many ways it resembled our ride through Sheep Creek Canyon and Flaming Gorge (only a couple hundred miles away, after all), beginning with high, bare red-rock walls on either side, the road following the meanders of the San Miguel River most deliciously, then opening up into more monumental formations, the view stretching wider over red, crimson, rust, and orange scrub, with patches of bright yellow aspen up high and occasional bursts of bright gold cottonwoods along the river.

And all the time we're turning and sweeping and winding along. Then into formations of gray rocks, perhaps changing from sandstone to limestone [shale, I just learned at the Moab museum], and towards Grand Junction, tumbled boulders and dry badlands. Get the picture? Oh yeah, and in that whole 100 miles or so, I passed maybe six other vehicles. Sublime.

Then I tried to find the back way into Moab, through Cisco, but the turnoff I thought would be it had a sign, "No Access to Moab," which was probably a lie, eh? Anyway, now I'm here, and it's still a great little town. And what a setting. Tomorrow I'm going to ride down to The Needles section of Canyonlands, for there's an 11-mile hike to "The Confluence" (of the Green and Colorado, of course), which would be great to see.

After that: well, I am still on my way to Vancouver, after all, so I'm trying to pick a route that will avoid the risk of snow (right now anywhere above 6,500 feet in the Cascades, so that shuts out the Sedro Woolley route, for example), and I guess, as usual, I'll make it up as I go along. The "Jazz Rider," improvising my way, eh?

But I want this to get mailed tomorrow (and have a Moab postmark), so I'm going to shut up now. Next time I'll tell you about the "Brutus Scale," in which your oil temperature gauge can tell the temperature outside. (Oh yes!)

El Viajero Fantomo

After another wonderful meal at the Center Café, a most unlikely gourmet restaurant in the middle of humble little Moab, I paid a return visit to the small museum, then returned to the excellent bookstore, Back of Beyond. This time I bought 10 "irresistible" books, most of which I boxed up and mailed to Vancouver the following morning, along with some T-shirts for Danny, Janette, Max, and the "new guy," Nick.

On a morning of heavy rain, I rode down to The Needles area of Canyonlands National Park, through spectacular scenery of rocky mounds and pinnacles, and stopped at the Visitors Center to get some hiking information. In the gardens around it the native plants were identified with little signs, so that when I began my hike I could put more names to the scenery around me. Rabbitbrush (big, yellowish), snakeweed (small green clump), big sage (smells *great* in rain), peppergrass (segmented stems, small clump), four-winged saltbush (sage-green, bigger, mesquite-like).

The rain tapered off, but I was glad of the cool overcast as I began a fairly strenuous hike, scrambling up and down canyon walls and through some sandy washes between formations of eroded red sandstone and scattered junipers and pinyon pines. A dark brown rabbit crouched under a ledge, and a few small lizards warmed themselves in brief spells of sunshine.

Five and a half miles took me to the breathtaking precipice of a high canyon wall, looking down on the confluence of the brown waters of the Colorado and the green of the Green, a clear line between them in midstream. I sat down on the rim to eat my lunch and fully take in this fabled and remote site, taking my imagination back to the tales of Major Powell's explorations in the late 19th century, from Wallace Stegner's *Beyond the Hundredth Meridian*.

Even more than 100 years later, there was still only one other way to reach that place: by water. Far below me I saw two colorful kayaks pulled up on a sandy crescent, and two tiny figures walking around.

That night, I tried a different Moab restaurant, the Poplar Place Pub and Restaurant, and it was crowded, as the whole town seemed to be — some big mountain bike race was coming up in a few days. Oiled pine décor with white plaster, native rock-art decorations (like I'd seen inscribed on the face of Newspaper Rock, which I stopped to look at on my way back from Needles), and rock music played, "thumping quietly."

I went to sit at the bar to eat (better light, and you could smoke), but you couldn't drink wine there, only beer. Utah. "Separate licences," explained the girl behind the bar. Hungry after my hike, I went to work on a big salad and shrimp scampi with pasta, but I noticed a young Jesuit-bearded, Roman-haired fellow staring at me from time to time, and soon his girlfriend came over to verify my "identity" for him. I wrote in my journal, "Now I want to run."

Talking to my brother Danny on the phone that night, assuring him that I was still on my way to Vancouver, he informed me that Canadian Thanksgiving was only a few days away, and urged me to arrive before then, to join them for the traditional turkey feast. So for the next few days I stepped up the pace, and piled up the miles, staying mostly on the Interstates.

Oct 8 Moab — Boise
128,565 (952 kms) [595 miles]

A long day, but relatively painless. A lot of Interstate at around 140 kph [88 mph]. Busy through Price, though in other direction, and awful around Salt Lake City. Massive highway construction continues there, plus it's Columbus Day long weekend, I've just learned.

Poor Utah. Growing too fast (fastest-growing state, I think I read), and no way to stop that kind of action. Turn away jobs for voters? I don't think so. Noticeable smog there today, probably at least partly from highway construction and for notoriously corrupt Olympics too. Too bad, though. Used to be so lovely there, and the people so active. Remember days of bicycling around there and noticing every car had a bike rack and/or ski rack. Also tough for them as Mormon majority gets watered down. Others don't necessarily share their hard-working values. Or wish to keep things nice. Neat, clean, and proper.

Reading Tim Cahill's Road Fever avidly. So . . . relatable.
Something going on here in hotel, a hockey game in town, and

appears to be a couple of bands staying here (one Australian) on night off. Now I know what it's like to have nice hotel invaded by bunch of low-lifes!

On another *rant: Might as well confess, Dear Diary, we're worried about the drinking lately. Since summer. Definitely gone up a notch, and bears watching.*
So: watch us drink . . .

Coffee in bar just as piano player goes off. Nothing else worth staying for. Creeps with cell phones, smoking and drinking aimlessly, but purposefully. Time to go again . . .

I slept poorly that night, and felt "moderately lousy" all the next day, feverish, aching mildly all over, with a knotted stomach. Still, I pressed on through another long ride (866 kilometres, 541 miles), to Vancouver, Washington, where I was able to call Danny and tell him, "I'm in Vancouver." The other one.

A low-grade fever often has a mildly hallucinogenic effect on the brain, and as I rode through surprisingly heavy traffic on the wide open sage desert of eastern Oregon, I found my thoughts were running in abstract directions.

And for once, I wasn't thinking about *myself*, but about the people around me — in the larger sense, the people of North America, and my dwindling hopes for their (*our*) future. (It could only have been a fever that made me stop thinking about my *own* life for awhile.) By then, I had travelled pretty widely in Canada and the United States, city and town and country, and I saw so many people every day, going about their lives, interacting with each other, and I realized that my overall opinion of them by that time was . . . not high.

So many men and women, young and old, looked and behaved in ways that seemed cruel (to each other, and especially to their *children*), petty, self-absorbed, self-righteous, and *smug*. "Smite the smug," I railed in my journal, but realized they were "unassailable, by their very nature." I sometimes found myself sharing the dark view of humanity expressed by Roger

Waters in Pink Floyd's *Animals,* in which he divided people into dogs, pigs, and sheep. While I would still have added another species, the few real *humans* who tried to look after that "barnyard" and be *nice* to the other animals, I had to admit that a lot of people, maybe even most, did not behave very well toward each other.

Most people spend their whole lives in a fairly narrow circle of like-minded friends and neighbors, where it is easy to accept the comforting illusion of human goodness (except for those damn *foreigners*). But if that insulation were suddenly stripped away, and the smug found themselves gridlocked in an eastern ghetto or south-central Los Angeles, or facing a mob of fundamentalist Muslims, their world might suddenly become a lot bigger, and a lot darker. It *is* a jungle out there.

At the same time, just as during my passage along the Healing Road I had eventually reached a certain stage of "Acceptance," however tormented, I also seemed to be gaining a sense of acceptance about the world-as-it-was. And as usual, my thoughts, my travels, my reading, and my writing all seemed to be intertwined.

Having enjoyed Alex Shoumatoff's *African Madness* a few years back, I had recently read his *Legends of the American Desert,* a collection of tales that seemed to be more about Mexico and New Mexico than the four actual deserts of the American West. In the book, Shoumatoff admitted that he had intended to write a "hydrography" of the Southwest, its history in terms of precious water, but kept getting "sidetracked," and had ended up with a book that was somewhat "schizophrenic." The writing and the stories were often excellent, no question, but in trying to capture the intricate tapestry of that vast and complicated region, he had set himself a task that was ultimately impossible — to *synthesize* all that material into some grand resolution.

All of those themes came together in my journal entry that evening:

> *It just* is, *that's what the book ends up saying, and that's the way I've started to feel about the world around me. It just* is.
> *Deal with it.*

I try, and at least I still have curiosity *to keep me going. If not hope. That seems to be gone, with idealism and faith. No more illusions. It just is.*

Deal with it.

Don't ask me; I'm just sympathizing
My illusions are a harmless flight
Can't you see my temperature's rising?
I radiate more heat than light

PRESTO, 1991

C·OAST RĪDER

All of us get lost in the darkness —
Dreamers learn to steer by the stars
All of us do time in the gutter —
Dreamers turn to look at the cars

THE PASS, 1991

Once again, Vancouver was a fine resting-place for the Ghost Rider (and for "the rest of us" too), back in the familiar guest room of the little red house in Kitsilano, with Danny and Janette. Max was three now, and I enjoyed getting down on the floor with him to play with blocks and toy cars — always good for the soul. I called him "Peewee;" he called me "Uncle Funny Man." The new arrival, Nick, was now four months old, and a remarkably placid little guy — the "Buddha-child," I called him.

Janette's parents, Stuart and Vera, were visiting from New Brunswick as

423

well, so it was nice to join their family group for Thanksgiving. I was also able to get a call through to Brutus, and we had another good, funny conversation. He was always able to find the humorous side of his situation, at least on the phone. Like me, he saved his complaining for the letters.

The mid-October weather was unusually fine in Vancouver, with a succession of cool, sunny days. Active as ever, Danny and Janette took me rowing in the Burrard Inlet again, and for the first time I tried a narrow racing-type shell. On a blustery, wavy day, it was a mixed experience, given my limited technique, for when I tried to "feather" the oars on the return stroke, one or the other would often fail to clear the waves; "catching a crab," as it's called. Later, Janette told me she could hear my bad words carrying far across the water.

I did a little better on my first attempt at inline skating, coached by Danny, the professional trainer and master-of-all-sports (except perhaps swimming and rowing), glad I never had to "use" the protective gear Danny urged on me, the kneepads, elbowpads, gloves, and helmet.

Then there was another hike with Danny up the Capilano River to the dam, and marching with Janette through the woods with the two Labrador retrievers, black, bossy Tara and yellow, dumb Barley, and some good restaurant and home-cooked dinners. By the end of the week, my faithful steed came back clean and shiny from the new BMW dealer, John Valk, with a new battery, starter (finally succumbed to the injuries resulting from the "diesel incident" in Alberta the year before), and oil sight glass, and it was time to get rolling again.

Travelling was obviously still the best thing for me, and I had decided I would try to stay out until after Christmas again, as I had the previous year, and work my way south through the States, then maybe explore some different parts of Mexico. Again, few plans, just some possibilities. The "South Park" guys had invited me to their annual Halloween bash in Los Angeles, and I decided that was a good enough excuse to go there, so I had booked a week at the Sunset Marquis starting October 27th, 10 days away.

With the weather already "unfriendly" in the mountains, maybe I would follow the coast highway all the way down to California. Brutus and I had ridden parts of it during the Rush tour, but I thought it would be good to ride the whole way, just to be able to say I'd "done it." People on the West Coast were forever asking, "Hey man, have you done the coast highway?"

I also phoned Steven and asked him if he might be interested in meeting me in Moab sometime soon, where we could rent a 4x4 and explore some of the remote parts of Canyonlands I didn't dare try to reach on my own. In turn, he suggested that he might be able to borrow Shelly's father's Humvee later in the year, and meet me for some back-road explorations in Baja California, maybe over Christmas. That sounded interesting, and we agreed to stay in touch as I travelled.

I also talked to Liam, the band's longtime "main man" (we just called him "the president"), and he was going to be spending a few days in Seattle, not so far away, starting a tour with another band (it was always good for my conscience to know that he, at least, was *working*).

Late on the morning of October 17th, I set off from Vancouver on the short ride down to Seattle, checked into the hotel where Liam was staying, the Paramount (just across the street from the old Paramount Theater, where Rush had played many times in the late '70s — before we "graduated" to the bigger arenas — and that brought back some memories too).

Liam wouldn't be back until the evening, so I took a walk through Seattle's pleasant downtown and market area, with the predictable coffee shops on every corner and a lot of "hipsters" of all ages — particularly noting a 50-year-old man with thinning purple hair, and summing up with the journal note, "Seattle is so . . . *Seattle.*"

Liam got back late to the hotel (full of stories about the band he was working for and their meddlesome ex-stripper wives), and we decided just to have a room-service dinner and get caught up over a few drinks. It always seemed to me that nothing much happened on my travels around the continent, but that night I seemed to go on (and on) telling stories for a couple of *hours,* from the hurricane in the Maritimes and its effect on my ferry crossing, to the Pony Express Highway across Kansas on a rainy-then-sunny Sunday as the Midwest changed abruptly to the Great Plains before my eyes, to the abrupt left turn at Atikokan that resulted in an

8,913-kilometre [5,571-mile] crossing of "Canada," to the glories of Moab and the myriad delights of Baja.

I hope I wasn't *too* boring.

At least I didn't have to worry about boring my friend Brutus, my "captive audience," and the next day I started travelling with him again, seeing things and making plans through his eyes once more.

Oct. 18, '99
Rockaway Beach, OR

Hey there Groovy Dude,

At last we're alone again . . .

Great.

However, of course we'll make the best of it, won't we?

And tonight we are; you are loving this place, amigo. The Silver Sands Motel is a modest but perfectly adequate kind of place, and it is *on* the ocean. Outside my window, there's a narrow strip of lawn, then some low hummocks of sand and dune grass, maybe 100 feet of smooth beach, then the surf and the curve of blue Pacific.

When I walked out there from my room when I arrived, butt and Macallan-on-ice in hand, I just stood and listened for awhile, and the Pacific makes such a wonderful music: a steady chord of mid-range breakers, high-frequency surf, and a low, powerful boom under it all. Hopefully we'll be lulled by that all night long. In our dreams . . .

So. I spent an enjoyable week with the Lindley-Pearts, and found them well. Max gets cooler all the time, and their new boy, Nick (Tank), is the Buddha-child: so calm and good-humored, yet responsive (to his "Uncle Funny Man"), and he seems to embody that "Desiderata" thing: "Go placidly amid the noise and haste . . ."

That's what he does, most of the time, and let that be a lesson to us all.

And, in fact, I have been thinking lately, or realizing, that I have adapted to a completely different mode of travelling. The Jazz Mode, perhaps, improvising, making it up as I go along, but more — responding to the other "players," weather, roads, traffic, my "rhythm section," you might say. As part of the "deal with it" mentality, and the necessity to *adapt*, a guy has to learn to improvise, rather than just playing a pre-written part.

I've been reading Bruce Chatwin's excellent *In Patagonia*, which I've been wanting to get to for years, and — speaking of books — I had a nice fax back from Bryan Prince, Bookseller, and it looks as though he's going to take care of your "six-pack" of books himself, even mailing it from Niagara Falls, New York, to avoid any unnecessary delay or hassle. I hope it works out, for there are some treasures there which might sustain you for awhile, as they did Your Humble Servant.

Glad to be here for you, brother.

And in the words of the great philosopher Forrest Gump, "That's all I have to say about that."

And now the sun is sinking, the surf is playing its chord, the glass is empty, my stomach is growling, and I'm going to find me some dinner.

Later, Bro.

Oct. 19, '99
Brookings Harbor, OR

Back at ya, Pilgrim —

You and I learned awhile back that a little coastline goes a long way. And takes a long time too. Think Pacific Coast Highway from

San Simeon to Monterey. Think Mexico from Puerto Angel (clobbered recently by that earthquake) to Mazatlán. Think Oregon 101 from Newport to Cannon Beach.

Well, I wanted to take a different route, and avoid the snow in the mountains, and now when annoying people ask if I've ever taken the "scenic" coastal route, I can assure them I have.

Some lovely vistas of blue ocean, surfswept stretches of beach, giant teeth of rock sticking up, conifers shaped to leeward by the wind, tall stands of Douglas fir, and all like that, certainly makes a beautiful sight. However, once you've seen it one or two times . . .

. . . from the end of a line of traffic backed up and crawling behind a big fat RV towing a sport-ute, or a double-trailer dumptruck. Or, just as the road finally opened up a little south of Coos Bay (nice name on ya), a bitter fog rolled in, hiding the road, the traffic, and the scenery. And making it 47°F out.

That's why my writing might be a little shaky; I've been here half an hour, had a drink and a smoke, and I'm still shivering!

Just a few miles from California. It will warm up soon.

I'm thinking I'll check out some big trees tomorrow (yeah, really!), then maybe swing around the "Lost Coast," and then think about whether I've had enough "coasting," and go find some mountains and deserts. Where real men ride. (Strangely, I've only seen maybe five or six other touring-type riders, yet *dozens* of long-distance cyclists.)

I think I told you I was invited to the "South Park" guys' Halloween party, so that gives me a kind of "target" to work around. I'd like to visit the Sonoma area again, maybe stay in St. Helena (still holding a position in Ellwood's Top Three Small Towns, with Moab and Loreto), try to get into the lodge at Yosemite for a couple of nights, do a hike there, and of course, there's always Death Valley. We'd still go there again anytime, wouldn't we?

I'll probably get Palm Springs in there somewhere too, then

after, drift a little eastward. Southern Arizona merits some more "jazz riding" (it occurs to me that one theory on the etymology of "jazz" is the French verb "jaser," to converse, and that's what I do: converse with the weather, traffic, and road, and decide where they want me to go). I'm still psyched on Big Bend [Texas], too, so we'll be wandering that way, then picking a new "gateway" to Mexico. Maybe "Gringo Pass," by Organ Pipe Cactus National Park, where I wouldn't mind camping again. Would you?

I'm just glad there's still lots of stuff that interests me enough to get me up in the morning to go have a *look* at it. Earlier in this western meander, I was harboring a doubt or two, wondering where I was going to go, what I was going to do, and it's still a big ol' riddle: Who am I? What am I supposed to be doing? Where am I going? When will it be over? And why — well, just why.

But no. I think we agreed not to trouble ourselves over that question. It's not about why, but *how*. Right? Du-uh!

Anyway, tonight we're seaside again, in a Best Western, with a cliffed cove of gravelly sand, hundreds of giant beached (and bleached) logs, the above-described chilly fog (no open window tonight, we fear), and occasional slo-mo waves breaking one at a time, 10 long seconds apart. You know, the *other* kind of Pacific scene.

I'm still maintaining that the Pacific *sounds* better than the Atlantic, as a shameless generality, but it seems increasingly true to me that the Atlantic *smells* better. Or at least richer. Dunno why that should be, but from Alaska to Mexico on this coast the ocean just seems to smell *bland* in comparison. Different tide patterns? Different intertidal species? Find out, willya?

And with that mission, I'll leave you for now. I'll get this mailed out tomorrow, from here in Oregon, where we are far too stupid to be allowed to dispense our own gasoline.

Ghost Rider

[Brutus again]

Oct. 20, '99
Mendocino, CA

Far out, rainbow crystal unicorn —

Like, wow dude, this place is a totally hip groove, sayin'? (Jive Across the Decades.) On another cool, foggy afternoon, I took a cruise around this hippy-Victorian, wheat germ, dream-catcher, B&B, cutesy-wootsy little town. And you know, we don't know *what* to think. We may have to stay another day, just to try to figure it out some.

Pretty splendid ride today, now that I think about it. (You know how it doesn't always feel that way at the time; can't really, I suppose, until it's over.) Cold and foggy this morning, and I just took it easy, kind of "felt my way" down the 101, riding only as fast as I could *see.*

And I'll tell you what: we've got to be selective about recommending that Lost Coast road. It's what we professional Ghost Riders call "very technical," sayin'? Narrow, lumpy, twisting, not particularly "engineered," you might say. Like some Mexican roads. Random scatterings of gravel, often in the tighter curves (of course), and often needing first gear in the switchbacks, with solid trees to either side, or wide open curves of meadow and fog, with steep dropoffs looming down into the . . . fog.

Last spring, Geddy asked me for recommendations on a five-day driving tour from Portland to Vancouver, and I'm sure I told you about the all-inclusive route I sketched out for him. He ended up not going, but of course that was one of the routes I recommended, based on my notes of our reaction. However, I reckon a good Ghost Rider has to look at the "rhythm section" a little differently when he's playing for an *audience,* you know? Weather, traffic, and roads are capable of many moods. And mood *swings.* Some people might not dig the vibe, man, or adapt so willingly (or resignedly). And then there's the "technical factor." We must be properly discriminating, for our discriminating clientele, n'est-ce pas? (Frog for "sayin'?")

Anyway, the redwoods were, once again, rather *tall.* And all around you going way up in the sky, with sunbeams (shafts, really) through the mist (briefly lighter fog, really), so big around it's *alarming* sometimes, kind of like looking at an elephant up close, or a whale, or . . . a really big tree. And lots of 'em, too, though all in named groves, like the big red cedars are on Vancouver Island. (Named after the philanthropists who *saved* them, no doubt.) Still, they are *there,* and you can cruise slowly through the "Monarchs of the Mist," as the picture-book called them (the one I saw in the Visitors Center, where I stopped to get the little "passport stamp" for the inside cover of my journal), and dig their delicate spice, and the somber, cathedral-like vibes from those impossibly tall and thick pillars. (I know, you're thinking, "Been there, done that, got the sticker," and no, I didn't have the heart to ride through the "Drive-Thru Tree," not without you.)

"Not without my Brutus!"

I meant what I said on the phone the other day, my furry freak brother. When I say "You're always with me," I don't mean nothin' glib or sappy, sayin'? I mean that I'm constantly thinking of where I am and what I'm doing vis-à-vis *you:* what you would say about it, what I'd say to you, how I can describe it and relate it to all the things that we know. And much that *only* we'd know, I'd venture. Or understand. So with regard to what I said about being there for *you,* I want you to know that you are here for *me* too, in a very real way, and it's good for me both to think about these letters, and to write them. And that's all I have to say about that.

And back to Mendocino. What mystified me, I realize now, is

that when I circled the 10 or 12 blocks of the town, I didn't see
anything "real." No McDonald's, no Super 8, no NAPA Auto Parts,
no Home Hardware, no supermarket. Just hippy-dippy Victoriana
and big old-style hotel (though yuppified, of course) called the
Hotel Mendocino. Remembering the Copper Queen Hotel in
Bisbee (a similar sort of town, now that I think about it), which
had been a good experience, I was tempted to give it a try, but
when I learned it was non-smoking, I passed (saying, with mock
innocence, "You mean you can't even smoke in *your own room?*"),
and went back a little outside of town to this place, Hill House. (It
might be overlooking the town, but I can't see through the fog!)

Anyway, it's pretty good. A big Victorianish main building
with restaurant and bar, and a couple of house-like modules to
either side, with maybe 50 rooms altogether. We had a nice dinner
of lentil and smoked pork soup, mesquite-grilled chicken with
potatoes and baked beans, and a nice selection of wines by the
glass. Now the fog has cleared a little, for I can see the three-
quarter moon and hear the distant surf. (Not that distant,
obviously.) Still cold though.

Oh yeah: one route we *will* recommend to our clients is
Highway 1 between Leggett and the coast. Sublime mountain road
of good pavement and engineered curves (e.g. second gear
switchbacks at full lean instead of first gear, and everything else a
notch less "technical"), and the odd lumber truck or RV to get by,
but mostly just great, and probably some fine views when it's not
so foggy. (Later in the day it was okay inland — I was actually hot
for about a half hour — but remained foggy off the ocean.
Probably that Humboldt Current. This is Humboldt County, after
all. Or maybe that Pacific effect called "La Puta.")

Probably, yeah.

And some fabulous groves of eucalyptus today, too, with that
fine medicinal tang, and sometimes the road ran through arching
tunnels of what I'd guess were cypresses. In the barren hills above

the Lost Coast, a peregrine falcon and some horned larks, and fog crawling up from the sea in moving shapes, like ghosts. Yeah.

Oct. 21, '99
Mendocino

Like ghosts, yeah. And still the same, a day later. And suitable, somehow, for there's definitely a "Twilight Zone" feel to this town. No convenience stores, but a good general store (they had no synthetic oil, but they did have the obsolete typing-paper tablets I've been scouring for in drug stores and stationery shops from coast to coast without success). No cheesy stickers, but The Macallan 18-Year-Old. No Gap, no Safeway, no Dairy Queen, no Rite-Aid, and certainly no *Walmart*. But there is a shop called "Sacred Symbols," offering Hypnotherapy/ Readings/ Energy Work.

And, of course, lots of things made of driftwood, stones, glass, and candles, and lots of expensive casual clothes. A decent museum and bookstore. Many little shops and café-bakeries, but few restaurants: basically only the hotel on Main Street and here, it seems.

What started to win me over is the setting. The whole headland surrounding the town to seaward is a state park, all rugged cliffs, arches, and sea caves, with a knee-high meadow of salt-resistant grasses. Through the moving shapes of fog I could just see the ocean, maybe 100 feet down, with thousands of those weird, snake-like kelp stalks moving in the slow surge, as if alive, and ripples and foam as a submerged rock was revealed, like some big animal surfacing. Nicely spooky, overall, and as I circled back toward town, facing the buildings along Main Street, too far away to note the vintage of the parked cars, but just the line of uniformly stylized shops, it could definitely have been, like, some other time, you know? Somewhere between, say, 1895 and 1967. It's starting to work for me, this place. Maybe it's just the fog.

But no, there's something more insidious at work, for in my mellow tripping through town after my cliff-side stroll, I bought a replacement for my travel-weary sweatshirt, and a tan ultra-suede going-out-to-dinner shirt. Plus a pair of cashmere socks (sounds so decadent, couldn't resist). Then, a coffee and cookies in a little café as I caught up on my journalizing.

Could I be, like, turning into my *brother* here? Scary.

Mendocino, by the way, is named for Mendoza, a Spanish regent-governor type in 16th century Mexico City. (And the cape was named first, long before the town 40 miles away.) Got its big start around 1850, hacking down redwoods to feed the boom in gold-rush-era San Francisco. One of my theories is that they're trapped in a timewarp in atonement for their previous sins against the mother planet. There are similarities to Nantucket, for example, or Lahaina on Maui. A history of butchering big things evolved into a picturesque shrine of romantic nostalgia.

Doing their Energy Work.

And it strikes me that it could be (shudder) an "artists colony." No, no, anything but that! (I overheard two aging hippie ladies at the post office talking about living there, and one of them said, "It's been so good for my *work*.") However, I've heard that epithet applied to Bisbee too, and I guess it's not necessarily the kiss of death. Never heard *Moab* called that though.

Oh yeah. It occurs to me that neither we nor our clients should stay anywhere with "Fort" in its name. I told you about the hellish atmosphere of Fort Frances, and yesterday I'd thought of stopping in Fort Bragg, but it seemed that the oceanview property was occupied by a Georgia Pacific lumber mill, and all the motels across the highway were facing *it*. So no Forts, except in the Northwest Territories — where there's little choice anyway!

But I digress. Repeatedly. Well, that's my job, eh? (Canuck for "sayin'?")

Consider this as a name for Mendocino's zoning restrictions: "Homeogothic." That works.

And now it's after six. Time to think about din-dins. I'll wrap up this rap for now, tribal brother. May you walk in vales of love, a peaceable kingdom, butterflies, songbirds, rainbows, surf-chords, redwood spirits, and mellow vibes.

Or maybe it's just the fog . . .

Fare-thee-well for now, Sunshine, and

> Keep the faith, brother
> *Ghost Rider*

["passport" stamp]
Oct. 24, '99
Yosemite National Park

Yo, Yo, Windigo —

That there's the "passport stamp" I was telling you about, and this here is the time-warp writing paper from Mendocino. We hope it will be nicer than that flimsy air-mail stuff we used to use. (It better be, because I bought two — in case I don't get back into the past again for awhile.)

Before I attempt to recount a busy couple of days, I want to bring you here: the Ahwanee, the supreme example of log-and-stone-walled "lodgeness" you can imagine, the palatial dining room with high log-trussed ceiling, triangular iron chandeliers outlined in electric faux candles, gigantic windows reflecting them, and tables enough to accommodate a few hundred people. Which, unfortunately, they're doing.

I believe that, after Yellowstone, this is the busiest of the national parks, and it feels like it, everywhere I've been so far. The road leading into the park was superb, a beautifully engineered mountain road on which third gear was nearly always fine, good banking on the tight turns, and perfect pavement everywhere, but a steady series of "clumps" of cars crawled along in my direction, and even more were coming out (Sunday afternoon), so passing was cautious and rare.

Truly epic scenery of high, gray, glacier-scoured rocks, through pines and cedars, and delicious air at 4,000 feet. A lovely lodge to arrive at, but all around it, and over by Yosemite Village (think Grand Canyon) and the Visitors Center (think Rushmore), just feels like, I don't know, a beautiful outdoor *mall* or something.

But I'll give a more objective report tomorrow, I'm sure, after I do a hike and calm down a little.

It was a strange couple of days. Yesterday morning I left Mendocino (which was definitely a "winner" destination, I think now), and carried on along Highway 1, near the coast. Some wonderful riding despite the unrelenting fog (about three days solid), especially when the road tucks inland to avoid building a bridge (I realize now), cutting through a ravine with a couple of whoop-de-doos, then a tight switchback at the bottom, then a couple more whoop-de-doos up to the next headland. Glorious — if you have it to yourself. You know the odds on a road like that. Slim.

However, I persevered (just to say I *done* it!) all the way down to Jenner (I think it was), where I turned inland through the dry yellow hills, eucalyptus, and groves of pine. Pretty, but with just a little too much traffic, habitations, driveways, cars, and "driveway-darters" out of nowhere. So, it was tense riding. Then through Santa Rosa and into the Sonoma Valley, where I'd thought I might stay a night or two — except that I'd made a typical Scooter Trash error, and thought it was Thursday, when it was Friday. Forget about it.

So, I stopped at the Jack London bookstore in Glen Ellen, cruised the town of Sonoma (nice), then picked somewhere nearby, and unpopular with San Franciscans. That would be Petaluma, and the inevitable Best Western and Carrow's Restaurant (both mediocre, and an exact echo of last May in Stockton, I recall. Great).

With another day in hand before I could get into this place (again, think weekend, and an easy day's drive from San Francisco), I thought I'd try something a little . . . off the beaten track. Say, or rather *sing*, "Saturday Night in Salinas." But first I'd swing by the Blackhawk Auto Museum, just outside Danville, which I'd visited last year.

Maybe I told you about it: the most beautiful car museum this reporter has ever seen, and I've seen all the "biggies." Every car in there is unique, in one way or another: one-off Ghia-bodied Chryslers; the choicest examples of Duesenberg, Packard, Pierce-Arrow, Bugatti, V-16 Cadillac, Isotta-Fraschini, Rolls, Hispano-Suiza, Mercedes; the one-and-only Jag xj-13 Le Mans prototype, Delage, Delahaye, Lagonda; you get the picture. And each one restored to jewel-like perfection, and presented on two floors of opulent polished stone salons, with excellent lighting and plenty of space for each one. (And about *150* of them.)

Then back into the suburban Interstate grind (no joy in the riding that day . . . though I take that back: I remember riding past San Pablo Bay, near Sears Point, and digging the shore birds along there — stilts, plovers, and sandpipers — and some of the on-ramps were . . . fun). But you know the gaff: they's the roads that takes you where you's goin'.

I was thinking of Steinbeck regarding Salinas, of course, and it occurred to me that it would make a worthy addition to the Ghost Rider's Tour of Ghost Writers (and *that's* a book, eh?). The National Steinbeck Center, at the edge of Old Town Salinas, was the best of its kind that I've seen. It presented the history of the region in the conventional way (like Yuma, Moab, Yarmouth, et al.), but through the lens of Steinbeck's writing, with imaginative selections and illustrations, from dioramas to hands-on props.

"For reasons too stupid to go into" (Riebling quote) I ended up at a substandard motel (the Travel Inn, $35, but I found a good meal).

And next morning, a good breakfast too, at "Tabacchi's Family Coffey Shoppe." Despite the spelling, it was a classic place, with a turquoise counter and booth tables, cantilever stools at the long counter, dark green naugahyde on the banquettes, and country music whining and moaning.

And here's my "thumbnail" map of the route I improvised coming from Salinas to here. [Hand-drawn map attached.] I know you're impressed by all the "special effects" in this letter, but I also suspect you'll be (secretly) impressed by this routing. Especially if you believe that I actually *did* it.

Though only after a *bitter* flail in the morning, casting about for County Road G-17, and a couple of lesser missteps later on (those county roads are not excessively identified in the fashion of numbered signage, as you know), I managed to do all that, *"and may I say, not in a shy way."*

Don't let me get started . . .

Anyway, that State Highway 25 is the one we took from Coalinga [Coaling Station A, origin of town name] on Mothers Day, 1997, and it occurred to me today how *spoiled* we were on that tour, riding amazing roads pretty well every day (thanks to you, of course; or, if I made it *possible,* you made it *happen*), and just accepting such sublimity as normal.

Well, now this here Ghost Rider knows better, for instead of snoozing away on a Prevost [tour bus] through the in-between miles, I'm *doin'* 'em, sayin'? It makes a difference. Parts of that 25 were brilliant (several gangs of Sunday sport-bike riders had obviously made the same choice), and the variations of scenery, from foggy Mexican suburbs during my flail (a space-warp to what the real Mexico could be like: *nicer!*) and into Steinbeck's

Long Valley, irrigated vegetable farms on a massive scale, stretching flat and green under the fog, and so fragrant with *life* (rather than just "food").

Then up again into the yellow-grass hills, with lots of lovely twisties (and no RVs or trucks, and few cars and pickups), then down into the Central Valley: cotton, lettuce, cabbage, artichokes, almonds, vineyards, and the wide, swift-moving, and dramatic (to me) California Aqueduct, then up into the piney mountains, which is where this tale began (I think).

Oct. 25, '99
Yosemite

Late the following afternoon . . .

Back from an all-day hike up the canyon wall, gaining 3000 feet (from 4,000 feet) in four miles, and about 13 miles altogether. Pleasantly tired all over now, with a couple of blisters — probably more from the downhill, for much of it was a hardpack surface of dried mud with a dusting of powdery sand and gravel. Given the steepness of the descent, you always had to be prepared to slip, with knees bent and weight back, like a skier, and that too was tiring. Glacier Point was the goal, an overlook above most of the valley, to Halfdome and the farther, unglaciated peaks, among the chaparral, pines, and firs.

However, the unfortunate thing was that you could also *drive* there, which of course most good Americans did, and they could simply park, walk (or waddle) 100 yards, look around, and drive away again.

I have to believe they don't share the same *experience* of that view, not being tired, sweaty, and footsore, but satisfied in having earned all that beauty, you know? And does your *lunch* ever taste good.

You know that I've been talking (to myself) for a long time

about turning these adventures into a book someday, and that was on my mind again today, as I wrote in my journal:

Thinking more and more these days about the great book I'm "supposed" to be writing. Don't know if that means anything, but the thought of trying to get everything I know (even about this trip) into a book is very daunting. Even everything I know about today would fill a good book. What I see, what I think, while I walk.

Millions of thoughts spin out, all connected, like a tape unreeling, then as soon as I stop, all gone. Snap. *Same with riding, now that I think about it.*

You know what it's like, all them thoughts whirling out of your brain, making sense and falling into shape, and you can just *see* how it ought to be.

Ah, but to "make it so," that's the hard part. It's going to take a long, long time, and make a serious hermit (emphasis on both words) out of me, and force me to put into words a lot of difficult stuff, so I'll have to make sure I'm ready, really ready, for all that.

Not yet, that's for sure, but maybe I'm building up to it. "Workin' out," eh? Now if I just had a *researcher,* I could get somewhere — one who's not, like, behind bars.

So hurry up and get out of that joint, willya? I got important *jobs* for ya!

And now I've moved over to the bar, for the cognac I so richly deserve. Still weird to me to be in a non-smoking *bar,* but — it's Kalifornia.

And say, how do you think I feel having a best buddy who's a non-smoking, non-drinking, celibate vegetarian? Oh, I know it's not all by *choice,* and I'm sure I'll be able to "rehabilitate" you in no time. Recorrupt you, like. (Though I'm afraid you're on your own with the *celibacy,* mate.)

More reasons to treasure the memories of that *Test For Echo* tour. I keep saying we were "spoiled," but I guess that's only so if you consider it being spoiled to have, like, a good life. Not hardly. It's just that things have gone *so* downhill since then, I guess. I certainly consider that tour to be the zenith of my career, and of my life. Everything was so right, and we made the most of it. Couldn't have done more.

Whenever people express anything like "envy" for my present nomadic existence (except *you*), I soon set them straight (gently, of course). This ain't no "joyous journey," but a desperate, restless *exile*. As I said, I'd rather be sitting at home, writing a great book. However . . . deal with it.

As we are, and will, right Windigo? (Native legend of spirit transformed by taste of human flesh, doomed to haunt the night and frighten children. See Stegner, I think.)

And that's it for now; I want to get this mailed. Off to Furnace Creek tomorrow, then L.A. (on the 28th now). Call me that week.

G.R.

Lately I had noticed another sure sign of the growth of my little baby soul — a renewed concern about the natural world I was travelling through. It will be apparent by now that I had maintained my *love* for nature, but that's not the same as *caring* about it. After life's betrayals had so completely undercut my faith and my ideals, for a long time I hadn't felt any *responsibility* for the world around me ("Aw, save your own planet!"). However, for many years before that, such environmental and philanthropic interests had been a big part of my life.

Every December, our bookkeeper Sheila would send me a long list of the previous year's charitable contributions, pages of them, and I would go over it all with Selena, showing her what "causes" we were contributing to, and how much, and explaining why. Children's diseases, environmental watch-dogs, rainforest salvation, women's shelters, clean water for Africa, AIDS research, community programs, that sort of thing. I wanted her to know and understand my "if you do well, do good" philosophy. However, I had also believed that "if you do good, you'll *get* good," which obviously hadn't worked out, and part of my shattered ideals meant that I remained generous to friends and street people, but lost all interest in organized charity.

Every Christmas, Jackie used to order whole *cases* of food and household goods and have them delivered to the local food bank (refusing to let them publicize her, as they once wanted to do), and earlier that year Deb had told me about a phone message at the Toronto house from "Mr. Case," wondering why he hadn't heard from Jackie, and hoping he hadn't offended her in some way.

At Selena's funeral, my brother Danny read a W.H. Auden poem, which Jackie and I later agreed to put on Selena's memorial (not knowing at the time it would be *Jackie's* memorial too — or not so soon). It was the famous lament which ends with, "Pour away the ocean/ And sweep up the woods/ For nothing now can ever/ Come to any good."

At the time I had certainly felt that way, as if the "end of the world" had come, so who needed stars, or oceans, or woods? Even after so many miles on the Healing Road, I still believed that "nothing now can ever come to any good," but slowly, slowly, I was becoming interested in the health of the oceans and the woods again.

Just east of San Francisco, on my way to Yosemite, I rode by a hideous, smoke-belching industrial park (obvious oxymoron), hidden well away from the city, and it got me thinking that just as modern people had become "separated" from natural life, distanced and desensitized from not only hunting and fishing, but from everything to do with the production of their food, the same thing was happening with *industry*. Increasingly, it was out of our sight, in "industrial parks," or in unpopulated areas — not only in the West, either, for I had seen the chemical plants in the hills of West Virginia, along the lower Mississippi, and in rural areas of the Midwest.

As I climbed the canyon wall to Glacier Point that morning, I noticed a layer of orange haze stretching across the Yosemite Valley, from rim to rim — smog. On the same hike I noticed a sign telling about someone called a Yosemite "guardian," who had dynamited the moraine on the floor of the valley in 1890, to "lower the water table." How did that "guard" the natural beauty of Yosemite, I wondered.

At that same time, I had been reading Aldo Leopold's *Sand County Almanac*, written in 1949, and considered to be one of the seminal books of ecological awareness. Leopold was no dilettante naturalist, but a keen hunter and outdoorsman who understood that *humans* were part of the natural world too. He didn't object to the use of natural resources, but only protested against the wholesale destruction of everything *around* them. "To keep every cog and wheel is the first rule of intelligent tinkering," he wrote.

As I wandered the backroads of the West, it became clear to me that each of those roads had been blazed by a miner, a logger, or a rancher, and yet now those same people were so obviously the *enemies* of the land they had pioneered — especially as they had grown into impersonal corporations dedicated to digging up piles of toxic slag, clearcutting the mountain forests, overgrazing the public lands, or damming every river. In Western Canada and the United States, forests, grasslands, deserts, valleys, rivers, canyons, mountainsides, and shorelines were still being swallowed up at a prodigious rate, and no end in sight.

"Chaos is the law of nature; order is the dream of man," wrote Henry Adams, and while this particular "disappointed idealist" (not to say "cynic") had learned to accept that nature, and life, were totally random, chaotic, and *heartless*, "order" was not my dream, only beauty. And maybe some peace . . .

It ought to be second nature —
At least, that's what I feel
"Now I lay me down in dreamland" —
I know perfect's not for real
I thought we might get closer —
But I'm ready to make a deal

SECOND NATURE, 1987

Chapter 17

TELESCOPE PEAK

Carry all those phantoms
Through bitter wind and stormy skies
From the desert to the mountain
From the lowest low to the highest high

GHOST RIDER, 2001

445

[Letter to Brutus]

["passport" stamp]
Oct. 26, '99
Death Valley National Park,
Death Valley, CA

Buenas Tardes, erstwhile sidekick,

Picture this: Furnace Creek Ranch laundromat, a cinder-block unit the size of a bathroom in a wayside rest stop, in the middle of a trailer camp, 5:45 p.m. [actually 4:45, I think], sun just behind the ragged casuarinas [actually tamarisk, I think] (some kind of dieback goin' on), and I'm waitin' here. Finding this sweltering little relic was not unlike my route to Yosemite, but you know the gaff: couldn't put it off another day!

But as I've said before, it's good to be here (well, not *here* — though it's not unpleasant on a picnic bench facing the narrow lane between the trailers and RVs (of the ones I can see, three from Nevada, one from California, and one from . . . South Dakota. And look at that: now I'm trapped in a parenthesis inside a parenthesis. Well, I'm breaking out with *one*. And I'm taking you with me).

There.

So, a good ride today. And what made it so wasn't just riding through the avenue of tall pines and firs in the park early this morning, or winding higher through the thinning forest with shafts of sunlight filled solid with smoke (from a "managed," or "prescribed" fire, the signs pointed out) and then to the edge of treeline on the Tioga Pass (tie-oga, I learned), at 9,942 feet, or winding down the other side over Mono Lake, with those weird Tufa formations along the shore. Nope, the finest part of the day was coming over the *next* pass (Sagehen maybe?) and out into the wide, open, sagey sea. And like a sea, when you're out there, time slows down. Every source of danger and every source of beauty is, literally, miles away.

And when the world opened up and slowed down like that, an audible sigh and a settling of my shoulders occurred, automatically, and I felt . . . better. How long since I've ridden along with my legs up on the cylinder heads? Can't even remember. Definitely not on the coast.

[SET CHANGE]

Now that's even better. Dining room, with last light over the Panamints and Telescope Peak, where I hope to stand tomorrow. Between my wash and dry cycles I stopped over to the Visitors Center, and the cute ranger-babe (oh those uniforms, eh?) told me it's about three hours up, gaining 3,000 feet in a short way (again! Parts of me are still a little sore from yesterday's climb), then maybe an hour down, and an hour's ride each way. This time, though, the elevation gain is from 8,000 to 11,000 feet, so that could be a bit serious. Still, gotta go for it. If I make it, why, tomorrow night I'll have *two* desserts!

I've been debating whether or not I should regale you with some of the meals I'm having, and I figure, hey, better you should know, or be reminded, of some of the stuff that's out here, in the "other world," waiting for you. Sayin'?

Funny thing: today I thought I was taking mostly *new* roads, like 120 over the Tioga Pass and east into Nevada. But, then I realized that *we* must have taken the one that connects Coaldale Junction with the Westgard Pass, and the one after that I had taken last year, between the Sonora Pass (better than Tioga, I reckon, both for scenery and "technicality") and Tonopah. Proof of the ceaseless freshness of the desert is that I was grooving along, quite satisfied, and then noticed one of those "historic" signs for the ruins of a ghost town called Palmetto (they thought the Joshua trees were little palms) I'd seen last year. It made me smile, and feel no less glad to be there.

Right now, there's an outline of paler sky along the sharp-edged silhouette of the Panamints, numinous, like.

So, tonight we're having a lobster taco, warm, with cold chile verde, a glass of Kendall-Jackson Chardonnay, and grilled scallops on angel hair pasta. Maybe dessert too — to "bulk me up" for tomorrow. You know, carbo-loading.

And I have to wonder why I love this place (Death Valley) so much. Already content to be riding along in the cool sunlight, watching the sage, the scattered cholla, a herd of five wild horses as I came down 264, ranches and irrigated hay farms, mines both abandoned and active, the sudden "boundary" where the Joshuas studded the sage at a certain line of elevation going up and coming down, and just past the Cottontail Ranch ("Always Open") at the junction with 95, the creosotes take over from sage as the "dominant biomass."

For the first time I took the road in from Scotty's Junction to Scotty's Castle, stopped to buy some of their cool old stickers and ask the ranger about those areas of eroded debris whose name had been eluding me for about an hour (alluvial fans, stupid), then continued down Grapevine Canyon and into the valley. I felt myself smile, and look over those stark, wrinkled hills and creosote flats, sand dunes and salt pans, and love them. Don't know why. Well, I probably do, but if you have to ask — then I'm saving it for the real book. (Not the bootleg version I hear you're publishing, called "Letters To Brutus.")

You should also know that while you're enjoying (or enduring) my volumes of communication lately, my journal is pouting:

"You used to write all that to *me*."

Who loves ya, baby?

I was just thinking about how some of those other biker-guys give the rest of us a bad name, you know? This morning at the Ahwanee I woke at about 6:30, windows open and chilly, pine-scented air keeping me under the covers for awhile, and while I enjoyed that first smoke, I heard an open-piped Harley exploding, one cylinder at a time, trying with repeated blats and concussions and finally igniting into a pulsing roar of potato-potato on fast idle, then rumbling off through the woods like a flathead Ford with a broken muffler (pretty good analogy, actually).

Then, just now, two of them show up at the dining room here, with beer-guts bulging out of their Hawaiian shirts, and when informed of the "casual elegance" dress code, they go huffing, throbbing, and blatting off to the Ranch. Low-lifes.

Lately I've noticed that the more I travel, and the more people I observe at work and play, the lower my overall assessment of humanity falls. This is profound. I have always been an idealist, a believer in the "improvability" of people, and the essential goodness of most people, so this change is as profound as, say, never wearing T-shirts with stuff on them, when before I never wore T-shirts or sweatshirts that *didn't* carry a message. Deep, man. If you follow me. I certainly encounter people I instinctively like, casually, and there are certainly those I know and value as "kindred spirits." But they are few. Most people, I seem to have decided, just spoil it for the rest of us, sayin'?

I bet you do. Though you've always been more *tolerant* than I have.

Is that the word? I still tolerate a lot, probably more than ever, but that doesn't mean I accept, admire, or *appreciate* what I see. I just try to put up with it.

Oct. 27, '99
Death Valley

[sticker with photo of Death Valley landscape] — Manley Peak, from Zabriskie Point, of course, and at the top left is Telescope Peak (snowy that day, apparently, but not today).

It began with a 65-mile ride over ever-worsening road; from the good paved state highway, to narrower, lumpier pavement, to a graded gravel road, then for the last few miles, to ungraded, aggressively vertical gravel. Just like that Hunter Mountain Road, with sand, gravel, rocks, ruts, and perilous curves ("curvas peligrosas") above steep dropoffs. (Signed "High-Clearance 4-Wheel Drive Only" — ha!)

And that was just to get to the trailhead, at 8,000 feet. Then seven miles on foot up to the summit, through ascending ranges of sage, then juniper, then pinyon pine, mountain mahogany (another tree, like the giant sequoias and ponderosa pines, that needs fire to germinate), limber pine above 9,000 feet, and finally, the ancient bristlecone pines, above 10,000 feet.

The summit itself was pretty much bare, jagged rock (though it felt pretty comfortable to lay on by the time I got there), with only a few grasses. But the view, of course, was stupendous. The whole valley so far down, the white floor around Badwater (the part they call the "chemical desert"), and the oasis of Furnace Creek just a tiny green smudge. And far below to the west, Panamint Valley, with its brown furrowed mountains, heaping of sand dunes at one end, the highway across it invisible except to my imagination, and somewhere way over there, Father Crowley Overlook.

Now, though, I'm tired and sore. Coming down was once again nearly as tough as going up — except it was easier to breathe, at least. At one point, I was enumerating my pains as I walked: neck, shoulders, back, lower back, hips, thighs, hamstrings, knees, calves, ankles, and, especially, feet. (Waaah!) But I made it without needing a helicopter rescue.

And at least there was no way to *drive* up there, so I only shared the experience with two other guys, who likewise sat quietly, ate their lunches, and looked around (I got one of them to take my photo, for proof), and I passed one other hiker on my way down. Checking the trail-log at the bottom I noticed that, on average, three people signed in every day, though some admitted they hadn't made it to the top.

Now, my brain is as tired as my body (all that thinking while I did all that walking) so I look forward to shutting it down for awhile in L.A. (ha!), and also heaping abuse upon my too-healthy body. That's enough "training," sayin'?

And there, I shall also certainly be speaking to *you*, so I'll save something for us to talk about. I was thinking today that one reason I've been doing so much letter-writing lately is that I've been staying in a better class of places, where the restaurants tend to have dimmer lighting. No good for reading, but okay for scribbling my heart out to you!

And now, after I tell you that I had corn and crabmeat chowder, Southwestern grill, with a petit filet, chicken, and shrimps with appropriate sauces and salsas, a glass of Benziger Cabernet, Indian River peaches with ice cream, coffee, cognac, and lots of water . . . I'll leave you alone.

Look forward to talking to you, muchacho, and hearing "wassup" with you.

From Death Valley, where the Ghost Rider does his laundry (where else better?), I bid you Buenos Noches.

G.R.

And did I but know it . . .

As I stood at the summit of Telescope Peak, Death Valley was before me, but Death Valley was *behind* me too. Yet again, big changes were on the horizon.

changes never end
hope is like an endless river
the time is now, again

CEILING UNLIMITED, 2001

EPİLOGUE: EVER AFTER

Love is born with solar flares
From two magnetic poles
It moves toward a higher plane
Where two halves make two wholes

THE SPEED OF LOVE, 1993

In less than a day I was in Los Angeles; in less than a week Andrew introduced me to Carrie, my *real* angel of redemption; in less than a month we were deeply in love, and in less than a year we were married in a fairy-tale wedding near Santa Barbara.

Carrie:

Beautiful, smart, cultivated, artistic, affectionate;

Deep green eyes, long dark hair, radiant smile;

Tall, slender, shapely, nicely put together;

Half English, half Swedish, all American, all mine.

The answer to a prayer I hadn't dared to voice, or even *dream*. Carrie. A friend, a soulmate, a lover, a wife, a new journey to embark upon, the greatest adventure.

Though even after we met I resisted this unlikely salvation for awhile, feeling myself by then to be still little more than a burned-out husk. That metaphor can also be stretched to embrace "once burned," and all that, and I guess this little baby soul had been burned more than once. But the East African people have a different saying about that, "Wood that has burned once is easier to set aflame." Or maybe it was more like the seeds of the ponderosa pine or sequoia, which must be touched by fire before they can produce new life.

After our first, awkward meeting at a Hollywood restaurant with Andrew and his date, Carrie and I were brought together again later that week by Andrew (a determined little matchmaker) for a hike in Topanga State Park with him and his dog, Bob, an amiable Jack Russell terrier. Carrie and I walked together the whole way (Andrew discreetly ahead with Bob: our chaperones) and talked about the world and our lives in it. But stubbornly, I still refused to consider this "dating," or that I was supposed to *do* anything, and the next day I continued blithely on my travels.

A week or two later, I somehow found myself circling back toward Los Angeles, and Carrie and I had our first date alone together at a restaurant in Laguna Beach, then drinks over at the Ritz Carlton. Again, we talked comfortably, growing friendly but not "flirty," until one moment when I chanced to see her from across the restaurant — that single, unforgettable glimpse of her unguarded face would stop time, and change everything. One telling moment melted my cool resolve and beckoned me back to the land of the loving.

But again, with a typical lack of self-awareness, I rode away (Carrie by now calling me her "conquistador," forever donning my black leather armor and riding off on my steed in search of adventures), and again I found myself wanting to circle back. This time I was less able to resist this woman's undeniable "rightness," and after a two-day visit to Santa Monica, where Carrie lived, it was all over for the Ghost Rider.

Still, the "conquistador" rode away again. Steven and I had arranged to meet in Tucson in mid-December to go Baja-bashing in his father-in-law's Hummer (a whole other story), but I couldn't stop thinking about Carrie. A few days into that trip I phoned her and asked her to meet me in Cabo San Lucas for a weekend. Then, once Steven and I had successfully "killed off" Christmas, I flew back to the house on the lake, and Carrie joined me there to ring in the new millennium with ardent love and hope aflame.

In January 2000, I moved to Santa Monica to be with Carrie, for she had a budding photographic career there, while I had only — her. I often had that "caught in a whirlwind" feeling once again, my emotions soaring toward a newfound joy one day, then diving into the old familiar misery the next, but the tendency was all upward, and I committed myself to building a new life with Carrie. I had found my little baby soul's true salvation, and once again I wanted to live *forever*. I joined the local YMCA, started yoga classes, stopped smoking, and even cut way down on my drinking. Anything can happen, and sometimes that's good.

On September 9, 2000, our families and closest friends gathered in the garden of a villa in Montecito, a day of sunshine, flowers, music, champagne, and dancing; a day of happiness, laughter, and triumph. For those who had helped me survive that long, lonely, road, like my parents, Geddy and Alex, Ray, Liam, Sheila, and Brad and Rita, there was so much joy.

As I stood under the arch of white flowers before the ceremony, the orchestra playing before Carrie's grand entrance, I looked out over the group of well-dressed, smiling guests, then behind to the trees and the blue expanse of the Pacific. For a moment, I thought about all that had brought me there, and my face began to crumble. But it was only a moment, a little turning point of realization, and then of peace, and I smiled with pride and happiness as I stepped down to the grass to take Carrie's hand.

And now, as I bring this tale to a close, it is January 2002. For a year I have been back working with Geddy and Alex in a small recording studio in Toronto, composing, arranging, and recording a new Rush album called *Vapor Trails*. The title grew out of a metaphor which first appeared in a letter to Hugh Syme, in the summer of 1999, as an off-handed reference to the ghosts of memory.

The song "Vapor Trail" was also one of the first lyrics I wrote for the project, for the first few songs I worked on necessarily had some philosophical and emotional "baggage" to sort through. Songs like "Sweet Miracle" and "Earthshine" reflected the joy of my new life, and then I moved on to less personal, more conceptual themes.

Carrie still had her life and work in Santa Monica, and we had made our home there, but we didn't want to be separated too much, so throughout the year she and I commuted between our townhouse in Santa Monica and a rented apartment in Toronto — her introduction to the dislocations of a musician's life (and a musician's wife).

With wonderful serendipity, Brutus was released on parole in January 2001, and started working at a photo studio in Toronto just as I arrived there. Once again we were best friends who could actually *see* each other, and the "letters to Brutus" written from lonely restaurant tables and distant motel rooms were replaced by evenings spent *together*, talking of where we had been, where we were, and where we hoped we might be going. Even dreaming of travelling together again one day.

Jackie's brother, Steven, remained a close friend (though distant, living in darkest Ohio); Keith continued to keep the house on the lake perfect for us (despite the rarity of our visits amid all that work and travel), and the only one who still seemed to have trouble letting me "move on" was Deb. We kept trying to heal the breach between us, but when I told her I was engaged to Carrie she seemed to feel abandoned, betrayed, and cut off from the memories we had shared, and reacted with an emotional letter that drove us farther apart. Even then, both of us tried to keep communicating as best we could, and Carrie even agreed to meet with Deb in hopes of helping her to accept the way things were now, but maybe it was one gap between past and future that could never be bridged. Still, we kept trying.

And I continued trying to build my own bridges, trying to put my experiences into words, as both continuing "therapy" and attempts at resolution. After a few weeks in the studio, I had a handful of lyrics finished, and wanted to let Alex and Geddy put some of them to music before I continued, so I started looking through my journal notes and letters from my travels. Before I knew it, I was working on the impossible task of translating all that material, and all I had survived, into this book. It was another long process, sometimes painful and always difficult, but it seemed to help me lay my ghosts to rest. The healing continues.

With that in mind, I look back to another turning point, a late afternoon soon after I moved to Santa Monica. I stood alone on the Santa Monica Pier looking out to sea, thinking of all that had happened, and how miraculously my life had turned completely around again. I thought about all those restless, often miserable miles (55,000 of them) I'd covered between the dock on Lac St. Brutus and that pier overlooking the Pacific Ocean. And the distance my little baby soul had travelled on that Healing Road too, from sitting on that dock with a cigarette and a Scotch and seeking meaning in a pair of duck-shaped rocks across the lake.

It occurred to me that all of my "characters" had found their separate redemption there too, and that I was gradually reuniting into one focused entity. The Hollywood party boy, Ellwood, was happy to have moved to California, like he always wanted to, and to be romancing a beautiful woman every single day (and night) of his life. John Ellwood Taylor, the wandering bluesman, was content to hang up his blues and sing a happier song for awhile, while little Gaia, our 14-year-old "inner girl," was all aglow with misty emotion and romantic poetry. Only one of us had no place in this sunny new world: the Ghost Rider.

As I stood on the Santa Monica Pier, the unofficial end of Route 66, the "Ghost Road," I saw that it was a fitting place to entertain the sudden realization that the Ghost Rider's road ended there too. A hermit no more, a gypsy no more, a splintered personality no more; I was growing into one man again (though no longer a man alone), with joy and meaning in my life, passing the days and nights in a place where I belonged — beside the woman who loved me so well. Carrie.

I had found my place of rest and redemption, and the Ghost Rider's work was done. He could keep on riding now, right off the end of that pier, into the sunset.

And if the music stops
There's only the sound of the rain
All the hope and glory
All the sacrifice in vain
If love remains
Though everything is lost
We will pay the price,
But we will not count the cost

BRAVADO, 1991

Acknowledgements

Some of life's journeys must be undertaken alone, but no open highway can soothe a battered soul like the open hearts of caring people. I wish to take this opportunity to formally thank the family members and friends who cared for me when I could not: my parents, Glen and Betty, sisters Judy and Nancy, brother Danny and his wife Janette, Deb and Mark, Steven and Shelly, Keith, Brutus and Georgia, Brad and Rita, David and Karen, Paul and Judy, Ray and Susan, Sheila, Pegi, Geddy and Nancy, Alex and Charlene, and Liam and Sharyn.

On the road, I was given hospitality and welcome diversion by some of the above, as well as by Dan and Laurie, Gump, Trevor, Nathalie, the Williams Family, Freddie, Rob and Paul, Andrew (Our Benefactor), the Hollywood ex-pats, the Rich family, the Nuttall family, and those who more directly helped to shape these pages: Lesley Choyce, Mark Riebling, and my brother Danny, who gave me astute and valuable advice. Paul McCarthy's editorial genius was unstintingly sympathetic, encouraging, insightful, and incisive, and drove me to keep trying to make my story deeper and richer.

My motorcycle and I would like to extend our special appreciation to BMW of Salt Lake, Iron Horse in Tucson, Shail's and John Valk in Vancouver, and McBride Cycle in Toronto.

Sometimes I can almost sustain the high-minded sentiment that it was worth the pain of losing Jackie and Selena for the joy of having known them. I don't know if I will ever be able to embrace that notion, but the important thing is that I embrace *today* — the joy of knowing Carrie, and the inspiration of being loved by her. Without her, *Vapor Trails* would not have been made, and this book would not have been written.

"Dedicated to the future, with honor to the past."